# RICHMOND VOLUNTEERS

The Volunteer Companies of the City of Richmond
and Henrico County, Virginia
1861 - 1865

by

Louis H. Manarin

and

Lee A. Wallace, Jr.

Official Publication No. 26
Richmond Civil War Centennial Committee
Richmond, Virginia

Westover Press
Richmond
1969

This volume is
affectionately dedicated to
J. AMBLER JOHNSTON

Chairman of the Richmond Civil War Centennial Committee and worthy son of a Confederate Veteran, for his long years of devotion to our history and his untiring efforts to the preservation of historic landmarks and recognition of historic events of lesser importance.

Library of Congress Catalog Card Number 72-100103

## SPONSORS

All of whom were operating in Richmond before or during 1865. Antecedents of those having changed their names since 1865 are indicated.

B'NAI B'RITH
CARDWELL MACHINE COMPANY
CHESAPEAKE AND OHIO RAILWAY
   Virginia Central Railroad
COKESBURY BOOK STORE
   The Methodist Publishing Company
CONNECTICUT MUTUAL LIFE INSURANCE COMPANY
DAVENPORT INSURANCE COMPANY
FIRST AND MERCHANTS NATIONAL BANK
   First National Bank
JOHN T. GODDIN & SONS, INC.
   Wellington Goddin
GORDON METAL COMPANY
MEDICAL SOCIETY OF VIRGINIA
RICHMOND, FREDERICKSBURG & POTOMAC RAILROAD COMPANY
RICHMOND HOTELS
   Central Hotel - St. Claire
RICHMOND NEWSPAPERS, INC.
   Richmond Dispatch
RICHMOND PAPER COMPANY
ROYAL GLOBE INSURANCE COMPANIES
   Virginia Fire & Marine Insurance Co., Liverpool, London and Globe Insurance Co., Ltd: Royal Insurance Co. Ltd.
SEABOARD COAST LINE RAILROAD COMPANY
   Petersburg Railroad Co., Richmond & Petersburg Railroad Co., Seaboard & Roanoke Railroad Co.
E. B. TAYLOR COMPANY
THALHIMERS
   Thalhimer Bros.
E. M. TODD COMPANY, INC.
UNITED VIRGINIA/STATE PLANTERS
   Planters National Bank
UNIVERSITY OF RICHMOND
   Richmond College
VIRGINIA HISTORICAL SOCIETY
WATKINS COTTRELL COMPANY

and one sponsor of the Years 1961-1965 by its surviving personnel

   RICHMOND CIVIL WAR CENTENNIAL COMMITTEE

RICHMOND CIVIL WAR CENTENNIAL COMMITTEE
PUBLICATIONS

1. MAP OF CIVIL WAR RICHMOND
2. MAP OF BATTLEFIELDS WITHIN 25 MILES OF RICHMOND
3. ADULT READING LIST
4. LIST OF 100 YEAR OLD BUSINESS FIRMS, ORGANIZATIONS AND CHURCHES
5. CHILDREN'S READING LIST
6. THE NATION'S MOST HISTORIC AIRPORT
7. WALKING TOUR MAP OF DOWNTOWN RICHMOND
8. RICHMOND 1861 - 1865
9. CATALOG OF CIVIL WAR PHOTOGRAPHIC NEGATIVES
10. THE CIVIL WAR HORSE
11. AIR ARM OF THE CONFEDERACY
12. LIBBY PRISON
13. CONFEDERATE INFLATION CHART
14. PANORAMIC PHOTOGRAPH OF CIVIL WAR RICHMOND
15. DIRECTORY OF CIVILIAN OFFICIALS: RICHMOND-HENRICO-CONFEDERATE
16. RICHMOND OCCUPIED  ENTRY OF THE UNITED STATES FORCES INTO RICHMOND, VA. APRIL 3, 1865 CALLING TOGETHER THE VIRGINIA LEGISLATURE AND REVOCATION OF THE SAME
17. RICHMOND AT WAR
18. INDEX TO THE PAPERS OF THE SOUTHERN HISTORICAL SOCIETY
19. FACSIMILE OF CIVIL WAR RICHMOND 60¢ CURRENCY
20. THE SIXTY-SEVEN HILLS OF RICHMOND
21. TROOP MOVEMENTS AT THE BATTLE OF COLD HARBOR
22. CONFEDERATE MILITARY HOSPITALS IN RICHMOND
23. TRENTON-RICHMOND FRIENDSHIP BOWLS
24. HISTORIC POINTS OF INTEREST IN RICHMOND
25. REPRODUCTION 1865 MAP OF RICHMOND
26. RICHMOND VOLUNTEERS

## RICHMOND CITY COUNCIL
## 1958 - 1966

### Mayors

| | |
|---|---|
| A. Scott Anderson | 1958-60 |
| Claude W. Woodward | 1960-62 |
| Eleanor P. Sheppard | 1962-64 |
| Morrill M. Crowe | 1964-66 |

### Vice-Mayors

| | |
|---|---|
| Robert J. Heberle | 1958-60 |
| Eleanor P. Sheppard | 1960-62 |
| Phil J. Bagley, Jr. | 1962-64 |
| Robert J. Habenicht | 1964-66 |

### Councilmen

| | |
|---|---|
| Phil J. Bagley, Jr. | 1958-60 |
| | 1964-66 |
| F. Henry Garber | 1958-60 |
| | 1960-62 |
| J. Edward Lawler | 1958-60 |
| George W. Sadler | 1958-60 |
| | 1960-62 |
| | 1962-63 |
| Eleanor P. Sheppard | 1958-60 |
| | 1964-66 |
| Robert C. Throckmorton | 1958-60 |
| | 1960-62 |
| | 1962-64 |
| | 1964-66 |
| Claude W. Woodward | 1958-60 |
| | 1962-64 |
| E. Elwood Ford | 1960-62 |
| | 1962-64 |
| Ben R. Johns, Jr. | 1960-62 |
| R. Hugh Rudd, Jr. | 1960-62 |
| J. Westwood Smithers | 1960-62 |
| | 1962-64 |
| Robert J. Heberle | 1962-64 |
| Ruth J. Herrink | 1962-64 |
| A. Scott Anderson | 1963-64 |
| | 1964-66 |
| B. A. Cephas, Jr. | 1964-66 |
| Henry R. Miller, III | 1964-66 |
| James C. Wheat, Jr. | 1964-66 |

### City Clerk

William T. Wells

### RICHMOND CIVIL WAR CENTENNIAL COMMITTEE

| | |
|---|---|
| J. Ambler Johnston - Chairman | 1959-65 |
| C. Hobson Goddin - Vice Chairman | 1959-65 |
| Robert C. Throckmorton | 1959-65 |
| Miss India Thomas | 1960-65 |
| William H. Stauffer | 1959-60 |
| Robert W. Waitt, Jr. | 1959-60 |
| Saul Viener | 1960-65 |
| Fletcher Cox - Ex Officio | 1959-61 |
| Fletcher Cox | 1961-65 |
| Rush Loving - Ex Officio | 1959-61 |
| Robert W. Waitt, Jr. Executive Secretary | 1960-64 |
| Mrs. Elizabeth Bacon Acting Executive Secretary | 1964-65 |

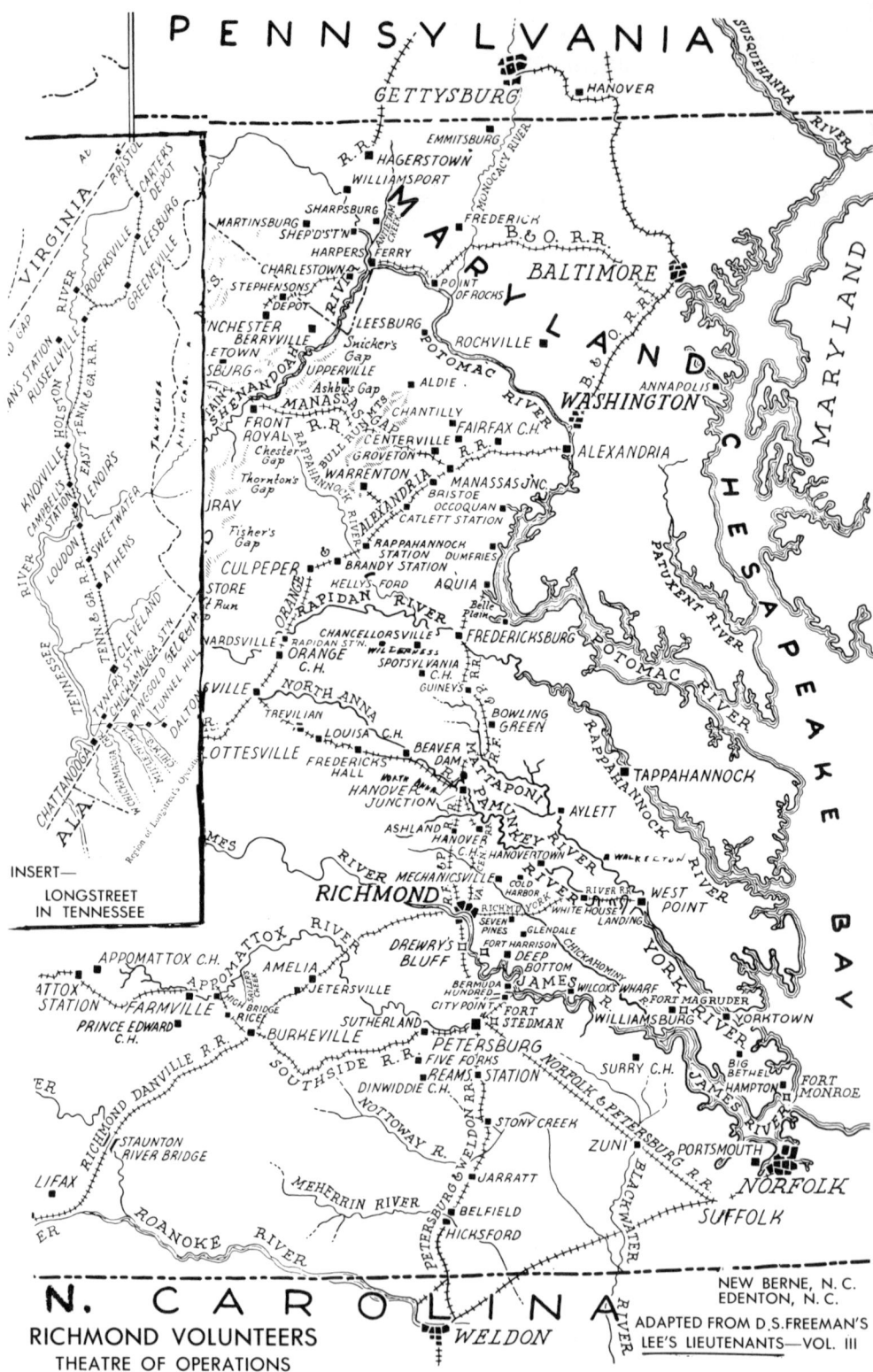

PREFACE

As the Centennial of the War of 1861-65 approached, the Congress of the United States created the Civil War Centennial Commission, leaving to then-President Eisenhower the appointment of the members. He appointed as Chairman, Major General (Retired) U. S. Grant III, and, at the same time, requested the Governors of all the States to form their own Civil War Centennial Commissions with such subordinate local organizations as they deemed proper. J. Lindsay Almond, then Governor of Virginia, introduced the necessary legislation in the General Assembly, resulting in the appointment of the Virginia Civil War Commission; which Commission in turn requested the various cities and counties to form their own local Civil War Centennial Committees.

A. Scott Anderson, Mayor of the City of Richmond at that time, forthwith appointed the Richmond Civil War Centennial Committee. During the whole period of the Centennial, this Committee operated as an agency of the City Council and with a most cordial cooperation between the two.

The Richmond Civil War Centennial Committee decided early after its appointment to concentrate its efforts on the preservation of the history of Richmond's participation in the War Between the States. The Committee sponsored no reenactments, no parades; but on two occasions it utilized the performing arts to add another dimension to the story of Richmond during that period. In conjunction with the Richmond Ballet Company, they presented in a local theatre, "An Evening of 19th Century Ballet." In June 1965 as a fitting climax to the cultural phases of the Centennial Observance, and in cooperation with the Department of Recreation and Parks of the City of Richmond, the Committee created and produced "Richmond Under Two Flags", an historical drama, presented in Dogwood Dell, Richmond's outdoor amphitheatre, for three performances before more than 12,000 people.

Every Friday night for three years, tours were conducted to the Confederate Museum, the Valentine Museum, St. Paul's Church, General Lee's home, and the State Captiol. At each a skit of about ten minutes was staged by local actors portraying pertinent incidents connected with each location. These became so popular that it was necessary to conduct four relays each evening. Approximately 12,500 people participated in these tours.

Meanwhile the Committee prepared, published and distributed gratuitously the publications listed on the following page, with the exception of numbers 17 and 26. After the close of the Centennial, No. 17 was published under the auspices of the University of North Carolina Press and has been subject to most favorable reviews everywhere in the English-speaking world.

When the National Commission made its final report to Congress it cited the Richmond Committee as the only one below State level awarded the medal for achievement.

We now come to the final publication, No. 26, RICHMOND VOLUNTEERS. Much of the work incident to its preparation was done during the life of the Committee; and all work incident to its preparation since that time has been done by Dr. Louis H. Manarin and Mr. Lee A. Wallace, Jr., together with the continuing voluntary work of the members of the Committee itself and its staff, which includes the former Acting Executive Secretary.

The existence of the Committee as an agency of the City of Richmond having expired it was no longer in order to expect the City to finance its publications so an invitation was extended to a selected list of business concerns and organizations operating in Richmond in 1865, who promptly and gratuitously made possible the bare cost of production, with no expectation of profit. A list of such SPONSORS appears on a following page.

We cannot conclude the Preface without a special reference to the rosters. There are perhaps thousands of present day Richmonders and people all over the nation whose ancestors are therein listed and many of them will be surprised to see grandpa was a private or maybe a corporal. We remember his always being addressed as Captain, or Major, never by a lesser title; but on closer study, we find he was in his teens or early twenties and did not acquire his title until the formation of the United Confederate Veterans, whereupon all of its officers were immediately promoted, even unto that of General!

Again, upon checking the list of youthful privates, we see many who became our leading citizens in later years.

In the name of the City Council of Richmond, its erstwhile Civil War Centennial Committee submits this volume as something long overdue in print. Dr. Manarin and Mr. Wallace have not only conducted the research and written this text; they have also been throughout the lifetime of the Committee an inspiration in scholarly research and attainment.

> J. Ambler Johnston
> Former Chairman
> Richmond Civil War
>     Centennial Committee

## INTRODUCTION

The City of Richmond has had a military tradition woven through the fabric of its history. Within fifty years after the landing at Jamestown, the Colony of Virginia had established militia laws which called for regular musters for peacetime and mobilization in emergencies. Under this early militia system, all freemen were organized into companies and regiments, and the officers were appointed by the Assembly. By 1652 the regiment of Charles City and Henrico Counties was in existence.

The town of Richmond was incorporated in the year 1737 and in 1779 Richmond was made the capital of Virginia. On May 8, 1792 the Congress of the United States passed "An Act to provide more effectually for the national defense, by establishing an uniform militia throughout the United States." Under this act, the militia of the City of Richmond was organized into a regiment and designated the 19th Regiment of Militia. In May 1848 a second militia regiment was organized in Richmond when all members of the 19th Regiment of Militia living east of Tenth Street were organized into the 179th Regiment of Militia. In May 1851 the uniformed volunteer militia companies from Richmond and the counties of Henrico and Chesterfield were organized into the 1st Regiment of Virginia Volunteers.

Within the militia system certain of the companies were known as volunteer companies. These volunteer companies were established by interested citizens and drilled at regular intervals at their own armories. Membership in the volunteer companies was strictly voluntary; thus the companies frequently took on the air of a fraternal organization. They existed only as long as the interest of the members lasted. After the company was organized and the officers elected, the men would select a uniform which was to be purchased by the individual volunteer. The color and design of the uniform usually reflected a rather gay, romantic approach to the sober art of war. Once a volunteer company was uniformed it could apply to the State for arms. At regular intervals, when the militia was required to drill, the companies would report with their regularly assigned battalion and regiment. Although the volunteer companies met and drilled as separate units at their own armories on their own time and according to their own schedule, they were still a part of the State militia system and were organized under and within that system. As such, they did not constitute a standing army for the State. It is of interest to note that prior to 1861 the State's "standing army" consisted of only one company of light infantry known as the Public Guard. In addition to the regular militia musters and their own meetings, the volunteer companies would take part in patriotic functions and ceremonies, after which they would usually participate in some sort of private social activities. The existence of the organized volunteer companies, plus the interest displayed by those who had participated in defunct volunteer organizations, provided a nucleus of trained and semi-trained men when the call came in 1861. With a population of 38,000 just prior to the war, the City of Richmond provided some forty companies of artillery, cavalry, and infantry. These units served with the armies in the field. In addition, many citizens enlisted in other regular units or served in staff and command positions, while others enlisted in local defense units organized during the war.

Originally intended to cover the companies from Richmond, this book was expanded to include those companies from the County of Henrico because of the past association of the Richmond and Henrico units and service of many Richmonders in units of that county. During the war, numerous local defense units were organized in Richmond; however, it was necessary to limit the scope of this work to the regular units. Historical sketches of the local defense units would well make a companion volume to this one.

The authors of the following unit histories have sought to record the activities of the individual companies and the brigades, divisions and armies in which they served. After dividing the companies in each branch of service, each author researched and wrote his chosen unit histories, which were later reviewed by both authors to ensure uniformity in editorial procedure. The style of each author remains.

In researching and writing these histories the authors used published histories of the companies and regiments, and memoirs of members of the units. In addition, all references in the War of the Rebellion; Official Records of the Union and Confederate Armies and the Southern Historical Society Papers were consulted. The local newspapers provided much on the early histories of many units, as well as pertinent information during the early phases of organization prior to muster in. The most valuable sources were the original company muster rolls and individually compiled military service records on file at the National Archives, Washington, D. C., Record Group 109. By regulation each company was required to fill out a muster roll every two months. Along with statistics on company strength and battle casualties, these rolls frequently contained information on the activities of the companies in the record of events column. The compiled military service records provided information on the individual officers and men, and frequently contained documents which pertained to the activities of the company. In addition, company record books and other primary sources were used. The authors have adhered to the policy of citing the source of quoted material by reference to the source prior to the incorporation of the quote.

The research on the various units brought out two interesting facts. In the past, Richmond's contribution has been frequently summed up with reference to the 1st Regiment Virginia Infantry. This publication will show that in addition to many individual companies, a second regiment (15th Regiment Virginia Infantry) was formed of local companies and served throughout the war. It was also discovered that the Orange Light Artillery, which has been credited to Richmond, was organized in Orange County and mustered in at Richmond. The latter event led to its being considered a Richmond unit.

The authors wish to acknowledge the assistance rendered by

Mr. Elmer O. Parker and Mrs. Sara Jackson, Army and Navy Branch, National Archives, Washington, D. C.; Miss Eleanor Brockenbrough, Confederate Museum, Richmond; and to the staffs of the Virginia State Library and the Valentine Museum, Richmond. These people graciously gave their aid and assistance by providing information on pertinent collections on file in the various institutions. Also, the following individuals provided assistance on various aspects of the study: William A. Albaugh III, Falls Church, Virginia; Colonel R. Bolling Batte, USAR (Retired), Midlothian, Virginia; Mrs. John Nicholas Brown, Providence, Rhode Island; Herbert L. Ganter, Williamsburg, Virginia; Robert L. Miller, Arlington, Virginia; William K. Kay, Richmond; and Fleming C. Fraker, Arlington, Virginia. A special note of thanks to Miss India Thomas for her interest and encouragement. Finally, we would be remiss if we failed to acknowledge those who assisted in preparing the manuscript in its final typed form. To Mrs. Betty Bacon and Mrs. Frances High we acknowledge our indebtedness for their labors in preparing the manuscript for publication.

Louis H. Manarin
Lee A. Wallace, Jr.

## TABLE OF CONTENTS

PREFACE
INTRODUCTION
ARTILLERY
    Howitzer Battalion . . . . . . . . . . . . . . . . . . . . . . . . 1
        1st Company . . . . . . . . . . . . . . . . . . . . . . . . . . 3
        2nd Company . . . . . . . . . . . . . . . . . . . . . . . . . 12
        3rd Company . . . . . . . . . . . . . . . . . . . . . . . . . 19
        4th Company . . . . . . . . . . . . . . . . . . . . . . . . . 28
    Courtney Artillery . . . . . . . . . . . . . . . . . . . . . . . . 30
    Crenshaw Battery . . . . . . . . . . . . . . . . . . . . . . . . 37
    Hampden Artillery . . . . . . . . . . . . . . . . . . . . . . . . 44
    Henrico Artillery . . . . . . . . . . . . . . . . . . . . . . . . . 52
    Letcher Artillery . . . . . . . . . . . . . . . . . . . . . . . . . 56
    Magruder Artillery . . . . . . . . . . . . . . . . . . . . . . . . 64
    Marion Artillery . . . . . . . . . . . . . . . . . . . . . . . . . 66
    Metropolitan Guard . . . . . . . . . . . . . . . . . . . . . . . 69
    Parker Battery . . . . . . . . . . . . . . . . . . . . . . . . . . 73
    Purcell Battery . . . . . . . . . . . . . . . . . . . . . . . . . 79
    Richmond Fayette Artillery . . . . . . . . . . . . . . . . . . . 89
    Richmond Flying Artillery . . . . . . . . . . . . . . . . . . . . 97
    Richmond Otey Battery . . . . . . . . . . . . . . . . . . . . . 98
    Thomas Artillery . . . . . . . . . . . . . . . . . . . . . . . . 104
CAVALRY
    Caskie Mounted Rangers . . . . . . . . . . . . . . . . . . . 108
    Governor's Mounted Guard . . . . . . . . . . . . . . . . . . 116
    Henrico Light Dragoons . . . . . . . . . . . . . . . . . . . . 124
    Henrico Mounted Guard
        Company A . . . . . . . . . . . . . . . . . . . . . . . . . 133
        Company B . . . . . . . . . . . . . . . . . . . . . . . . . 138
    Henrico Mounted Rangers . . . . . . . . . . . . . . . . . . . 142
    Texas Rangers . . . . . . . . . . . . . . . . . . . . . . . . . 143
INFANTRY
    1st Regiment Virginia Infantry . . . . . . . . . . . . . . . . 152
        Company B-Richmond City Guard . . . . . . . . . . . . 164
        Company C-Montgomery Guard . . . . . . . . . . . . . 168
        Company D-Old Dominion Guard . . . . . . . . . . . . . 173
        Company G . . . . . . . . . . . . . . . . . . . . . . . . . 177
        Company H-Richmond Grays, No. 2 . . . . . . . . . . . 180
        Company I . . . . . . . . . . . . . . . . . . . . . . . . . 183
        Company K-Virginia Rifles . . . . . . . . . . . . . . . . 188
        Band . . . . . . . . . . . . . . . . . . . . . . . . . . . . . 193
        Drum Corps . . . . . . . . . . . . . . . . . . . . . . . . . 198
    15th Regiment Virginia Infantry . . . . . . . . . . . . . . . . 203

|   |   |
|---|---|
| Company A-Henrico Grays | 211 |
| Company B-Virginia Life Guard | 214 |
| Company D-Henrico Guard | 217 |
| Company F-Emmett Guard | 220 |
| Company G-Southern Guard | 222 |
| Company H-Young Guard | 225 |
| Company K-Marion Rifles | 228 |
| F Company | 231 |
| Jackson Guard | 242 |
| Richmond Grays | 248 |
| Richmond Light Guard | 257 |
| Richmond Light Infantry Blues | 263 |
| Richmond Sharpshooters | 275 |
| Richmond Zouaves | 284 |
| Varina Artillery | 291 |
| Virginia Guard | 294 |
| Index | 297 |

### BELL HOUSE - CAPITOL SQUARE

Built during the winter of 1824-1825, the Bell House served the Public Guard as a sentry post and a means of summoning assistance in times of emergency. Besides its use as an alarm, the bell functioned as Richmond's official timekeeper and it was rung at the commencement of General Assembly sessions and for Sunday religious services. After the Civil War, the Bell House became a storehouse, armory and post office. It is now under the care of the Capitol Police Force.

# Artillery

## HOWITZER BATTALION

Captain George Wythe Randolph's Howitzer Battery, designated as Company H, 1st Regiment of Virginia Volunteers, was enlisted in State service on April 21, 1861. This battery, known as the Richmond Howitzers, had been raised and sent to Harpers Ferry just after John Brown's raid in 1859. Being called into active service, the battery was stationed at the Spotswood Hotel when it was mustered in. On the 21st of April the battery was ordered to Wilton Bluff, eight miles below Richmond, when the rumor spread that the U. S. sloop Pawnee was moving up the James. When the ship failed to materialize, the battery returned to Richmond on the 23rd. After a brief period at the Spotswood Hotel, the company was sent to the Richmond College artillery barracks. Randolph's Battery was reported at the Baptist College on April 29, 1861 with 225 men and six Dahlgren Howitzers. Applications for membership in the Howitzers increased until it was decided to transfer the company out of the 1st Regiment and expand it into a battalion. Captain Randolph was appointed major, and between May 8-10, 1861 three companies were formed and designated as 1st, 2nd, and 3rd Companies, Howitzer Battalion. A fourth company was started in July, and was to be designated the 4th Company, but was disbanded in August when efforts to recruit it to full strength failed. The battalion staff included: Dr. Theodoric Pryor Mayo, 1st Lieutenant and formerly first sergeant of the 1st Company, Adjutant; W. E. Randolph, Surgeon; J. B. Timsley, Jr., Sergeant Major; W. B. Smith, Quartermaster; and Rev. Thomas Ward White of the Presbyterian Church, Chaplain.

Soon after its organization, the Howitzer Battalion left Richmond College and went into camp at Howard's Grove. By May 21 the battalion was encamped on Chimborazo Heights, near Griffin's Spring, overlooking the James River, Rocketts, and the suburban town of Fulton. The battalion's guns were placed on the plateau above the camp. Reporters from the Daily Dispatch visited the camp, and found "the boys," numbering about 170, in good spirits and health. They also noted that:

> The culinary operations, for dinner, were progressing during our stay. Two or three sable cooks were preparing the beef, corn bread, and coffee, in regular camp style, and, we doubt not that the food was eaten and relished, with a zest which more luxurious dishes could not have so well imparted, with the exercise and mode of life to which the Howitzer boys are now subject.

Chaplain White, they reported, "has evidently entered fully into the spirit of the campaign and while rejecting Puritanism as a characteristic of Yankee Pharisees, will diligently attend to his ministerial and preceptive duties on all proper occasions."

On May 24 the 1st Company left Richmond to join General Johnston's army at Manassas Junction. The 2nd Company joined General Magruder's forces at Yorktown on May 27, and on June 3 the 3rd Company was ordered to proceed to the lower Peninsula. On June 10, 1861 the 2nd and 3rd Companies, under Major Randolph, served together in the battle at Bethel Church. In September 1861 the 1st Regiment Virginia Artillery was organized. Major Randolph was appointed colonel, commanding the regiment, to which the 2nd Company was assigned as Company A, and the 3rd Company as Company D. The creation of the 1st Regiment terminated the existence of the Howitzer Battalion for the duration of the war.

Courtesy Confederate Museum

Captain George Wythe Randolph is seated at the lower right. Armed, but with nondescript dress, the newly organized Howitzers were sent to Charlestown November 1859.

## HOWITZER BATTALION

## 1ST COMPANY

On November 9, 1859 the "Howitzer Battery" was partially organized at a meeting held in the office of the clerk of the Circuit Court, James D. Ellett, in the State Court House on Capitol Square. George Wythe Randolph, who conceived the idea of the company, was elected captain. Born in 1818 at Monticello, the home of his maternal grandfather Thomas Jefferson, Randolph was appointed a midshipman at the age of thirteen, and served in the navy for six years. Afterwards he studied law at the University of Virginia, and in 1850 moved to Richmond to practice his profession. In addition to the election of a captain, Gaston C. Otey was elected first sergeant. On November 16 the company met at Military Hall, over the First Market, elected a secretary and treasurer, and held their first drill.

On November 19 the Howitzers, although without uniforms, were quickly armed by the State and sent to Charlestown with other Richmond companies. Rumors of plots to rescue John Brown and his raiders from the jail at Charlestown had prompted Governor Henry A. Wise to send more troops there. At Charlestown, where they were quartered in the basement of the Presbyterian Church, the organization of the Howitzers was completed with the election of 1st Lieutenant John C. Shields and 2nd Lieutenant John Thompson Brown.

By July 4, 1860, when they paraded for the first time with the 1st Regiment of Virginia Volunteers, the company had procured uniforms of gray frock coats and trousers, similar to those worn by the other companies in the regiment. Late in 1860 the Howitzers were designated in the 1st Regiment as Company H.

On May 25, 1860 six Dahlgren 12-pounder Boat Howitzers, one of which was rifled, were shipped to Captain Randolph from the Washington Arsenal. The guns, purchased by the State expressly for the Howitzers, were designed to be drawn by the cannoneers; however, new light field-carriages to be drawn by two horses to each piece were constructed at the State Armory. On February 22, 1861 the Howitzers, numbering seventy-four men, paraded with its battery of six pieces.

The Howitzers, on April 19, 1861, went into quarters in the basement of the Spotswood Hotel, at the corner of Main and Eighth streets. On April 21 the company was mustered into the service of the State for one year. On the same day, a Sunday, rumors had it that the Federal sloop Pawnee was on its way up the James to shell Richmond. Bells rang, whistles blew, and the Howitzers, with the Fayette Artillery, Richmond Grays, and Company F, were called out, and sent to Wilton's Bluff, about eight miles down the river. The Pawnee never arrived, and after some target practice at Wilton's, the Howitzers returned on the 23rd. "Pawnee Sunday," however, was remembered for many years in Rich-

'mond. Soon after their return to the city, the Howitzers were sent to the artillery barracks which had been established at Richmond College.

About May 3, 1861 Lieutenant Brown was ordered with the battery's left section, which included the rifled piece, and forty-seven men, to Gloucester Point, where on May 7 they opened fire on the United States steamer <u>Yankee</u>. Only a few rounds were exchanged before the steamer withdrew, but they were apparently the first hostile shots of the war fired in Virginia.

The Howitzers increased in numbers, and during May 8-10, the command, now detached from the 1st Regiment, was divided into three companies, forming the Howitzer Battalion under Major Randolph. The original company, reorganized on May 8 with the election of Captain John C. Shields, was thereafter known as the 1st Company. At this time, the battalion, less Lieutenant Brown's detachment at Gloucester Point, was sent from Richmond College to a camp at Howard's Grove. From there it was moved to Chimborazo Heights by May 21.

On May 24 the 1st Company left Richmond by railroad, and reached Camp Pickens at Manassas Junction on the next day. The company on June 29 moved to Fairfax Court House, where they were attached to General Milledge L. Bonham's Brigade, of the "advance forces," Army of the Potomac. On July 17 they fell back and took up positions at Mitchell's Ford on Bull Run. The four guns comprising the battery were placed so as to command the approach to the ford; and about 9:30 A. M. the company underwent their baptism of enemy artillery fire when Federal batteries opened up; but as the enemy did not move within the range of the Howitzers, the battery did not reply. This attack proved to be but a feint, as the main attack was launched at Blackburn's Ford on the right, and within sight of the company. The battery remained in position at Mitchell's Ford, and on July 21 stood by anxiously while the battle of First Manassas raged over on their left. After the retreat of the Federals began, the right section of the battery, under Lieutenant William P. Palmer, was sent with Bonham's Brigade in pursuit to Centreville, but returned without having fired a shot.

On August 9 the 1st Company was transferred to Brigadier General N. G. Evans' Brigade, which it joined on the 10th at Leesburg, Loudoun County, and went into camp at nearby Mead's Farm. Later, Lieutenant Edward S. McCarthy's section moved to Big Spring on the other side of town. During August the sections of the battery went on several expeditions to harass the enemy in the vicinity of Lovettsville, White's Ferry, and Point of Rocks. On October 9 Lieutenant Palmer's right section was moved to Edwards' Ferry road, near Fort Evans, where a rifled iron gun of the battery was posted. By this time the battery had been increased to six guns. Lieutenant Palmer's section was ordered to Carter's Mill on Goose Creek, October 17, but was soon afterwards returned to the Edwards' Ferry road. Meanwhile, the left section participated in Ashby's attack on Harpers Ferry. On November 17 Lieutenant Palmer was elected captain of the company, replacing Captain Shields, who was promoted to lieutenant colonel and sent to command Camp Lee at Richmond. In late December the company went into winter quarters, the right section erecting huts at Fort Evans, and the other two sections at Goose Creek.

About March 7, 1862 the forces at Leesburg, now under Brigadier General D. H. Hill, left the town and moved eastward to join the main army under General Johnston. In early April Johnston's army moved out to join General Magruder's forces on the Peninsula.

The 1st Company arrived in Richmond about April 10, and was encamped at Camp Lee, where its former captain, now Colonel Shields, provided them with a "long remembered" dinner, accompanied by a "fine flow of wits and spirits," toasts, and speeches. Discipline was relaxed at Camp Lee, and the men were allowed to visit their families and friends in the city. Within a few days the company left by steamer down the James River for the Peninsula lines, where, during the attack on April 16, the battery was hurried into position at Dam No. 1, where it was exposed to severe artillery fire and sharpshooting. While at Dam No. 1 the twelve months enlistment period expired, and the company was re-enlisted and reorganized. An election of officers was held, and 1st Lieutenant McCarthy was elected captain. Captain Palmer, who desired to go on the medical staff of the army did not seek re-election. On May 2 the artillery, moving in advance of the infantry, was withdrawn from the lines and on the 4th two pieces of the battery were placed at Fort Magruder, near Williamsburg. Here, on the 5th, they served in repelling the attack on General Longstreet's command, serving as the rear guard for the army moving up the Peninsula toward Richmond. Firing next to the guns of the 1st Company were three pieces of the Richmond Fayette Artillery. At Williamsburg the 1st Company acquired a 3-inch iron rifle which had been abandoned by the enemy.

After crossing the Chickahominy, the company went into camp near Richmond, and remained there until May 17 when they left for picket duty at Meadow Bridge, the Christian farm, the Friend House, and Garnett's field. From the first two locations the battery delivered harassing fire against the Federals across the Chickahominy, and from Garnett's two pieces participated in as much of the action of the battle of Seven Pines as occurred in that area.

During the Seven Days' Battles the 1st Company served with Griffith's Brigade, Magruder's Division, to which it had previously been assigned. The company was under fire at Fair Oaks Station on June 29, but was not engaged. Three pieces of the battery were ordered to the front at Malvern Hill, and were engaged until their ammunition was exhausted. One 6-pounder was damaged by a 12-pounder solid shot which struck the face of the muzzle, and several of the battery's gun carriages were considerably damaged by shell fire.

In August the 1st Company's left section remained near Richmond waiting for new equipment while the right section, attached to Barksdale's Brigade, McLaws' Division, moved with Longstreet's Corps to

Gordonsville. It was not until after Second Manassas that the sections were united. The battery during the Maryland Campaign was reported as being comprised of two 10-pounder Parrotts and two 6-pounders. Only two pieces, however, were apparently brought into action on September 17 at Sharpsburg. These guns, served by one officer and thirty-two enlisted men, remained in line of battle all day, losing one killed and one wounded.

The artillery of Lee's army was in poor condition after the Maryland Campaign, and the fall of 1862 was spent in rebuilding its strength. For some time the 1st Company remained in camp near Culpeper Court House, and in November moved with Longstreet's Corps to Fredericksburg. On December 13, the day of General Burnside's attack, the two 10-pounder Parrotts were among the guns firing from the hill in rear of the Howison House, to the right of Marye's Heights and the Telegraph Road. The battery's two 6-pounders were in position, but were not engaged.

In the general reorganization of the artillery in April 1863, the four batteries of McLaws' Division were formally organized into a battalion under Colonel Henry C. Cabell. On April 29 when part of Sedgwick's Corps crossed the river below Fredericksburg, the battalion was in position on Lee's Hill. On May 1, when it became apparent that the Federal main attack was in the direction of Chancellorsville, Major S. P. Hamilton, commanding the battalion, brought up the batteries of Captains McCarthy and Manly with the division. On May 2 they relieved Pegram's Battalion on the turnpike within view of the Federals at Chancellorsville. Later in the day the line fell back, and after its re-establishment the battery's two 6-pounders were ordered to the front. On the morning of the 3rd they were joined by the two Parrotts. Late, on the same day, the battery moved with the division to meet the threat which had developed at Salem Church. The battery was again engaged on the 4th, and on the morning of the 5th reported to Kershaw's Brigade for further duty. During the fighting at Chancellorsville the 1st Company had two killed and two wounded.

After Chancellorsville, General Lee took the offensive, and on June 3 the 1st Company, with Longstreet's Corps, started on the march which would ultimately take them into Pennsylvania. The Potomac was crossed on June 26, and on July 1 they were encamped within a few miles of Gettysburg. The battery moved up with the division on the 2nd, and the rifle section commenced firing about 4:00 p.m., with the Napoleon section in reserve nearby. Two hundred rounds were fired, and both sections were exposed to the heaviest artillery fire they had ever experienced. Seven men were wounded, and the battery lost thirteen horses. The battery went into position on the morning of the 3rd, about 350 yards in advance of the skirmishers; and, firing twenty rounds, succeeded in driving back a Federal advance. At 1:30 p.m. the battery, which had moved to another location, opened up in the general artillery fire preceeding Pickett's assault. Both sections of the battery were engaged during the day. One of the rifles was disabled when a wheel was shot away, and a caisson had to be abandoned when its team was killed. The company lost two men killed and two wounded. Ten horses were killed on the 3rd. During July 2 and 3 the rifle section fired about 600 rounds, and the two Napoleons expended 264 rounds. On the return march to Virginia the battery went into position at Hagerstown on the 6th, but was not engaged. During the period of inactivity following the Gettysburg Campaign, the company was encamped successively at Bunker Hill, near Winchester, Millwood, Gaines' Cross Roads, and on July 25 arrived at Culpeper Court House. The severe winter of 1863-64 was spent at Morton's Ford on the Rapidan.

Early on May 6, 1864 the 1st Company moved with Cabell's Battalion to Parker's Store, and later in the day proceeded on to New Hope Church, as no suitable ground was found for their employment in the Wilderness. In the fighting at Spotsylvania Court House the battery was located on an elevated position on the left of Longstreet's Corps, on the right of General Ewell. The fighting here on May 10 was about the bitterist yet experienced by the company. On one occasion the Federals broke through the lines, and, believing it was being flanked, the infantry fell back. Just at the right moment, Sergeant E. G. Steane, whose piece was on line with the infantry entrenchments, turned his gun and poured an enfilading fire of double canister into the Federal ranks, which, with the help of the infantry, drove the enemy back and restored the line.

The operations of the armies moved south toward Richmond, and on May 28 the company went into position 200 yards in front of Pole Green Church, Hanover County, on Totopotomoy Creek, where a considerable amount of skirmishing and sharpshooting took place. From this point the company moved south, across Old Church Road, to cooperate with Kershaw's Division near Old Cold Harbor, where the battery was heavily engaged June 1-3, especially in the repulse of the Federal general assault on the-3rd. On June 4, while the battery was in position just east of Gaines' Mill Pond, Captain McCarthy was instantly killed by a Minie ball through the head. The company remained with the battalion on the lines east of Richmond until about June 15, when they proceeded toward Petersburg, then under attack by General Grant.

During the operations around Petersburg the 1st Company was encamped at the Dunn House, opposite Port Walthall Junction, about halfway between Richmond and Petersburg. The company was then under Captain Robert M. Anderson, and its battery at this time consisted of four 12-pounder Napoleons. During the winter of 1864-65 the battery saw little, if any, action. On the night of April 2, 1865 the lines at Richmond and Petersburg were evacuated. The battery's horses were in bad condition, and many gave out by the time they reached Amelia Court House. The caissons were abandoned and destroyed, leaving the horses to be used as gun teams, which restricted the ammunition supply to that which could be transported in the limbers. At Amelia Court House Cabell's batteries were placed in the advance of the artillery train under

General Reuben L. Walker, and were not engaged until April 8 near Appomattox Station. Here, during a rest period when the teams were unhitched, the train was completely surprised by Federal cavalry. The guns were quickly unlimbered and loaded with canister, which, with the artillerymen now armed with muskets, drove away the attacking force. The column proceeded on towards Lynchburg, and, on April 10, upon learning of the surrender at Appomattox Court House, the guns were spiked and buried, the carriages and harness destroyed, and the 1st Company disbanded.

Courtesy Virginia State Library

John Esten Cooke

John Esten Cooke, who had established his reputation as a writer before secession, enlisted in the Howitzers in 1859. On January 31, 1862, he was discharged as 2nd sergeant, 1st Company, and afterward served as a volunteer aide to General J. E. B. Stuart. Cooke was commissioned as a first lieutenant, artillery, on May 19, 1862 and on July 25, 1862 was promoted to captain. He served as chief of ordnance, Stuart's cavalry division, 1862-1863; and from 1864-1865 as assistant adjutant general Artillery Corps, Army of Northern Virginia.

# 1ST COMPANY RICHMOND HOWITZERS

## CAPTAINS

McCarthy, Edward S.   Palmer, William P.   Shields, John C.

## LIEUTENANTS

Anderson, R. M., 1st Lieut.
Armistead, Robert, 2nd Lieut.
McCarthy, Dan S., 2nd Lieut.

Nimmo, John, 2nd Lieut.
Poindexter, George H., Lieut.D.M.
Williams, Henry S., Jr., 2nd Lieut.

## NON-COMMISSIONED OFFICERS AND PRIVATES

Anderson, J. C., Pvt.
Adkisson, C. E., Pvt.
Adams, Lewis, Cook
Anderson, J. H., Pvt.
Anderson, John, Cook
Anderson, L. C., Pvt.
Anderson, T. B., Jr., Pvt.
Arents, F. S., Pvt.
Armistead, Thomas S., Pvt.
August, James A., Pvt.
Ayers, E., Pvt.
Ayres, John G., Pvt.
Ayres, Samuel B., Pvt.
Ayres, T. E.
Baird, J. D., Pvt.
Ballard, F. S., Pvt.
Ballard, William P., Pvt.
Barksdale, T. W., Pvt.
Barnes, E. F., Pvt.
Barnes, F. J., Pvt.
Barnes, Hy. C., Pvt.
Barnes, J., Pvt.
Barnes, J. W., Pvt.
Barr, David, Pvt.
Barr, John W., Pvt.
Baxter, G. W., Pvt.
Bean, W., Pvt.
Bell, J. C., Pvt.
Bennett, Albert B.
Berrell, H. L., Pvt.
Binford, James H., Pvt.
Binford, Napoleon B., Pvt.
Blackadar, William H., Sergt. Major
Booker, George Jr., Pvt.
Booker, I. R., Pvt.
Booker, R. M., Pvt.
Boudar, H. B., Pvt.
Bowen, J. J., Pvt.
Bowman, S. H., Pvt.

Byrd, W. T.
Bradley, A. S., Pvt.
Brander, James T., Pvt.
Bransford, John, Pvt.
Bugg, Wilson N., Pvt.
Burr, H. D., Pvt.
Camm, Charles, Pvt.
Care, Riter G., Pvt.
Carter, H. C., Pvt.
Carter, James T., Pvt.
Carter, Lewis W.
Carter, Sam'l J., Pvt.
Cary, W. L., Pvt.
Chesterman, A. D., Pvt.
Close, Robert, Pvt.
Colburn, William S., Pvt.
Cooke, John Esten, Sergt.
Coyle, C., Pvt.
Crew, W. H.
Crouch, F. N., Pvt.
Croxton, C. C., Pvt.
Crump, George R., Corpl.
Cullingworth, Joseph N., Pvt.
Dame, W. M., Pvt.
Daniel, F. S., Pvt.
Davis, Decatur O., Artificer
Davis, J. C., Pvt.
Davis, Wm. H., Pvt.
Denman, A. M., Pvt.
Denny, George H., Pvt.
Dibrell, Anthony, Corpl.
Dibrell, W. S., Pvt.
Doggett, D. L. Jr., Pvt.
Dooley, C. W., Pvt.
Drewry, John W., Pvt.
Dudley, C., Pvt.
Dupuy, B. N., Pvt.
Early, George W., Pvt.

Edmondson, H. C., Pvt.
Eggleston, J. C., Pvt.
Ellett, James M., Pvt.
Ellis, George, Pvt.
Ellyson, W. P., Pvt.
Eustace, W. T., Pvt.
Exall, G. B., Conscript.
Farr, J. K., Pvt.
Finney, E. W., Pvt.
Fitch, Hy., Pvt.
Flournoy, Charles
Ford, John R., Pvt.
French, Marcellus, Pvt.
Friend, Charles N., Pvt.
Gibson, James W., Pvt.
Goodin, Ed. C., Pvt.
Gravatt, E. W., Pvt.
Gray, Charles J., Pvt.
Gray, Edward, Pvt.
Gray, J. T., Pvt.
Gray, S., Pvt.
Gretter, William P., Pvt.
Grigg, George L., Pvt.
Grundy, T. B., Pvt.
Guigon, A. B., Pvt.
Hardy, William J., Pvt.
Harrington, Charles A., Pvt.
Harris, B. F., Pvt.
Harris, B. W.
Harris, T. H., Pvt.
Harrison, Geo. E., Pvt.
Harrison, Henry, Pvt.
Harrison, Wm., Cook
Harrison, W. J., Pvt.
Harrison, W. L., Pvt.
Hart, Franklin, Pvt.
Harvey, M. L., Pvt.
Harwood, C. W., Pvt.
Herring, Elbridge, Pvt.
Herring, John H., Pvt.
Herring, William D., Pvt.
Higgason, A. E., Pvt.
Howard, Charles, Pvt.
Howard, J. C.
Johnston, J., Pvt.
Kean, William C., Pvt.
Kelly, R. J., Pvt.
Kepler, Henry, Pvt.
Kepler, Walter A., Pvt.
Kerr, J. M., Pvt.
Keyser, A. S., Pvt.

Kingsolving, C. J., Pvt.
Knight, E. C., Pvt.
Knight, R. D., Pvt.
Lambert, J. Ben., Pvt.
Lamkin, W. A., Pvt.
Leake, P. S., Pvt.
Lee, George, Pvt.
Lewis, C. M., Pvt.
Lewis, William T., Pvt.
Macon, Thomas J., Pvt.
Madden, James S., Pvt.
Maloney, John, Pvt.
Maloy, William, Pvt.
Marsden, (unknown), Pvt.
Marston, George P. P., Pvt.
Martin, S. Taylor, Pvt.
Martin, Thomas, Pvt.
Massie, Henry L., Pvt.
Mathews, John, Pvt.
Maury, R. H., Pvt.
Mayo, John C., Act.Asst. Surg.
McCabe, George R., Pvt.
McCabe, James E., Pvt.
McCandlish, Robert
McCreery, John Van Lew., Sergt.
McKenna, John T., Pvt.
McMillan, C. N., Pvt.
McNamee, George W., Pvt.
McReynolds, T. M., Pvt.
Meade, H. L., Pvt.
Meade, Peyton, Pvt.
Michaud, Paul, Pvt.
Michie, William E., Pvt.
Miller, Henry J., Pvt.
Minor, J. B., Pvt.
Moncure, T. D., Sergt.
Moore, E. D., Pvt.
Moore, Ro F., Pvt.
Moore, William S., Pvt.
Moran, Michael C., Pvt.
Morrison, M., Pvt.
Morton, Allan, Corpl.
Morton, G.Nash, Pvt.
Mosby, O. A., Pvt.
Moseley, John M., Corpl.
Niven, T. M., Pvt.
Page, C., Pvt.
Page, John W., Pvt.
Page, W. H., Pvt.
Pallard, B. G., Pvt.
Palmer, W. W., Pvt.

Parker, William H., Pvt.
Parrott, C. G., Pvt.
Peachy, Thos, G., Jr., Pvt.
Perry, William H., Pvt.
Petticord, S. M., Pvt.
Pleasants, Charles M.,Pvt.
Pleasants, John W., Pvt.
Pleasants, William A., Pvt.
Poindexter, Charles, Pvt.
Powell, Edward W., Pvt.
Powell, H. L., Pvt.
Powell, Junius L., Pvt.
Price, O. M., Pvt.
Puryear, William H., Pvt.
Rahm, F. H., Pvt.
Read, N. C.,
Redd, A. L., Pvt.
Reynolds, J. M., Pvt.
Richardson, A. M., Pvt.
Richardson, George T., Pvt.
Richardson, Ro E., Pvt.
Robinson, Leigh
Rogers, H. P., Pvt.
Rowland, R. G., Pvt.
Royall, J. B., Pvt.
Royall, R. W., Pvt.
Schooler, John H., Pvt.
Schlater, Lemuel H., Sergt.
Scott, Charles, Pvt.
Scott, J. A., Pvt.
Sears, Dewitt, Pvt.
Sears, L. L.,Pvt.
Seay, J. L., Pvt.
Seay, Jno. W.
Selden, Charles Jr., Pvt.
Seldon, N. W., Pvt.
Simms, W. E., Pvt.
Simpson, James H., Pvt.
Skinner, E. C.. Pvt.
Smith, B. L.,
Smith, William P., Pvt.
Snead, E. B., Pvt.
Snead, A. H., Pvt.
Snead, James W., Pvt.
South, T. J., Pvt.
Steane, E. G., Corpl.

Stiles, E. W.
Stiles, R. A., Pvt.
Stiles, R. R., Corpl.
Sublett, Harrison, Corpl.
Taliaferro, W. T., Pvt.
Tatum, John C.
Tatum, William H., Pvt.
Terrell, H. L., Pvt.
Thompson, John, Pvt.
Todd, Charles L., Sergt.
Todd, John W.
Todd, William R., Pvt.
Townsend, H. C., Corpl.
Trabue, Charles C., Sergt.
Trent, S. W.
Tucker, Ben L.
Tyler, J. H., Pvt.
Vaden, Sam'l E., Pvt.
Vest, Geo. S.
Waddill, W. L., Artificer
Wade, Edwin W., Pvt.
Washington, Wallace,Pvt.
Wayt,William, Pvt.
Wharton, R. G., Pvt.
White, Wm. G., Pvt.
Whiting, Thomas L., Pvt.
Wildt, Charles, Pvt.
Williams, E. A., Pvt.
Williams, Edgar, Cook
Williams, F. H., Conscript
Williams, F. S., Pvt.
Williams, J., Pvt.
Williams, James P., Corpl.
Williams, John N., Pvt.
Williams, Joseph G., Pvt.
Williams, W. L., Pvt.
Williamson, J. A., Pvt.
Wingo, Charles E., Pvt.
Wise, John B., Pvt.
Wise, L. A., Pvt.
Wortham, R. C., Pvt.
Wyatt, John W., Pvt.
Wyatt, R. W.,Q.M. Sergt.
Wyatt, Thomas B., Pvt.
Wynne, A. L., Pvt.
Yancey, John P., Corpl.

## HOWITZER BATTALION

## 2ND COMPANY

The 2nd Company, Richmond Howitzer Battalion, was organized on May 9, 1861 at the Richmond College artillery barracks. Lieutenant John Thompson Brown of Captain Randolph's original company was elected captain. At the time of his election he was in command of two detachments of the Howitzers stationed at Gloucester Point. The company, as formed in Richmond, joined the two detachments on May 27 at Yorktown. About this time Captain Brown received two of the original company's six Boat Howitzers, which, added to the two pieces he had taken to Gloucester Point about May 3, gave the 2nd Company a battery of four 12-pounder howitzers, one of which was rifled.

When it was learned on June 4 that Federal troops were at Bethel Church, about 15 miles from Yorktown, a small force including a detachment of the 2nd Company was sent out, but on arriving at the church they found that the Federals had left. On June 5 infantry and the remainder of the 2nd Company arrived; and later, Colonel D. H. Hill's 1st North Carolina Regiment and Major George Wythe Randolph with the 3rd Company, Howitzer Battalion.

Federal troops appeared before the lines at Bethel Church on June 10, and at 8:45 a.m. the opening shot of the battle, aimed by Major Randolph, was fired. Both companies of the Howitzer Battalion were conspicuously engaged in the cannonade which continued, with intervals of suspensions, until about 1:30 p.m. when the Federals withdrew. Colonel Hill, in his report, singled out the performance of the rifled howitzers detachment under Lieutenant Henry Hudnall and Sergeant S. B. Hughes of the 2nd Company, which was posted near the North Carolinians. Across the creek from the church, Captain Brown directed the fire of another howitzer under Sergeant Wharton. In the course of firing the piece was accidentally spiked when the priming wire, inserted in the vent too soon, was bent by the cartridge being rammed home. The disabled piece was hidden in the bushes, and the supporting infantry fell back across the creek. Later it was replaced by another piece from the 3rd Company, and, after the battle, the disabled howitzer was recovered and unspiked. Elsewhere on the field another of the battery's howitzers, under Sergeant Crane, routed with one shot a column of the 5th New York Zouaves advancing toward the ford about a mile below the bridge.

In September 1861, with the organization of the 1st Regiment Virginia Artillery, the 2nd Company was assigned to it and designated as Company A. Lieutenant Hudnall was promoted to captain, replacing Captain Brown, who was appointed as major of the regiment.

On October 3, when the troops under General Magruder were assigned outpost positions on the lower Peninsula, the rifled howitzer of the battery was posted at Ship Point on the Poquosin River and the other guns were posted at Harwood's Mill. By the time of General McClellan's attack of April 5, 1862, the 2nd Company was at Wynn's Mill, on the line extending from Yorktown along the Warwick River to Mulberry Point on the James River. On May 1 the 2nd Company, which had re-enlisted, reorganized and elected 2nd Lieutenant David Watson of Company H, (Albemarle Artillery), 1st Regiment Virginia Artillery, as their new captain.

The artillery evacuated the Peninsula lines on May 2, to begin the retreat toward Richmond. On May 30 the battery left camp at the Fairfield Race Course near the city, and on the 31st, with Hill's Division, was engaged at Seven Pines. In June the 2nd Company was back on duty with the 1st Regiment, now under Colonel Brown, their former captain. The regiment comprised part of the Reserve Artillery of which little use was made during the Seven Days' Battles. The 2nd Company was in the field, within the sound of battle, from June 26 until June 30 when they returned to camp at Blakey's Mill, near Richmond. After Malvern Hill the battery's teams were used to carry off captured ordnance. The 2nd Company was among the batteries, totaling thirty-two field pieces, that accompanied General Pendleton across the James River on July 29, and from Coggins Point and Maycox's, on the 31st, shelled Federal vessels and the camps on the other side of the river. After about 1,000 rounds had been expended, the batteries left and went into camp near Petersburg.

On August 19 the Reserve Artillery left Richmond, and on September 3 rejoined Lee's army near Manassas. During the Maryland Campaign the 1st Regiment was assigned to Jackson's Corps as reserves. The 2nd Company at this time was armed with two 10-pounder Parrott rifles, one 12-pounder howitzer, and a "Hotchkiss" rifle. En route to Sharpsburg, Colonel Brown's batteries were ordered on the 15th to guard the fords at Williamsport. The 2nd Company was ordered to Sharpsburg but was not engaged in the battle of the 17th.

Jackson's Corps began moving into the lines at Fredericksburg on the morning of December 12, and on the 13th, the day of Burnside's attack, Colonel Brown's batteries were held in readiness to go when and where they were needed. About one o'clock, two 10-pounder Parrotts and a bronze rifle from the 2nd Company, with a 3-inch rifle from the Powhatan Battery, all under charge of Captain Watson, were sent to support the guns already in action at Hamilton's Crossing, the right of Hill's Division and of the Confederate line. Later they were joined by two rifles from the 3rd Company, sent in to replace some guns which had been withdrawn for want of ammunition. The 2nd Company lost one man killed and seven wounded in the day's fighting. On December 16 the company, with the 1st Regiment, moved to Grace Church, Caroline County, and by January 1, 1863 was in winter quarters near Bowling Green, where they remained until April 29.

On the morning of May 1, 1863 the battery was in the line of march for Chancellorsville, and on the 2nd moved with Jackson on the flank march against the Federal right. Near Catherine Furnace the rear of Jackson's column was attacked by Federal infantry but a portion of the

1st Regiment, including the 2nd Company, went into position and drove them back. On May 3 the battery participated in the general attack against Hooker at Chancellorsville, losing four men wounded and four horses killed.

In the reorganization of the Army of Northern Virginia after the death of General Jackson, the 1st Regiment was assigned to the Reserve Artillery of Ewell's Corps. On June 10 the 1st Virginia Artillery left Culpeper Court House with Ewell's Corps for the march which would take them into Pennsylvania. The regiment was engaged in the capture of Winchester, and on July 1 it arrived at Gettysburg too late to participate in the first day's fighting. In the disposition of the batteries early the next morning, the 2nd Company was placed on the left of the railroad cut, and was engaged from about 4:00 p.m. until dark. On the 3rd the battery went into position on the right of the Fairfield road and commenced firing about 2:00 p.m. That night the batteries of the regiment went into camp in the rear, and on the night of the 4th started on the return march to Virginia. The battery's four 10-pounder Parrotts at Gettysburg fired 661 rounds; casualties were two killed on the 3rd.

A welcomed period of inactivity behind the Rapidan River followed the Gettysburg Campaign. The 1st Regiment spent most of August at Blue Run Church, Orange County, In September they were sent to Orange Court House, Morton's Ford, and Pisgah Church. After the battle of Bristoe, October 14, in which the 2nd Company was present but not engaged, they moved to Culpeper Court House and then to Brandy Station. Following a period of picket duty at Rappahannock Bridge, the company went into camp at Slaughter Mountain. In December, after the Mine Run operations, they went into winter quarters at Fredericks Hall, Louisa County.

On February 27, 1864 Captain Watson was promoted to major and second in command of the regiment, which, at this time, was also known as Hardaway's Light Artillery Battalion. 1st Lieutenant Lorraine F. Jones was appointed captain of the 2nd Company on the same day.

The battery moved with Ewell's Corps artillery into the Wilderness on May 5, but was not engaged until the 10th at Spotsylvania Court House, where they went into position on General Rodes' line. They remained on the line of battle during the 11th, and were again engaged in driving back the Federal attacks of the 12th and 18th.

Moving towards Richmond, the company went into camp on the Mechanicsville Turnpike about eight miles from the city on May 29. The company was held in reserve during the first and second days of the battle of Cold Harbor; however, on June 3 it was heavily engaged with the battalion in driving back the Federal assaulting columns, firing from positions south of Old Church Road. After Cold Harbor, and during June, when the fighting shifted south of Petersburg, Hardaway's Battalion remained on the lines east of Richmond.

In July the 2nd Company was transferred from Hardaway's Battalion to Major Wilford E. Cutshaw's Battalion, which consisted of the Charlottesville Battery, the Courtney Artillery from Henrico County, and

Courtesy Confederate Museum

Private John Werth, 2nd Company, Howitzer Battalion; wounded at Big Bethel on June 10, 1861 while serving the battery's rifled Dahlgren howitzer.

Virginia, 1864
By William Ludwell Sheppard, who served first as a private and later as 2nd lieutenant, 2nd Company, Howitzer Battalion, 1861-1865.

the Staunton Artillery. On August 9 Cutshaw's Battalion left Richmond for Gordonsville to join General Early's forces in the Valley. After participating in the operations around Winchester and Charlestown, the battalion, with Kershaw's Division, moved east of the Blue Ridge through the Luray Valley to Culpeper Court House and Gordonsville, rejoining Early on September 25 at Brown's Gap. On October 19, at Cedar Creek, the battery was among the last to leave the field, not moving until the infantry had been swept past and the Federals were within 300 yards of the guns. The order was given to limber up the guns, and moving on to the road they found it blocked by a wagon train. The Federals gained possession of the road and the guns. It was then every man for himself. The remnants of the company went into camp near New Market on the 31st. In December the company went into winter quarters on the Hamilton farm near Fisherville. The men were offered furloughs until spring with the provision that each take with him a battery horse to care for during the winter. Applicants, needless to say, exceeded the number of horses.

The battalion returned east in February 1865 and went on duty as heavy artillery at Fort Clifton on the Appomattox River. On March 7 the 2nd Company, numbering about sixty-six men armed with muskets, marched with the battalion to Petersburg. From there they proceeded by rail to Lynchburg where on the 9th they occupied positions on the line opposite the town. The company remained at Lynchburg until March 13, when they left by rail for High Bridge, remaining there until the 16th. On March 17 they returned to Fort Clifton.

Cutshaw's Battalion evacuated Fort Clifton on April 2 at 10:00 p.m. and, armed as infantry, marched westward with General Ewell's forces. On April 6 they fought at Deatonsville, where Major Cutshaw lost a leg. Those who escaped capture moved on through High Bridge and Farmville. Before the end, 1st Lieutenant Henry S. Jones was mortally wounded and others were killed, wounded or captured. On April 9 the 2nd Company, after fighting its last battle, surrendered. Captain Jones and forty-four of his company received their paroles at Appomattox Court House.

## 2ND COMPANY RICHMOND HOWITZERS

### CAPTAINS

Jones, Lorraine F.

### LIEUTENANTS

Angel, Joseph C., 2nd Lieut.
Jones, Henry S., 1st Lieut.

McRae, Wallace, 2nd Lieut.

### NON-COMMISSIONED OFFICERS AND PRIVATES

Abell, James D., Pvt.
Ackerman, James J., Pvt.
Allen, Henry C., Pvt.
Allgood, Edward A., Pvt.
Allgood, John J., Pvt.
Allgood, Samuel D., Pvt.
Attkisson, James T., Pvt.
Attkisson, J. M. N., Pvt.
Attkisson, William J., Pvt.
Barnes, Harvey G. H., Pvt.
Barnes, Luther R., Pvt.
Barnes, Silas W., Pvt.
Binford, James E., Pvt.
Blake, John L., Pvt.
Blanton, William E., Pvt.
Booker, Thomas, Pvt.
Bosher, E. Jeter, Pvt.
Bosher, Robert S., Sergt.
Brady, Philip, Pvt.
Brent, T. Carroll, Pvt.
Brown, George W., Artificer
Bryan, St. George, Pvt.
Buchanan, William, Pvt.
Burnley, Charles T., Pvt.
Burnley, Henry M., Pvt.
Butler, Elijah, Pvt.
Calyo, John A., Pvt.
Carson, J. C., Pvt.
Carter, George A., Pvt.
Casey, John W., Pvt.
Chapman, John E., Pvt.
Chappell, Joseph E., Sergt.
Christian, George L., Sergt.
Clark, David B., Corpl.
Cock, Erasmus R., Pvt.
Cocke, Calvin E., Pvt.
Cocke, Joseph S., Corpl.
Coleman, J. L. Pvt.
Crane, Henry R., Pvt.
Cross, James B., Pvt.
Davis, Creed T., Pvt.
Davis, Thomas J., Pvt.

Davis, William L., Pvt.
Dillard, Thomas J., Pvt.
Dunn, William W., Pvt.
Duval, Alexander, Pvt.
Eastin, William B., Pvt.
Ellett, John S., Sergt.
Elliott, C. F., Pvt.
Ellyson, James T., Pvt.
England, C. S., Pvt.
Faxon, John W., Pvt.
Fitzgerald, Nehemiah, Pvt.
Fleming, Abram, Pvt.
Fleming, John S., Pvt.
Foster, James B., Pvt.
Franklin, Lloyd B., Pvt.
Gardner, J. B., Pvt.
Gouldin, Samuel R., Pvt.
Grigg, James A., Pvt.
Hagan, James, Pvt.
Hamilton, William H., Pvt.
Hansborough, B. H., Pvt.
Harlow, Hudson M., Pvt.
Harris, M. V., Pvt.
Hines, John, Pvt.
Holladay, F. H., Pvt.
Hudson, William D., Pvt.
Hughes, George P., Pvt.
Hundley, Joseph W., Pvt.
Hutcheson, Hugh M., Pvt.
Hutchinson, William K., Pvt.
Jackson, Abel, Pvt.
James, John W., Pvt.
Jesse, James. M., Pvt.
Johnson, William R., Pvt.
Jones, E. L., Pvt.
Jones, John T. Pvt.
Jones, John W., Pvt.
Jones, Laney Jr., Sergt. Major
Jones, Peter L., Pvt.
Justice, David O., Pvt.
Kemp, Wyndham, Pvt.
Kersey, Robert

Lawrence, Samuel R., Pvt.
Lawson, Alexander, Pvt.
Lee, W. P., Pvt.
Lee, W. W., Pvt.
Leftwich, Thomas R., Pvt.
Lemon, William, Pvt.
Lewis, Theodore, Pvt.
Lipscomb, Spotswood, Pvt.
Lumpkin, Trueman, R., Pvt.
Mann, William J., Pvt.
Mason, James S., Pvt.
Maxey, Joseph E., Corpl.
Mayo, John B., Pvt.
McCarthy, Carlton, Pvt.
McCarthy, Julian, Pvt.
McCarthy, William H., Corpl.
McKinney, James S., Pvt.
Miller, Charles M., Pvt.
Miller, J. A., Pvt.
Mills, John, Pvt.
Moody, E. M., Pvt.
Mordecai, George W., Corpl.
Mordecai, John B., Pvt.
Mordecai, William Y., Q. M. Sgt.
Morris, Walter, H. P., Pvt.
Neighbors, William, Pvt.
New, John W., Pvt.
Norvell, S., Pvt.
O'Brien, William, Pvt.
Palmer, Charles T., Pvt.
Palmore, Thomas W., Pvt.
Parrack, Thomas C., Pvt.
Pattison, Richard G., Pvt.
Pleasants, Reuben B., Sergt.
Potts, John, Pvt.
Price, W. D., Pvt.

Pryor, John, Pvt.
Puryear, H. H., Pvt.
Ragland, John S., Pvt.
Roark, Elisha, Pvt.
Robinson, Andrew R., Pvt.
**Robinson**, Thomas V., Pvt.
Rodenheiser, J. C., Pvt.
Scruggs, George F., Pvt.
Semple, G. W., Pvt.
Shook, Henry C., Pvt.
Singleton, John C., Pvt.
Smith, Thomas S., Pvt.
Smith, William A., Pvt.
Swann, Thomas J., Pvt.
Taliaferro, John C., Pvt.
Tatum, Lucien B., Pvt.
Terrell, Joseph, Pvt.
Tinsley, James G., Pvt.
Tompkins, M. W., Pvt.
Trent, Stephen A., Pvt.
Vanname, Peter M., Pvt.
Waldrop, John, Pvt.
Walfor, Edward F., Pvt.
Walker, H. T., Pvt.
Watkins, Samuel V., Pvt.
White, William T., Pvt.
Williams, Joseph G., Corpl.
Wingfield, W. T., Pvt.
Winston, James D., Pvt.
Winston, William C., Pvt.
Wood, R. W., Pvt.
Worsham, Luther W., Pvt.
Worsham, W. G., Pvt.
Yates, James A., Pvt.
Yeatts, T. B., Pvt.

## HOWITZER BATTALION

## 3RD COMPANY

    The 3rd Company, Richmond Howitzer Battalion, was organized at the Baptist College artillery camp, Richmond, on May 10, 1861 with the election of Robert C. Stanard as captain. As frequently occurred, the company was also referred to as Stanard's Battery, after its captain. Soon after its organization, the Howitzer Battalion was transferred to Howard's Grove. By May 21, the battalion was encamped on Chimborazo Heights, near Griffin's Spring, overlooking the James River, Rocketts, and the suburban town of Fulton.
    The company left Richmond on June 4, 1861 for Yorktown. Traveling by railroad and steamer, the company arrived on the 5th and was sent to Bethel Church on the next day. Here they joined the 2nd Company Richmond Howitzers and North Carolina infantry under Colonel D. H. Hill. Federal troops appeared before the lines at Bethel Church on June 10, and at 8:45 a.m., the opening shot of the battle, aimed by Major Randolph, was fired. Both companies of the Howitzer Battalion were conspicuously engaged in the cannonade which continued, with intervals of suspensions, until about 1:30 p.m., when the Federals withdrew. On the 11th the 3rd Company withdrew to Yorktown and returned to Bethel Church on the 13th. It remained on guard duty until the 19th when it returned to Yorktown. The Company Clerk reported on August 31, 1861 that "since that time a part or all of the company have participated in the various expeditions towards Hampton, Newport News, &c. At this time two of the guns with their detachments are at Mulberry Island and two at Ship Point." On the 1st of September the company was divided and one section was stationed at Deep Creek and the other at Camp Curtis. In September 1861, with the organization of the 1st Regiment Virginia Artillery, the 3rd Company was assigned to it, and designated as Company D.
    The sections of the company remained divided on outpost duty at their respective stations for the rest of the year. On October 27, 1861 Captain Stanard died of disease, and 1st Lieutenant Edgar F. Moseley was appointed captain on November 16. Remaining as stationed on September 1, the two sections went into winter quarters, where they remained until March 4, 1862 when ordered to move to Suffolk. The company was reunited on the 5th and moved to Petersburg by way of City Point. From Petersburg it went by rail to Suffolk, arriving on the 7th. This move transferred the company from the Army of the Peninsula, under Magruder, to the Department of Norfolk, under Huger. The force collected at Suffolk was a reserve, and had been created to support the troops at Norfolk and defend the railroad and the town of Suffolk from raiding parties. The company was mustered in for the war on March 25, 1862 and remained at Suffolk until April 21, when it moved with a small force to Sandy Cross, N. C., where it remained until the 2nd of May when it returned to Suffolk. With the evacuation of Norfolk, General Huger withdrew his forces to

Petersburg. One section of the company withdrew from Suffolk on May 8, while the other section was moved east of the town into defensive works. On May 12 the works were evacuated and the troops retired to Petersburg, where the company was reunited on the 16th. It remained at Petersburg until the 28th when it was marched to Richmond where it went into camp on Williams' farm, below the city. At this time the 1st Regiment Virginia Artillery was assigned to the Reserve Artillery; however, as a battle was imminent, some companies of the 1st Regiment Virginia Artillery were assigned to infantry brigades. The 3rd Company, now under Captain Benjamin H. Smith, Jr., was assigned to Brigadier General Winfield S. Featherston's Brigade, Longstreet's Division, on June 25. The company was under a new captain by reason of Captain Moseley's promotion to major and 1st Lieutenant Benjamin H. Smith, Jr., to captain on June 22, 1862. The activities of the company were reported by Colonel J. Thompson Brown, 1st Regiment Virginia Artillery, as follows:

>...The...3rd Howitzers, Captain B. H. Smith, having been ordered to join Featherston's brigade, General Longstreet's division, reached Mechanicsville at 10 p.m. on Thursday, June 26.
>
>On Friday, 27th, it was engaged with good effect at Catlin's house, one section being in the orchard and the other to the right of the house. They continued their fire until the enemy left the field.
>
>In the evening of the same day it was again engaged at Gaines' Farm, the three howitzers being stationed on the brow of the hill, near the barn, whence they shelled the enemy's position in the woods. The Parrott piece on the right of the barn engaged one of the enemy's batteries on the south side of the Chickahominy, thus drawing a raking fire away from our infantry while charging the enemy's position. The Parrott gun continued to fire until the enemy's battery became silent, but I myself, being accidently present, withdrew the howitzers early in the evening. They were inefficient against the battery because of their short range, and they could no longer shell the enemy's infantry without endangering our own troops.
>
>This battery was subsequently [withdrawn back to Hogan's farm on the night of June 27-28, where it remained until] engaged on this side of the Chickahominy in the battle of Monday, 30th, near Enroughty's house. It fired but a few rounds, still it was much exposed to the fire of artillery and infantry.
>
>The battery was not engaged on Tuesday, and has now rejoined the regiment....

The company returned to camp on July 4 and remained there until August 6 when the troops were advanced to Malvern Hill to confront

McClellan's army. The move by McClellan proved to be a feint and he retired soon after the Confederates began making contact with his skirmishers. With McClellan drawing back into his base, the Confederate troops were ordered back to Richmond. The 3rd Company returned to Richmond on August 8. When General Lee moved Longstreet's command to reinforce Jackson, the Reserve Artillery was left in the defenses of Richmond. On August 15 the company was sent to Petersburg, where it remained until the 22nd when it was ordered back to Richmond.

The Reserve Artillery remained at Richmond until August 26 when it was ordered to join the Army of Northern Virginia. After a long arduous march, the Reserve Artillery joined the army on Manassas plains on September 3. The 3rd Company, with the remaining companies of the 1st Regiment Virginia Artillery, arrived at Gainesville on the 4th and moved to Leesburg on the 6th. The next day they crossed the Potomac and moved to Frederick, Md. From Frederick the company moved with Longstreet's command toward Hagerstown, while Jackson's command moved to capture Harpers Ferry. The action at Boonesboro Gap forced Lee to recall Longstreet's leading elements, and to concentrate Longstreet's command in an effort to hold McClellan while the rest of the army retired toward Sharpsburg and Jackson completed the siege and capture of Harpers Ferry. The 1st Regiment Virginia Artillery was ordered to guard the ford at Williamsport, arriving at that point on September 15. The next day they moved to Shepherdstown and returned to Williamsport where they were engaged on the 19th and 20th of September.

During this campaign the company was reported equipped with two 10-pounder Parrotts and two 20-pounder Parrotts. With the withdrawal of the Army of Northern Virginia from Sharpsburg and its return to Virginia, the 1st Regiment Virginia Artillery moved to join the army encamped near Bunker Hill.

The company remained in camp after rejoining the army. The rifle section left camp en route for Charlestown where it arrived October 2, and was ordered on picket duty on the Harpers Ferry and Charlestown Turnpike. It remained until October 16 when a skirmish took place and the Confederate forces retreated to Charlestown. During the action the rifle section suffered one killed and three wounded, one of the latter being Captain Smith who was wounded in the foot as he was bringing off the second gun. Because of the nature of the wound, Captain Smith's foot was amputated, and he was left at Charlestown where he was captured. Captain Smith was paroled at Charlestown and returned to Richmond to await his exchange. During his absence the company was commanded by 1st Lieutenant James S. Utz. After this action the rifle section returned to camp near Bunker Hill. On October 28 the company broke camp and joined Jackson's Corps.

When McClellan moved across the Potomac, Lee moved Longstreet's Corps east of the mountains, leaving Jackson in the Valley. When the Federal army, now under Burnside, moved toward Fredericksburg, Lee moved Longstreet to that town. Jackson remained in the Valley until ordered to join the army at Fredericksburg. Leaving Winchester on November 20, the company arrived at Guiney's Station on the 3rd of December. The next day it moved in the direction of Port Royal. On December 10 the company moved near Port Tobacco and fired a few shots at the enemy's gunboats on the Rappahannock and returned to Port Republic. Leaving Port Republic on the 12th, the company moved in the direction of Fredericksburg, and arrived on the field in rear of Hamilton's Crossing about 4 a.m. on the 13th. The rifled 10-pounder Parrott section of the company was ordered to Major John Pelham on the extreme right of the line. The section went into action about 11 a.m. and remained in action until about 8 p.m., withdrawing once for a short time for ammunition. During the action the guns under Pelham received heavy firing from the Federal artillery across the river. However, they concentrated their fire on the Federal infantry. By the end of the day the 3rd Company had lost three killed and three wounded. Among those killed was 1st Lieutenant Utz. 2nd Lieutenant Henry Clay Carter was promoted to 1st Lieutenant and assumed the duties of commanding officer. The smoothbore howitzer section did not see action on December 13; however, it was moved up on the infantry line on the 14th in the expectancy of another attack. The rifled section remained on the right on the 14th. On December 16 the company was moved back to camp at Grace Church, Burnside having withdrawn to the north side of the Rappahannock. The company was sent on picket duty on the Rappahannock and remained until the 29th when it moved to camp near Bowling Green, Caroline County. On the 30th the artillery moved to a regular camp near Bowling Green, and went into winter quarters.

The routine of winter quarters was broken on January 19, 1863 when the company was ordered to Grace Church. The Federal army's move up the north side of the Rappahannock made it necessary to move some of the troops closer to Fredericksburg. The mud forced Burnside to cancel his plans. With the return of the Federals to their base, the company returned to its camp near Bowling Green on January 27. Here, on February 15, 1863, the 1st Regiment Virginia Artillery was assigned to Jackson's Corps as Colonel J. Thompson Brown's Battalion (Reserve). An inspection report, dated February 20, 1863 lists the company equipped with two 10-pounder Parrotts and two 12-pounder Navy howitzers. It remained in camp until ordered to report to Hamilton's Crossing on April 29. Joining Jackson's Corps, the company moved with that command to reinforce General Anderson at Salem Church. General Hooker had moved his army up the north side of the Rappahannock, crossed over, and was moving east on the rear of Lee's army. With Anderson's and Jackson's troops Lee moved against Hooker, and the latter retired to Chancellorsville. The company, with Captain Smith in command, was in the rear of Jackson's column on the move to flank Hooker's position at Chancellorsville on the night of May 1-2. During the march the artillery was engaged at Catherine Furnace and cut off from the infantry. However, infantry reinforcements succeeded in driving the Federals back and the artillery continued the march. Jackson's infantry advanced and rolled up Hooker's right flank before the 3rd Company arrived on the field. When the fighting died down on the 2nd, the Federals were in a strong defensive position. The next day, the 3rd Company was ordered to Hazel Grove, where the Confederate artillery was massed to enfilade the strong Federal position. The fierce infantry attacks, combined with the heavy artillery bombardment, forced the Federals to retire to a defensive line north of Chancellorsville. Hooker's army retired north of the Rappahannock and back to their camps opposite Fredericksburg. Lee moved his army back to Fredericksburg, and the 3rd Company was stationed near Hamilton's Crossing.

Following the death of Jackson, the Army of Northern Virginia was reorganized and the 1st Regiment Virginia Artillery, known as Brown's Battalion, was assigned to Ewell's Corps Reserve Artillery. Ewell's Corps was chosen to be the advance element of Lee's army on his march into Pennsylvania. On June 4, 1863 the 3rd Company left Hamilton's Crossing for Culpeper Court House. Arriving on the 8th, the company left on the 10th for the Valley. Advancing with Early's Division, the company was engaged on the west of Winchester on June 14. It was at Winchester, on June 17, that the 3rd Company exchanged its two 10-pounder Parrotts with the 2nd Company for two 3-inch rifled guns. It now had four of the latter. On June 22 the company crossed the Potomac and advanced with Ewell's Corps through Maryland and into Pennsylvania. On June 29 it was in camp near Carlisle. The next day it was ordered back, and, following Ewell's Corps, arrived on the field at Gettysburg in the evening of July 1. On the 2nd the battery was placed in position near the seminary and shelled the Federal lines. On July 3 it was moved to the right of the Fairfield road, where it shelled the enemy lines during the unsuccessful attempt to break their center. Retiring with the army on the next day, the company recrossed the Potomac on July 14, minus the company wagon which had been captured on the retreat. From Winchester, the army moved to Culpeper Court House, and on August 2 the company was stationed at Blue Run Church, Orange County. Here the company remained until September 13 when it moved to within three miles of Rapidan Station, and marched to Morton's Ford on the 19th. On the 23rd the company left Morton's Ford and marched to Pisgah Church. On October 8 it left Pisgah Church and joined the army in the move against Meade's army which terminated in the battle of Bristoe Station on October 14, 1863. Unsuccessful in his efforts to cut off Meade's retreat, Lee withdrew his army to the south side of the Rappahannock. When Meade advanced in late November, Lee retired to a defensive position along Mine Run. The Federals advanced to this line but did not attack. On December 1-2 Meade withdrew north of the Rapidan. The 3rd Company was actively engaged during this campaign and on December 21 marched to Frederick's Hall and went into winter quarters. With the exception of a move to Orange Court House on February 6, 1864 and return on February 11, the company remained at Frederick's Hall until the beginning of the spring campaign in 1864.

With the coming of spring, the company left Frederick's Hall on April 18 and camped near Barboursville on the 20th. Official returns show that the company was still in Brown's Battalion, Ewell's Corps. On May 4 the artillery was moved toward the Wilderness battlefield, but was not engaged because of the terrain. On the 7th the company was ordered to Spotsylvania Court House and went into position in front of the Harris House on the 10th. Here the battery was engaged in shelling the enemy's skirmishers and in replying to one of his batteries nearly all day on the 10th. About 6 p.m. on the 10th a Federal assault column broke through the Confederate infantry on the right of the battery, thus coming upon the right and rear of the battery, which necessitated the temporary abandonment of the guns. General W. N. Pendleton reported that: "The captain had fought his battery until he was actually seized by soldiers from the enemy's ranks, and some of his men were carried off by the retreating foe and not recovered." A Confederate counterattack drove the Federals out of the lines and the guns were recovered. At the end of the day the battery's losses totaled six killed, nine wounded, twenty-four captured (including Captain Smith), and twenty-four horses killed and disabled. Men from Captain Asher W. Garber's Company, Virginia Light Artillery, were sent to assist the survivors in manning the guns. The company again fell under the temporary command of 1st Lieutenant Carter. On May 14 the company went into position a few hundred yards to the left of the Harris House, where it was engaged on the 18th in repulsing a Federal assault. The 3rd Company left its position on the line on May 21 and moved in the direction of Hanover Junction, where it went into position near the railroad depot on the 25th. The moves of the company after this date were recorded by the company clerk as follows:

> 27th moved towards Atlee's Station. 28th moved to Cold Harbor road 7 1/2 miles from Richmond. May 31 moved to Cowardin's farm. June 1st went into position in front of Pole Green Church, in the evening the enemy charged, but were easily repulsed with considerable loss. No casualties. 2, 3, 4 remained in camp at Cowardin's farm. 5th went into position to left of Johnson House. 7th went in front of our lines to right of Johnson House and opened enfilading fire on enemy's lines. 8th moved to Gaines' farm. 13th crossed the Chickahominy at McClellan's Bridge and camped near Savage Station. 17th moved to camp near Chaffin's farm.

When Lee moved the bulk of his army to Petersburg, Brown's Battalion, now under Lieutenant Colonel Robert A. Hardaway and known as Hardaway's Battalion, remained north of the James River. The company was put in position on New Market Heights on June 26 where it aided in repulsing a Federal advance on August 16. On September 2 the 1st Regiment Virginia Artillery was redesignated the 1st Battalion Virginia Light Artillery, and the 3rd Company became Company D of the battalion. Also Captain Smith returned to command the company after being paroled and exchanged on September 22. However, illness prevented his active presence with the company, and 1st Lieutenant Carter continued as acting commanding officer.

Owing to the capture of Fort Harrison on September 29, the artillery had to be withdrawn to the intermediate lines. On that day, the 3rd Company retired up New Market road supported by Brigadier General Martin W. Gary's Cavalry. The cavalry and artillery made a stand at Laurel Hill Church and fought until they were flanked on the left and compelled to withdraw. Subsequently the battery went into position on the intermediate line to the left of Fort Gilmer and remained until October 16 when it was ordered to take position to the left of the Henrico Poor House on the new line extension from Fort Gilmer across the New Market, Darbytown, and Williamsburg roads. In October the 1st Battalion Virginia Light Artillery was reported in Longstreet's Corps. On the evening of October 27 the enemy made an assault upon an angle of the works occupied by one gun of the battery, but after reaching within one hundred yards of the gun was forced to retire, leaving thirty-eight dead in front of the gun. The detachment manning the gun lost two killed and two wounded. The company remained in position in the lines between the New Market and Darbytown roads through December. On December 28 it was reported equipped with four 12-pounder Napoleons.

By Special Orders No. 14, paragraph 18, Adjutant and Inspector General's Office, dated January 18, 1865, the 1st Battalion Virginia Light Artillery was disbanded and the companies became independent batteries. The 3rd Company was officially designated Captain Benjamin H. Smith's Battery, Virginia Artillery. The battery remained in the Richmond defenses until April 2, 1865 when the lines were evacuated. Passing through Richmond, the company joined the army under Lee, retreating westward from Petersburg. At Deatonville, on April 6, the battery was engaged in a half hour skirmish with Federal cavalry. On April 8 the 3rd Company camped within four miles of Appomattox Court House. That evening the members assisted in the burial of several guns belonging to companies of the old 1st Battalion Virginia Light Artillery. Moving to Appomattox Court House on the 9th, the company went into position on the line and replied in kind to Federal batteries. On that day the Army of Northern Virginia was surrendered, and ninety-five members of the 3rd Company Howitzers were paroled.

# 3RD COMPANY RICHMOND HOWITZERS

## CAPTAIN

Smith, Benjamin H., Jr.

## LIEUTENANTS

Carter, Henry C., 1st Lieut.  
Payne, William P., 2nd Lieut.

Read, William M., 2nd Lieut.

## NON-COMMISSIONED OFFICERS AND PRIVATES

Alsop, Baswell, Pvt.
Anderson, Joseph J., Pvt.
Andrews, Andrew J., Pvt.
Armistead, William M., Pvt.
Austin, John M., Pvt.
Austin, Thomas H., Pvt.
Barksdale, Henry W., Pvt.
Barksdale, Thomas W., Pvt.
Barnard, Dudley W., Pvt.
Bass, Hubert O., Pvt.
Bass, Robert P., Pvt.
Blackburn, W. S., Pvt.
Blanks, Glendon, Pvt.
Bohannon, Joseph T., Pvt.
Boisseau, C. C., Pvt.
Boisseau, Theoderick, Pvt.
Bowles, John T., Pvt.
Breeden, Hoskins, Pvt.
Breeden, William Jr., Pvt.
Brent, W. E., Pvt.
Brooke, Richard, Pvt.
Brooks, Thomas V., Corpl.
Bugg, John R., Pvt.
Bullington, Heger, Pvt.
Burwell, Dandridge S., Pvt.
Cardoza, Edward S., Pvt.
Casey, Jesse R., Pvt.
Chamberlayne, Richard C., Pvt.
Chastain, James B., Pvt.
Chew, Hugh P., Pvt.
Clarke, James E., Pvt.
Clarke, S., Pvt.
Cattrell, Henry L., Pvt.
Cottrell, Joseph F., Pvt.
Courtney, William B., Pvt.
Cropper, George T., Pvt.
Crump, Edward M., Pvt.
Crump, John A., Pvt.
Cullen, Edward F., Pvt.
Davis, Samuel H., Pvt.
Donnan, David, Pvt.

Eaton, P. J., Pvt.
Ellett, Edwin J., Pvt.
Evans, Henry J., Pvt.
Fisher, W. H., Pvt.
Flournoy, Henry W., Pvt.
Flournoy, John J., Corpl.
Foster, George M., Pvt.
Fourqureau, Charles B., Pvt.
Fourqureau, Joseph M., Pvt.
Fourqureau, Matthew W., Pvt.
French, James H., Pvt.
Gambal, Robert J., Pvt.
Gardner, Henry D., Pvt.
Gardner, Miles H., Corpl.
Gardner, Miles H., Pvt.
Goode, Robert B., Pvt.
Goode, William E., Pvt.
Green, William H., Pvt.
Green, William W., Pvt.
Gretter, Frederick P., Pvt.
Gretter, William B., 1st Sergt.
Hammond, John T., Pvt.
Hardwick, John T., Pvt.
Harris, James L., Pvt.
Harris, John C., Pvt.
Herring, C. O., Pvt.
Herring, William D., Pvt.
Hogg, Thomas, Pvt.
Hunt, Claiborne B., Corpl.
Hutcherson, John H., Pvt.
Jean, Cincinnatus, Pvt.
Jeter, Francis A., Pvt.
Johnson, G. E., Pvt.
James, Alfred O., Pvt.
Jones, Edward V., Pvt.
Jones, Henry, Pvt.
Jones, I. L., Pvt.
Jones, Thomas S., Pvt.
Jones, Wiley J., Pvt.
Jones, William R., Pvt.
Keesee, F. M., Pvt.

Keesee, Thomas, Pvt.
Lane, George T., Pvt.
Lear, John S., Pvt.
Lear, William W., Pvt.
Levy, Daniel A., Pvt.
Liggon, Samuel H., Pvt.
Lorraine, Edward C., Pvt.
Lumpkin, Leonzio, Sergt.
Lyell, George J., Pvt.
Lyne, William H., Pvt.
Mahoney, Elias N., Pvt.
Mahoney, Francis J., Pvt.
Major, S. C., Pvt.
Manders, James M., Pvt.
Manders, John, Pvt.
Mayo, Thomas T., Pvt.
Mayo, William C. A., Pvt.
Miller, Thomas M., Pvt.
Mitchell, Richard B., Pvt.
Morgan, John H., Pvt.
Morris, Edlow P., Pvt.
Morrison, Charles R., Pvt.
Moultry, James, Pvt.
O'Connor, Patrick, Farrier
Pagard, Thaddeus, Pvt.
Page, Carter B., Pvt.
Pagua, I., Pvt.
Parker, George J., Pvt.
Parkhill, Charles, Pvt.
Piet, William A., Pvt.
Plume, Augustus H., Pvt.
Plumer, Henry, Pvt.
Porter, David E., Pvt.
Porter, George W., Pvt.
Porter, Peter B., Pvt.
Porter, Wallace D., Pvt.
Powell, James P., Pvt.
Powell, Thomas L., Pvt.
Powell, T. P., Pvt.
Puller, William B., Pvt.
Quarles, Thomas H., Sergt.
Roberts, Robert R., Corpl.
Roberts, William H., Pvt.
Rollin, W., Pvt.
Roper, George K., Pvt.
Santas, F., Pvt.
Saunders, William, Pvt.
Sclater, William M., Pvt.
Scott, George T., Pvt.
Sheppard, Sterling C., Pvt.
Sizer, John J., Jr., Pvt.
Smith, J. N., Pvt.
Smith, Oscar V., Corpl.
Soublette, James D., Pvt.
Sublett, C. T., Pvt.
Sublett, Edward H., Pvt.
Sublett, Peter A., Corpl.
Sublett, William B., Pvt.
Swann, Robert B., Pvt.
Sydnor, Roger J., Pvt.
Sydnor, William J., Q.M.Sergt.
Taliaferro, A. F., Pvt.
Thaxton, George D., Sergt.
Thompson,
Trice, J. J., Pvt.
Tyler, E. G., Pvt.
Wakeham, Alfred, Corpl.
Wakeham, William, Pvt.
White, Robert C., Pvt.
White, William S., Sergt.
Whitlock, Thomas, Pvt.
Winfree, Powhaton, Pvt.
Winfree, Reuben, Pvt.
Winn, Edwin A., Pvt.
Winn, John, Pvt.

## HOWITZER BATTALION

## 4TH COMPANY

In June 1861 Private Napoleon B. Binford of Captain John Thompson Brown's Company of Artillery (2nd Company, Richmond Howitzer Battalion) was commissioned a captain by Governor Letcher and authorized to raise a company of artillery, which was to be designated the 4th Company, Richmond Howitzer Battalion. On June 27, 1861 Captain Binford advertised in the Richmond Dispatch that he needed twenty-two men to complete the company. By July 5 he had forty-five men and officers on the roll, and on July 18 the company was enrolled in the artillery service and stationed at Camp Lee, just west of the city, where it was hoped the company could be completed. However, on August 29, 1861 the company was disbanded by order of Governor Letcher, because it was under strength with still only forty-five men on the muster roll.

Courtesy National Archives

Confederate Artillerymen at Dinner.
Drawing by Allen C. Redwood.
Reproduced from Battles and Leaders of the Civil War.

## 4TH COMPANY RICHMOND HOWITZERS

### CAPTAIN

Binford, N. B.

### LIEUTENANTS

Armistead, George W., 1st Lieut.  
Kirby, J. L. S., Jr., 1st Lieut.  
Michie, William E., 2nd Lieut.

### NON-COMMISSIONED OFFICERS AND PRIVATES

Boyd, J. P., Pvt.
Chandler, Linsay T., Pvt.
Chum, George H., Pvt.
Clay, Richard S., Pvt.
Darland, Nicholas, Pvt.
Dunn, Richard S., Pvt.
Duval, Robert R., Pvt.
Edwards, A. C., Corpl.
Fitzgerald, William, Pvt.
Ford, F. W., Pvt.
Ford, William T., Pvt.
Green, John L., Pvt.
Green, William C., Pvt.
Hall, A. J., Sergt.
Hall, J. T., Sergt.
Harlow, D. W., Pvt.
Harlow, J. W., Pvt.
Higgeson, Albert E., Pvt.
Holt, John D., Pvt.
Lambert, S. Ben, Pvt.
Lipenskie, Joseph, Pvt.

Luz, Fridolin, Pvt.
Madison, Melvill, Pvt.
Mahone, D. W., Pvt.
Malory, J. P., Pvt.
Morriss, George P., Pvt.
Place, William B., Pvt.
Pryneer, B. F., Pvt.
Robinson, James, Pvt.
Sheel, Charles E., Pvt.
Skinnen, William W., Pvt.
Snead, R. J., Pvt.
Sullens, A., Pvt.
Tomkies, A. J., Pvt.
Twiford, Rivel, Corpl.
Van Dyke, J., Sergt.
Watts, J. Thomas, Pvt.
Wharton, W. A., Corpl.
Winston, E. T., Pvt.
Yarbrough, C. B., 1st Sergt.
Yarington, C., Corpl.

## COURTNEY ARTILLERY

Captain Alfred R. Courtney's company of light artillery, which included men from Henrico County and the City of Richmond, enlisted on July 8, 1861, and was first stationed at the Richmond College artillery barracks. On August 28, 1861 the company was ordered to Manassas Junction for duty with the army there under General Joseph E. Johnston.

During the winter, General Johnston's Army of the Potomac was organized into four divisions, and Courtney's Battery was assigned to General Trimble's Seventh Brigade, Third Division, of which Major General R. S. Ewell assumed command on February 12, 1862. Ewell's Division joined General Jackson in the Valley on May 21, and at Front Royal on the 23rd, the battery's one rifled gun was brought into action under Lieutenant Joseph White Latimer, who as a cadet at the Virginia Military Institute had received gunnery instruction from Jackson. The battery was engaged at Winchester on May 25, and on the retreat to Port Republic took its turn in serving with Ashby's cavalry in the rear guard. On June 8 the battery was among those engaged at Cross Keys, firing until its ammunition was exhausted, and leaving the field with two killed and ten wounded. In his report of the battle at Cross Keys, Trimble recorded:

> Of the heroic conduct of the officers and men of Courtney's battery, commanded by Captain Courtney, with Lieutenant Latimer as first lieutenant, in holding their position under the incessant fire of four batteries at one time, I cannot speak in terms which would do them full justice. The fact that they stood bravely up to their work for over five hours, exhausted all their shot and shell, and continued their fire with canister to the end of the battle, speaks more in their favor than the most labored panegyric. The most admirable position selected for the battery alone saved it from total destruction, if a special Providence did not guard it from harm.

Jackson's Army of the Valley District, with Ewell's Division in advance, reached Lee's forces east of Richmond on June 27, in time for the second of the Seven Days' Battles, known as Gaines' Mill. Late in the afternoon, Lieutenant Colonel Stapleton Crutchfield, Jackson's Chief of Artillery, ordered in three batteries, including Courtney's, to engage the Federal batteries which were firing on the infantry. The fire of Crutchfield's artillery was effectively directed, and soon the batteries were able to continue their work, advancing by "half battery" with the infantry. By nightfall, the Federals were in retreat. Trimble's Brigade was on the extreme left of the line at Malvern Hill on July 1, and Courtney's Battery, going into position about 5:00 P.M., was engaged for about a half an hour, firing effectively until they were "withdrawn reluctantly" by an order, as it was later learned, intended for another battery.

Ewell's Division, on July 13, was ordered to proceed with Jackson to check the advance of Pope, moving from the direction of Orange Court House. Crutchfield's batteries moved with the infantry by railroad, and arrived at Gordonsville on July 19. On the 20th, Captain Courtney was promoted to major, commanding the batteries of Ewell's Division, and Lieutenant Latimer was promoted to captain, replacing Courtney. At this time the battery consisted of two 3-inch rifles and two Napoleon 12-pounders.

On August 9, at Cedar Mountain, the battery, brought up early in the battle, was engaged in a duel with Federal batteries, which lasted for almost two hours. Casualties in the battery amounted to five wounded. Jackson's Corps, forming the left wing of Lee's army, moved northward, and on August 28-30, at Second Manassas, inflicted a defeat on Pope which sent the Federals in retreat to Centreville. Latimer's Battery did not participate in the fighting of the 28th, but was actively engaged throughout the next two days.

After the battle of Chantilly, in which the battery was not engaged, the army moved into Maryland. At Harpers Ferry on September 14, Crutchfield skillfully placed his batteries, including Latimer's, into a position from which, on the 15th, they delivered an effective fire into the rear of a battery on the federal left on Bolivar Heights. The battery, for lack of horses, and two disabled guns, was left at Harpers Ferry, while Crutchfield moved on to Sharpsburg. He later returned and replenished the battery with horses and two 3-inch rifles, replacing the two 10-pounder Parrotts, which had burned out vent plugs from the action on the 15th. The battery then proceeded to Sharpsburg, but did not arrive in time to take part in the fighting on the 17th.

On December 13, at Fredericksburg, Captain Latimer, acting as Chief of Artillery of the Division, was placed in command of a battery of five rifled guns, posted in an exposed position on the left of Jackson's Corps, across Deep Run from Pender's Brigade. Two of the guns, under Lieutenant William A. Tanner, were from Latimer's battery. They were constantly engaged from about 11:00 A. M. until dark. The Courtney Artillery lost one private killed, seven men, including Lieutenant Tanner, wounded, and had eight horses disabled.

In February 1863 the battery was on duty with Trimble's Division near Rappahannock Academy. Its armament then consisted of two 3-inch Dahlgren rifles and two Napoleons. With the reorganization of the artillery in April, the battery was assigned to Lieutenant Colonel Hilary P. Jones' Battalion, attached to Trimble's Division of the Second Corps. Lieutenant Tanner was promoted to captain of the battery, replacing Latimer, who was promoted to major and assigned to Andrew's artillery battalion of the same corps.

The battery, which was not engaged at Chancellorsville until the third day, was apparently by this time equipped with four Napoleons. On the morning of May 3 two of these guns were detached from the battery and participated in the fighting at Hazel Grove. The remaining two pieces, under Captain Tanner, served with Jones' Battalion, not being relieved until after the Federals had been driven from their positions in front of the Chancellor House.

In the reorganization of the army, May 30, 1863, Jones' Battalion of four batteries, which included Tanner's, was assigned to Early's Division, Ewell's Corps. On June 4 the second invasion of the North began with the departure of Ewell from Hamilton's Crossing near Fredericksburg. On June 27 the Courtney Artillery was attached to Gordon's Brigade, and on the 28th was engaged in battle near Wrightsville. The battery rejoined the division on the 30th, and on July 1 took part in the first day's battle at Gettysburg. The battalion was not actively engaged on the 2nd and 3rd. On the return march to Virginia, the battery successfully repulsed a number of attacks on the wagon train before rejoining the battalion at Williamsport.

The battery participated in the skirmish at Summersville Ford, on the Rapidan River, September 14, and on October 14 was brought into action at Bristoe Station, where Captain Tanner was wounded. He was taken to Warrenton, but, because of his wound, could not be removed when the army withdrew, and was taken prisoner. The battery went into camp near Brandy Station, remaining there until November 4, when it marched to the vicinity of Cedar Mountain. On November 27 the battery was engaged at Mine Run where three men were wounded, and three horses were killed. In December the Courtney Artillery was in camp near Fredericks Hall, on the Virginia Central Railroad, Louisa County.

On May 5, 1864, the artillery battalions of the Ewell's Corps were at Locust Grove in preparation to moving eastward into the Wilderness. Jones' Battalion was now commanded by Major Wilfred E. Cutshaw, and the Courtney Artillery was under 1st Lieutenant R. C. Maxwell, who had been in command since the wounding of Captain Tanner. The battery was not engaged in the Wilderness, but in the subsequent fighting at Spotsylvania Court House it was brought into position on the left of the salient, where two officers, including Lieutenant Maxwell, and twenty-seven men were captured on the 12th. Remaining with the army, Cutshaw's Battalion was engaged at North Anna, Hanover Junction, Cold Harbor and in the lines in front of Richmond.

On August 9 Cutshaw's Battalion left Richmond to join General Early's forces in the Valley. At the end of the month near Winchester, the battery, now under Lieutenant Giles C. Courtney, had one officer, three corporals and eighteen privates present for duty; five non-commissioned officers, the bugler and forty-nine privates were shown on the rolls as being on detached service. The battalion moved east of the Blue Ridge with Kershaw's Division and rejoined General Early at Brown's Gap on September 25. After the disaster at Cedar Creek on October 19, the artillery encamped at New Market; and in December, went into winter quarters near Fisherville. As the inspection reports for December 31, 1864 do not include the Courtney Artillery, it is probable that they lost their guns at Cedar Creek and the men were assigned to duty with another battery.

In February 1865 the battalion returned east and was assigned to duty as heavy artillery in Fort Clifton on the Appomattox River. On March 6 Cutshaw applied to have his battalion converted into cavalry, but instead, about March 16, it was decided to issue them horses from disbanded batteries and bring them back into the field as light artillery. The Courtney Artillery does not appear among the organizations surrendered at Appomattox, and, as Lieutenant Courtney was paroled as second lieutenant of the Staunton Artillery of Cutshaw's Battalion, it appears that the battery was not revived and that the men were assigned to duty with the other companies, the remnants of which surrendered at Appomattox Court House on April 9, 1865.

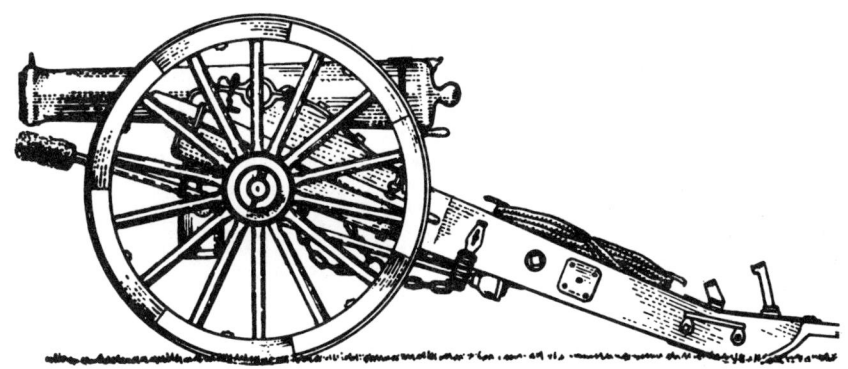

## COURTNEY ARTILLERY

### CAPTAINS

Courtney, Alfred R.   Latimer, Joseph W.   Tanner, William A.

### LIEUTENANTS

Courtney, Giles C., 2nd Lieut.
Crosley, John E., 2nd Lieut.
Heath, Roscoe B., 2nd Lieut.
Maxwell, Benjamin C., 1st Lieut.
Vaughan, Richard W., 3rd Lieut.
Vaughan, Robert H., 1st Lieut.

### ASSISTANT SURGEON

Ingram, S. L.

### NON-COMMISSIONED OFFICERS AND PRIVATES

Abbott, James T., Pvt.
Abbott, John H., Pvt.
Alley, David, Pvt.
Alley, Edward, Pvt.
Alley, Henry, Pvt.
Alley, Isaac N., Pvt.
Alley, Richard, Pvt.
Alley, William B., Pvt.
Anderson, John B., Pvt.
Atkinson, George A., Pvt.
Baptist, John, Pvt.
Bass, Claiborne M., Pvt.
Bawsell, William C., Pvt.
Bennett, Benjamin W., Sergt.
Berry, George W., Pvt.
Blackburn, James, Pvt.
Blankenship, William B., Pvt.
Blanton, John A., Pvt.
Blanton, Joseph J., Pvt.
Blunt, William R., Pvt.
Bowman, R. C.
Bowman, William A. D., Pvt.
Bradley, Ephraim T., Pvt.
Brady, Patrick, Pvt.
Brimmer, Frederick, Pvt.
Brock, William Richard, Pvt.
Brooks, James H., Pvt.
Browder, Philip B., Pvt.
Brown, Benjamin M., Pvt.
Browning, John, Pvt.
Bryant, George F., Pvt.
Buchanan, James, Pvt.
Burke, James, Pvt.
Burruss, William B., Pvt.
Butler, William F., Pvt.
Carter, Henry L., Pvt.
Carter, Lewis M., Pvt.
Cash, John B., Pvt.
Cheatham, Alfred B., Corpl.
Cheatham, James W., Pvt.
Clarke, Edward S., Pvt.
Clarke, James A., Pvt.
Clarke, Sherley H., Pvt.
Conner, John T., Q.M. Sergt.
Conway, Samuel W., Pvt.
Cornett, George W., Pvt.
Cornett, Henry, Pvt.
Cornett, James W., Pvt.
Cornett, Watson G., Pvt.
Cornett, William I., Pvt.
Courtney, Peter C., Pvt.
Courtney, Thomas L., Pvt.
Cross, John W., Pvt.
Crostic, John H., Pvt.
Crostic, Thomas O., Pvt.
Davis, Samuel, Pvt.
Day, William H., Pvt.
Delany, John T., Pvt.
Delany, Samuel M., Pvt.
Denton, Garland, Pvt.
Denton, Samuel B., Pvt.
Drumheller, John L., Pvt.
Duke, John M., Sergt.
Dunavant, Archer, Pvt.
Dunaway, Beverly R., Pvt.
Dunnaway, Henry H., Pvt.
Dyson, Francis A., Pvt.
Edwards, John, Pvt.
Ellis, John H., Pvt.
Emery, Edward, Pvt.
England, Robert J., Pvt.
English, William L., Pvt.

Epps, George H., Pvt.
Evans, Theodorick, Pvt.
Farmer, F. C. D., Pvt.
Ford, A. H., Pvt.
Ford, Cledoma, Pvt.
Ford, John T., Pvt.
Ford, Lemuel, Pvt.
Ford, Macon S., Pvt.
Ford, Royal, Pvt.
Ford, Samuel F., Pvt.
Ford, Seth, Pvt.
Ford, Simeon, Pvt.
Ford, William J., Pvt.
Foster, John H., Pvt.
Foster, Samuel, Pvt.
Francis, David E., 1st Sergt.
Franck, Benjamin T., Pvt.
Franklin, George W., Pvt.
Franklin, Walter W., Pvt.
Frith, Thomas D., Pvt.
Furcron, James M., Pvt.
Furcron, John F., Pvt.
Furcron, Junius A., Pvt.
Garnett, L. B. S., Pvt.
Gentry, Edward, Pvt.
Gentry, William, Pvt.
Gibbs, Thomas E., Pvt.
Glenn, Thomas, Pvt.
Golding, Thomas W., Sergt.
Grymes, William, Pvt.
Hall, John W., Corpl.
Hamilton, James M., Pvt.
Hanover, Henry B., Pvt.
Harlern, William H., Pvt.
Harlow, Damascus M., Pvt.
Harlow, William E., Pvt.
Harlow, William G., Pvt.
Harris, John W., Pvt.
Haskins, Thomas H., Pvt.
Heise, Julius J., Pvt.
Hodges, J. T., Pvt.
Holcombe, Joseph L., Pvt.
Holder, Mathew T., Pvt.
Holt, William H., Pvt.
Hooper, Mathew J., Pvt.
Hopkins, Edward B., Corpl.
Hotze, William H., Pvt.
Houston,
Houston, J. H., Pvt.
Houston, John, Pvt.
Hugand, Cornelius, Pvt.
Huband, Henry C., Pvt.

Hutchinson, H. L., Pvt.
Hutchinson, William H., Bugler
Jarvis, Francis, Pvt.
Jeator, James A., Pvt.
Jenkins, W. G., Pvt.
Jimmerson, Zachariah, Pvt.
Johnson, James M., Pvt.
Johnson, Robert A., Corpl.
Johnson, Thomas R., Pvt.
Joice, David, Pvt.
Jones, Thomas, Pvt.
Jordan, DeWitt C., Pvt.
Journey, Lysander J., Pvt.
Keith, James T., Pvt.
Kell, James M., Pvt.
Kelly, Andrew, Pvt.
Kelly, James M., Pvt.
Kersey, James, Pvt.
Kersey, William, Pvt.
Kinstrey, William, Pvt.
Lacy, John S., Pvt.
Lacy, Thomas, Pvt.
Lacy, William H., Pvt.
Lannon, M. J., Pvt.
Lawrence, George W., Pvt.
Lawrence, Mosby W., Pvt.
Leonard, Rich T., Pvt.
Lewis, C. M., Pvt.
Love, William P., Pvt.
Lowry, Ro J., Pvt.
Lynch, John, Pvt.
Mack, James W., Pvt.
Maddox, H. L., Pvt.
Mason, Howard, Pvt.
McGee, Charles W., Pvt.
McNamara, James, Pvt.
Metcalf, Joseph, Pvt.
Middleton, DeCalb J., Pvt.
Miller, David M., Pvt.
Miller, Joseph B., Pvt.
Miller, Peter R., Pvt.
Monroe, John, Pvt.
Moody, Benjamin, Pvt.
Morrisett, Beverly F., Sergt.
Murdon, Green H., Pvt.
Orange, A. J., Pvt.
Orange, Pleasant, Corpl.
Osborn, William A., Pvt.
Ostrander, William J., Pvt.
Palmer, John, Pvt.
Pate, Samuel M., Pvt.
Perry, A. H., Pvt.

Perry, C. T., Sergt.
Pitts, Thomas G., Pvt.
Pond, Magnus W., Pvt.
Powell, George, Pvt.
Reeves, John M., Pvt.
Reynolds, John J., Artificer
Rose, William L., Pvt.
Rose, W. Z., Pvt.
Rosse, William John, Pvt.
Rushbrook, Joseph W., Pvt.
Saddler, Robert B., Pvt.
Sales, Anthony, Sergt.
Saunders, R. W. C., Corpl.
Scarborough, J. C., Pvt.
Scott, Roger, Pvt.
Scott, William, Pvt.
Seaton, William E., Corpl.
Shepherd, George W., Pvt.
Shepperson, James A., Pvt.
Shepperson, Jesse F., Pvt.
Shield, Alfred, Sergt. Major.
Smoot, Samuel B., Pvt.
Snead, Andrew J., Pvt.
Sneed, James W., Sergt.
Sowell, Benjamin D., Pvt.
Spence, James, Pvt.
Sprouse, Jeremiah, Pvt.
Sprouse, Pleasant, Pvt.
Stanley, Paul, Pvt.
St. Clair, John A., Pvt.
St. Clair, Q. W., Pvt.
St. Clair, William T, Pvt.
Stone, A. F., Pvt.
Strom, William B., Pvt.
Sutton, C. W., Pvt.
Tate, Samuel M.
Tennelle, James T., Pvt.
Thorp, George W., Pvt.

Thorp, James V., Pvt.
Thorp, John C., Pvt.
Thorp, Robert D., Pvt.
Thorp, William J., Pvt.
Tibbs, Marcus, Pvt.
Timberlake, Charles M., Pvt.
Tinsley, Charles A., Pvt.
Tinsley, William, Pvt.
Traylor, Joseph, Pvt.
Turner, James, Pvt.
Turnley, James W., Pvt.
Tyler, James P., Pvt.
Tyler, Joseph F., Pvt.
Tyler, Thomas A., Pvt.
Vest, Aurelius, Pvt.
Waddell, Robert, Pvt.
Wade, William M., Pvt.
Wallace, George P., Pvt.
Wallace, James H., Pvt.
Wamach, P. F., Pvt.
Warbriton, John T., Pvt.
Warbriton, Martin Van Buren, Pvt.
Warner, Geo. W., Pvt.
Weaver, George W., Pvt.
Webb, B. L., Pvt.
West, William, Pvt.
Williams, David, Pvt.
Williams, E. A., Pvt.
Williams, Gentry, Pvt.
Williams, Herbert, Pvt.
Williams, John, Pvt.
Williams, Moses, Pvt.
Willix, William T., Pvt.
Wilson, James, Corpl
Winstry, William, Pvt.
Withers, Edward A., Pvt.
Worthan, John W., Pvt.
Young, Jeremiah, Pvt.

# CRENSHAW BATTERY

The Crenshaw Battery, a company of light artillery, was organized in March 1862 at the warehouse of Messrs. Crenshaw & Company, on the Basin between Tenth and Eleventh streets. The battery was named for William G. Crenshaw, its first captain, who outfitted the company with "handsome uniforms," overcoats, and shoes; and who advanced the necessary funds to the Confederate government for the purchase of horses and guns. His generosity enabled the battery to reach the field earlier than was usually the case of a new organization. The battery, numbering about eighty men, enlisted on March 14 and went into camp at Camp Lee west of Richmond. Later, the battery received two 10-pounder Parrott rifles, two 12-pounder bronze Howitzers, and two 6-pounder bronze smoothbore guns.

On April 29, 1862 the battery was ordered to proceed to Guiney's Depot on the Richmond, Fredericksburg & Potomac Railroad. Early in May, near Fredericksburg, the battery was attached to Brigadier General Maxey Gregg's South Carolina Brigade, which on May 24 left for Richmond, where, in June, they were assigned to Major General A. P. Hill's Light Division.

The Crenshaw Battery, moving with Gregg's Brigade, crossed Meadow Bridge on June 26, and, although shelled by Federal batteries, did not participate in the day's fighting. Soon after crossing the bridge at Gaines' Mill on the 27th the battery was brought into action, and moved to another position after having lost two men killed, three wounded, and eleven horses. They continued firing until two guns were disabled by broken axles and two others became "too hot to fire with safety." The battery retired, recovering the disabled pieces, and that night proceeded to Richmond, where they went into camp on the hill at the intersection of Venable Street and the Mechanicsville Turnpike. Here the battery was refitted, and on July 3 moved out to rejoin the brigade, which they found on the road returning from Malvern Hill.

On July 29, Hill's Division left Richmond by railroad for Gordonsville to reinforce General Jackson in checking the advance of Pope's army moving from Orange Court House. The armament of the battery at this time consisted of one 12-pounder Howitzer, one 12-pounder Napoleon, and two 6-pounder smoothbores. Captain Crenshaw's Battery was held in reserve at Cedar Mountain on August 9, and did not become engaged. Moving northward with Jackson's Corps, it participated at Second Manassas on August 29-30, and was present at Chantilly on September 1, but took no part in the action.

The Army of Northern Virginia moved across the Potomac into Maryland on September 5-6. Jackson was ordered to seize Harpers Ferry on September 9, and on the 14th, Hill's Chief of Artillery, Lieutenant Colonel Reuben L. Walker, placed the division's batteries on Bolivar Heights, west of the village. In the attack of the 15th, Captains Crenshaw and Pegram (Purcell Battery) brought their batteries to within four hundred yards of the Federals and poured in a devastating enfilading fire. Within a very short time, the Federal commander gave the surrender order. Moving in advance of Hill's infantry, Colonel Walker brought four of his batteries, including Crenshaw's, on the battlefield at Sharpsburg on the 17th, at about 3 o'clock in the afternoon. They were immediately sent into action south of the town near the lower bridge.

After Lee's forces withdrew across the Potomac into Virginia, the battery went into camp near Winchester, where it remained until November 20, when the division moved to a position near Fredericksburg. By order of the Secretary of War, Captain Crenshaw left the battery on November 30, and was sent to England as a government purchasing agent. He did not resign as captain until April 15, 1863.

On December 12, a section of the battery was placed in position with the Purcell Battery and the Pee Dee (S.C.) Battery on Prospect Hill, which formed the right of Hill's Division. In the battle of the 13th, 1st Lieutenant James Ellett and one private were killed, and two corporals and six privates were wounded. The other section of the battery was in position, but as the guns were of short range, did not fire. Two days later the battery moved to Moss Neck, and on January 1, 1863 went into winter quarters at Camp Maury, about four miles from Bowling Green in Caroline County.

In April 1863, with the general reorganization of the artillery, the batteries of Hill's Division were organized into a battalion, commanded by Colonel Reuben L. Walker, which was comprised of the Crenshaw Battery, Letcher Artillery, and the Purcell Battery, from Richmond, and the Pee Dee (S.C.) Battery and Fredericksburg Artillery.

The battery marched with the battalion towards Chancellorsville on May 1, but was not engaged until the next day, when Major Willie J. Pegram, commanding the battalion, sent Lieutenant J. Hampden Chamberlayne with two Napoleons from the battery to support McGowan's Brigade south of the Plank Road. The battery was again engaged on the 3rd and 4th, and on the 7th returned to the lines at Fredericksburg. During the fighting at Chancellorsville, it lost one killed, five wounded, and had seven horses disabled.

On June 16 the battalion, now one of the two comprising the Reserve Artillery of Hill's Third Corps, broke camp near Fredericksburg to begin the long march into Pennsylvania. Near Fayetteville, Pa., Lieutenant Chamberlayne and three enlisted men of the battery were captured while out on a foraging party to procure horses. The battery was engaged at Gettysburg on July 1-3, losing fifteen men wounded, thirteen horses, and one gun permanently disabled. On the evening of the 4th the battery took up the line of march to Hagerstown, arriving on the 7th. There, on the 11th, the battery went into position, and remained until the night of the 13th, when it resumed the march and crossed the Potomac at Falling Waters. During this march a caisson had to be abandoned for want of horses to draw it. An even more serious misfortune occurred when the axle of a gun carriage broke, and the gun had to be brought off on the limber. This left the battery with only two serviceable pieces, a 10-pounder Parrott and a captured U. S. 3-inch rifle. After reaching Virginia, the battalion remained in the Valley until July 21. By the end of August it was in camp near Orange Court House, under Lieutenant A. B. Johnston.

On October 9 the battery was again on the march, and on the 14th went into position at Bristoe Station shortly before the fighting ended. On November 2, 1863 1st Lieutenant Thomas Ellett was promoted to captain to rank from April 15, 1863. The battery now became known as Ellett's Battery. Several men were wounded in action on the Rappahannock on November 8, and on the 27th, the battery marched to Verdiersville to meet the Federals who had crossed the Rapidan. It remained in line of battle behind Mine Run for three days. In December, following the Mine Run operations, the battery went into winter quarters at Camp Taylor, Albemarle County.

The battery, under Captain Thomas Ellett, was still equipped with only two pieces, when on May 5, 1864, it moved toward the Wilderness with Hill's Corps. On the 6th the battery was in position with the battalion on Hill's left, and on the 9th arrived at Spotsylvania Court House, where they cooperated with the cavalry in driving back the Federals until Hill's positions on the right of the line could be established. At Spotsylvania Court House the battery was heavily engaged during the fighting of the 10th and 18th.

As a result of Grant's efforts to outflank Lee's army, the fighting shifted to Cold Harbor east of Richmond. On June 3, the battalion, in position on Turkey Ridge, assisted in the bloody repulse of the general assault by Grant's army. After the failure at Cold Harbor, General Grant moved his army south across the James River with Petersburg as his objective. The battalion under Pegram, now a lieutenant colonel, reached Petersburg on the 18th, and was sent into the defenses east of the city.

After the frontal attacks on Petersburg, June 15-18, failed, the Union army began to extend their lines southwestwardly around the city and by the end of August had reached the Petersburg and Weldon Railroad. On September 30, the battery, with the Letcher Artillery, took part in General Heth's attack on Federal forces advancing westward in the vicinity of Peebles' Farm. The battery was again in action on October 2, repulsing attacks on Heth's lines. In another move westward, the Federals made good progress until they met Confederate opposition at Burgess' Mill, twelve miles southwest of Petersburg, where the Boydton Plank Road crossed Hatcher's Run. Here, on October 27, Ellett's Battery was engaged in checking the enemy's advance. The battalion afterwards went into winter quarters at Burgess' Mill, and on February 6-7, 1865, participated in the Battle of Hatcher's Run.

Colonel Pegram took the Crenshaw Battery with him on March 30, when ordered to move with Pickett's Division. At Five Forks, on April 1, about fourteen miles west of Petersburg, Lieutenant E. G. Hollis had charge of one gun, posted in the center of the line at the cross roads, with a section from Braxton's Battalion nearby. To the right, opposite Gilliam's field, were the three remaining pieces of Ellett's Battery. The guns at the cross roads opened up with double canister when Sheridan attacked in the late afternoon. Riding up and down the line, directing the fire of his guns, Colonel Pegram fell mortally wounded, and by nightfall Pickett's positions had been carried. Lieutenant Hollis and his cannoneers were captured, but the others of the battery managed to escape. Petersburg was evacuated on April 2, and on the 9th, about six miles from Appomattox Court House, the Crenshaw Battery destroyed their guns and disbanded.

Private John O. Farrell

Private John O. Farrell, Crenshaw Battery, enlisted March 14, 1862; was promoted to corporal in 1864; captured at Five Forks April 1, 1865.

Courtesy Hirst D. Milhollen

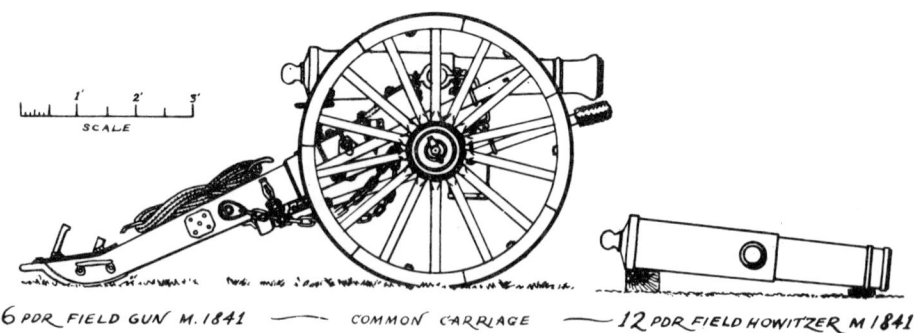

6 PDR FIELD GUN M. 1841 — COMMON CARRIAGE — 12 PDR FIELD HOWITZER M 1841

# CRENSHAW BATTERY

## CAPTAINS

Crenshaw, William G.
Ellett, Thomas

## LIEUTENANTS

Ellett, James, 1st Lieut.
Hobson, Charles L., 1st Lieut.
Johnston, Andrew B., 1st Lieut.

Allen, William B., 2nd Lieut.
Chamberlayne, J. H., 1st Lieut.
Hollis, Edward G., 2nd Lieut.

## NON-COMMISSIONED OFFICERS AND PRIVATES

Adkinson, J. E., Corpl.
Allegre, William R., Sgt.
Allen, R. E., Pvt.
Almarode, S. H., Pvt.
Anderson, Ludlaw G., Pvt.
Arvin, George A., Pvt.
Anvil, H. D., Pvt.
Ballowe, R. T., Pvt.
Barbary, James, Pvt.
Barbary, Perry, Pvt.
Blevens, Samuel, Pvt.
Britton, Samuel, Pvt.
Burgess, Benjamin, Pvt.
Burgess, William R., Bugler
Burroughs, T. H., Pvt.
Caldwell, James J., Pvt.
Caldwell, M. A., Pvt.
Calvert, Cary A. B., Pvt.
Campbell, James H., Pvt.
Carter, James M., Pvt.
Cary, A. R., Pvt.
Cary, D. H., Pvt.
Cary, John S., Pvt.
Cary, Miles, Pvt.
Casey, Bryan, Pvt.
Catlett, Thomas J., Pvt.
Coghill, George L., Pvt.
Coleman, G. F., Pvt.
Coleman, James A., Pvt.
Coleman, John C., Pvt.
Coleman, L. L., Corpl.
Coleman, Walker, Pvt.
Colquitt, Joseph H., Pvt.
Connor, J. E., Pvt.
Cooper, Jonathan, Pvt.

Crenshaw, Joseph H., Pvt.
Dalton, F. S., Pvt.
Dalton, Walter G., Pvt.
Davies, Henry L., Pvt.
Davis, Hector, Pvt.
Dillard, Isaiah J., Pvt.
Dillard, John R., Pvt.
Douglass, John L., Pvt.
Duerson, S. K., Pvt.
Duncan, B., Pvt.
Dunn, N. H., Pvt.
Ellett, Robert, Sgt.
Emett, T. A., Pvt.
Farrell, John O., Corpl.
Feltner, George W., Pvt.
Ferguson, E. C., Pvt.
Ferneyhough, Edward S., Corpl.
Fleming, Archibald, Pvt.
Franklin, Benjamin, Pvt.
Frick, Theodore, Pvt.
Gary, W. T., Pvt.
Gentry, W. W., Pvt.
Gibson, Daniel W., Pvt.
Gibson, E. D., Pvt.
Gibson, John W., Pvt.
Gibson, T. C., Pvt.
Gilbert, W., Pvt.
Goolsby, John C., Pvt.
Graves, B. V., Pvt.
Graves, Thomas E., Bugler
Gray, John T., Pvt.
Greer, T. L., Pvt.
Grooms, James W., Pvt.
Hackley, A. S., Corpl.
Hall, Thomas J., Pvt.

Hancock, E. A., Pvt.
Hargrove, William E., Pvt.
Hart, James M., Pvt.
Hatcher, E. M., Pvt.
Herndon, J. C., Pvt.
Herndon, R. S., Pvt.
Hicks, W. J., Pvt.
Hilman, G. L., Pvt.
Hines, R. N., Pvt.
Hogan, R. D., Pvt.
Holland, H. W., Pvt.
Hudson, John, Pvt.
Hughes, P. S., Pvt.
Jackson, John A., Pvt.
Johnson, Austin, Pvt.
Johnson, G. G., Pvt.
Johnson, John A., Pvt.
Johnson, J. W., Sgt.
Johnson, R. J., Pvt.
Johnson, T. T., Pvt.
Johnson, William R., Pvt.
Joiner, M. J., Pvt.
Jones, E. M., Pvt.
Jones, Thaddeus M., Pvt.
Jones, William Ellis, Pvt.
Jones, William G., Guidon
Kendall, H. L., Pvt.
Knowles, Marion, Pvt.
Lancaster, Daniel M., Pvt.
Langley, James, Pvt.
Lankford, Thomas S., Pvt.
Latham, R. G., Pvt.
Leary, Emile, Pvt.
Lee, Daniel E., Pvt.
Lewis, John, Pvt.
Lewis, William T., Pvt.
Loving, Taliaferro, Pvt.
Luck, Marcellus, Pvt.
Lumsden, C. L., Pvt.
Lumsden, G. G., Pvt.
Lumsden, H. C., Pvt.
Lynham, E. N., Pvt.
Mallory, R. H., Sgt.
Mallory, Thomas J., Pvt.
Mann, M. B., Pvt.
Mayo, John A., Pvt.
McIntosh, William, Pvt.
McLeod, Alex O., Pvt.

Meyer, Frederick, Pvt.
Mitchell, J. G., Pvt.
Morgan, William P., Pvt.
Moss, John F., Pvt.
Moyer, A. J., Pvt.
Murray, Daniel F., Pvt.
Nesbitt, Edgar M., Pvt.
Newman, A. G., Pvt.
Newman, James F., Corpl.
Nubie, E. C., Pvt.
Nuckoles, Lewis B., Pvt.
Nuckols, E. L., Pvt.
O'Roark, G. W., Pvt.
Parker, William A., Pvt.
Parsel, Isaac, Pvt.
Parsons, J. L., Pvt.
Payne, John A., Pvt.
Peacher, J. H., Pvt.
Pemberton, Charles, Pvt.
Perry, William H., Pvt.
Pettit, Joseph, Pvt.
Phillips, Alonzo, Corpl.
Pleasants, B. F., Pvt.
Procter, Austin, Pvt.
Proffitt, W. W., Pvt.
Purcell, O. G., Pvt.
Purnell, F., Pvt.
Quesenberry, Joseph N., Pvt.
Ratcliff, W. T., Pvt.
Ratcliff, W. J., Sgt.
Rawlings, B. C., Pvt.
Redford, John R., Sgt.
Rider, M. T., Pvt.
Roudenboush, S. D., Pvt.
Rowland, J. R., Pvt.
Ruffin, J. R., Corpl.
Scott, W. C., Sgt.
Seaton, M. V., Pvt.
Seeley, R. S., Pvt.
Self, Job, Pvt.
Sharp, Samuel, Pvt.
Sizer, J. Irving, Pvt.
Smith, C. D., Pvt.
Smith, H. D., Sgt.
Smith, W. W., Pvt.
Snead, William D., Corpl.
Straughan, J. J., Pvt.
Straughan, J. L., Pvt.

Strother, R. I., Pvt.
Strother, Sidney, Corpl.
Tankersley, C. W., Pvt.
Thomas, J. J., Sgt.
Thomason, William, Pvt.
Vass, Benjamin W., Pvt.
Vass, H. J., Corpl.
Vass, John W., Pvt.
Venable, Thomas, Pvt.
Walden, R. C., Corpl.
Walker, Thomas G., Pvt.

Ware, George W., Pvt.
Warner, G. W., Pvt.
Watkins, T. W., Pvt.
Weisiger, Junius K., Pvt.
Weisiger, Powhatan, Pvt.
Wheeler, John J., Pvt.
White, C. M., Pvt.
White, M. J., Corpl.
Wood, Thomas, Pvt.
Young, Charles P., Pvt.
Young, George S., Corpl.

# HAMPDEN ARTILLERY

Organized early in May 1861, the Hampden Artillery was named for the English patriot John Hampden and was mustered into service for one year on May 11, 1861 with Lawrence S. Marye as captain. Although officially designated Hampden Artillery, it was also known as Captain Marye's Battery. On May 18, 1861 the Richmond Dispatch reported the company stationed at the Baptist College, and added: "The company numbers seventy-four men, are uniformed in grey cloth, and are armed with four 6 pounders."

In July 1861 the Hampden Artillery was ordered to Staunton to join General W. W. Loring's Army of Northwestern Virginia. Upon its arrival the battery was ordered to Elk Mountain. On September 8 it was assigned to the 2nd Brigade, Army of Northwestern Virginia, commanded by Brigadier General Samuel R. Anderson. One section was assigned to the 3rd Brigade under Brigadier General Daniel S. Donelson. During the unsuccessful drive on Cheat Mountain on September 11-17, the sections moved with their respective brigades. When General Loring moved with a portion of his army to support General Floyd, the Hampden Artillery remained on the Greenbrier River line. In December 1861 the battery, now in Colonel William Gilham's Brigade, Loring's army, moved to join General Thomas J. Jackson's command at Winchester.

With his force General Jackson moved to reoccupy Romney. On January 2, 1862 he advanced on Bath and occupied the town on the 3rd and 4th. After bombarding Hancock on the 5th, Jackson moved on Romney, and occupied the town on January 10. Leaving Loring's army at Romney, Jackson returned with his original force to Winchester. However, early in February, Jackson was directed by the Secretary of War to order Loring's command back to Winchester. With the commands united, Jackson withdrew from Winchester on March 11 and retired to Woodstock. He then moved on a Federal force at Kernstown where he was engaged on March 23. After an unsuccessful attempt to drive the Federals, Jackson retired to Newtown. Immediately before the move on Kernstown the battery had been detached and ordered to Brigadier General Turner Ashby, with whom it remained on outpost duty until Ashby's death on June 6, 1862. On April 21, 1862 the battery was reorganized for the war and William H. Caskie, a merchant by profession, was elected captain. The battery was then designated as Caskie's Battery.

After the action at Kernstown, Jackson, now reinforced by Ewell's command, moved down the Shenandoah Valley. After defeating the Federals at McDowell on May 8, Jackson moved against a Federal force at Front Royal and defeated it on May 23. On May 25, at Winchester, Jackson routed the Federals under General Banks. The Hampden Artillery, still with Ashby's cavalry, was engaged at Front Royal, and during the engagement at Winchester pursued the Federals to Stevenson's Depot where the artillerymen mounted the artillery horses to join a final charge on the retreating foe. However, they were called back before the charge was made. Jackson then withdrew up the Valley to avoid being cut off and to meet a Federal thrust from western Virginia. On June 2 the battery was engaged at Woodstock and was engaged at Cross Keys and Port Republic on June 8 and 9, when Jackson defeated Federal forces under Fremont and Shields, respectively.

With the defeat of the Federals in the Shenandoah Valley and the presence of McClellan's army in front of Richmond, General Lee ordered Jackson to move to Richmond for an attack on McClellan's right. The series of battles which followed and succeeded in driving McClellan from in front of the capital are known as the Seven Days'. Throughout this campaign, June 26-July 1, the Hampden Artillery was attached to Brigadier General J. R. Jones' Brigade of Jackson's Division, Jackson's command. It is not known what part they took in the engagements, but they were on the field.

After the engagements around Richmond, the artillery was organized into battalions and the Hampden Artillery was incorporated in Major R. Snowden Andrews' Battalion of Artillery, Brigadier General William B. Taliaferro's (Jackson's old) Division. Lee dispatched Jackson's command to confront a Federal force under General John Pope moving in the direction of Gordonsville. The Hampden Artillery, now in Major R. Snowden Andrews' Artillery Battalion of Taliaferro's Division, moved with Jackson and was actively engaged at Cedar Mountain on August 9, when Jackson defeated Pope's advance. During the battle Major Andrews was wounded and Major Lindsay M. Shumaker assumed command of the battalion. Lee, finding McClellan evacuating the Peninsula and moving to reinforce Pope, determined to join Jackson in an effort to defeat Pope before he could be reinforced. A move was made on August 21, and artillery was engaged, but Pope retired behind the Rappahannock. Sending Jackson around Pope's right to attack his base of supply at Manassas Junction, Lee reasoned that Pope would retire to protect his line of supply. Jackson executed the move and retired to Groveton. Pope retired to confront Jackson and Lee moved with Longstreet to join Jackson. The Hampden Artillery moved with Jackson, and during the battle of August 28-29 it was left at Sudley Mill "on the opposite side of the Catharpin Run in position to command the ford there for the security of the wagon train." On August 30 it was engaged in repulsing an enemy attack on Sudley Ford. It remained in this position throughout the engagement.

Lee now determined to move his army into Maryland and Shumaker's Battalion of Artillery, still in Taliaferro's Division, which was now commanded by General J. R. Jones, encamped near Frederick, Md., on August 7. Three days later the battery moved with Jackson to capture Harpers Ferry, which surrendered on the 15th. Jackson left one division to carry out the necessary administrative work while he marched with the rest of his command to join the main army at Sharpsburg. Arriving on the field at Sharpsburg on the 16th, Jackson's command was ordered to the left of the Confederate line. General Jones' Division was on the left of Jackson's line with Shumaker's artillery in support. During the battle on the 17th General Jones reported that all the batteries of Shumaker's Battalion were heavily engaged. At this time the Hampden Battery was equipped with one 10-pounder Parrott and three 6-pounder guns.

Lee retired from Sharpsburg during the night of September 18-19 and moved his army in the vicinity of Winchester where it was allowed to receive a much needed rest. In October the battery received replacements when Captain Edwin J. Anderson's Battery, Virginia Light Artillery (Thomas Artillery) was disbanded and the men, horses, and two senior lieutenants were assigned to it. On October 10 Major Shumaker was relieved and ordered to North Carolina and Captain J. B. Brockenbrough assumed command of the battalion.

In late October 1862 McClellan moved his army across the Potomac River east of the Blue Ridge. Lee divided his army and moved Longstreet east of the mountains, leaving Jackson in the Shenandoah Valley to guard the mountain passes and threaten McClellan's communications. On November 9 General Ambrose E. Burnside assumed command of the Federal army and began shifting the army toward Fredericksburg. Lee moved Longstreet to that town and succeeded in occupying the heights just west of it before Burnside's army was up, thus preventing him from taking the town. Jackson was ordered from the Valley when it was determined that Burnside intended a move on Richmond from Fredericksburg. Jackson's force was placed south of the town to guard avenues of advance should Burnside determine to move south, avoiding a crossing at Fredericksburg. When Burnside began crossing the Rappahannock at Fredericksburg on December 11, Lee moved Jackson up on Longstreet's right to extend his line southward along the heights just west of the town. The Hampden Artillery was placed in position on Jackson's line near the Bernard cabins. Burnside launched his attack on December 13 and failed to break through the Confederate line. The Hampden Artillery was engaged throughout the 13th, having one rifled gun disabled when the axle broke from the recoil of the gun. Defeated, Burnside withdrew to the north bank of the Rappahannock.

By the end of December 1862 the armies were busy constructing winter quarters. Captain Brockenbrough had been wounded on the 13th, and Major R. Snowden Andrews returned to command the battalion. The Hampden Artillery was sent to Essex County to obtain forage. On March 14, 1863 the Hampden Artillery was transferred from Major R. Snoden Andrews' Battalion of Artillery, Jackson's Corps, to Major James Dearing's Battalion of Artillery, Longstreet's Corps. Dearing's Battalion was attached to Major General George E. Pickett's Division and was operating with that division against Suffolk when the Hampden Artillery joined the battalion. It remained in Southeastern Virginia until after the battle at Chancellorsville, and moved with Pickett's Division when Lee advanced his army into Pennsylvania. Arriving on the field at Gettysburg during the night of July 2-3, the battalion was engaged on the 3rd in the general bombardment of the Federal lines before Pickett's charge. Exhausting its ammunition, the Hampden Artillery remained on the field until the army retired on the next day. During the engagement on the 3rd it suffered a loss of three men wounded and seven horses killed. Retiring with the army, Dearing's Battalion recrossed the Potomac on July 14. On July 21 the Hampden Artillery was engaged at Chester Gap on a move to Culpeper Court House by Pickett's Division. By August 4 Lee's army was in camp south of the Rapidan River.

On September 9 Longstreet's Corps left the Army of Northern Virginia to reinforce General Braxton Bragg in Tennessee. Pickett's Division, with Dearing's Battalion of Artillery, was assigned to duty along the James River. On the 23rd, Pickett was assigned to command the Department of North Carolina and Southern Virginia, with headquarters at Petersburg. The battalion remained with Pickett and was to remain on detached service in the Department of North Carolina and Southern Virginia until September 1864. On January 2, 1864 General Lee proposed that a move be made to capture New Bern, N. C. Chosen to lead the expedition, Pickett began concentrating his force at Kinston. Dividing his troops into three commands, Pickett moved in the direction of New Bern on the morning of January 30. The Hampden Artillery moved with Brigadier General Robert F. Hoke's Brigade and was engaged at Batchelder's Creek on February 1, successfully driving the enemy. Only one of Pickett's columns moved with success. Faced with the failure of two of his columns, Pickett withdrew his forces from New Bern.

After the failure of the New Bern expedition, General Pickett returned to Virginia, and General Hoke took command of the troops operating against New Bern. With the assistance of the ironclad ram "Albemarle," Hoke moved to invest Plymouth, N. C., on April 18. Arriving on the 19th, the "Albemarle" drove off the Federal boats, and on April 21 the town of Plymouth was surrendered to General Hoke. Following this victory, Hoke turned his attention to New Bern, and had the city under attack when orders arrived in early May to abandon the siege and return to Virginia.

While in North Carolina the battery underwent organizational changes. On March 19 it was reported in Colonel Hilary P. Jones' Battalion of Artillery, Major Dearing having been promoted. On April 9, 1864 Captain Caskie was promoted and 1st Lieutenant John E. Sullivan became captain. In early May 1864 Major John P. W. Read was assigned to command the battalion when Colonel Jones was promoted, and the battalion was officially designated the 38th Battalion Virginia Artillery. The Hampden Artillery was designated Company C within the battalion. As such, the battalion was assigned to Major General W. H. C. Whiting's Division of General Beauregard's command in the Petersburg line in early May. From May 15 to 21 it acted under Beauregard in repelling General B. F. Butler on the Bermuda Hundred line. On May 30 the battalion was ordered from Drewry's Bluff to accompany Hoke's Division north of the James to reinforce Lee at Cold Harbor. There on June 1-3 the battalion was engaged in the Battle of Cold Harbor. Remaining with the army, the battalion was moved to Petersburg when Grant crossed to the south side of the James and moved on that city. Arriving on June 17, the battalion was ordered into action near the Hare House. After the initial engagement it was placed in the Petersburg line.

The battalion remained in the defenses at Petersburg for the balance of the war. General Beauregard left in late September 1864, and the artillery of the old Department of North Carolina and Southern Virginia was assigned to General Richard H. Anderson's Corps. In November 1864 the battery was reported in Major Joseph G. Blount's Battalion of Artillery, Anderson's Corps. The battery was reported equipped with four 12-pounder Napoleons on December 28, 1864 and in January 1865 it was reported in Major Robert M. Stribling's Battalion of Artillery, Anderson's Corps. On April 2, 1865 Lee evacuated Petersburg and retired westward. Joined by the troops from Richmond, the army retreated to Appomattox Court House where it was surrendered on April 9. When surrendered, the battery was reported in Major Stribling's Battalion of Artillery, Anderson's Corps.

# HAMPDEN ARTILLERY

## CAPTAINS

Marye, Lawrence S.
Caskie, William H.
Sullivan, J. E.
Sutton, William

## LIEUTENANTS

Archer, William S., 2nd Lieut.
Booker, Lewis, 2nd Lieut.
Caskie, James A., 1st Lieut.
Chapman, S. F., 1st Lieut.
Duvall, Theodore C., Jr., 1st Lieut.
Mahone, James H., Lieut.
McCurdey, Thomas B., 1st. Lieut.
Pleasants, James, 1st Lieut.
Thomas, George L., 2nd Lieut.
Watson, David S., 1st Lieut.

## NON-COMMISSIONED OFFICERS AND PRIVATES

Acorn, Peter, Pvt.
Adams, B. P., Pvt.
Addington, A. J., Pvt.
Allen, John, Pvt.
Allen, Lafayette W., Pvt.
Aylward, Edward, Pvt.
Baker, J. V., Pvt.
Baker, Robert, Pvt.
Barker, Benjamin, Pvt.
Barker, William C., Sergt.
Barnum, Charles T., Pvt.
Baughman, E. A., Pvt.
Baughman, Greer H., Sergt. Major
Beers, Henry H., Q.M. Sergt.
Bell, S.A., Pvt.
Blain, Joseph A., Pvt.
Blair, Joseph A., Pvt.
Bootwright, James K., Corpl.
Boswell, Richard, Pvt.
Bowe, George A., Pvt.
Bowling, Arthur, Pvt.
Boze, Jesse, Pvt.
Bozel, Richard, Pvt.
Bradley, Johnston T., Pvt.
Brady, Daniel, Pvt.
Brady, James T., Pvt.
Braxton, A. C., Pvt.
Breadlove, William F., Pvt.
Breeden, Horace S., Pvt.
Bridgewater, O. C., Pvt.
Brooks, Albert, Pvt.
Brooks, Allen J., Pvt.
Brown, George W., Pvt.
Brown, Lucius, Pvt.
Brown, Thomas J., Pvt.
Brown, William, Pvt.
Brunt, Robert W., Pvt.
Burton, M. L., Pvt.
Carbary, James, Pvt.
Cave, Elias, Pvt.
Champion, Z., Pvt.
Childress, Edward, Pvt.
Chumley, O. E., Pvt.
Clarke, William, Pvt.
Clayton, George B., Pvt.
Clifton, A. S., Corpl.
Cocke, John B., Pvt.
Congdon, George W., Pvt.
Cottrell, William R., Pvt.
Cox, John F., Pvt.
Davidson, Robert S., Corpl.
Davis, Robert S., Pvt.
Davis, W. H., Pvt.
Davis, William R., Corpl.
Dean, Thomas C., Pvt.
Doherty, Matthew, Pvt.
Dunn, James, Pvt.
Dunn, Woodson, Pvt.
Duvall, Melville J., Pvt.
Easley, Fleming, Pvt.
Enroughty, B., Pvt.
Etting, Samuel M., Sergt.
Eve, E. Dorsay, Pvt.
Farmer, A., Pvt.
Fields, James, Pvt.
Fields, Thomas B., Pvt.
Fisher, Samuel, Pvt.
Fitzpatrick, James, Pvt.
Fletcher, George W., Pvt.
Floyd, John J., Pvt.

Ford, Robert M., Pvt.
Ford, Simon P., Pvt.
Ford, Thomas E., Pvt.
Fraysier, William H., Pvt.
Fugate, A. S., Pvt.
Gentry, Paron D., Pvt.
George, W. L., Pvt.
Gill, James A., Pvt.
Gill, James A., Pvt.
Glass, Anthony, Pvt.
Glass, James E., Pvt.
Glass, Thomas, Pvt.
Goode, George W., Pvt.
Goode, William H., Pvt.
Grady, Preston F., Pvt.
Green, William, Pvt.
Halsey, Charles A., Pvt.
Hancock, Wm., Pvt.
Harris, Charles L., Pvt.
Harris, James O., Pvt.
Harris, M. W., Pvt.
Hawley, John A., Corpl.
Heckler, W. T., Pvt.
Herndon, L. T., Pvt.
Hopkins, Frederick, Sergt.
Hopkins, John D., Pvt.
Hughes, William H., Pvt.
Hutchinson, W. R., Pvt.
Jennings, Benjamin, Pvt.
Johnson, Charles, Pvt.
Jones, David N., Sergt.
Jones, Eli H., Pvt.
Jones, Reuben A., Corpl.
Jones, Richard, Pvt.
Jones, Thomas, Pvt.
Jones, Walter D., Pvt.
Kearney, John, Pvt.
Keatts, John R., Artificer
Kelley, William H., Pvt.
King, John, Pvt.
Kirby, Matthew, Pvt.
Lee, Levi, Pvt.
Leitch, Benjamin P., Pvt.
Leitch, Elijah, Pvt.
Limerick, William, Pvt.
Lindsey, Jeter J., Pvt.
Loving, Benjamin V., Pvt.
Luck, John H., Pvt.
Magovrin, Edward, Pvt.
Maloy, James, Pvt.
Mantle, Henry, Pvt.
Martin, Carter, Pvt.

Martin, George D., Pvt.
Master, James, Pvt.
Matthews, Thomas, Pvt.
McCook, William H., Pvt.
McCurdey, John H., Sergt.
McDonald, Jno., Pvt.
McGhee, Richard, Pvt.
McGinness, Phillip B., Pvt.
McLaughlin, John D., Artificer
McLearen, A. H., Pvt.
Meegan, Patrick, Pvt.
Melton, Benjamin B., Pvt.
Melton, Matthew, Pvt.
Melton, Reuben, Pvt.
Melton, Samuel M., Pvt.
Merritt, T. J., Pvt.
Meyer, Charles, Pvt.
Miller, Charlton, Pvt.
Miller, David, Pvt.
Miller, John R., Pvt.
Miller, Levi W., Pvt.
Mills, R. W., Pvt.
Mills, William T., Pvt.
Moore, George J., Pvt.
Moore, Walter, Pvt.
Morris, Joseph B., Pvt.
Morris, W. H. P., Sergt.
Nash, W. F., Pvt.
Nichols, George H., Bugler
Nunnally, E. D., Pvt.
Oakes, F. B., Pvt.
Oakley, James K., Pvt.
Oakley, Thomas, Pvt.
Otey, George, Pvt.
Ott, Henry, Pvt.
Pates, John A., Pvt.
Penny, William, Pvt.
Phillips, Richard W., Pvt.
Powell, James E., Pvt.
Ragland, Joseph H., Corpl.
Raynor, C. T., Corpl.
Reid, James W., Pvt.
Reins, B. F., Pvt.
Rey, William T., Pvt.
Roane, Patrick, Pvt.
Roberts, Richard F., Pvt.
Robertson, A. G., Pvt.
Robertson, Joseph R., Pvt.
Rogers, John, Pvt.
Rose, James, Pvt.
Rountree, Daniel R., Pvt.
Rowe, George W., Pvt.

Schleiser, Conrad, Pvt.
Schliesar, G. W., Pvt.
Shannon, John P., Pvt.
Shelton, William A., Pvt.
Shunley, O. E.
Slater, John, Pvt.
Smiley, G. W., Pvt.
Smith, Charles, Pvt.
Smith, Emmett P., Corpl.
Smith, George W., Pvt.
Smith, Herbert, Pvt.
Smith, Samuel L., Pvt.
Snead, Jesse L., Pvt.
Snellings, George T., Pvt.
Staiars, Preston M., Pvt.
Stanley, Charles A., Pvt.
Stanley, H. M., Pvt.
Stanley, J. D., Pvt.
Stanner, Frederick, Pvt.
Steger, William D., Pvt.
Stewart, Charles, Pvt.
Sturgis, W. D., Pvt.
Sudsbury, M. W., Pvt.
Sullings, Richard, Pvt.
Sullivan, George A., Pvt.
Sullivan, Mordecai, Pvt.
Sullivan, Woodson J., Corpl.
Tennent, Charles B., Pvt.
Tennent, Julian R., Sergt.
Tenser, Charles, Pvt.

Terrell, Berry, Pvt.
Thomas, James R., Pvt.
Thorp, James H., Pvt.
Thorpe, George W., Pvt.
Traylor, J. L., Pvt.
Trewolla, Alfred P., Pvt.
Trewolla, Samuel P., Pvt.
True, Dolpin, Pvt.
Tucker, Thomas, Pvt.
Tucker, William, Pvt.
Tyler, George P., Corpl.
Tyler, Robert, Pvt.
Tyler, Samuel G., Pvt.
Vaughan, John T., Pvt.
Walthall, R. E., Pvt.
Warbritton, Major, Pvt.
Weinhold, Henry, Pvt.
West, James T., Pvt.
Wheeler, John H., Pvt.
White, Henry, Corpl.
Wicker, Elisha, Pvt.
Williams, Charles, Pvt.
Williams, Joseph H., Sergt.
Wood, William W., Pvt.
Woods, Michael, Pvt.
Woodson, Aylett R., 1st Sergt.
Wright, Carter, Pvt.
Wright, Charles, Pvt.
Wright, David, Pvt.
Yancey, J. R., Pvt.

# HENRICO ARTILLERY

The Henrico Artillery was organized in early May 1861 under Captain Johnson H. Sands, a twenty-four year old Henrico County lawyer. It was reported on May 10 as Company B, 33rd Regiment (Henrico County) Virginia Militia. However, on May 13 the company, numbering 85 men, was mustered into State service for one year.

In late July 1861 the company was ordered to Brigadier General John B. Magruder's command on the Peninsula, and in the fall was assigned to Colonel George W. Randolph's 1st Regiment of Virginia Artillery. On October 3 the battery was ordered to Young's Mill on Deep Creek, beyond Warwick Court House. General Magruder reported on the 25th of November that a Federal regiment had been routed about three miles from Hampton by a small body of cavalry and three rounds fired by a section of the Henrico Artillery under Lieutenant Walter H. Robertson. After this skirmish it remained relatively inactive on the Warwick line until March 1862.

In April 1862, when McClellan's army moved against the lines, which extended along the Warwick River to Yorktown, the three 6-pounders of the Henrico Artillery were stationed at Lee's Mill, while the 10-pounder Parrott, under Lieutenant William B. Ritter, was placed in a redoubt on the extreme right of the position at the mill. There the battery was engaged in repelling an attack of April 16.

On April 30 the battery was reorganized following their re-enlistment, and Lieutenant Ritter was elected captain. A lawyer by profession, Captain Ritter had been a member of the Richmond Fayette Artillery.

Magruder's artillery was withdrawn from the lines on May 2, and on the next day the remainder of the army began moving up the Peninsula toward Richmond. After reaching the Chickahominy River the army was reorganized, and the Henrico Artillery with the 1st Regiment Virginia Artillery, now under Colonel John Thompson Brown, was assigned to General Pendleton's Reserve Artillery. However, about June 23, the Henrico Artillery, although still a part of the 1st Regiment, was assigned to the artillery of General Magruder's Division, commanded by Colonel Stephen D. Lee. The battery at this time was comprised of one officer and 43 men present for duty, and had 48 horses, about half the number required for a four-gun battery. Colonel Lee's report of June 24 shows the battery, then stationed at the farm of a Mrs. Price on Nine Mile Road, as being attached to Toombs' Brigade; but General Toombs' report of the Seven Days' Battles does not mention the battery, nor, for that matter, is the battery mentioned in any of the reports for that period. Presumably, the battery was present on the field, but saw little action.

On July 5 the Henrico Artillery was returned to Colonel Brown's Regiment of the Reserve Artillery. The Reserve Artillery, which had not moved with the army to confront General John Pope in Northern Virginia, was ordered on August 18 to join the Army of Northern Virginia by way of Gordonsville. Leaving their camp near Richmond on the 19th, and moving at the rate of twenty miles a day, the Reserve Artillery rejoined General Lee's forces near Manassas on September 3, after the 2nd Battle of Manassas.

The Henrico Artillery, much depleted in strength and efficiency, was left at Leesburg, and did not accompany the army into Maryland. On October 2 with only one officer present, the battery was reported as being "apparently efficient." Captain Ritter was ill, and some of the officers were reported as "still in Richmond, or Petersburg." The men of the battery were ordered to be dispersed among the other batteries of the regiment by Special Order No. 209, Headquarters, Army of Northern Virginia, dated October 4, 1862. Although the dissolution of the battery was considered as being temporary, the Henrico Artillery was never reorganized.

Captain Greenlee Davidson

Captain Davidson, of the Letcher Artillery, was mortally wounded at Chancellorsville May 3, 1863.

# HENRICO ARTILLERY

## CAPTAINS

Sands, Johnson H.
Ritter, William B.

## LIEUTENANTS

Crump, Sylvanus, 1st Lieut. (Jr.)
Crump, William B., 2nd Lieut.

Fontaine, William H., 1st Lieut.
Robertson, Walter H., 2nd Lieut.

## NON-COMMISSIONED OFFICERS AND PRIVATES

Acree, W. J., Pvt.
Adams, John W., Pvt.
Askew, Henry S., Pvt.
Austin, C. E., Pvt.
Ballard, John W., Pvt.
Barnberry, Henry, Pvt.
Barny, Peter, Pvt.
Bennett, John P., Pvt.
Bland, William C., Pvt.
Bossieux, James, Pvt.
Boswell, James P., Pvt.
Bowler, Nebby, Pvt.
Breeden, Bartlett B., Pvt.
Breeden, Rufus, Pvt.
Bridgewater, Robert, Pvt.
Bridgewater, Patrick H., Pvt.
Brown, Washington, A., Pvt.
Burns, Nicholas, Pvt.
Burrows, Howard L., 1st Sgt.
Cardy, John, Pvt.
Cheatham, William T., Pvt.
Clark, Robert J., Pvt.
Cocke, Charles, Pvt.
Cole, Robert, Pvt.
Collins, John, Pvt.
Crawley, Wallace B., Pvt.
Cray, William R., Pvt.
Crenshaw, L. S., Corpl.
Darly, Thomas, Pvt.
Daugherty, Anthony, Pvt.
Daugherty, Charles, Pvt.
Daugherty, John, Pvt.
Daugherty, Patrick, Pvt.
Dayley, Robert, Pvt.
Decassy, James, Pvt.
Digges, John M., Pvt.
Duncan, James, P., Pvt.

Enroughty, Madison, Pvt.
Enroughty, Nelson, Pvt.
Enroughty, Richard, Pvt.
Enroughty, Walter, Pvt.
Eubank, George W., Pvt.
Ferrell, H. O., Pvt.
Finn, William, Pvt.
Flippen, M. V., Pvt.
Gaines, A., Pvt.
Gaines, William H., Pvt.
Geddy, G. W., Pvt.
Gleason, Charles, Pvt.
Gleason, A., Pvt.
Gleason, Thomas, Pvt.
Grady, John, Pvt.
Graham, James, Pvt.
Grovan, Charles, Pvt.
Harman, John E., Pvt.
Harrard, William T., Pvt.
Harvey, James A., Pvt.
Harvey, Martin, Pvt.
Hazlewood, G. W., Pvt.
Heilsman, Julius F., Pvt.
Henderson, Alex, Pvt.
Henderson, C. D., Pvt.
Henderson, C. N., Pvt.
Johnston, Thomas J., Pvt.
Jones, Henry, Sgt.
Lacy, William D., Corpl.
Lawson, Thomas, Pvt.
Leathers, John W., Pvt.
Lewis, Robert E., Pvt.
Lipscomb, James A., Pvt.
Lyons, Jerry, Pvt.
MacDearman, Bernard, Pvt.
Madison, James, Pvt.
Maloney, Patrick, Pvt.

Martin, Alpheus, Pvt.
Meighan, Roger, Pvt.
Moore, G. W., Pvt.
Moore, Thomas H., Pvt.
O'Neal, Simon, Pvt.
Pollard, George B., Corpl.
Pollard, Leonidas C., Pvt.
Quarles, George W., Pvt.
Regnault, Charles H., Corpl.
Reynolds, J. G., Pvt.
Richardson, E. D., Pvt.
Satterfield, J. O., Pvt.
Seimms, Frederick D., Pvt.
Shackleford, Lanson, Pvt.
Sherman, Edward A., Pvt.

Smith, James, Pvt.
Smith, John W., Pvt.
Smith, Joseph, Pvt.
Smyth, Henry B., Corpl.
Sparkie, George W., Pvt.
Spicer, James Franklin, Pvt.
Sullivan, Michael, Pvt.
Taylor, James, Pvt.
Waltrif, B. J., Pvt.
Welsh, Thomas, Pvt.
Wildt, Charles, Pvt.
Wilkinson, C., Pvt.
Woodward, John R., Pvt.
Wootton, George D., Pvt.

# LETCHER ARTILLERY

The Letcher Artillery was the only company of light artillery raised for the Provisional Army of Virginia, a component of the State's military forces created by the State Convention on April 27, 1861. This distinction was nominal, however, as the battery was mustered into the service of the Confederate States and integrated with the other forces in the field.

The battery was raised in Richmond by Colonel Greenlee Davidson, Aide-de-Camp to Governor John Letcher, for whom the battery was named. When mustered into service on February 17, 1862 the battery was comprised of five officers and 141 enlisted men. On the following day, the battery was ordered to the Camp of Instruction at Camp Lee, on the western edge of Richmond.

On April 19, 1862 the Letcher Artillery was ordered to Hanover Junction (now Doswell), and from there proceeded to the vicinity of Fredericksburg where it was attached to Brigadier General Joseph R. Anderson's command. On May 26 General Anderson withdrew to Richmond, where his command was assigned to Major General A. P. Hill's Light Division.

The battery went into the Seven Day's Battles equipped with two 3-inch rifles, two bronze 6-pounder smoothbore guns, and two 12-pounder Howitzers. Only two rifled guns, were engaged on June 26 at Beaver Dam Creek (Mechanicsville). At Gaines' Mill, on the 27th, the battery was on the field but was not engaged; however, Anderson's report indicates the battery took part in the battle, but not with his command. At Frayser's Farm, on the 30th, the battery was under fire but not engaged. On July 1, at Malvern Hill, it was heavily engaged and suffered severely. From June 26 to July 1 the battery lost three killed and sixteen wounded. Among those killed was Lieutenant Charles Ellis Munford, who fell at Malvern Hill. He was the son of Colonel George Wythe Munford, Secretary of the Commonwealth and formerly a captain of the Richmond Light Infantry Blues.

Hill's Division was ordered to reinforce General Jackson, confronting Pope's army moving south towards Gordonsville. The division arrived to save the day at Cedar Mountain on August 9, and the Federals were driven back. During this move the Letcher Artillery was held in reserve, and was not committed to action. However, their opportunity on August 24, near Warrenton Springs, where batteries of the division's artillery, under Lieutenant Colonel Reuben L. Walker, drove back heavy columns of Federal infantry, scattering them "in the greatest of confusion." The battery was engaged in the fighting at Groveton on the 29th, and at Second Manassas on the 30th, where it assisted in driving back several attacks on the division's left. Although present at Chantilly (Ox Hill) on September 1, it took no part in the action.

After Chantilly, Lee's army crossed the Potomac River into Maryland. The Letcher Artillery, which moved with Hill's Division, Jackson's

Corps, was at this time armed with one 3-inch rifle, two Napoleons, and one 6-pounder smoothbore. The battery participated in Jackson's capture of Harpers Ferry, September 14-15, one section taking part in the final and successful assault against the Federal positions on Bolivar Heights. Remaining at Harpers Ferry with an infantry brigade, the battery was not present with the division at the Battle of Sharpsburg on September 17. Hill's Division, covering the retirement of Lee's army, recrossed the Potomac on September 19, and bivouacked about five miles from Shepherdstown. The battery, which had rejoined the division, was under fire during the battle near Shepherdstown on the 20th, but was not actively engaged.

On the day of Burnside's attack at Fredericksburg, December 13, 1862, Captain Davidson's battery was placed with Braxton's Fredericksburg Artillery on the left of Hill's Division. Three charges were made on their positions and all were hurled back with canister. The battery remained in position until nightfall and suffered severely in casualties and in the loss of horses. After the battle, the battery went into winter quarters on the Rappahannock, near Bowling Green.

During the winter of 1862-1863, the Letcher Artillery received two Napoleons, replacing the two bronze 6-pounder smoothbores, one of which seems to have been left behind after the Seven Days' Battles. These two pieces were cast in March 1862 from old French guns which had been cast during the Revolution and later stored at the State Armory in Richmond. When Major General Francis H. Smith, Superintendent of the Virginia Military Institute, learned that the old French guns were being melted down he protested and was successful in having the remaining pieces sent to Lexington, where they were placed in front of the cadet barracks. Two 6-pounders cast from the melted French guns were, by order of Governor Letcher, issued to Captain Davidson's battery. In January 1863 these two 6-pounders were inscribed with the names of the battles in which they were used, the names of the battery's officers with the date January 1, 1863, and sent to Lexington, where they stand today (1965), with the French guns, in front of the barracks.

In the spring of 1863 the batteries attached to the Army's divisions were formed into organized battalions. Lieutenant Colonel Reuben L. Walker's Battalion was comprised of five batteries, three of which, including the Letcher Artillery, were from Richmond.

Walker's Battalion, with Hill's Division, reached the battlefield near Chancellorsville on May 1, but it was not until the next day that the Letcher Artillery was engaged. It was on the 3rd, a day of vigorous action for the battery, that Captain Davidson was mortally wounded, at the time the Federals were being driven from the field to an intrenched position north of Chancellorsville.

With the reorganization of the Army of Northern Virginia in early June 1863, the battalion was assigned to the Artillery Reserve of Hill's Corps. On June 16 the battalion, now under Major William J. Pegram, left its encampment near Fredericksburg to begin the march northward

Courtesy Library of Congress

Governor John Letcher
of Virginia

Governor John Letcher, for whom Captain Davidson's battery was named.

into Pennsylvania. The battery, now under Captain Thomas A. Brander, was engaged at Gettysburg, July 1-3, during which time it had three killed, eleven wounded, and had eleven horses killed. One of the battery's Napoleons was disabled and was afterwards reported as being captured with the wagon train on the return march to Virginia; but in January 1864 it was learned that the piece had been recovered and brought off the field by the Chief of Ordnance, Army of Northern Virginia.

After the Mine Run operations of November and December 1863, the battalion went into camp for a month on the farm of a Major Lee near Madison Run, Madison County, and afterwards moved into winter quarters about ten miles west of Gordonsville. As late as March 7, 1864 the battery was reported as being armed with only three Napoleons.

By May 5, when Pegram's Battalion joined Hill's Corps in the march to the Wilderness, they were no longer designated as Reserve Artillery. Because of the dense growth, the battalion saw little action in the Wilderness; but on the 10th they were severely engaged in driving back General Hancock's attacks at Spotsylvania Court House. The battery was engaged at Cold Harbor on June 3; and on the 18th was sent into the lines at Petersburg, then under attack by General Grant.

Brander's Battery and the Purcell Battery were sent with Mahone's Division to Reams Station on the Weldon and Petersburg Railroad on June 28. Here they engaged Wilson's cavalry. These two batteries were again in action along the railroad on August 18, this time near the Davis House, where they had been sent to support the divisions of Heth and Mahone. Pegram's Battalion participated in the attack at Poplar Spring Church on August 21, and on the 24th the battery, with the Purcell Battery, was sent to attack the Federals at Reams Station, near where they were destroying the railroad. The two batteries again served together, October 1-2, with the divisions of Heth and Wilcox, southwest of Petersburg. The battalion remained in the Petersburg lines throughout the winter.

At the end of February 1865 the Letcher Artillery had two officers and sixty-nine men present for duty. On March 1, Captain Brander received his promotion to major and was transferred to Lieutenant Colonel William T. Poague's Battalion; Lieutenant James E. Tyler was placed in command of the battery. In the final days of the fighting at Petersburg, the battery was with the battalion in the lines which ran southwest to Burgess Mill. After the evacuation of Petersburg on April 2, the battery, which was not paroled at Appomattox, presumably reached Lynchburg with Walker's artillery train and was disbanded.

## LETCHER ARTILLERY

### CAPTAINS

Brander, Thomas A.
Davidson, Greenlee

### LIEUTENANTS

Barker, William C., Jr., 2nd Lieut.
MacMurdo, Richard C., 1st Lieut.
Munford, Charles Ellis, 2nd Lieut.
Munford, John H., 1st Lieut.
Tanner, William E., 2nd Lieut.
Tyler, James E., 2nd Lieut.
Tyler, John H., 1st Lieut.
Worsham, Thomas R., 1st Lieut.

### NON-COMMISSIONED OFFICERS AND PRIVATES

Adams, James, Pvt.
Adams, John, Pvt.
Adams, Josiah, Pvt.
Allen, John, Pvt.
Arnold, John, Pvt.
Baird, James P., Pvt.
Banks, Stephen, Pvt.
Barksdale, Chas. H.
Barrett, George, Pvt.
Barrett, James H., Pvt.
Batten, John T., Pvt.
Bazzel, Michael, Pvt.
Beers, James H., Corpl.
Bellem, James, Bugler
Bennett, James, Pvt.
Bernard, Frank, Pvt.
Berry, Travers J., Pvt.
Blackeley, Thomas J., Pvt.
Blankenship, Louis, J.
Bolt, John, Pvt.
Bonner, Daniel, Pvt.
Boyd, Alexander, Pvt.
Brady, Nicholas B., Pvt.
Brander, Auguste, Pvt.
Brander, Carter, Q.M.S.
Bridges, David Jr., Sergt.
Broderick, James, Pvt.
Brown, Edward, Pvt.
Brown, George, Pvt.
Brown, John, Pvt.
Brown, Thomas, Pvt.
Bruce, Brad B., Pvt.
Bryan, William, Pvt.
Burnett, Malvin, Pvt.
Burton, Robert, Pvt.
Butler, George, Pvt.
Byrd, Henry C., Pvt.
Byrd, Richard W., Pvt.
Calloway, James G., Corpl.
Camps, Antonio P. C., Pvt.
Carpenter, Henry, Pvt.
Carpenter, James, Pvt.
Carroll, William F., Pvt.
Carter, Charles J., Corpl.
Carter, Thomas, Pvt.
Casey, Bryan, Pvt.
Cassey, Patrick, Pvt.
Cates, De Sidney, Pvt.
Ceeley, George, Pvt.
Champion, John J., Pvt.
Chapman, Mathias J., Pvt.
Clark, Charles, Pvt.
Clark, James A., Pvt.
Clary, Dennis, Pvt.
Coleman, John A., Pvt.
Coles, Edward W., Pvt.
Connell, George M., Pvt.
Connelly, John, Pvt.
Conner, Robert B., Pvt.
Cooper, John W., Comsy. Sergt.
Corneal, John, Pvt.
Cornell, Charles A., Pvt.
Cotton, Charles H., Pvt.
Courtney, Patrick, Pvt.
Coyle, Thomas, Pvt.
Curbo, Francis, Pvt.
Curran, Timothy, Pvt.
Cusack, Dennis, Pvt

Daley, William, Pvt.
Dalton, Alexander, Pvt.
Dalton, Harvey, Pvt.
Cameron, Zachariah, Corpl.
Daniel, Joel A., Pvt.
Daniels, Thomas, Pvt.
Davidson, Albert, Sergt.
Davis, John, Pvt.
Dawson, John L., Pvt.
Delaney, Frank, Pvt.
Dempsey, Austin N., Pvt.
Devoy, Charles H., Pvt.
Dickey, Robert D., Pvt.
Dickson, John, Pvt.
Dillon, Francis, Pvt.
Doll, John W., Bugler
Douglass, Martin, Pvt.
Duffy, Francis T., Pvt.
Duffy, James B.
Durfee, Thomas, Pvt.
Egan, Patrick, Pvt.
Egan, Thomas, Pvt.
Entsminger, David E., Pvt.
Estes, James, Pvt.
Estes, John A., Pvt.
Exall, Charles H., Sergt.
Fallon, John, Pvt.
Faust, Anton, Pvt.
Ferriter, James T., Pvt.
Fick, Peter G., Pvt.
Fisher, Thomas N., Pvt.
Flarherty, Thomas, Pvt.
Ford, James W., Pvt.
Fourd, William, Pvt.
Friedman, Jacob, Pvt.
Fulford, James R., Pvt.
Gage, David L., Pvt.
Gallagher, William H., Corpl.
Garnett, Alex, Pvt.
George, William, Pvt.
Gibson, Charles, Pvt.
Gill, William, Pvt.
Gilliam, J. W., Pvt.
Glow, John A., Pvt.
Goodall, Thomas J., Pvt.
Gordon, Arthur R., Pvt.
Gorman, John, Pvt.
Gough, Arthur
Grant, Thomas, Pvt.
Graper, Henry, Pvt.
Grayson, Edward, Pvt.
Greenwalt, Samuel

Grinnan, Eugene R., Pvt.
Habberman, John, Pvt.
Hackett, James H., Pvt.
Hall, Manville, Pvt.
Haynes, Samuel, Pvt.
Haywood, Thomas, Pvt.
Heinenger, Joseph, Pvt.
Henry, William W., Pvt.
Herren, Thomas, Pvt.
Hill, William, Pvt.
Hinks, Francis, Pvt.
Hollern, John O., Pvt.
Holloway, C. D., Pvt.
Houseman, Henry, Pvt.
Houseman, John A., Pvt.
Hoxter, Melvin C., Pvt.
Hoy, Michael, Pvt.
Hudson, Francis E., Pvt.
Hummel, Joseph, Pvt.
Jacobs, John F., Pvt.
Jarrell, James M., Pvt.
Johnson, John A., Pvt.
Johnson, Richard, Pvt.
Johnson, William, Pvt.
Jones, Albert S., Pvt.
Jones, Thomas D., Pvt.
Jones, William, Pvt.
Jones, William E., Pvt.
Joyce, Festy, Pvt.
Kaldenback, James H., Pvt.
Karrie, Francis, Pvt.
Kearns, Burton, Pvt.
Keegan, Michael, Pvt.
Kell, Frederick, Guidon
Kelly, Henry, Pvt.
Kelly, John, Pvt.
Kemp, William, Pvt.
Kierans, Michael, Pvt.
King, James, Pvt.
King, J. C.
Kinne, Edmond D., Pvt.
Klees, Henry, Pvt.
Krugh, Samuel, Pvt.
La Belle, O., Pvt.
Layton, Joseph M., Pvt.
Liekens, Gabriel, Pvt.
Lohr, Henry, Pvt.
Lohr, John, Pvt.
Lohr, Martin, Pvt.
Londree, Joseph, Pvt.
Lowery, Benjamin, Pvt.
Loyd, St. Clair, Pvt.

Lynch, John, Pvt.
MacMurdo, Charles J., Pvt.
Mannin, Michael, Pvt.
Marr, John H., Pvt.
Martin, Thomas M., Pvt.
Mason, Alexander, Pvt.
Mauck, Robert F., Pvt.
May, Lewis A., Pvt.
Mc Anally, John, Pvt.
McCarthy, James, Pvt.
McCarthy, Jeremiah, Pvt.
McCauley, William H., Pvt.
McDermott, James, Pvt.
McGinnis, Joh, Pvt.
McKinney, Icelius, Sergt.
Meade, Thomas, Pvt.
Meade, Thomas, Pvt.
Miller, Stephen, Pvt.
Mills, Henry, Pvt.
Mitchell, William G., Pvt.
Moore, Charles, Pvt.
Moore, William R., Pvt.
Morrissey, John, Pvt.
Mosier, Samuel H., Pvt.
Moussa, Ali B., Pvt.
Mullins, F. M., Pvt.
Munford, Robert B., Q.M. Sergt.
Murphy, John, Pvt.
Nicholson, Lewis A., Pvt.
O'Brien, John, Pvt.
O'Conner, Jeremiah, Pvt.
O'Donoghur, Joseph, Pvt.
Outland, Calvin L. R., Pvt.
Outland, Richard W., Pvt.
Parkhurst, John M., Pvt.
Parkinson, William, Pvt.
Parsons, Andrew J., Pvt.
Patton, George, Pvt.
Payne, Thomas G., Pvt.
Pfaw, Frank, Pvt.
Pierce, John, Pvt.
Platt, Robert C., Pvt.
Powers, William, Sergt.
Price, David, Pvt.
Reilley, Patrick, Pvt.
Richard, Charle, Pvt.
Richards, Andrew J., Pvt.
Roberts, Frank, Sergt.
Robinson, Thomas W., Pvt.
Rodgers, William, Pvt.
Rose, Robert, Pvt.
Rosser, Samuel, Pvt.
Rosson, Joel F., Pvt.
Rosson, Yancey P., Pvt.
Rover, Peter T., Pvt.
Runkwitz, Otto, Pvt.
Ryan, John J., Sergt.
Ryan, Patrick, Pvt.
Sanders, Joseph, Pvt.
Savage, William L., Pvt.
Schaeffer, Benjamin K., Pvt.
Scholl, Emile, Pvt.
Semmes, Charles W., 1st Sergt.
Shannon, Thomas, Pvt.
Shea, John, Pvt.
Shelton, John, Pvt.
Shields, Thomas, Pvt.
Simpson, Robert, Pvt.
Sims, W. E., Pvt.
Skinner, William H., Pvt.
Slade, John F., Pvt.
Slaughter, John, Pvt.
Small, Benjamin, Pvt.
Smith, David T., Pvt.
Smith, Frank (1), Pvt.
Smith, Frank (2), Pvt.
Smith, Henry F., Pvt.
Smith, James, Pvt.
Smith, Thomas, Pvt.
Smith, Thomas W., Pvt.
Smith, William, Pvt.
Sparks, John, Pvt.
Spaulding, Francis W., Pvt.
Spencer, Daniel M., Pvt.
Staite, Opie, Pvt.
Stallings, William F., Pvt.
Stanton, Charles H., Pvt.
Stelle, Thomas, Pvt.
Stillwell, Vincent, Pvt.
St. John, Charles, Pvt.
Sullivan, John, Pvt.
Szcarbinowsky, Charles A., Pvt.
Taylor, Asbury, Pvt.
Taylor, William, Pvt.
Thurman, M. B., Pvt.
Tilden, Samuel, Pvt.
Tillman, Thomas A., Pvt.
Timberlake, David, Pvt.
Tooman, James, Pvt.
Travers, John M., Pvt.
Tucker, Henry P., Pvt.
Tucker, James, Corpl.

Tucker, John, Pvt.
Turner, William, Pvt.
Tyler, William, Pvt.
Utz, George W., Pvt.
Vonberger, Henry, Pvt.
Walker, Samuel F. C., Pvt.
Watson, James W., Pvt.
Weaver, J. B., Pvt.
Weaver, John F., Pvt.
Weaver, Wenzel, Pvt.
Weimar, August, Pvt.
Welsh, John, Pvt.
Welsh, John H., Pvt.
Wheeler, Albert, Pvt.

White, John, Pvt.
Wilkie, Alexander, Pvt.
Williams, George W., Pvt.
Williams, John, Pvt.
Williams, Thomas M., Pvt.
Wilson, Andrew J., Pvt.
Wilson, James S., Pvt.
Wilson, Wallace, Pvt.
Winston, John G., Pvt.
Wood, William G., Pvt.
Woodall, George W., Pvt.
Woodard, T. S., Pvt.
Wyatt, Doctor J., Pvt.
Yowell, Joshua, Pvt.

# MAGRUDER ARTILLERY

Organized on the Peninsula by order of General John B. Magruder on March 31, 1862, this company of light artillery was composed of men who re-enlisted for two years or the war. With Thomas Jefferson Page, Jr., as captain they were stationed on Magruder's line near Yorktown on April 5, 1862, and on April 16, 1862 were ordered in support of the infantry engaged at Lee's Mill (also known as Dam No. 1). They remained in the line until the Confederate forces, now under General Joseph E. Johnston, began their withdrawal up the Peninsula.

Remaining a part of Magruder's command, the company, numbering only forty-eight men, retired up the Peninsula. During this period the batteries were organized into battalions, and the Magruder Artillery was assigned to Colonel S. D. Lee's Battalion, Magruder's Division. On June 24 the company rolls reported only twenty-nine men present to man its 3-inch rifle and 6-pounder gun, and was stationed "left of Nine Mile road, in clover field, beyond New Bridge road." Two days later, on June 26, it was engaged with the enemy on Garnett's farm. It is not known what part, if any, it played in Magruder's move on Savage Station, as that general failed to employ his artillery effectively. On July 1, at Malvern Hill, the company was held in reserve.

After the Seven Days' Battles around Richmond the battery was placed in general reserve. General Magruder requested that the battery be ordered to remain with his command, but it was ordered to join Lee's army in Northern Virginia in its move to engage General John Pope. One gun of the company was reported engaged at South Mountain, Maryland on September 15, 1862, but the company did not see any sustained action during the campaign. Because of the reduced condition of many of the batteries with the Army of Northern Virginia, General Lee ordered they be consolidated. By Special Order No. 209, Headquarters, Army of Northern Virginia, dated October 4, 1862, the Magruder Artillery was disbanded and the men and horses distributed among other companies of Colonel S. D. Lee's Battalion of Artillery, Longstreet's Corps. Forty-six men of the company were assigned to Captain Tyler C. Jordan's, afterwards Captain John Donnell Smith's, Company Virginia Light Artillery, known as the Bedford Light Artillery. Captain Page was promoted to major and later commanded a battalion of artillery in the Army of Northern Virginia.

## MAGRUDER ARTILLERY

### CAPTAIN

Page, Thomas Jefferson, Jr.

### LIEUTENANTS

Magruder, Georger Allen, 1st Lieut.  Yancey, Stephen D., 2nd Lieut.
Smith, John Donnell, Jr., 1st Lieut.

### NON-COMMISSIONED OFFICERS AND PRIVATES

Allen, James S., Pvt.
Barker, Benjamin F., Pvt.
Belmer, Herman, Pvt.
Bishop, Thomas, Pvt.
Bledsoe, Robert H., Ord. Sergt.
Blum, Ernest, Sergt.
Bonhomme, Jean, Corpl.
Bormet, John, Pvt.
Brady, John, Pvt.
Bremo, Joseph, Pvt.
Brown, Dixon, Sergt.
Bulman, Francis W., Pvt.
Callis, Daniel, Pvt.
Camelo, August, Pvt.
Carleton, John W., Pvt.
Chapman, William P., Pvt.
Cobb, Richard H., Pvt.
Curl, William, Pvt.
Dew, R. H., Pvt.
Dillon, Francis, Corpl.
Driscoll, Daniel, Corpl.
Flick, George, Pvt.
Flynn, (unknown), Pvt.
Goode, Joseph H., Pvt.
Graves, John, Pvt.
Green, Peter, Pvt.
Griffin, J., Pvt.
Hall, Smith, Pvt.
Haswell, George W., Pvt.
Herring, B., Corpl.
Hogan, Timothy, Pvt.
Hogg, John W., Pvt.
Hogge, Addison R., Pvt.
Hottinger, S., Pvt.
Howard, Thomas C., Sergt.
Hurt, Joseph S., Pvt.
Johnson, J., Pvt.
Jones, Henry F., Sergt.
Jones, James L., Pvt.
Keifer, (unknown), Pvt.
Kimpleton, Eadon, Pvt.
Laforge, (unknown), Pvt.
McBride, (unknown), Pvt.
McKay, John, Sergt.
Meloth, Christian, Pvt.
Meyer, Cort, Pvt
Miles, Richard, Corpl.
Milliron, A. R., Pvt.
Mills, C. W., Pvt.
Mitchell, Charles, Pvt.
Moore, J. Ellett, Pvt.
Moore, William R., Corpl.
Morizoli, Bernard, Pvt.
Murphy, (unknown), Pvt.
Murray, William C., Pvt.
Newnan, Thomas, Corpl.
Oliver, Juan, Pvt.
Pitzenberger, Vincenz, Bugler
Prout, John, Pvt.
Reiler, Charles, Pvt.
Schneider, Frederick, Pvt.
Schweizer, (unknown), Pvt.
Sherwell, William, Pvt.
Smith, G. N., Pvt.
Smith, G. W., Pvt.
Sommer, John, Pvt.
Stansbury, Charles, Pvt.
Strasser, Jacob, Pvt.
Swartz, George, Pvt.
Thomas, William, Pvt.
Twiggs, Richard T., Pvt.
Warner, John, Pvt.
West, Alancy
Wright, James, Pvt.
Wright, John, Pvt.

## MARION ARTILLERY

This company of heavy artillery was mustered into Confederate States service on December 15, 1861 for three years or the war, with Thomas P. Wilkinson as captain. Officially designated the Marion Artillery, it was also known as Company A, Marion Artillery, and Company A, Richmond Local Guard. The latter name described its true nature. Stationed on Marion Hill east of the city, the company served in the defensive line, and doubtless received its name from the position it occupied.

By Special Order No. 37, Adjutant and Inspector General's Office dated February 14, 1862, the company was disbanded and the men were mustered out of service. However, the men of the company soon re-enlisted into other Virginia organizations. Eighteen joined a new company organized by Captain Wilkinson on March 24, 1862 which was officially designated Company C, 10th Battalion Virginia Heavy Artillery, while thirteen of the men enlisted in Company C, 3rd Regiment Virginia Artillery, Local Defense. Six men joined Captain Thomas A. Brander's Battery Virginia Artillery and others enlisted individually in various units.

## MARION ARTILLERY

### CAPTAIN

Wilkinson, Thomas P.

### LIEUTENANTS

Montgomery, Alexander, 2nd Lieut.
Quinn, Michael J. C., 3rd Lieut.

Wilkinson, James, 1st Lieut.

### NON-COMMISSIONED OFFICERS AND PRIVATES

Adams, William M., Pvt.
Allen, Charles, Pvt.
Allen, Robert P.
Anderson, Josiah, Pvt.
Anderson, Robert, Pvt.
Atkins, Andrew J., Pvt.
Atkins, Austin, Pvt.
Barnley, William, Pvt.
Barry, George, Pvt.
Baugh, Thomas, Pvt.
Bayley, Alfred, Pvt.
Bayley, Patrick H., Pvt.
Belcher, Leroy W., Pvt.
Brandes, Augustus, Pvt.
Bransford, William, Pvt.
Brown, William, Pvt.
Chalkley, Robert, Pvt.
Cheatham, William T., Corpl.
Clarke, Leroy, Pvt.
Cockrill, Robert H., Pvt.
Cole, George W., Pvt.
Collins, Daniel, Pvt.
Cooper, David L., Pvt.
Cotton, Alexander, Pvt.
Cotton, Joseph, Pvt.
Crowder, Gregory, Pvt.
Davidson, Reuben, Pvt.
Denton, Melchesedeck, Pvt.
Dodson, Jackson W. B., Sergt.
Dyer, William A., Pvt.
Elliott, Thomas, Pvt.
Eubank, Joseph, Pvt.
Farren, William, Pvt.
Foster, James, Pvt.
Freeman, William, Pvt.
Gage, Dennis L., Pvt.
Gentry, Benjamin W., Pvt.
Gentry, Edward, Pvt.
Gentry, James D., Pvt.
Goyne, George, Pvt.
Graham, Patrick, Pvt.
Harding, William, Pvt.
Haskins, John, Pvt.
Henderson, Charles N., Pvt.
Henderson, Pleasant T., Pvt.
Henry, Edward J., Corpl.
Herrin, Thomas, Pvt.
Hollins, Michael, Pvt.
Horseley, Thomas H., Pvt.
Johnson, George W., Pvt.
Johnson, Robert D., Sergt.
Landrum, John Y., Pvt.
Laurinson, John, Pvt.
Leary, John, Pvt.
Loury, John S., Pvt.
Maloney, Edward, Pvt.
McDermott, James, Pvt.
Merriman, James, Sergt.
Miller, James
Montgomery, Alexander P., Corpl.
Montgomery, Devereaux, Corpl.
Moore, Benjamin, Pvt.
Normant, John, Pvt.
Outland, Calvin, Pvt.
Outland, Richard W., Corpl.
Pace, Andrew Jackson
Pace, Henry, Pvt.
Pankey, Charles F., Pvt.
Perdue, William, Pvt.
Perrin, Patrick P., Pvt.
Price, Richard, Pvt.
Rose, Robert, Pvt.
Ryan, Jeremiah, Pvt.
Samuels, Temple, Pvt.
Sandridge, Alfred L., Pvt.
Sandridge, Thomas O., Pvt.
Shea, Patrick, Pvt.
Smith, Beverly T., 1st Sergt.
Snead, William, Pvt.
Stansfield, James W., Pvt.

Stansfield, William W., Corpl.
Starke, Thomas, Pvt.
Sullivan, Daniel, Pvt.
Taylor, Robert, Pvt.
Thacker, Carodin, Pvt.
Thornberry, William, Pvt.
Tinsley, Milton, Pvt.
Tinsley, William, Pvt.
Utley, Henry C., Pvt.
Walback, John B., Pvt.
Wallace, John G., Pvt.
Walsh, John, Pvt.

Walthall, George W., Pvt.
Warburton, Martin V. B., Pvt.
Ware, William H., Sergt.
Watkins, Edward, Pvt.
Watkins, Thomas, Pvt.
Watson, Joseph E., Pvt.
Wilkinson, Samuel, Pvt.
Wilson, John, Pvt.
Winston, John G., Pvt.
Wooldridge, Henry C., Pvt.
Wooldridge, Leroy S., Pvt.

## METROPOLITAN GUARD

The Metropolitan Guard, under Captain Joseph Barlow, was organized in Richmond, apparently during February and March 1862. On March 17, 1862 this company of heavy artillery was mustered into Confederate States service at Richmond, for the duration of the war, with four officers and 88 enlisted men. Soon after being mustered in, the company was sent to Jamestown Island, where it was assigned as Company A, 10th Battalion Virginia Heavy Artillery, commanded by Major William Allen.

The battalion evacuated Jamestown Island on May 4, 1862, and was transported up the James River to Richmond, where they arrived on May 7. Evacuation orders were so sudden that only six 32-pounders and three 9-inch Dahlgrens were removed from the island. When the battalion arrived at Richmond, it was sent to Camp Winder. On the next day, it was ordered to occupy the defensive works around the city. Company A was assigned to Battery 2, Marion Hill, on the Osborne Turnpike; Company B was assigned to Battery 4 on the eastern edge of the city; and Companies C and E were stationed at Battery 3 on the Williamsburg Road. Company D was placed in Battery 10 at Camp Lee; by July, however, it was at Battery 2. The companies were shifted about from time to time, but generally remained east of the city in that portion of the defenses known as the "First Division, Inner Line." On August 19, 1862 Major Allen resigned and Major James O. Hensley was appointed to command the battalion.

Aside from the routine duties in the defenses, the battalion was often called upon to furnish large details for guard duty in Richmond. This service restricted battalion training, and seems to have had a bad effect on the morale of the troops.

The long period of inactivity along the defenses was broken in May 1864 when the fighting between the armies in the field moved closer to Richmond. On May 17 Company A engaged Federal cavalry on the Mechanicsville Turnpike, and on June 21 the company was ordered out on the Williamsburg Road to where the Chaffin's Bluff lines crossed just beyond the Mill Road. On June 23 they moved to White Oak Swamp, and then back to near Fort Gilmer. On June 24 they returned to Richmond and on July 23 moved out with the battalion to the Chaffin's Bluff lines on the Williamsburg Road. When the Federal II Army Corps crossed the James River at Deep Bottom on July 27, the battalion moved to positions on the "Fourth Line" near Varina, but returned to the Inner Line on the next day.

On September 29 Federal cavalry appeared in Roper's field on the Darbytown Road. All of the guns which could reach them opened up, and the Federals turned northward, passing a mile in front of the Williamsburg Road batteries, from which a few shots were fired. The battalion was next engaged on October 1, when Federal infantry and artillery appeared near Roper's field. The Federal artillery fired on the battalion's positions, but a few rounds from the batteries on the Darbytown Road forced the Federals to retire.

The battalion was ordered to Chaffin's farm, in front of Fort Harrison, on October 27. They apparently remained here until the evacuation of Richmond on April 2, 1865. Of the 52 enlisted men reported present for duty in Company A in February 1865, only 13 remained to be paroled at Appomattox Court House on April 9, 1865.

# METROPOLITAN GUARD

## CAPTAIN

Barlow, Joseph W.

## LIEUTENANTS

Holland, Henry, 2nd Lieut.
Russell, Thomas, Jr., 2nd Lieut.
Satterwhite, William L., 1st Lieut.

Tyler, Washington H., 2nd Lieut.
Whitman, Michael G., Sr. 2nd Lieut.

## NON-COMMISSIONED OFFICERS AND PRIVATES

Acree, Leroy, Pvt.
Agan, John, Pvt.
Allen, Robert, Pvt.
Anderson, Henry P., Pvt.
Ashbrook, John R., Sergt.
Aubinoe, Samuel N., Pvt.
Auld, Joseph H., Pvt.
Austin, John L., Pvt.
Austin, Samuel T., Pvt.
Ball, Lewis C., Pvt.
Barley, James D., Pvt.
Barlow, James T., Pvt.
Bennett, John P., Pvt.
Bingham, Lycurgus A., Pvt.
Bowden, George E., Pvt.
Breeden, William F., Pvt.
Britton, James F., Pvt.
Brooks, John T., Pvt.
Brooks, John W., Pvt.
Brown, John, Pvt.
Burns, Thomas, Pvt.
Burroughs, Thomas J., Pvt.
Burton, John J., Pvt.
Burton, William T., Pvt.
Cammack, John H., Pvt.
Chambers, J., Pvt.
Chevallie, John A., Pvt.
Clarke, James E., Pvt.
Clarke, John W., Pvt.
Cordle, James J., Pvt.
Cosby, Benjamin F., Pvt.
Crafton, James H., Sergt.
Crouch, Jackson, Pvt.
Curry, John W., Pvt.
Dahart, Fred, Pvt.
Davis, Charles F., Pvt.
Davis, James B., Pvt.
Davis, Thomas L., Pvt.

Davis, W., Pvt.
Davis, William E., Jr., Drummer
Davis, William E., Sr., Pvt.
Davis, William L., Pvt.
Dilliard, John R., Pvt.
Dunn, William A., Pvt.
Eason, Hiram, Pvt.
Eubank, John N., Pvt.
Farmer, James A., Pvt.
Farrisee, Jeremiah, Pvt.
Figg, Benjamin W., Pvt.
Fitzpatrick, John, Pvt.
Florence, Henry, Pvt.
Francis, Emanuel, Sergt.
Franklin, Robert B., Pvt.
Franklin, William W., Pvt.
Frayser, George D., Pvt.
French, William, Pvt.
Gagen, Christ, Pvt.
Garthwright, William C., Pvt.
Gary, Montgomery, Pvt.
Gatewood, Lewellyn, Pvt.
Gatewood, Marcellus, Pvt.
Gayle, John W., Pvt.
Gentry, Matthew G., Pvt.
Gilmore, Cornelius P., Pvt.
Godwin, Thomas V., Pvt.
Gorman, James, Pvt.
Grant, John B., Pvt.
Greenstreet, William, Pvt.
Hagan, John, Pvt.
Hagan, John Jr., Sergt.
Hancock, Josiah A., Pvt.
Hancock, Obediah, Pvt.
Hancock, William T., Sergt.
Heckler, Christian, Pvt.
Heckler, John, Pvt.
Hicks, Henry T., Pvt.

Hines, John G., Pvt.
Hogan, James, Pvt.
Howard, Henry, Musician
Hubbard, George W., Pvt.
Hubble, Bernard, Pvt.
Hudgins, Samuel W., Pvt.
Hudgins, Thomas E., Pvt.
Hudgins, William H., Pvt.
Hughes, Josiah, Pvt.
Hughes, William H., Pvt.
Hurley, Thomas, Pvt.
Jacobs, Llewelyn W., Corpl.
James, Robert, Pvt.
Jenkins, Andrew J., Pvt.
Jenkins, James H., Pvt.
Jenkins, Solomon B., Pvt.
Johnson, Alexander W., Pvt.
Johnson, Joseph E., Pvt.
Johnson, William, Pvt.
Kilburn, Patrick, Pvt.
Kinker, John B., Pvt.
Kirby, L. C.
Knight, John G., Pvt.
Kritzer, Phillip, Pvt.
Lambert, Philip, Pvt.
Lea, William A., Corpl.
Leahman, Rudolph B., Pvt.
Liggon, William, Pvt.
Lindsey, William H., Pvt.
Mack, Thomas, Pvt.
Madison, P., Pvt.
McCook, Joshua, Pvt.
McCormick, James, Pvt.
McDermott, James, Pvt.
McDonald, Stephen, Pvt.
McKune, Peter, Pvt.
Miller, William, Pvt.
Minson, Dandridge, Pvt.
Mountcastle, Soanes M., Pvt.
Mundin, Edward L., Pvt.
Mewman, Sehppard, Pvt.
Newton, Tazewell, Pvt.
O'Hare, Dennis, Pvt.
O'Neal, John, Pvt.
Page, George W., Corpl.
Palmore, Albert B., Sergt.
Palmore, James M., Pvt.
Palmore, Thomas W., Pvt.
Palmore, William H., Pvt.
Pedestra, John, Pvt.
Perkinson, Emmitt, Corpl.
Perrin, Patrick, P., Sergt.
Pollard, Thomas L., Pvt.
Porter, H. A., Pvt.
Porter, William A., Pvt.
Powers, Jefferson, Pvt.
Quarles, James P., Pvt.
Raine, Henry, Pvt.
Redford, Marcus L., Pvt.
Rhodes, Holden, J., Pvt.
Rhodes, Philip B., Pvt.
Richardson, Charles, Pvt.
Robinson, Elias L., Pvt.
Ryan, Robert E., J., Pvt.
Sandridge, Alfred L., Pvt.
Sandridge, Thomas O., Pvt.
Satterwhite, John G., Pvt.
Sherer, Charles E., 1st Sergt.
Slaughter, Peter, Pvt.
Smith, James N., Pvt.
Snead, Benjamin R., Pvt.
Solari, Antonio, Pvt.
Synco, Edward P., Pvt.
Taylor, William H., Sergt.
Thacker, William, Pvt.
Thompson, Edwin F., Pvt.
Tibbs, Philip, Pvt.
Tisdale, Henry, Pvt.
Traylor, Theophilus, Pvt.
Trimmer, George W., Pvt.
Trimmer, James, Pvt.
Trimmer, Joseph H., Pvt.
Vance, Henry P., Pvt.
Wade, Hosiah D., Pvt.
Walker, Jesse G., Pvt.
Walton, Minjam H., Pvt.
Warren, John H., Pvt.
Weaver, Christ, Pvt.
West, Richard E., Pvt.
White, Patrick, Pvt.
Wicker, Elliott F., Pvt.
Willeroy, Edwin S., Pvt.
Wood, Charles, Pvt.
Woody, John L., Pvt.
Wren, John
Wright, Thomas, Pvt.
Wright, William B., Pvt.
Yarbrough, Philip L., Pvt.

## PARKER BATTERY

On the night of March 14, 1862, in the City of Richmond, this company was mustered into Confederate States service with Dr. William Watts Parker as captain, and was "received as a portion of Virginia's quota." A common practice of the time was for a unit to be known by its captain's name, thus it was officially designated the Parker Battery. Mustered-in for three years or the war, the battery was ordered to Camp Lee, west of Richmond. Originally the company was intended for the infantry service, as Captain Parker had served as 3rd Lieutenant, Company B, 15th Virginia Infantry. At Camp Lee the company was transferred to the artillery branch. On March 18, 1862 nineteen men from Company A, and seven from Company B, 52nd Virginia Militia were transferred to the battery.
During this period the battery was reported as Company D and E, Fitzgerald's 1st Regiment C. S. Artillery, which was a proposed organization never formed nor recognized by the Adjutant and Inspector General's Office. Afterwards it was mustered as a component of the 4th Regiment Virginia Light Artillery, which appears to have been another proposed organization never formed or recognized by the Adjutant and Inspector General's Office.
Without field pieces, the battery was ordered to report to the Army of Northern Virginia on May 20, 1862. They were assigned to the inner line of defenses and encamped on Stoney Run, four miles from Richmond. From Stoney Run they were ordered to Redoubt No. 4, thence to Camp Steward on Brook Turnpike, four miles from Richmond, where they remained during the engagements around Richmond.
After the Seven Days' Battles the battery was furnished light artillery pieces and on July 5 assigned to Nelson's Battalion of Artillery, C.S.A.,(also known as the 31st Battalion Virginia Light Artillery and the 3rd Battalion Reserve Artillery) which was a field organization composed of independent batteries. Seven days later, on July 12, Parker's Battery was assigned to General Lafayette McLaws' Division, Longstreet's command. Within the division it was assigned to Major Delaware Kemper's Battalion of Artillery and was reported as Company D of that battalion. In mid July the battalion was ordered to Malvern Hill where it received orders to join the Army of Northern Virginia, then moving against General John Pope. In route it was engaged briefly in an artillery duel near Warrenton. Arriving on the field of Second Manassas at 2 a.m. on the night of August 30, it went into position between Jackson's and Longstreet's commands. It was actively engaged on the 31st. During the fighting Major Kemper was wounded, and Colonel S. D. Lee was assigned to command of the battalion.
Moving with the army into Maryland, the battery advanced with Longstreet's command toward Hagerstown. When the army retired to Sharpsburg, the battery was placed in position in front of Dunkard Church

"on the right of the Sharpsburg-Hagerstown road." Here the men of the battery placed their two 3-inch rifles and two 12-pounder Howitzers in position. Heavily engaged on the 17th in front of Dunkard Church, the battery lost twenty-one men killed and wounded and twelve horses. When the fighting subsided on their front, one section was pulled out and moved to the right of the town to support the forces opposing General A. E. Burnside. Here they were engaged until A. P. Hill's men came on the field to drive Burnside back.

From Sharpsburg the battery retired to Winchester with the rest of the army. Here they went into camp, and during their stay the composition of the battery changed. Because of the ages of the original enlistments, the battery was referred to as the "Boy Company." Of the 116 originally mustered in on March 14, 1862, forty-one were nineteen years old or younger. The youngest was Private Otho L. Butler, who was fourteen when he enlisted. Private Joseph M. Richardson, a lad of fifteen years, had been killed at Sharpsburg. Now depleted after a long campaign, which included two major battles, some of the boys took advantage of their age and were discharged. Those who remained were joined by older recruits. On November 6 Colonel Lee left the battalion and Colonel E. P. Alexander was assigned to its command.

In November 1862 Longstreet's command was moved to Fredericksburg, where it was joined by Jackson's Corps to face General A. E. Burnside. The Parker Battery was placed on the left of Longstreet's line. One gun was concealed at the Stansbury House. During the battle on December 13 it saw little action. After the battle, when the armies went into winter quarters, the battery was sent to Camp Carmel, near Carmel Church, Caroline County. Here they went into winter quarters. To while away the hours several of the men formed a string band, which proved popular in camp.

On April 29, 1863 the battery moved from Carmel Church to join the army at Fredericksburg. When it arrived, word was received that a portion of the Federal army under General Joseph Hooker had crossed the upper Rappahannock River and was moving to attack the rear of Lee's army. Lee decided to leave a small holding force in the lines at Fredericksburg while he moved the balance of the army against Hooker. One section of the Parker Battery, under Lieutenant J. Thompson Brown, was sent to man two 10-pounder Parrotts of Captain A. B. Rhett's Battery, which had been detached from the battalion. These guns were on the right of Marye's Hill, and had been left in position by order of General Lee. On May 1 Captain Parker moved with the rest of the battery and two guns at the head of Jackson's infantry toward Chancellorsville to engage Hooker. Parker's section was actively engaged throughout the the Battle of Chancellorsville.

While Lee and Jackson were successfully driving Hooker, the Federal force at Fredericksburg attacked the thin Confederate line on Marye's Heights. Lieutenant Brown's section was actively engaged in repulsing two Federal assaults. When the Federals broke through the

Confederate line, Lieutenant Brown's entire section was captured. Three weeks later it was paroled and exchanged. General Lee succeeded in driving Hooker from Chancellorsville, and, turning on the Federals advancing from Fredericksburg, drove them across the Rappahannock.

The captured men of Lieutenant Brown's section joined the battery in time to take part in the Gettysburg Campaign. Advancing with the army, the Parker Battery was placed in position on Longstreet's right at Gettysburg on July 2. Here they were engaged on the 2nd and 3rd, firing an estimated 1,142 rounds of ammunition. On July 3 they suffered three killed and ten wounded. On the 4th they retired with the army without further loss.

In September 1863 Alexander's Battalion accompanied Longstreet's Corps to Tennessee. Due to delays in transit, the artillery arrived too late to take part in the Battle of Chickamauga; but the Parker Battery, under Dr. Parker, rendered assistance to the wounded. Later it was ordered up Lookout Mountain with the 3-inch rifles. Here they fired on Federal positions in the valley below. On or about November 10 the battalion received marching orders. They moved to Sweetwater and took part in Longstreet's advance on Knoxville. The Parker Battery was actively engaged at Campbell's Station and in front of Knoxville, but Longstreet was forced to retire after Bragg was defeated at Missionary Ridge and Federal forces began moving toward Knoxville. On December 14 the Parker Battery saw action in the engagement at Bean's Station. Throughout the winter of 1863-1864 Longstreet's command was engaged in sporadic fighting. In February 1864 E. P. Alexander was promoted to Brigadier General and Colonel Frank Huger assumed command of the battalion.

On April 7, 1864 Longstreet was ordered to rejoin the Army of Northern Virginia. During the Battle of the Wilderness, the Parker Battery was on the field but not engaged. Equipped with four rifled pieces, the battery saw action at Spotsylvania Court House on the left of Lee's line. In the campaign that followed they were engaged at North Anna, Hanover Junction, and Cold Harbor. In June they crossed south of the James River with General George E. Pickett's Division to Bermuda Hundred and went into position near the Howlett House on the Howlett line. They remained in the Howlett line with their four 3-inch rifles until the line was evacuated on April 2, 1865. From June, until they retired, the battery saw sporadic action. When the battery withdrew, it was under the command of J. Thompson Brown, who had been promoted to captain after Captain Parker was promoted on February 18, 1865. Joining the main army retiring from Petersburg, the battery saw its last action at Sayler's Creek on April 6. Here two detachments were captured. Those who remained with the army were surrendered at Appomattox Court House on April 9 when Lee surrendered the Army of Northern Virginia. The parole list shows that forty-two men and two officers of Parker's Battery, now under command of Lieutenant E. S. Woolridge, were surrendered as a unit, while four men absent on detail were also surrendered. Those captured at Sayler's Creek were confined at Point Lookout, Md., and released in June 1865.

# PARKER BATTERY

## CAPTAINS

Franklin, Peter A., Capt. & A.Q.M.
Parker, William W.

## LIEUTENANTS

Brown, J. Thompson, 1st Lieut.
Tucker, Sylvester J., Sr., 1st Lieut.
Parkinson, Jordan C., Jr., 1st Lieut.
Wooldridge, Edwin S., Jr., 2nd Lieut.
Savill, George E., 2nd Lieut.

## NON-COMMISSIONED OFFICERS AND PRIVATES

Adams, Frederick, Pvt.
Adams, Samuel, Pvt.
Adkins, A. J., Pvt.
Alfriend, Thomas L. O. S.
Amory, Edward T., Pvt.
Anderson, H. T., Pvt.
Angle, Francis E., Pvt.
Arrington, James, Pvt.
Atkinson, C., Pvt.
Atkinson, Henry A., Pvt.
Atkisson, J. Rosser, Pvt.
Backhurst, James, Pvt.
Banks, William A., Pvt.
Baptist, Frank, Pvt.
Baptist, John R., Pvt.
Barker, Andrew J., Pvt.
Baughan, William G.
Bell, Thomas R., Pvt.
Belvin, Winchester, Pvt.
Berry, David H., Pvt.
Bidgood, Ro. W., Pvt.
Blankenship, J. C., Pvt.
Bolton, Henry W., Pvt.
Bolton, Washington, Pvt.
Bowery, William J., Pvt.
Bradley, James A., Pvt.
Brooks, William, Pvt.
Brown, Christopher, Pvt.
Brown, David A., Pvt.
Brown, Noah, Pvt.
Bryant, Robert A., Pvt.
Butler, Otho L., Pvt.
Cannon, Montraville, Pvt.
Cardwell, John T., Pvt.
Carlton, George W., Pvt.
Carter, I. A., Pvt.
Carter, John T., Pvt.

Cavnaugh, John, Bugler
Chick, O. B., Pvt.
Clark, Gibson, Corpl.
Clarke, Robert N., Corpl.
Clay, W. Henry, Pvt.
Clayton, James, Pvt.
Clayton, William G., Pvt.
Cogbill, John A., Sergt.
Cogbill, William B., Sergt.
Condry, Madison E., Sergt.
Conklin, W. J., Pvt.
Cook, William, Pvt.
Craddock, R. A., Pvt.
Creery, John W., Pvt.
Dalton, W. C., Pvt.
Darden, James C., Corpl.
Davis, Richard, Pvt.
Denny, Thomas A., Pvt.
Denson, R. H., Pvt.
Duffey, Edward S., Pvt.
Dunaway, Robert E., Corpl.
Egge, William W., Pvt.
Eggeling, William, Bugler
Elder, Richard F., Pvt.
Estes, John James, Pvt.
Estis, Anderson F., Pvt.
Evans, Thomas, Pvt.
Evans, William M., Pvt.
Farriss, Robert P., Pvt.
Fenley, H., Pvt.
Figg, Royal W., Pvt.
Filbates, Benjamin, Pvt.
Floumery, F., Pvt.
Flournoy, C. H., Pvt.
Folkes, George W., Pvt.
Forsett, Thomas, Pvt.

Francisco, Marion, Pvt.

Gary, John S., Pvt.
Gill, Annanias, Pvt.
Glenn, John W., Pvt.
Goff, George W., Pvt.
Gordon, William H., Pvt.
Green, N. L., Pvt.
Gregory, William T., Pvt.
Hallowell, Joshua C., Sergt.
Halstead, Richard B., Pvt.
Halstead, Robert N., Pvt.
Hampton, Joshua, Pvt.
Hancock, George W., Pvt.
Harris, Alexander, Pvt.
Harrison, W. L., Pvt.
Harrisson, Andrew F., Pvt.
Hart, William F., Pvt.
Harton, Horace, Pvt.
Hays, Joseph T., Pvt.
Hewett, John H., Pvt.
Hewett, Joseph H., Pvt.
Hightower, John A., Pvt.
Hix, John T., Pvt.
Holland, W. H. G., Pvt.
Holloway, Lucius H., Pvt.
Houk, John, Pvt.
Howard, Theodore C., Pvt.
Jackson, William F., Pvt.
Jones, George W., Corpl.
Jones, James, Pvt.
Jones, James H., Pvt.
Joslin, Alfred R., Pvt.
Kirtley, Thomas J., Pvt.
Knight, Samuel, Pvt.
Lambeth, Charles W., Corpl.
LaPrade, G. W., Pvt.
Loughridge, James B., Pvt.
Luck, Lewis, Pvt.
Lyle, James R., Pvt.
Madison, George W., Pvt.
Madison, James H., Pvt.
Martin, Edward T., Pvt.
Martin, Thomas, Pvt.
Matthews, George G., Pvt.
Mays, William J., Pvt.
McKenny, Fleming, Pvt.
McKenny, Nathaniel, Pvt.
McKinney, John W., Pvt.
McNeil, Patrick, Pvt.
Merrow, John, Pvt.
Miller, Charles H., Pvt.
Miller, George H., Pvt.

Moody, John W., Pvt.
Moore, Charles, Pvt.
Moore, Edward, Pvt.
Moore, John C., Pvt.
Moore, William S., Pvt.
Mountcastle, Sylvester, Pvt.
Murray, Charles E., Pvt.
Nash, William F., Pvt.
Newell, William T., Corpl.
Nunez, Moses Israel, Pvt.
Oliver, Elijah, Pvt.
Orange, James C., Pvt.
Parker, S. H., Cadet
Parr, William J. C., Pvt.
Pearce, John F., Pvt.
Pearman, James F., Pvt.
Peers, James C., Pvt.
Pemberton, Thomas W., Q.M. Sergt.
Perdue, William T., Pvt.
Perkins, Charles W., Pvt.
Philips, James G., Pvt.
Pleasants, James G., Pvt.
Powers, John J., Pvt.
Quinlin, Lucius J., Pvt.
Ransom, William A., Pvt.
Richardson, David C. Corpl.
Richardson, Joseph M., Pvt.
Roach, Benjamin F., Pvt.
Roach, James A., Pvt.
Roach, John B., Pvt.
Roach, John H., Pvt.
Roach, Joseph E., Pvt.
Roach, Robert, Pvt.
Robertson, Mortimore, Pvt.
Robinson, R. F., Pvt.
Robinson, Robert S., Pvt.
Royall, Thomas E., Sergt.
Royall, T. M., Pvt.
Samuel, Albert T., Pvt.
Scherer, John F., Pvt.
Scherer, Philip V., Corpl.
Schonfield, David, Pvt.
Seay, James T., Pvt.
Sheppard, William E., Pvt.
Shields, H. C., Pvt.
Sieker, Lambertine, Pvt.
Slater, Osear L., Pvt.
Sleicher, John, Pvt.
Smith, Isaac T., Pvt.
Snellings, D. A., Pvt.
Spence, Michael, Pvt.

Stubbs, John S., Pvt.
Stubbs, Silas H., Pvt.
Taylor, Huey, Pvt.
Timberlake, T. W. B., Pvt.
Todd, Thomas J., Corpl.
Tompkins, James H. F., Pvt.
Trainer, Bernard J., Pvt.
Trueman, John, Pvt.
Tucker, Leonidas R., Pvt.
Tunbridge, John S., Pvt.
Turner, F., Pvt.
Turner, John R., Pvt.
Turnley, William F., Pvt.
Tyler, Henry, Pvt.
Tyler, James M., Sergt.
Tyree, R. F., Pvt.
Vaden, P. F., Pvt.
Valentine, William G., Pvt.
Verlander, James W., Corpl.
Waddill, John A., Pvt.
Walton, Nathan T., Pvt.

Warburton, George, Pvt.
Waymack, Edward C., Pvt.
Weisiger, S. Carter, Pvt.
Weisiger, Samuel P., Pvt.
Wheeley, Sylvester, Pvt.
Whitehead, William H., Pvt.
Whitehurst, A. J., Pvt.
Wilkerson, R. T., Pvt.
Wilkes, W. H., Pvt.
Williams, J., Pvt.
Williams, John T., Pvt.
Williams, R. L., Pvt.
Williams, William A., Pvt.
Willis, John J., Pvt.
Woodall, Reuben, Pvt.
Woody, George A., Pvt.
Wooldridge, A. B., Pvt.
Wooldridge, D. S., Pvt.
Wright, George S., Pvt.
Wright, John D., Pvt.

Frank Baptist in 1862

Detailed from Parker's Light Artillery to report to the Post Office Department for service at Archer & Daly's, where he printed the **FIVE CENTS** blue from the De la Rue plates.

## PURCELL BATTERY

The organization of the Purcell Battery, a company of light artillery, was begun in Richmond about April 20, 1861. Raised largely by the efforts of Daniel Hagerty, the battery was named for John Purcell, a wealthy Richmond merchant who financed much of its equipment. The battery was sent to Fredericksburg in April, before it had been fully recruited and equipped. Before leaving Richmond, the battery was issued four 10-pounder Parrott rifles.

By May 20 the Purcell Battery was fully organized, and was mustered into State service for one year while still at Camp Mercer, near Fredericksburg. Reuben Lindsay Walker, a graduate of the Virginia Military Institute (Class of 1845), Civil Engineer, and New Kent County planter, was made captain, and Daniel Hagerty first lieutenant. As frequently occurred, the battery was also known as Walker's Battery, after its captain. William R. J. Pegram, a University of Virginia law student who had been sent to the battery from Captain R. Milton Cary's Company F as a drillmaster, was elected second lieutenant. In time Lieutenant Pegram would rise to become one of the Confederacy's most distinguished artillerists. On May 22 Colonel Daniel Ruggles, commanding the Department of Fredericksburg, reported that the battery, the only field battery in the department, was not prepared for field service. However, by the end of the month the Purcell Battery was stationed at Aquia Creek and was brought early into the action of May 31 when the batteries there were attacked by Federal steamers. In late June the battery was on duty at Mathias Point.

On July 18 Walker's Battery left for Manassas Junction with Holmes' Brigade, which was ordered on the 20th to Camp Wigfall as a reserve for Ewell's Brigade at Union Mills, on the right of Beauregard's line. The brigade was ordered up to the battlefield of First Manassas on July 21, at about 2:00 p.m., but did not become engaged. The Purcell Battery, however, was ordered forward to fire on the enemy retreating across Cub Run.

After the Battle of First Manassas the Purcell Battery returned to the Aquia Creek District; and on August 23 was ordered to Marlborough Point, at the mouth of Potomac Creek, where they were engaged on that day for about an hour with the Federal armed steamers <u>Yankee</u> and <u>Release.</u> At the end of August the battery was at Dumfries with a strength of four officers and seventy-seven enlisted men present for duty. On September 13 Walker's Battery was assigned to General Trimble's command at Evansport, and on the 25th participated in the engagement with an armed tug at Freestone Point. The battery continued on duty in the Aquia District until the spring of 1862.

In the reorganization of the artillery before the Seven Days' Battles the Purcell Battery was assigned to the artillery of General A. P. Hill's Division, and was attached to Field's Brigade. Captain Walker was promoted to Major, Chief of Artillery, for the division. Lieutenant

Pegram was promoted to captain, and the battery became known as Pegram's Battery. At Mechanicsville on June 27, after crossing Beaver Dam Creek, the Purcell Battery was subjected to the severe fire of about thirty guns of the Federal artillery. Nightfall found Pegram's Battery with forty-seven casualties, many of its horses killed, and two disabled guns. Captain Pegram, with great energy and determination, put his battery into condition to fight the next day at Gaines' Mill. The battery was engaged at Frayser's Farm, and on July 1, at Malvern Hill, it was brought up to support the right of the line at the Crew Farm. "No men could have behaved better than Captains Pegram and Grimes (Portsmouth battery)," reported General Armistead, "they worked their guns after their men were cut down, and only retired when entirely disabled." During the Seven Days' Battles, the battery lost seven killed and fifty-three wounded, out of a total of about eighty men.

Hill's Division, on July 27, 1862, was ordered to the support of General Jackson, confronting Pope's army, which was reported to be moving south toward Gordonsville. On August 9, at Cedar Mountain, Pegram's Battery was brought forward to a position in front of Early's Brigade, and during the fighting, repulsed several attempts by the enemy to capture their guns. After dark, and with the aid of a full moon, the battery, with Field's Brigade, set out in pursuit of the enemy. The four guns of the battery opened with shell and canister, which resulted in confusion and disorder among the Federals; however, three batteries opened up on the Purcell Battery, and for two hours they fought. At about 10 o'clock the guns of Captain Pegram were silenced. The battery suffered two killed, including Lieutenant Mercer Featherston, and twelve wounded. In the fighting at Groveton, near the battlefield of First Manassas, on August 28, Pegram's guns were almost continuously in action, repulsing the enemy's assaults on Jackson's positions behind the unfinished railroad embankment. On August 29 the fighting was even more severe, lasting all day. With two pieces of the battery Pegram engaged an entire enemy battery until a shell burst and disabled one of the gun crews. Pegram wrote: "It was the worst shot I ever saw...killing two of my best men, wounding two, stunning the remainder, killing three horses, disabling a wheel & cutting through a tree."

In early September the Army of Northern Virginia crossed the Potomac into Maryland. At Harpers Ferry on September 14, the batteries of Hill's Division were placed on high ground commanding the Federal left on Bolivar Heights. In the attack of the 15th Pegram and Crenshaw moved their batteries to within 400 yards of the Federals and poured a devasting enfilading fire into their ranks. On the 17th Hill's artillery, in advance of the infantry, arrived on the field at Sharpsburg, and was brought into action near the lower bridge almost at once. In the fighting on the west side of the bridge, a brigade of Wilcox's Division was observed in an isolated position. Pegram, with the only gun left with ammunition, and Braxton's Battery were ordered to a position on high ground just north of the Shively House, from where they poured a devasting enfilading fire into the Federals at about 500 yards range. Among the casualties of the day's fighting was Captain Pegram, who received a slight wound in the head. Within two weeks, however, he was back on duty with his battery.

After Sharpsburg the army recrossed the Potomac and the Purcell Battery went into camp with the division near Bunker Hill, north of Winchester. The battery was so reduced in strength that it was threatened with disbandment. However, on October 4 Chapman's Dixie Battery, which had been reduced to thirty-two men, was disbanded, and the men and horses assigned to Pegram's Battery. At the end of October the Purcell Battery, in camp near Berryville, had four officers and ninety-one enlisted men present for duty.

At Fredericksburg, on December 12, Hill's Division relieved that of General Hood. The division's right was on the road from Hamilton's Crossing to the Port Royal road, and the batteries of Captains Pegram and McIntosh, with sections from others, were placed on the heights near the railroad. Although subject to artillery fire on the morning of the 13th, Pegram and McIntosh held their fire until the enemy's infantry attack about noon, after which the batteries drove back two Federal advances. At 3:00 p.m. all guns were relieved by fresh batteries, except one section of the Purcell Battery which remained in action until nightfall. The battery had three killed, including Lieutenant Zacharie C. McGruder, during the day's fighting.

In March 1863 the Purcell Battery turned in its two 3-inch rifles for two 12-pounder Napoleons, giving them a total of four. With reorganization of the artillery of the Army of Northern Virginia in April, the batteries of Hill's Division were organized into a battalion under Lieutenant Colonel Walker. Captain Pegram was promoted to major, and second in command of the battalion, which, besides the Purcell Battery, included the Pee Dee (S. C.) Battery, Crenshaw Battery, Letcher Artillery, and Captain Marye's Fredericksburg Battery.

At dawn on May 1, 1863 Walker's Battalion moved with Hill's Division toward Chancellorsville. The battery, under 1st Lieutenant Joseph McGraw, was the only one in the battalion engaged in the first day's fighting, when for a short time they assisted in driving Hooker's men back to Chancellorsville. At 6:30 a.m. on May 2, while going into position on General Anderson's right to shell the Federal infantry in the woods, the batteries of McGraw and Captain Brunson became engaged in a long range duel with two Federal batteries. After about twenty minutes, Major Pegram reported the firing to be but a waste of ammunition, and the batteries were ordered withdrawn; whereupon, they followed Jackson's flanking column which was already on the march. On May 3 the battery was engaged south of the Plank Road, shelling Federal infantry and artillery positions. That night, with its ammunition chests replenished, the battery was placed in position on the Plank Road. Federal batteries opened up on them the next morning, but were soon silenced. During the four days at Chancellorsville the Purcell Battery lost three killed, and eight wounded, two of whom later died. Lieutenant McGraw was promoted to captain around April 20, 1863, and the company became known as McGraw's Battery.

In early June 1863 the artillery of the Army of Northern Virginia was again reorganized. Colonel Walker was appointed Chief of Artillery for Hill's Corps; and his battalion, under the command of Major Pegram, was assigned as one of the corps' two battalions of reserve artillery.

On June 16 Pegram's Battalion left its encampment near Fredericksburg to begin the march into Maryland and Pennsylvania. By June 27 it was encamped near Fayetteville, Pa., and on July 1 arrived at Gettysburg where it was engaged throughout the three-day struggle. The battalion expended 3,800 rounds during this time and had ten killed, thirty-seven wounded, and thirty-eight horses killed. The Purcell Battery lost one killed, five wounded, and had thirty-five horses killed or disabled. On the return march to Virginia the battery engaged Federal cavalry at Amesville, and on July 13 recrossed the Potomac.

After the Mine Run operations of November and December 1863, the battalion went into winter quarters at Lindsay's Depot, on the Virginia Central Railroad, in Albemarle County.

In early 1864 Captain McGraw was promoted to major and second in command of the battalion under Pegram, who had been promoted to lieutenant colonel. Lieutenant George M. Cayce was promoted to captain and the company became known as Cayce's Battery.

On May 5, 1864 Pegram's Battalion joined Hill's Corps and moved down the Plank Road toward the Wilderness to meet Grant's army. The dense growth of the area restricted the employment of artillery, but on the 6th the battalion went into a position on Hill's left to oppose Federal attempts to penetrate between Hill's left and Ewell's right. The battalion arrived at Spotsylvania Court House on May 9 and went into position with the infantry, where the lines crossed the Fredericksburg Road near the court house. On the 10th it assisted in driving back a fierce attack by Meade's infantry. During the artillery duel of the 18th, when Meade assailed Hill's line, Major McGraw was severely wounded, losing an arm which he courageously ordered amputated without the benefit of anesthetic.

The fighting shifted south and closer to Richmond. On June 3 the battalion occupied a position on Turkey Ridge, where they were engaged in checking Grant's costly assault at Cold Harbor. Near Riddell's Shop on June 13, the battalion was placed in line of battle to check the Federal advance, and here Colonel Pegram, with his old battery under Captain Cayce, made a superb attack upon the enemy.

The battalion reached Petersburg on June 18 and was sent into the lines east of the town. On June 28 Colonel Pegram, with the Purcell Battery and Captain Brander's Letcher Artillery, accompanied Mahone's Division to Reams Station on the Weldon Railroad, where they were effectively used against Wilson's cavalry. These two Richmond batteries were again engaged on the Weldon Railroad near the Davis House on August 18, where they had been sent under Colonel Pegram to cooperate with the divisions of Heth and Mahone. The battalion participated in an attack at Popular Spring Church on the 21st of August; and on the 24th, the batteries of Cayce and Brander served together in support of the at-

Colonel Reuben Lindsay Walker, the first captain of the Purcell Battery. Promoted to major in 1862, he rose to brigadier general in 1865.

Courtesy Library of Congress

Captain William Ransom Johnson Pegram, who commanded the Purcell Battery from 1862-1863. At the age of 23 he was commissioned as colonel of the artillery about one month before being mortally wounded at Five Forks on April 1, 1865.

Courtesy Confederate Museum

tack on Reams Station. On October 1-2 these two batteries saw heavy fighting with the divisions of Heth and Wilcox southwest of Petersburg. The battalion remained in the trenches during the winter, serving, in addition to their field pieces, two 8-inch mortars and two 24-pounder mortars. The end of February 1865 found the Purcell Battery with three officers and fifty-eight enlisted men present for duty.

Well deserved promotions for the three former captains of the battery were made before the end of the fighting at Petersburg. On March 1 the promotions of Colonel Walker to brigadier general and Lieutenant Colonel Pegram to colonel, both to rank from February 18, were announced. Major McGraw, who had returned to duty after recuperating from his wound, was promoted to lieutenant colonel and second in command of the battalion.

On April 1 at Five Forks, Colonel Pegram, accompanied by his adjutant and beloved friend, Captain Gordon McCabe, was mortally wounded while directing the fire of his guns. The death of the 23-year-old artillerist was an irreplaceable loss for the Army of Northern Virginia. As the Purcell Battery was not among those paroled at Appomattox Court House, it is presumed that it reached Lynchburg with General Walker's column and there cut down its carriages, buried its guns and disbanded.

## PURCELL BATTERY

### CAPTAINS

Cayce, George M.
McGraw, Joseph

Pegram, William J.
Walker, R. L.

### LIEUTENANTS

Allen, William A., 1st Lieut.
Crow, Charles E., 1st Lieut.
Dabney, William J., 2nd Lieut.
Featherston, Mercer, 2nd Lieut.
Fitzhugh, Henry M., 1st Lieut

Hagerty, Daniel, 1st Lieut.
McClintock, Richard D., Sr., 2nd Lieut.
McGruder, Zephaniah C., Lieut.
Walsh, James E., Jr., 2nd Lieut.

### NON-COMMISSIONED OFFICERS AND PRIVATES

Ackerly, James H., Pvt.
Adams, William H., Pvt.
Alderslade, George E., Pvt.
Allen, James R., Pvt.
Allen, Thomas, Pvt.
Anderson, William A., Pvt.
Ashby, Philip, Pvt.
Ayleshire, David F.
Bailey, Albert, Pvt.
Bailey, John, Pvt.
Bailey, Parks, Pvt.
Baker, George
Baker, Jacob, Pvt.
Ball, James H., Sergt.
Barker, Richard, Pvt.
Barry, John, Pvt.
Beck, Jamerson, Sergt.
Beckham, William J., Pvt.
Behrends, Charles, Pvt.
Bell, Thomas R., Pvt.
Berry, William F., Pvt.
Berry, William Thomas, Pvt.
Blankenship, John, Pvt.
Bohn, Dabney, Pvt.
Boulware, A. M., Pvt.
Bowyer, Robert H., Pvt.
Boyd, Theodore, Pvt.
Bradford, Henry C., Pvt.
Bradford, Hill C., Corpl.
Bradley, Charles F., Pvt.
Bragg, John G., Pvt.
Branch, James E., Pvt.
Brooks, Abraham, Pvt.
Brown, E., Pvt.

Brown, Henry, Pvt.
Brown, Valentine Jr., Pvt.
Broy, William P., Pvt.
Brunson, E. B., Pvt.
Bryan, Edwin, Pvt.
Buckley, James, Pvt.
Bullington, Henry N., Pvt.
Burks, Albert S., Pvt.
Burner, Jacob, Pvt.
Burns, Thomas, Pvt.
Burns, Thomas H., Pvt.
Butler, Walter F., Pvt.
Caldwell, J. L., Pvt.
Caldwell, John M., Pvt.
Callaghan, John T., Pvt.
Camden, Matthew, Pvt.
Campbell, F. M., Pvt.
Campbell, Robert, Pvt.
Campbell, Thomas, Pvt.
Campbell, Thomas J., Pvt.
Carter, Charles, Pvt.
Cash, John, Pvt.
Cavanaugh, William Y., Pvt.
Cayce, Edgar M., Q.M. Sergt.
Chamberlayne, J. Hampden, Sergt.
Chapman, E. G., Pvt.
Cheatham, Stephen, Pvt.
Clarke, Michael, Pvt.
Cobb, James Henry, Pvt.
Conner, James, Pvt.
Cook, Andrew J., Pvt.
Cook, William
Couch, William, Pvt.
Crawford, William, Pvt.

Creasy, N. G., Pvt.
Cubbage, John, Pvt.
Cubbage, Thomas, Pvt.
Cullers, R. M., Pvt.
Dager, Richard, Pvt.
Daniels, Samuel A., Pvt.
Davis, David, Pvt.
Davis, James, Pvt.
Davis, Robert J., Pvt.
Day, Francis, Pvt.
Delarue, Joseph, Corpl.
Dixon, Charles C., Pvt.
Dobbins, Thomas, Pvt.
Dockerty, George, Corpl.
Doherty, Anthony, Pvt.
Donahoe, Patrick, Pvt.
Dougherty, William, Pvt.
Drewry, Albert, Comsy Sergt.
Eddins, Hillary H., Pvt.
Eddins, John A., Pvt.
Eddins, R. H., Pvt.
Eddins, W. Hardy, Pvt.
Ege, Henry L, Pvt.
Ellis, Andrew J., Pvt.
Ellis, James, Pvt.
Elly, Benjamin, Pvt.
Elly, Charles, Pvt.
Elly, John, Pvt.
English, Thomas, Pvt.
Evans, J. Budd, Pvt.
Evans, John S., Pvt.
Farmer, E., Pvt.
Farmer, Patrick, Pvt.
Farrar, William D., Pvt.
Fassett, William P., Corpl.
Ferneyhough, John T., Pvt.
Finnell, Thomas, Pvt.
Fitzgerald, George, Pvt.
Flemming, William, Pvt.
Flint, Edward S., Pvt.
Flint, William T., Pvt.
Foster, Peter, Corpl.
Foster, Thomas R., Pvt.
Fowler, Thomas C., Pvt.
Fuller, David, Pvt.
Fuqua, C. T., Pvt.
Fuqua, N. A., Pvt.
Fuqua, Walter M., Sergt.
Faines, John, Pvt.
Gaines, William E., Sergt.
Gentry, William, Sergt.

Goode, G. B., Sergt.
Goode, H. P.
Grigsby, Caldwell, Pvt.
Grigsby, Mott C., Pvt.
Grotz, John, Pvt.
Groves, Joseph, Corpl.
Gurridge, Henry, Pvt.
Guy, James, Pvt.
Habron, Charles, Pvt.
Hackman, B. F., Pvt.
Haley, Joseph, Pvt.
Hall, William J., Pvt.
Hammond, M., Sergt.
Harris, Samuel H., Pvt.
Harrow, James S. M., Pvt.
Hart, Lewis, Pvt.
Hawkins, William E., Pvt.
Herring, Anthony, Pvt.
Higgs, N. C., Pvt.
Hill, Enoch, Pvt.
Hoffman, Albert, Pvt.
Hoffman, F. C., Pvt.
Holland, Albert, Corpl.
Horton, A. H., Pvt.
Horton, James M., Pvt.
Hotinger, John, Pvt.
Howard, George H., Pvt.
Hudson, George, Pvt.
Hughes, Samuel, Pvt.
Hughn, J., Pvt.
Hurt, John F., Pvt.
Hurt, S. C., Pvt.
Jackson, John W., Pvt.
James, Stephen C., 1st Sergt.
Jenkins, Daniel, Pvt.
Jenkins, Philip, Pvt.
Job, Thomas, Pvt.
Johnson, C. H., Pvt.
Johnson, George W., Pvt.
Johnson, James F., Pvt.
Johnston, William, Pvt.
Jones, Daniel P., Pvt.
Jones, Edward P., Pvt.
Jones, Henry B., Pvt.
Jones, John E., Pvt.
Jones, Stephen J., Pvt.
Jones, Wesley, Pvt.
Jones, William B., Pvt.
Jordan, J. H., Pvt.
Joyce, John, Pvt.
Kane, Michael, Pvt.

Kelso, John, Pvt.
Keyser, Ed., Pvt.
Keyser, Joseph, Pvt.
Kimball, Stephen H., Pvt.
Kinstry, James, Pvt.
Kirby, Edmond, Sergt.
Knox, Andrew J.
Krebbs, Henry B., Pvt.
Krebs, Charles, Pvt.
Kuper, William A., Pvt.
Lee, Charles, Pvt.
Lee, William H., Pvt.
Lewis, Edward, Pvt.
Limerick, Strother D., Pvt.
Lipscomb, Augustus B., Pvt.
Littleton, Harp, Pvt.
Logwood, John C., Sergt.
Lumpkin, Richard, Pvt.
Mahoney, James, Pvt.
Markham, James M., Pvt.
Markham, P. W., Pvt.
Martin, Daniel, Pvt.
Martin, Jarvis D., Pvt.
Mason, James B., Pvt.
Mathews, William, Pvt.
Matthews, Joseph, Pvt.
Matthews, Lazarus, Pvt.
Matthews, Munson
McClintock, E. L., Pvt.
McCook, Samuel, Pvt.
McDowell, Edward, Pvt.
McKenzie, John, Pvt.
McLean, Thomas B., Pvt.
McLeod, William H., Pvt.
Messler, Henry, Pvt.
Miffleton, Anthony, Pvt.
Miffleton, William, Pvt.
Miller, John H., Pvt.
Miller, L., Pvt.
Mitchell, James, Corpl.
Mitchell, Luther, Pvt.
Moon, Samuel, Pvt.
Moore, Samuel, Pvt.
Moren, James
Morris, James E., Pvt.
Morton, Levi, Bugler
Mosby, Benjamin F., Corpl.
Mosingo, Hezekiah, Pvt.
Mullen, William H., Pvt.
Murphy, James, Pvt.

Murphy, Michael, Corpl.
Neal, Isaac, Pvt.
Nelson, James, O., Pvt.
Newcomer, J. Clinton, Pvt.
Newman, William, Pvt.
Nolan, Jeremiah, Pvt.
Norman, G., Pvt.
Norman, William, Pvt.
Nunally, Emmet, Pvt.
Nunnelly, Caiphas, Pvt.
O'Brien, Thomas, Pvt.
O'Neil, John
Otey, A. W., Pvt.
Otey, James W., Pvt.
Partington, William E., Corpl.
Payne, George, Pvt.
Payne, Gustavus, Pvt.
Pearson, John Q. Q., Pvt.
Pence, Isaac, Pvt.
Pence, Wesley, Pvt.
Perry, Charles W., Pvt.
Perry, Lewis K., Pvt.
Peterson, John, Pvt.
Pilcher, George M., Pvt.
Pippin, John, Artificer
Plum, George W., Pvt.
Pollard, Henry W., Pvt.
Price, Frank S., Pvt.
Price, William A., Pvt.
Redford, Smith, Pvt.
Reynolds, John, Pvt.
Richie, James J., Pvt.
Ricketts, Augustus, Pvt.
Riley, And. J., Pvt.
Robertson, William, Pvt.
Robinson, Benjamin, Pvt.
Rogers, William
Rose, Heistin, Pvt.
Rose, Howard E., Pvt.
Rose, Lovell, Pvt.
Rose, Stephen, Pvt.
Royall, George, Pvt.
Sacrey, Andrew J., Pvt.
Sale, R. D. M., Pvt.
Saunders, Thaddeus W., Pvt.
Scott, Charles, Pvt.
Scott, Richard L., Pvt.
Scott, Thomas, Pvt.
Seymore, William, Pvt.
Short, Benjamin F., Pvt.

Short, James W., Pvt.
Simms, James, Pvt.
Simms, Joshua F., Pvt.
Sindlinger, Henry, Pvt.
Smith, George B., Pvt.
Smith, Henry, Pvt.
Smith, William T., Pvt.
Snapp, Joseph K., Corpl.
Snellings, William, Pvt.
Snyder, Joseph, Pvt.
Southall, George D., Pvt.
Southard, John M., Pvt.
Squires, John O., Pvt.
Stanford, John, Pvt.
Stanley, James T. C., Pvt.
Stanley, John, Pvt.
Stanley, Thomas, Pvt.
Stephens, Robert
Sterling, John, Pvt.
Stewater, James, Pvt.
Stillman, William, Pvt.
Stoneberger, James F., Pvt.
Stoneberger, J. V. B., Pvt.
Strole, Abraham, Corpl.
Stroop, George W., Pvt.
Stroop, John W., Pvt.
Stroop, William, Pvt.
Sutton, Archibald, Bugler
Taylor, Charles, Pvt.
Taylor, John E., Pvt.
Temple, Bernard M., Pvt.
Temble, W. Skyren, Sergt.
Thomas, George S., Pvt.
Thomas, John A., Pvt.

Thompson, Charles, Pvt.
Thompson, Gardner G., Pvt.
Thompson, Thomas H., Corpl.
Thomson, N. W., Pvt.
Thornton, Charles, Pvt.
Thorpe, William, Pvt.
Tilman, James A., Corpl.
Todd, George R. C., Pvt.
Totty, Robert T., Pvt.
Trevena, William, Pvt.
Tucker, Charles, Pvt.
Turner, C. T.
Turner, Jesse, Pvt.
Turner, John S., Pvt.
Tyler, William H., Pvt.
Uren, Joseph, Pvt.
Vaden, Thomas, Pvt.
Waldron, Burwell, Pvt.
Waldron, Jacob, Pvt.
Watkins, Charles B., Pvt.
Watkins, John C., Pvt.
Watson, Alexander, Pvt.
Watts, George, Pvt.
Weaver, John A., Pvt.
Wells, John
Wharton, W. G. Pvt.
White, William, Pvt.
Wilde, William, Pvt.
Williams, John, Pvt.
Wilson, John T., Pvt.
Winston, Lucien D., Pvt.
Yager, Thornton P., Pvt.
Zimmerman, William, Pvt.

# RICHMOND FAYETTE ARTILLERY

The Fayette Artillery was originally organized as the "Richmond Light Artillery" on May 3, 1821, and on May 29, Governor Thomas Mann Randolph signed the commission of Captain John Rutherfoord and other company officers. The company belonged to the 4th Regiment of Artillery, Virginia Militia, which was composed of all artillery companies within twenty-eight southeastern counties, and was attached to the 19th Regiment of militia (City of Richmond) for musters, drills, and parades. In July 1824, the company changed its name to the "Richmond Fayette Light Artillery" in honor of the Marquis de La Fayette, who had been invited to visit the Old Dominion in October of that year.

For many years the Fayette Artillery was Richmond's only artillery company. On patriotic anniversaries, and other occasions, it fired salutes on Capitol Square, and paraded with the other volunteer companies in the city. In May 1851 the Fayette Artillery, under Captain Robert McCandlish Nimmo, was included in the organization of the 1st Regiment of Virginia Volunteers.

The future of the Fayette Artillery seemed doubtful in March 1859, when the Richmond Daily Dispatch reported that the company was without a captain and almost in a state of disorganization. Colonel Thomas H. Ellis, 4th Regiment Artillery and a former captain of the Fayette Artillery, called a meeting for the company's reorganization in November 1859. On January 8, 1861 the revived company, under Captain Henry Coalter Cabell, turned out with two guns and marched in front of the 1st Regiment. On February 22, the company made an even better showing, with four pieces of artillery and 43 men.

On April 25, 1861 the Fayette Artillery was mustered into State service for one year, with four officers and 108 enlisted men. It was first stationed at the Baptist College artillery barracks. In May the company was sent to Gloucester Point, where it remained during the summer. At the end of June 1861, the battery, equipped as light artillery with four brass 6-pounders, was reported as being "well uniformed in Blue flannel, & well equipped; discipline: good; drill: excellent."

In September 1861 the Fayette Artillery was assigned to the 1st Regiment Virginia Artillery, in which it was designated as Company I. Captain Cabell was appointed lieutenant colonel of the regiment, and on September 24, 1st Lieutenant Miles C. Macon was promoted to captain of the company.

On April 4, 1862 the Fayette Artillery was placed in position at Wynn's Mill on General Magruder's defensive line on the lower Peninsula, where, on the following day, it assisted in repulsing a Federal attack. The battery was constantly engaged throughout April, but suffered no casualties. On May 4, following the evacuation of Yorktown, the battery was placed at Fort Magruder, at Williamsburg, where it served on the 5th in the repulse of the attack on General Longstreet's rear guard.

Anne S. K. Brown Military Collection

Captain Thomas H. Ellis

Captain Ellis as pictured on the cover to "Capt. Ellis' Artillery Quick Step," composed and dedicated to the Richmond Fayette Artillery by Harvey B. Dodworth; published in Richmond in 1846. Ellis was commissioned as lieutenant in the Fayette Artillery in 1836 and served as its captain from 1842 to 1847 when he was appointed major in the 4th Regiment of Artillery, Virginia Militia. He was appointed lieutenant colonel of the regiment in 1851 and colonel in 1855. In May 1861 he organized and commanded the Richmond Home Guard Artillery Battalion.

Colonel Micah Jenkins, commanding at Fort Magruder, reported: "The Fayette Artillery suffered particularly and acted with great gallantry."

In the general reorganization of the artillery in June 1862, the 1st Regiment Virginia Artillery was placed in Brigadier General William N. Pendleton's Reserve Artillery, Army of Northern Virginia. Scant use was made of the Reserve Artillery during the Seven Days Battles, June 26-July 1, 1862, and the batteries of this regiment saw little action. The Fayette Artillery was placed in position on June 30 and July 1, but was not ordered to fire, even though it was exposed to heavy artillery fire.

Shortly before the Maryland Campaign, the Fayette Artillery was detached from the Reserve Artillery, and assigned to Major General Lafayette McLaws' Division, Longstreet's Corps. The battery at this time was equipped with two 10-pounder Parrotts and four 6-pounders. Following the victory at Second Manassas, Lee moved his army into Maryland. Forced to divide his army in order to capture Harpers Ferry to ensure the safety of his proposed route of supply, and to maintain the initiative, Lee advanced northward toward Hagerstown while troops under Jackson advanced on Harpers Ferry. The rapid Federal advance forced Lee to return to defend the mountain passes. The two Parrott guns, with a rifled piece from Page's Battery, all under Captain Macon, were sent to Crampton's Gap, Maryland, on September 14, where they played a conspicuous part in checking the Federal advance. Colonel E. B. Montague, commanding elements of Semmes' Brigade, reported that "Captain Macon, the senior artillery officer managed his guns most handsomely, and he and his juniors are entitled to all the credit of the occasion..." After checking the Federal advance, Lee retired to Sharpsburg, Maryland, where he determined to fight a defensive battle. Under the direction of their former captain, Colonel Cabell, Chief of Artillery, McLaws' Division, the Fayette Artillery went into action at Sharpsburg on the morning of September 17, occupying a position in a pasture about 500 yards west of the Hagerstown Pike, and about 100 yards south of its intersection with Bloody Lane. Known surviving records are silent on details of the Fayette Artillery's part in the battle. Antietam Battlefield Board maps, published in 1904, indicated that only two guns of the battery were engaged. After the battle the battery retired south of the Potomac River with the army.

The Fayette Artillery, on December 8, 1862, was transferred to the artillery attached to Major General George E. Pickett's Division, Longstreet's Corps. On December 13, 1862, the day of Burnside's attack at Fredericksburg, the battery, with the exception of one Parrott, was placed in position on the hill in rear of the Howison House.

On February 18, 1863 Pickett's Division, with its artillery under Major James F. Dearing, along with Major General John B. Hood's Division, was sent to Petersburg. In the reorganization of the artillery of the Army of Northern Virginia the Fayette Artillery was assigned to Major Dearing's Battalion on April 16, 1863. On April 21 the four iron 6-pounders were replaced by four Napoleon 12-pounders. Shortly afterwards, the battalion left with the divisions of Pickett and Hood for operations in the vicinity of Suffolk, Virginia. Here it remained until ordered to Culpeper Court House in preparation for Lee's second invasion of the North.

About June 15 Dearing's Battalion left Culpeper Court House to join Pickett's Division, Longstreet's Corps, for the march into Pennsylvania. Arriving on the morning of July 3, Dearing moved his battalion on the battlefield at Gettysburg. When the signal guns for the general attack were fired, Dearing brought his batteries forward to positions on the Emmittsburg Road, near the Klinger House. In the day's fighting, the Fayette Artillery had three men killed, three wounded, and eight horses killed.

By November 10, 1863 Dearing's Battalion had been designated as the 38th Battalion Virginia Artillery, in which the Fayette Artillery was denominated as Company B. The battalion was assigned to the Department of North Carolina under command of General Pickett, whose headquarters were at Petersburg. In December 1863 the Fayette Artillery appears to have been detached for a short period of duty at Chaffin's Bluff, serving in Lieutenant Colonel J. L. Maury's Battalion of artillery.

Near the end of December 1863 the battalion left their winter quarters at Petersburg and marched to Goldsboro, North Carolina, from which place they were taken by train to Kinston, on the Neuse River. On January 30, 1864 the battalion, then under Major John P. Read, moved from Kinston with the forces under General Pickett to capture New Bern. They arrived before New Bern on February 1, and the Fayette Artillery, under command of Lieutenant William Clopton, with the other batteries, unlimbered and moved their pieces by hand to the bank of Bachelor's Creek, where they opened fire on a blockhouse on the other side. Here occurred an event unprecedented in the history of artillery during the war. The Fayette Artillery charged the Federal blockhouse, moving the guns by hand, stopping occasionally to fire a shot, and reloading as they advanced. The battery crossed the creek and went into position about 75 feet from the blockhouse, but before they could fire, a section of Federal artillery hurriedly left the fort for New Bern, about eight miles distant. The horses of the Fayette Artillery were brought up, the pieces limbered, and the battery started in pursuit of the Federals, who, however, managed to reach the town safely. In the confusion of the day's fighting, Sergeant Major Robert J. Fleming of the Fayette Artillery captured Lieutenant Colonel John F. Fellows of the 17th Regiment Massachusetts Volunteers, as well as his adjutant and orderly. On the next day, the Fayette Artillery, with Stribling's Battery and the 30th Regiment Virginia Infantry, moved against a fort at Beech Grove, at the junction of the Washington and New Bern roads. The formal surrender of the fort was received by Lieutenant Clopton and Sergeant Major Fleming. The prized trophies were two 3-inch steel rifled guns, which, a few days later, were presented to the Fayette Artillery by General Pickett. These guns replaced the four Napoleons, and were retained, with the two Parrotts, until the end of the war. The attack on New Bern was abandoned, and Pickett's forces returned to Kinston.

The Fayette Artillery accompanied the forces of Brigadier General

Robert F. Hoke in operations against Plymouth, North Carolina, April 17-20, 1864. On the 19th the battery lost two men killed and two wounded. The fall of Plymouth resulted in another, but also unsuccessful, attempt to capture New Bern.

On May 5 the Fayette Artillery left the vicinity of New Bern, and on May 14, after a march of 220 miles, arrived at Petersburg. On May 16 the battery, with General Whiting's Division, participated in the fighting at Port Walthall Junction, and, on the following day, moved into position with the battalion on the Bermuda Hundred lines, between Richmond and Petersburg.

Major Read's Battalion, on May 30, accompanied General Hoke's Division to Mechanicsville, and on June 1 went into action at Cold Harbor. General Pendleton, Chief of Artillery, singled out the battalion's part in the fighting on June 3: "Read's guns, on Hoke's line...though exposed to a fierce fire of infantry and artillery, were used with great energy and success." On June 13 the battalion marched from Cold Harbor to Petersburg, then threatened by an attack.

The battalion reached the Petersburg Lines on June 14, and on the next day, the Fayette Artillery went into position near the Avery House, on the right of the defense line. On the 17th the battery fell back to the Rives House, where they remained through the next day. About June 23 they were placed on the right of General Gracie's salient where they remained throughout the summer.

From October 1864 until the evacuation of Petersburg, the 38th Battalion served in the artillery attached to General "Dick" Anderson's Corps. With the promotion and transfer of Major Read in December 1864 the command of the battalion was given to Major Robert M. Stribling. Although actively engaged almost daily, the battalion did not serve in the parts of the lines heavily assaulted by the Federals until near the end of the fighting at Petersburg. In March 1865 the Fayette Artillery, under Lieutenant Clopton, had three officers and 73 enlisted men present for duty.

On April 2, 1865 Lee's army withdrew from Petersburg and retreated westward. He surrendered his army at Appomattox Court House on April 9. Only 24 men of the 38th Battalion, then under Major Joseph G. Blount, were paroled at Appomattox. Three full batteries, including the Fayette Artillery, escaped to Lynchburg. There, across the river on the Staunton road, they spiked their guns and cut down the carriages.

# RICHMOND FAYETTE ARTILLERY

## CAPTAINS

Cabell, Henry C.
Macon, Miles C.

## LIEUTENANTS

Clopton, William I., 1st Lieut.
Fleming, Robert J., Jr. 2nd Lieut.
Johnston, Peyton Jr., Jr. 2nd Lieut.

Jones, William Winston Jr., Jr. 1st Lieut.
Robinson, Benjamin H., 2nd Lieut.

## NON-COMMISSIONED OFFICERS AND PRIVATES

Allen, James L., Pvt.
Allen, William A., Pvt.
Alt, A., Pvt.
Andrews, Thomas H., Pvt.
Angle, A. M., Pvt.
Baker, Lewis W., Pvt.
Barnes, James, Pvt.
Barnes, Joseph, Pvt.
Barton, A. Pvt.
Benton, George, Pvt.
Black, James, Pvt.
Blunt, James T., Pvt.
Blunt, Joseph E., Q.M. Sergt.
Bohannon, G
Boyle, John, Pvt.
Brown, Charles, Pvt.
Brown, George W., Pvt.
Bruce, James, Pvt.
Brumfield, John M., Pvt.
Buckleman, Henry C., Pvt.
Burke, John, Pvt.
Burrows, Charles D., Pvt.
Butler, Isham, Pvt.
Butler, Solomon, Pvt.
Byron, Rudolph J., Sergt.
Carr, Jesse, Pvt.
Carter, Leonard H., Q.M. Sergt.
Carter, Thomas R., Pvt.
Carver, F. N., Pvt.
Clark, Samuel B., Pvt.
Clark, William G., Pvt.
Clayton, Henry, Pvt.
Clements, William, Pvt.
Cocke, Edwin, Pvt.
Cole, Haley, Artificer
Costello, James, Pvt.
Cox, B. M., Pvt.

Danzey, Thomas H., Pvt.
Dashields, G. H., Pvt.
Day, Walter C., Pvt.
Delume, Hilume, Pvt.
Dishman, L. L., Pvt.
Dowden, Richard B., Pvt.
Doyle, George P., Pvt.
Doyle, Thomas, Pvt.
Dunn, James, Pvt.
Eacho, Delaware A., Pvt.
Edwards, A. C., Sergt.
Edwards, D. C., Pvt.
Edwards, James H., Pvt.
Ellett, A., Pvt.
Ellington, John, Pvt.
Ellis, John H., Pvt.
Epperson, Joseph B., Pvt.
Eubank, Benton, Pvt.
Eubank, Carter H., Pvt.
Fercron, Archer, Pvt.
Finland, Thomas, Pvt.
Fitzgerald, D., Pvt.
Fitzgerald, William, Pvt.
Ford, Frederick W., Pvt.
Fowlkes, Richard H., Pvt.
Frayser, John S., Pvt.
Fritz, Peter, Pvt.
Gaines, David H., Pvt.
Gaines, E. W., Sergt.
Gay, William C., Pvt.
Gill, Henry H., Pvt.
Gilliam, Robert, Pvt.
Graves, Thaddeus C., Pvt.
Griddell, Henry C., Pvt.
Grubbs, A. B., Pvt.
Hall, John, Pvt.
Hardman, John, Pvt.

Hartman, J., Pvt.
Hartsberger, Peter A., Corpl.
Hawkins, Charles H. C., Pvt.
Hays, Robert, Pvt.
Heath, W. L., Pvt.
Heileman, Julius F., Sergt.
Herndon, G. A., Pvt.
Hix, A. L., Pvt.
Hix, George F., Pvt.
Hoeter, Dennis, Pvt.
Hogan, Joseph Pvt.
Holmes, Julius C., Pvt.
Holt, John D., Pvt.
Hood, John T., Pvt.
Horseley, B. F., Pvt.
Howard, Thomas J., Pvt.
Howle, John, Pvt.
Hunt, Michael, Pvt.
Ingraham, S. H., Pvt.
Irby, Morgan G., Pvt.
Jacobs, Strother, Pvt.
Jarvis, Ottaway, Corpl.
Jemmings, George F., Pvt.
Jones, A. H., Sergt.
Jones, B. S., Corpl.
Jones, James C.
Kane, John, Pvt.
Keene, James H., Pvt.
Kuis, August, Sergt.
Lamb, W. D., Pvt.
Lampkin, J. W., Pvt.
Leary, John H., Corpl.
Lillas, Thomas, Pvt.
Lilly, James, Pvt.
Lipscomb, A. C., Pvt.
Long, Reuben, Pvt.
Lucas, William D., Pvt.
Mallow, Jacob, Pvt.
Manning, William T., Pvt.
Martin, Patrick K., Pvt.
Martin, Washington O., Pvt.
Martin, William T., Pvt.
Maybright C., Pvt.
McCann, Daniel C., Pvt.
McCrea, William H., Pvt.
McCurdey, Peter, 1st Sergt.
McDonald, N. P., Pvt.
McGee, James H., Pvt.
McKennon, William, Corpl.
McMims, Andrew, Pvt.
McNamara, Thomas S., Pvt.

Middleton, John, Pvt.
Miller, John, Pvt.
Morefield, P. H., Pvt.
Morris, George P., Pvt.
Morris, W. L., Pvt.
Moseley, Thomas F., Pvt.
Mullins, Joseph, Pvt.
Munda, James E., Corpl.
Myers, C. A., Pvt.
Newman, Alexander, Pvt.
Newton, George A., Pvt.
Perdue, Andrew J., Pvt.
Pettus, William B., Pvt.
Phoeny, Anthony, Pvt.
Pippin, Elijah, Corpl.
Pollard, E. S., Pvt.
Pollock, Richard D., Pvt.
Pope, Charles W., Sergt.
Ramy, T. G., Pvt.
Ratcliffe, Ro K., Pvt.
Rayford, A. C., Pvt.
Reese, Richard, Pvt.
Reeves, Daniel D., Pvt.
Rex, C. M., Pvt.
Robertson, J. J., Pvt.
Robinson, James C., Pvt.
Robinson, William H., Pvt.
Rogers, William H., Pvt.
Rohrbaugh, James, Pvt.
Roper, Edwin, Pvt.
Rourke, John, Pvt.
Seaton, Fleming W., Pvt.
Seaton, W. S., Pvt.
Shell, Richard, Pvt.
Shell, William, Pvt.
Shook, James B., Pvt.
Smith, Thomas L., Pvt.
Smith, Zachariah, Pvt.
Sneed, Thomas W., Pvt.
Southard, Richard, Pvt.
Spencer, William B., Artificer
Stonesheet, A., Pvt.
Sutton, John C., Pvt.
Thomas, James D., Pvt.
Thomas, Milburn, Pvt.
Thompson, J. S., Pvt.
Tompkins, C. H., Pvt.
Totty, John H., Pvt.
Twyford, Revel T., Pvt.
Tyree, James H., Corpl.
Udurley, Moses, Pvt.

Vaden, George P., Pvt.
Vaughan, James C., Pvt.
Vernon, Joseph C., Pvt.
Walsh, John H., Pvt.
Walsh, William R., Pvt.
Webber, John S., Corpl.
West, William H., Pvt.

White, James P., Pvt.
Whitworth, Thomas, Pvt.
Williams, Milton G., Sergt.Major
Wilson, Alexander J., Pvt.
Wilson, Andrew J., Pvt.
Woodward, Robert A., Pvt.
Wright, Pleasant, Pvt.

# RICHMOND FLYING ARTILLERY

Captain Thomas T. Cropper's Company, Virginia Light Artillery, known as the Richmond Flying Artillery, enlisted on March 18, 1862. It was temporarily attached to the 24th Regiment Virginia Infantry before it was accepted into Confederate States service on May 21, 1862 and assigned to the 24th Battalion Virginia Partisan Rangers, known as Scott's Rangers. At this time the company was at Howard's Grove, near the city. On June 3, 1862 the Secretary of War ordered Brigadier General J. H. Winder to send an officer to muster the company into service, with instructions to enroll only the men between 18 and 35, should the company be below seventy rank and file. On June 5 Cropper's Company was disbanded, but on the 9th he protested in a letter and asked for time to inform Major John Scott, commander of the battalion. The Secretary of War directed General Winder to keep the company as organized until Captain Cropper could discuss it with Major Scott. However, the Secretary of War directed General Winder "to send the company to the field if necessary." General Winder's endorsement to the instructions was received by the Adjutant & Inspector General's Office on June 24, 1862, and reads: "The men of this company have all been assigned to other companies and Captain Cropper's Company no longer exists." Following the original instructions of June 3, General Winder had transferred twenty-five men to Captain Thomas H. Carter's Battery Virginia Artillery and ten to Company F, 1st Regiment Virginia Artillery.

A roster of the Richmond Flying Artillery has not been located.

# RICHMOND OTEY BATTERY

This company of light artillery was organized March 14, 1862 with George Gaston Otey as captain, and mustered into Confederate States service on March 22, 1862. A common practice of the time was for a unit to be known by its captain's name, thus it was officially designated the Otey Battery. Since there was already a company from Staunton serving as artillery under a Captain C. C. Otey, the company from Richmond was officially designated the Richmond Otey Battery. On the day the company was organized Captain Otey received a letter from Colonel, later Brigadier General, Henry Heth, commanding the District of Lewisburg, informing him that four unassigned guns would be available for his company at Lewisburg. Captain Otey informed the Adjutant and Inspector General on March 19 of Colonel Heth's letter and requested that his company be sent to the Baptist College Artillery Camp to organize and drill before reporting to Colonel Heth. However, on March 21 the Richmond Otey Battery was ordered to report directly to Colonel Heth at Lewisburg.

When the company arrived at Lewisburg, they were attached to Heth's small force, called the Army of New River. Early in May 1862 a Federal force advanced to cut the Virginia & Tennessee Railroad. Heth was ordered to defend the approaches to Dublin Depot and General Humphrey Marshall, commanding the District of Abingdon, was ordered to advance on Princeton to intercept the Federal advance. On May 10 Heth's force drove a Federal force from Pearisburg (Giles Court House). Heth then moved to threaten the rear of the Federal force at Princeton. With Marshall driving in front and Heth moving in rear, the Federal commander, General Jacob D. Cox, retreated from Princeton. After the occupation of Princeton, on May 16, General Marshall retired. The Federal advance had been defeated. Heth then marched on Lewisburg, now occupied by a Federal force under Colonel George Cook. Once in position, on May 23, Heth's initial attack progressed well, when "one of those causeless panics for which there is no accounting seized upon my command." Defeated, Heth retired toward Union, leaving four pieces of his artillery in enemy hands. Throughout this campaign of the Army of New River the Richmond Otey Battery served with distinction.

During the summer of 1862 the scattered Confederate forces were organized into the Army of Western Virginia under Major General W. W. Loring. The Richmond Otey Battery was incorporated in this force under Loring's Chief of Artillery, Major J. Floyd King. When General Lee advanced the Army of Northern Virginia into Northern Virginia, General Cox was ordered to retire down the Kanawha Valley and to send troops to the main Federal army under General John Pope. Captured documents informed Lee of this move, and he ordered Loring to advance down the Kanawha Valley. On September 6, 1862 Loring began his advance which culminated in the capture of Charleston on September 16. One piece of the Richmond Otey Battery was assigned to the advance while the rest of the artillery was held in reserve. At Fayetteville, on September 10, Loring defeated a Federal force and continued his advance on Charleston. During the advance one 12-pounder Howitzer of the Richmond Otey Battery was left at Gauley, while one section moved with the forces up the right bank of the Kanawha River and one section moved with the forces up the left bank. On September 16 Loring's forces drove the Federals from Charleston. During this campaign the Richmond Otey Battery sustained a loss of three killed and eleven wounded.

Under orders from Richmond, General Loring prepared to advance his force northward to join General Lee. Loring's infantry retired eastward to proceed northward by way of Lewisburg. Lee's withdrawal from Sharpsburg and increased Federal activity necessitated the retention of Loring's force in the Kanawha Valley. However, Loring had withdrawn all but his cavalry from Charleston. Loring was relieved on October 15 and General John Echols placed in command. Under their new commander the Confederates began a second advance on Charleston on the 17th. This advance met stiff opposition, and Echols soon retired to the Princeton-Lewisburg line. In December 1862 Major General Samuel Jones was placed in command of the department, and his troops went into winter quarters. The Richmond Otey Battery was stationed at Dublin Depot, and reported seventy-five men present in December 1862. The battery was now commanded by David N. Walker, who was promoted to captain after Captain Otey's death at Lynchburg on October 21, 1862.

Although there was much activity in southwestern Virginia during the winter and spring of 1863, the Richmond Otey Battery remained at Dublin Depot. On June 1, 1863 it was ordered to Piney to reinforce Colonel John McCausland's command. From there they were ordered to Wytheville, where they remained on the defensive until September 14 when they were ordered to Saltville. In October 1863 the battery was reported in Lieutenant Colonel J. Floyd King's Artillery Battalion, Army of Western Virginia and Eastern Tennessee, which was attached to General Longstreet's forces in East Tennessee. After a frustrating campaign Longstreet retired to Bristol and in April 1864 received orders to return with his corps to the Army of Northern Virginia.

The Richmond Otey Battery did not remain long in its old department. On May 7, 1864 Colonel King received orders to report to Longstreet's Chief of Artillery, Brigadier General E. P. Alexander, with two batteries from the Army of Southwestern Virginia and East Tennessee. One of those he chose was the Richmond Otey Battery. This battery and two other independent batteries were organized into a battalion under Colonel King and officially designated the 13th Battalion Virginia Light Artillery; the Richmond Otey Battery being designated Company C of the battalion. On July 31, 1864 the battalion was assigned to Longstreet's Corps. Now a part of the Army of Northern Virginia, the battery took part in the engagements which culminated in the occupation of the Richmond-Petersburg line, and was placed in the lines at Petersburg. In October 1864 the battalion was assigned to A. P. Hill's Corps. In addition to manning the battery's four 12-pounder Napoleons, the men were assigned three Coehorn mortars.

After the evacuation of Petersburg on April 2-3, 1865 the battery joined the retreating army. During the retreat the men were relieved of their artillery pieces and armed as guards with muskets. On April 8 they successfully drove off a Federal force attempting to capture the artillery train. Those who remained with the army were surrendered at Appomattox Court House on April 9, 1865.

# RICHMOND OTEY BATTERY

## CAPTAINS

Otey, George G.
Walker, David N.

## LIEUTENANTS

Balling, Archibald, 1st Lieut.
Gunn, Richard B., 2nd Lieut.
Langhorne, John B., 2nd Lieut.
Norvell, Edward, 1st Lieut.

## NON-COMMISSIONED OFFICERS AND PRIVATES

Anderson, R. P., Pvt.
Bagby, Henry B., P
Baldwin, Herman R., Pvt.
Ball, A. W., Pvt.
Ball, George P., Q.M. Sergt.
Barney, W. H., Pvt.
Batey, John, Farrier
Baughman, Charles C., Corpl.
Beall, E. S., Sergt. Maj.
Benson, C. E., Pvt.
Binford, Alfred R., Corpl.
Binford, Charles T., Pvt.
Binford, James H., Pvt.
Binford, Julian, Pvt.
Blair, Lewis H., Pvt.
Blair, William T., Pvt.
Booker, G. Y., Pvt.
Bridges, C. C., Pvt.
Briggs, R. T., Pvt.
Brooks, Cyrus, Pvt.
Buren, Henry C., Pvt.
Burnett, Henry C., Pvt.
Burnett, S. E., Pvt.
Burton, H. W., Pvt.
Burton, R. C., Pvt.
Butler, R. E., Pvt.
Campbell, W. J., Pvt.
Caperton, John, 1st Sergt.
Cardoza, Julian H., Pvt.
Carter, James M., Pvt.
Chalkley, Thaddeus A., Pvt.
Chamberlaine, James, Pvt.
Chamberlayne, Curtis, Pvt.
Cheatham, Andrew J., Pvt.
Clopton, S. C., Pvt.
Conrad, W. S., Pvt.
Cooke, Edwin B., Pvt.

Cox, Henry W., Corpl
Crane, T. C., Bugler
Crockett, H. E., Pvt.
Davies, W. W., Pvt.
Denney, R. S., Pvt.
Dupuy, R. R., Pvt.
Edmunds, Nathaniel S., Pvt.
Farley, Alfred A., Sergt.
Farley, Richard G., Pvt.
Farrar, Chastine B., Pvt.
Fendley, T. M., Pvt.
Finney, Edwin B., Corpl.
Fisher, E. C., Pvt.
Flournoy, James, Pvt.
Flournoy, P. P., Pvt.
Flournoy, R. W., Pvt.
Flournoy, Samuel, Pvt.
Ford, Edward L., Pvt.
Ford, William B. B., Pvt.
Frederick, J. C., Pvt.
Gay, H. E., Pvt.
Givens, A. J., Farrier
Glazebrook, Robert L., Pvt.
Glazebrook, Robert M., Sergt.
Goldsby, T. M., Pvt.
Gordon, Edward C., Sergt.
Gordon, John N., Jr., Pvt.
Gouldman, Edward, Pvt.
Gouldman, Henry E., Pvt.
Grant, Alexander, Sergt.
Grant, George W., Pvt.
Graves, R. M., Pvt.
Guathmey, R. W., Pvt.
Guerrant, W. G., Pvt.
Haney, J. W., Pvt.
Harper, Richard G., Pvt.
Harris, Alfred T., Jr., Pvt.
Harrison, Samuel J. Jr., Corpl.

Hart, H. R., Pvt.
Hart, William A., Corpl.
Hartman, Addison C., Pvt.
Harvey, Samuel M., Pvt.
Harwood, William F., Pvt.
Henry, A. K., Pvt.
Hewitt, H. C., Pvt.
Hooper, Benjamin W., Pvt.
Jamieson, R., Sergt.
Jefferson, E. C., Pvt.
Johnson, Adolphus M., Pvt.
Johnson, T. R., Pvt.
Keesee, Thomas B., Pvt.
Kennedy, John A. B., Pvt.
Kennon, William H., Pvt.
Kent, Charles E., Pvt.
Kerr, William M., Pvt.
Kershner, Madison M., Pvt.
Kirk, C. T., Pvt.
Lancaster, John J., Sergt.
Lancaster, L. W., Pvt.
Leake, William P., Pvt.
Leftwick, George W., Pvt.
Libby, George W., Pvt.
Ligon, W. H., Pvt.
Link, James A., Corpl.
Mahoney, D. H., Pvt.
Mahood, F. F. Corpl.
Mason, R. J., Pvt.
Maury, Richard W., Pvt.
Mayse, Robert G., Artificer
McCarthy, Samuel H., Pvt.
McClerman, John H., Pvt.
McCoy, Richard D., Pvt.
McKenney, Joseph B., Pvt.
McLance, R. G., Pvt.
Miller, James P., Pvt.
Miller, William G., Pvt.
Morris, Edward R., Pvt.
Mumford, William, Pvt.
Murkland, A. W., Hospital Steward
Nicholas, Spear, Corpl.
Nolting, James M., Pvt.
Nottingham, L. J., Pvt.
Page, James B., Corpl.
Painter, G. W., Pvt.
Painter, J. C., Pvt.
Perdue, James R., Corpl.
Pilcher, W. S., Pvt.
Pollard, J. S., Pvt.
Puckett, James C., Pvt.
Ralls, Charles E., Pvt.
Reid, J. H., Pvt.
Roberts, H. G., Pvt.
Roberts, J. C., Pvt.
Roberts, J. M., Pvt.
Ruffner, R. S
Rutherford, Thomas, Pvt.
Ryan, Thomas, Pvt.
Sarvay, William G., Pvt.
Saunders, Howard, Pvt.
Savage, George, Pvt.
Sclater, James B., Pvt.
Seibt, J., Artificer
Sharp, John H., Pvt.
Sheppard, William Z. Jr., Pvt.
Sims, Onslow B., Pvt.
Slaymaker, Henry C., Pvt.
Slaymaker, William A., Pvt.
Smith, Alfred W., Pvt.
Smith, C. M., Pvt.
Smith, Henry, Pvt.
Smith, P. B., Pvt.
Snider, William P., 1st Sergt.
Spence, C. A., Pvt.
Spence, William H., Pvt.
Starke, John L., Pvt.
Storrs, Robert Q., Pvt.
Stratton, Thomas E., Pvt.
Stratton, William H., Pvt.
Stuart, George C., Pvt.
Stuart, J. W., Pvt.
Tabb, W. S., Pvt.
Talbott, J. M. Jr., Pvt.
Talbott, Samuel G., Pvt.
Taylor, G. W., Pvt.
Taylor, John L., Pvt.
Templin, W. W., Pvt.
Thompson, C. H., Pvt.
Thompson, R. W., Pvt.
Thompson, Thomas R., Pvt.
Thompson, W. T., Pvt.
Tompkins, Wesley K., Hosp.Steward
Tompkins, Wilson, Pvt.
Tucker, B. D., Pvt.
Tyler, Stanley R., Pvt.
Valentine, Richard J., Pvt.
Waddy, George M., Pvt.
Walton, W. W., Pvt.
Watkins, Charles T., Pvt.
Watkins, John F., Pvt.
Webster, J. P., Pvt.
Wells, Dennis C., Pvt.
Wells, James M., Pvt.

West, Montgomery, Pvt.
Weymouth, John H., Pvt.
Wharton, Charles D., Pvt.
White, J. J., Pvt.
Wilbar, G. H., Pvt.
Williams, David W., Pvt.
Wood, J. B., Pvt.
Wood, Robert B., Pvt.
Woodhouse, J. G., Pvt.
Woods, J. T., Pvt.
Woods, Willie F., Pvt.
Wright, R., Pvt.
Yancey, Alexander, Pvt.
Yancey, C. K., Pvt.
Yancey, Francis M., Pvt.
Young, Nathaniel F., Pvt.

# THOMAS ARTILLERY

The Thomas Artillery, a company of light artillery, was organized on April 25, 1861 with the election of Captain Philip Beverly Stanard, a Virginia Military Institute graduate of the Class of 1856. The company was named for James Thomas, a wealthy citizen of Richmond, who fully equipped and uniformed it in gray at a cost of $2,000. On May 10 the company enrolled for active duty, and was apparently mustered into State service on the 17th, for a period of one year. At sunrise on July 4, the Thomas Artillery, then at Camp Chimborazo, overlooking Griffin's Spring, fired eleven rounds in honor of each state in the Confederacy.

On July 10 the battery left Richmond, traveled by railroad to Strasburg, and from there marched to Winchester, where it was assigned to the artillery of Brigadier General Joseph E. Johnston's Army of the Shenandoah. On July 18 the battery left for Manassas Junction, arriving there less than 48 hours later, after a foot march covering 60 miles. Equipped with one 10-pounder Parrott rifle, a brass rifled piece, and two bronze 6-pounder smoothbore guns, the battery reached the Manassas battlefield on July 21, and went into position on the left of General Jackson's line. Seven hundred rounds were reported fired during the battle in which Lieutenant Edgar Mann was killed, and six enlisted men were wounded, one mortally. A shell exploded one of the battery's caissons, and several of the others were perforated by small shot. Five disabled horses were left on the field.

The end of August 1861 found the battery in camp near Bristoe with a strength of four officers and 77 enlisted men present for duty. On September 17 the battery moved to Centreville, remaining there until October 15, when it moved to a new camp on Cub Run.

In the organization of the troops of the Potomac District under General Beauregard, during the winter of 1861-1862, the Thomas Artillery was assigned to Brigadier General Cadmus M. Wilcox's Brigade of the Second Division, commanded by Major General Gustavus W. Smith, which in February was redesignated as the First Division, Army of the Potomac.

The Thomas Artillery re-enlisted in March 1862 for "two years or the war;" and was reported in camp "near Richmond" at the end of April. During the Seven Days' Battles the battery served with Wilcox's Brigade, then designated as the Fourth Brigade, Longstreet's Division. At the battle of Mechanicsville, on June 26, the battery was brought into action and expended 150 rounds on the Federal infantry. One man, Corporal Bartlet, was killed by a sharpshooter. The total casualties suffered by the battery during the Seven Days' Battles were one killed and two wounded.

Soon after August 13 Longstreet's Corps was at Gordonsville, and on the 19th, with Jackson's Corps, started advancing towards General John Pope's Federal forces, which had retired behind the Rappahannock. On August 21 Wilcox's Brigade, with the Thomas Artillery, now under Captain Edwin J. Anderson, encountered an enemy force of cavalry near Mountain Run. Several of its charges were repulsed by Wilcox's infantry, the last of which sent the Federals scattering over an open field for a mile or more. In time, they re-formed on high ground in an open field on the opposite side of the run. Wilcox then ordered Captain Anderson to place his Parrott rifle under cover of some pine and open fire on them. What ensued was described by General Wilcox as follows:

> It has never been my pleasure to witness such beautiful shots as the first half dozen shell that were thrown at them. Each shell burst at the right place and time, and seemed to create more confusion and inflict greater loss upon them than the infantry fire. This artillery fire drove them entirely out of view, and nothing more was seen of them until about 5 p.m., when the cavalry reappeared. Three rifled pieces were now placed in position and after a few rounds the cavalry fled again in confusion.

The battery's Parrott was again engaged on the 23rd when it was placed with two Parrotts of the Loudoun Artillery, and the 3rd Company of the Washington Artillery Battalion of New Orleans, on the Rappahannock, to the left of Beverly's Ford. The firing commenced about 6 a.m., and a vigorous duel with Federal batteries across the river soon developed, continuing for about an hour.

The Thomas Artillery was among the depleted batteries ordered to be detained at Leesburg, and so did not participate in the Maryland Campaign; 27 men, however, had been detached to the Washington Artillery Battalion prior to their march northward. Presumably the battery was sent to Winchester for recruits and horses, both of which were not easily obtained in late 1862. The men and horses of the battery were assigned to Captain Caskie's Hampden Artillery on October 4, 1862 when the battery was disbanded. Although this arrangement was considered temporary, the Thomas Artillery was never reorganized.

## THOMAS ARTILLERY

### CAPTAINS

Anderson, Edwin J.
Stanard, Philip B.

### LIEUTENANTS

Macon, Edgar, 2nd Lieut.
Massenburg, James Jr., 2nd Lieut.
Thornton, Charles H., 1st Lieut.

### NON-COMMISSIONED OFFICERS AND PRIVATES

Acorn, Peter, Pvt.
Adams, B. P., Pvt.
Allen, John A., Pvt.
Anderson, Alfred A., Pvt.
Babb, Rufus K., Pvt.
Baker, J. V., Pvt.
Baker, Robert, Pvt.
Bartlett, Richard T., Pvt.
Batkins, Robert E., Pvt.
Blair, Joseph A., Sergt.
Bootwright, James K., Pvt.
Bosher, James G., Pvt.
Botteller, Walter P., Pvt.
Bowe, George A., Pvt.
Bradley, Johnston T., Pvt.
Brady, Anthony, Pvt.
Bridgewater, Oscar C., Pvt.
Broach, Benjamin F., Pvt.
Brockmeyer, Charles A., Sergt.
Bruden, Horace S., Pvt.
Brunt, Robert W., Pvt.
Champion, Zackins, Corpl.
Childress, William W., Pvt.
Congdon, George W., Pvt.
Conner, Christopher, Pvt.
Conner, James M., Pvt.
Conover, John, Corpl.
Cooke, Nicholas, Pvt.
Cottrell, William R., Pvt.
Cummings, John, Pvt.
Davidson, Robert, Pvt.
Davis, William A., Pvt.
Dellaway, William H., Pvt.
Dillard, Thomas, Pvt.
Dixon, John B., Pvt.
Doherty, Mathew, Pvt.
Duffy, Frank, Pvt.
Dunn, James, Pvt.
Easly, Flemming, Pvt.
Enroughty, Barister, Pvt.

Ferguson, J. F., Pvt.
Fitzgerald, Charles, Pvt.
Floyd, John J., Pvt.
Ford, Flemming H., Pvt.
Forney, T. H., Pvt.
Fraysier, William H., Pvt.
George, Lee, Pvt.
George, William L., Pvt.
Glenn, William H., Pvt.
Goode, William H. H., Pvt.
Green, William, Pvt.
Haley, Wellington, M., Pvt.
Harris, John, Pvt.
Harris, Marcellus W., Pvt.
Heckler, William T., Pvt.
Henderson, William, Pvt.
Herzog, Lewis, Pvt.
Holcom, James, Pvt.
Hopkins, Frederick M., 1st Sergt.
Houseman, John, Pvt.
Hoyt, A., Pvt.
Hunt, Thomas T., Pvt.
Hutchison, William P., Pvt.
Johnson, Charles, Pvt.
Johnson, Samuel, Pvt.
Jones, Nathan, Pvt.
Keizer, Christian, Pvt.
King, John, Pvt.
Kinny, William, Pvt.
Levy, Elias L., Pvt.
Maloy, James, Pvt.
Mantle, Henry, Pvt.
Marshall, John W., Sergt.
McCarthy, Florence, Corpl.
McCook, William H., Pvt.
McCoy, John Joseph, Pvt.
McCurdey, Thomas B., Sergt.
McCurdy, John H., Corpl.
McLaughlin, John D., Pvt.
Melton, William T., Pvt.

Meyer, Christopher, Pvt.
Miller, John, Pvt.
Montcastle, George H., Pvt.
Moore, George J., Pvt.
Nichols, George H., Pvt.
Oakley, James K., Pvt.
Oakley, Thomas, Pvt.
Parker, Joseph, Pvt.
Peers, James C., Pvt.
Peney, William, Pvt.
Pohleman, Christopher, Pvt.
Power, Edward, Pvt.
Power, Patrick, Pvt.
Powers, John H., Pvt.
Ragland, Joseph H., Pvt.
Rayner, Cyrus T., Corpl.
Rey, William T., Pvt.
Reynolds, Robert, Pvt.
Roane, Patrick, Pvt.
Robertson, Joseph R., Pvt.
Rock, William, Pvt.
Rogers, John, Pvt.
Rose, James H., Corpl.
Rowe, George W., Pvt.
Saunders, George T., Pvt.
Schofield, Robert C., Pvt.
Simpson, E. F., Pvt.
Slicer, Conrad, Pvt.
Smiley, James W., Pvt.

Smith, C. J., Pvt.
Smith, Thomas J., Pvt.
Smith, William H., Pvt.
Smith, William H., Pvt.
Stevinson, James R., Pvt.
Stratten, James, Pvt.
Stratton, Thomas E., Pvt.
Strickler, J. C., Pvt.
Sullivan, John E., Sergt.
Sutton, William, Pvt.
Taylor, Samuel, Pvt.
Tennent, Charles B., Pvt.
Tennent, Julian R., Pvt.
Tenser, Charles, Pvt.
Terrell, Berry, Pvt.
Thomas, Frances, Pvt.
Thomas, Joseph E., Pvt.
Thompson, Francis B., Pvt.
Topp, William, Pvt.
Troester, Jacob, Pvt.
Vest, J. K.
Walker, John H., Pvt.
Waller, Edwin M., Pvt.
Walthall, Richard E., Pvt.
Ward, Sedge T., Pvt.
Watkins, James H., Pvt.
Woods, W., Pvt.
Woodson, Aylett R., Pvt.
Young, William T., Pvt.

# Cavalry

### CASKIE MOUNTED RANGERS

This company was organized at a meeting of the Mounted Rangers, held at Old Broad Street Hotel on April 23, 1861 when John Fry was elected captain and the company was designated Fry's Mounted Rangers. On May 3, 1861 another election was held after the company completed its organization and Robert Alexander Caskie, a 27 year old merchant, was elected captain. At this time the company designation was changed to Caskie's Mounted Rangers. The company was mustered into Confederate States service at Richmond on June 9, 1861 for the term of "the war with the United States."

Assigned to General Henry A. Wise's Legion, the company proceeded to Lewisburg, where it arrived on July 17, 1861 for service in the Kanawha Valley. In late July or early August the cavalry of the Legion was organized into the 1st Regiment of Cavalry, Wise Legion, under Colonel J. Lucius Davis. The Caskie Mounted Rangers were designated Company C of the newly organized regiment. On August 5 General John B. Floyd's command joined the Wise Legion at White Sulphur Springs. General Floyd, as senior in command, was soon determined to move into the Kanawha Valley against the Federals. The offensive got under way and on August 8 Captain Caskie "with some forty to fifty troopers" was reported "in Raleigh...with a body of militia" under orders to "move toward Fayette Court House." During the advance the cavalry was used to scout all roads along the route of advance. Floyd advanced to Meadow Bluff on the 10th and ordered Wise to join him on the 14th. Crossing the Gauley River at Carnifax Ferry, Floyd defeated a Federal force at Cross Lanes on August 26. After this action Floyd remained inactive at Carnifax Ferry, waiting for reinforcements. Moving as if to join Floyd, Wise started conducting his own campaign against Federal positions at Hawk's Nest. On August 27 Captain Caskie's company successfully attacked a Federal outpost on Cotton Hill. Failing to drive the Federals from Hawk's Nest, Wise took a position at Dickersons, covering Miller's Ferry, some fifteen miles southwest of Floyd's position. On September 4 General Wise reported that he had "ordered Caskie, with General [Alfred] Beckley's militia, down the Loop, and by this time they are there. The day before yesterday they fought the enemy at Cotton Hill, and drove them within 2 miles of Montgomery's Ferry." The next day, September 6, Captain Caskie's company rejoined Wise's command.

After the battle at Carnifax Ferry on September 10, Floyd and Wise fell back to Sewell Mountain, arriving there on the 14th. General Floyd, however, withdrew his forces twelve miles eastward to Meadow Bluff on the 16th. General Lee arrived at Meadow Bluff on September 21, and arrived at Sewell Mountain on the 24th with reinforcements for Wise, in whose front the enemy were advancing in force. During an enemy demonstration on September 25, General Wise was handed an order from the War Department directing him to hand over his command to General Floyd and report to Richmond. On October 6 the Federals retired to the Gauley River and General Floyd moved out against them, taking all troops with the exception of the Wise Legion, which he found "to be in such a state of insubordination and so ill-disciplined as to be for the moment unfit for military purposes." The Legion was sent to Meadow Bluff, where it guarded the road to Lewisburg. General Floyd's operations were soon abandoned and General Lee left for Richmond on the 30th. The Kanawha Valley campaign, a failure, was over.

On December 4 the Wise Legion, under Colonel Davis, was ordered to Richmond, but the cavalry did not arrive there until almost two months later. On December 10 Colonel Davis was ordered to proceed to Lynchburg with the Legion, and, on the 21st of that month, to proceed to Richmond. By January 28, 1862 the regimental headquarters had been established at Richmond.

In early February 1862 four companies of Colonel Davis' regiment were encamped at the New Fair Grounds at Richmond, one company was at Lynchburg, one at Staunton and one at Petersburg. On February 12 five companies of Colonel Davis' regiment, including Captain Caskie's company, were ordered to Garysburg, N. C. By Special Orders No. 72, Adjutant and Inspector General's Office, March 29, 1862, Colonel Davis was officially assigned to command the Wise Legion Cavalry and ordered to proceed with four companies of the Legion Cavalry, including Caskie's, and two independent companies, to report to General Magruder at Yorktown. Magruder was informed on April 3, 1862 that two companies had left that morning and three would start on the next day. On April 23 General Magruder reported Colonel Davis' command in the Right Wing, Army of the Peninsula. The lines on the lower Peninsula were evacuated on May 3 and on the 4th, at Williamsburg, Colonel Davis' command won much praise for their charge and hand-to-hand battle with Federal cavalry near Saunder's Pond. Afterwards, Colonel Davis' command moved with the army toward Richmond. On May 16 the four companies of Davis' regiment, operating in North Carolina, were ordered to rejoin the regiment before Richmond. Colonel Davis' Regiment had been assigned to General Wise's newly formed brigade on May 10, but on May 28 it was placed under the command of Brigadier General J. E. B. Stuart. The regiment was officially designated the 10th Regiment Virginia Cavalry, and Captain Caskie's company was designated Company A.

During the Seven Days' Battles, the 10th Regiment, detached from

Stuart's Brigade, served with General Magruder's command, guarding the right flank of the army, and operating down the Williamsburg and Charles City roads. The company clerk reported that the "company scouted from Yorktown to Richmond and were on picket duty from River to Charles City Road to 13th June 1862—Were the advance guard of General Huger's Division in Tuesday and Sunday's action." After the Seven Days' Stuart's command was reorganized into a division of two brigades. The 10th Regiment was assigned to Brigadier General Wade Hampton's First Brigade, which spent most of the summer of 1862 on outpost duty below Richmond, watching McClellan. In a skirmish at White Oak Swamp Bridge on August 5, fifteen men of the company were captured. The regiment remained on outpost duty until Hampton's Brigade was ordered to rejoin the army in Northern Virginia.

Hampton's Brigade joined Stuart in Fairfax County on September 2, after the Battle of Second Manassas, and crossed the Potomac River into Maryland on the 5th. Beyond the fact that the 10th Regiment served with Hampton during the campaign in Maryland, we know little about the regiment specifically, and next to nothing about Caskie's Mounted Rangers. Records are equally vague on the history of the regiment at the time of Stuart's expedition into Maryland and Pennsylvania, October 9-12, 1862; however, General Hampton reported that one hundred and fifty men of the 10th Regiment participated in the expedition. On October 19, 1862 Caskie's Mounted Rangers were detached from the 10th Regiment and ordered to Staunton, Va. on guard duty. While the company was absent, the cavalry was reorganized into two divisions. The 10th Regiment was assigned to Brigadier General W. H. F. "Rooney" Lee's Brigade. The company remained at Staunton throughout the winter of 1862-1863, while the army confronted Burnside at Fredericksburg. The company clerk reported on the March-April 1863 muster roll:

> Company A, 10th Virginia Regiment Cavalry on detached service in and around Staunton, Va. Guarding and superintending labor of prisoners sentenced by court martial.

The company rejoined the regiment, guarding the fords of the upper Rappahannock River, in late May 1863. The 10th Regiment Virginia Cavalry, still assigned to General W. H. F. Lee's Brigade, participated in the battle of Brandy Station (Fleetwood) on June 9, 1863 and moved with Stuart's command during the Gettysburg Campaign. On the May-June 1863 muster roll the company's movements were reported as follows:

> The company picketted at Kelly's Ford on Rappahannock up to the 9th June, on that day was engaged in battle at Fleetwood and suffered severely.
>
> Picketted afterwards at Freeman's Ford on Rappahannock. From there marched to Middleburg and was en-

gaged in all the cavalry actions around that place [June 19] and Upperville [June 21]. From there crossed the Potomac River at Senaca Falls with General Stuart and were with him in all the cavalry engagements in which the brigade was engaged. [Principally at Hanover, Pa. on June 30.] Arrived at Gettysburg from Carlisle June 2, 1863.

On July 3 the regiment participated in the cavalry battle at Gettysburg. On the return march to Virginia, the regiment was engaged in the cavalry actions at Hagerstown on July 6 where Colonel Davis was captured, at Williamsport, Funkstown, Beaver Creek Bridge near Boonsborough, and at Shepherdstown.

Captain Caskie was promoted to major of the regiment on August 8, 1863, and 1st Lieutenant Edwin A. Fulcher was promoted to captain of the company. By the end of August the company was encamped at Raccoon Ford after having "been picketting at Brandy Station and Woodville and also scouting toward Orleans." In September, with the reorganization of the cavalry into a corps of two divisions, General W. H. F. Lee's Brigade, now under Colonel J. R. Chambliss, Jr., was assigned to Major General Fitzhugh Lee's Division. The Bristoe Campaign opened on September 13 when Meade's cavalry crossed the Rappahannock into Culpeper County. Stuart drove them back and then General Lee took the offensive. The 10th Regiment, with Chambliss' Brigade, participated in the Bristoe Campaign, October 11-21, which took them north to the old battlegrounds near Manassas Junction, and were engaged at Buckland on the 19th. Following this action the brigade recrossed the Rappahannock. After the Mine Run operations, November 28-December 1, the army went into winter quarters behind the Rapidan. The November-December 1863 muster roll, dated January 16, 1864, shows that the company was stationed at Ivy Depot, Virginia Central Railroad.

On May 7, 1864 the 10th Regiment, with Chambliss' Brigade, was engaged in the fighting at Todd's Tavern. While the infantry of the two armies were engaged at Spotsylvania Court House on May 9, General Sheridan's cavalry, about 12,000, started south toward Richmond with the main purpose of drawing Stuart's cavalry away from the flanks of Grant's army. Within three hours, the Confederate cavalry had overtaken them. Clashes occurred along the way as Stuart tried to obstruct Sheridan's advance; and on May 11, in the battle at Yellow Tavern, near Richmond, where Stuart was mortally wounded, the Confederate cavalry defeated Sheridan, forcing him to discontinue his move southward.

After the battles around Spotsylvania Court House, Grant moved east and southward toward Richmond. A frontal attack on Lee's positions at Cold Harbor, about eight miles east of Richmond, was repulsed with severe losses on June 3. The 10th Regiment, with W. H. F. Lee's Division, remained east of Richmond when the cavalry under Hampton left on June 8 in pursuit of Sheridan, who had set out for Charlottesville to destroy the Virginia Central Railroad. After the fighting around Trevilian Station, in Louisa County, Sheridan, followed by two divisions under Hampton, returned east. Chambliss' Brigade rejoined Hampton and on June 24, at Samaria Church and Nance's Shop, attacked Gregg's Division of cavalry. Among the 10th Regiment's dead at Samaria Church was Sergeant J. Lucius Davis, Jr., the 22-year-old son of the regimental commander.

Hampton crossed the James and on June 27 moved off to intercept Wilson's cavalry, returning from their raid to rejoin Grant's army. On the 28th, the 10th Regiment charged with Chambliss' Brigade against Wilson's raiders at Sappony Creek, a few miles west of Stony Creek Depot on the Weldon Railroad south of Petersburg. The Federals were driven back to Sappony Church, where they were again engaged by the brigade, fighting dismounted. After the rout of Wilson, the 10th Regiment was in no significant operations until August 14, when they were sent with W. H. F. Lee's Division to meet a Federal advance east of Richmond. On August 16 they were engaged at White Tavern, eight miles from the city on the Charles City Road, where General Chambliss was killed.

On August 25, Hampton's Division co-operated in the attack on the Federal II Corps at Reams Station, where they were engaged in destroying the Weldon Railroad. The 10th Regiment, with the brigade, now under Colonel Davis, was heavily engaged throughout the fighting. Captured on the return march from Gettysburg, Colonel Davis had been exchanged in March 1864, and after the death of Chambliss, commanded the brigade until his resignation from the army in February 1865. The 10th Regiment, with W. H. F. Lee's Division, co-operated with General Heth of Hill's Corps in the engagements fought along the Vaughn and Squirrel Level roads south of Petersburg, on September 29, known as the Battle of Peebles' Farm. Again, on October 27, the regiment was engaged in the fighting at Burgess' Mill, where the Boydton Plank Road crossed Hatcher's Run southwest of Petersburg. Remaining on the right of Lee's army, W. H. F. Lee's Division was engaged at Hicksford (now Emporia), where the Weldon Railroad crossed the Meherrin River, and successfully prevented the further destruction of the railroad by Gregg's cavalry and elements of Warren's V Corps.

The regiment remained in the vicinity of Hicksford until March 13, 1865, when the division was sent to the right of the lines at Petersburg. On the fatal day, April 1, at Five Forks, Lee's Division was on Pickett's right and was heavily engaged against Custer's Division of Sheridan's cavalry. Pickett's forces were routed and W. H. F. Lee's Division fell back toward the South Side Railroad. Petersburg was evacuated by General Lee's forces on April 2, and throughout the retreat westward the division was constantly employed in scouting and screening the movements of the army. Their last fight was on April 9 near Appomattox Court House, where the army surrendered. When the army was paroled at Appomattox Court House, none of the members of Company A, 10th Regiment Virginia Cavalry were reported on the parole roll.

## CASKIE MOUNTED RANGERS

### COLONEL

Caskie, Robert A.

### CAPTAINS

Fulcher, Edwin A.
Hawley, Louis J.

### LIEUTENANTS

Capston, J. L., 1st Lieut.
Doyle, John, 1st Lieut.
Hawley, S. B., 2nd Lieut.
Mott, William V., 2nd Lieut.

Neidt, H. C., 1st Lieut.
Sterrett, F. F., 2nd Lieut.
Tyndall, Mark A., 1st Lieut.

### NON-COMMISSIONED OFFICERS AND PRIVATES

Abshire, J. C., Pvt.
Allen, John, Pvt.
Allen, R., Pvt.
Amos, Berry B., Pvt.
Andrew, William, Pvt.
Barrett, Richard, Pvt.
Barry, Richard, Pvt.
Beard, David S., Pvt.
Beecher, Benhard, Pvt.
Berry, E. T., Pvt.
Berry, George E., Sgt.
Bethel, William M., Pvt.
Blunt, William R., Pvt.
Bradshaw, Wm. E., Pvt.
Brown, William, Pvt.
Buckley, J., Pvt.
Bupiew, William, Pvt.
Burmaster, Henry, Com. Sgt.
Burton, Marshall, Pvt.
Burton, Mortimer L., Pvt.
Burton, Wm. E., Pvt.
Butler, John, Corpl.
Camp, Charles, Pvt.
Carnagey, William A., Corpl.
Chamberlayne, S. D., Pvt.
Chapman, Charles, Pvt.
Chappell, John T., Pvt.
Childress, Charles B., Pvt.
Childress, Joseph H., Pvt.
Childress, William H., Pvt.

Christian, A. G., Pvt.
Chucrian, J., Pvt.
Churchman, G. R., Pvt.
Clark, William L., Pvt.
Cochran, James, Pvt.
Connor, John
Cook, Charles, Pvt.
Crawfort, W. B., Pvt.
Crossmore, Oliver, Sgt.
Crow, William L., Pvt.
Crump, George W., Pvt.
Curry, Richard, Pvt.
Daniels, Ferdinand, Pvt.
David, M., Pvt.
Davis, J. Lucius Jr., Pvt.
Dehart, Charles F., Pvt.
Delzer, Joseph
Denney, Charles F., Pvt.
Deshazo, William T., Pvt.
Dickinson, N. B., 1st Sgt.
Dilks, J. Henry, Sgt.
Doddin, R. S., Pvt.
Draifouse, Leon, Pvt.
Dunlap, George B., Pvt.
Ehlers, F., Corpl.
Eismann, L., Pvt.
Elmore, James, Pvt.
English, John, Pvt.
Eytel, Louis, Pvt.
Fairland, Francis, Pvt.

Farrell, J. P., Pvt.
Fisher, Charles, Pvt.
Fitzsimmons, John F., Pvt.
Foster, Charles, Pvt.
Foye, George, Pvt.
Frayser, L. T., Pvt.
Frick, G., Pvt.
Fulcher, John C., Pvt.
Furgerson, T. R., Pvt.
Galloway, Robert, Pvt.
Gay, James W., Pvt.
George, Alex S., Sgt.
Gibblin, M., Pvt.
Gill, Joseph N., Pvt.
Grant, James, Pvt.
Green, M., Pvt.
Hale, J., Pvt.
Halfpenny, George W., Pvt.
Hall, J., Pvt.
Hanselman, John, Pvt.
Harlow, Thomas, Pvt.
Harrison, J., Pvt.
Harvey, Harry
Heckler, G., Pvt.
Hedger, George W., Pvt.
Hegtly, W., Pvt.
Heineman, Herman, Pvt.
Hicks, James, Pvt.
Hubbard, J. W., Pvt.
Hubbard, W., Pvt.
Hubbell, Step, Pvt.
Hudnall, Benjamin F., Pvt.
Hudnall, Philip, Pvt.
Hudnall, William H., Pvt.
Hutchinson, J. M., Pvt.
Hutchinson, W. R., Pvt.
Israel, Julius, Pvt.
James, Greene W., Pvt.
Johnson, James, C., Pvt.
Jones, Thomas, Pvt.
Jones, William W., Pvt.
Jordan, Charles, Pvt.
Kale, John, Sgt.
Kane, Peter, Pvt.
Kassell, George, Pvt.
Katen, A., Pvt.
Kelley, Timothy, Corpl.
Kennedy, William F., Pvt.
Kenth, Jacob, Pvt.
Kirwin, Frank, Pvt.
Kincaid, Chs., Pvt.
Lambert, James, Pvt.
Lambert, J. H., Corpl.
Lambert, William, Pvt.
Law, C. W., Pvt.
Leber, William H., Pvt.
Lee, Daniel, Pvt.
Lee, John, Pvt.
Loughborough, James H., Pvt.
Mahoney, John, Pvt.
Malone, W. R., Pvt.
Maloy, Cornelius, Pvt.
Magel, Andrew, Pvt.
Markle, Andrew, Pvt.
McKenna, James, Pvt.
McKenney, William, Pvt.
McKenzie, William, Pvt.
Monnan, W. H., Pvt.
Moore, Michael, Pvt.
Moore, William R., Pvt.
Morris, Daniel W., Pvt.
Murphy, Michael, Pvt.
Myers, B., Pvt.
Myers, William J., Pvt.
Nelson, W. J., Pvt.
Nessler, Julius, Sgt.
Nott, Roger, Pvt.
Osgood, Francis S., Pvt.
Page, S., Pvt.
Parker, Joseph, Pvt.
Pate, N. T., Pvt.
Peasley, William, Pvt.
Pendergrass, Charles, Pvt.
Pondexter, S. F., Pvt.
Pondexter, William C., Pvt.
Potts, William I., Pvt.
Powell, R. W., Pvt.
Ramsey, J. O., Pvt.
Ray, Patrick, Pvt.
Reilly, O., Pvt.
Ressell, G., Pvt.
Ricks, Joseph, Pvt
Roberts, Benjamin D., Pvt.
Robertson, J. R., Pvt.
Roye, John, Musician
Scott, Joseph, Musician
Sedgewick, William J., Pvt.
Shafer, William, Pvt.
Shell, T. W., Pvt.
Smith, John F., Pvt.
Stein, M., Pvt.
Tabb, John P., Pvt.
Taylor, T. H., Sgt.
Thomas, Maurice O., Pvt.

Tichenor, F. W., Pvt.
Tucker, Jacob, Pvt.
Tyree, W. W., Pvt.
Vanderlip, Elias, Pvt.
Vanhorn, Shelley, Pvt.
Viehmeyster, William, Pvt.
Vondelehi, John, Pvt.
Wagner, Frank, Pvt.
Walsh, Malachi, Pvt.
Watson, Joseph, Pvt.
Whitehead, Henry, Pvt.

Widemayer, Adolph, Pvt.
Williams, Mastern, Pvt.
Williams, W. P., Pvt.
Wilson, C., Pvt.
Wilson, James, Pvt.
Winant, Richard, Pvt.
Windsor, Anderson, Pvt.
Wingfield, P. G., Pvt.
Woolffe, Henry, Pvt.
Woolridge, Peter, Pvt.
Wright, H. S., Pvt.

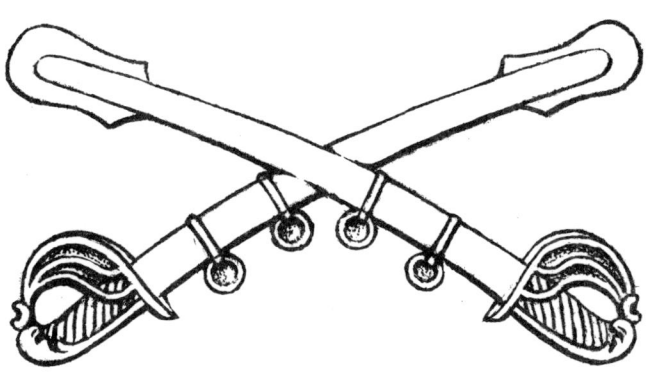

Cavalry insignia of 1860.

Source: drawn from an original by Robert L. Miller, Arlington, Va.

## GOVERNOR'S MOUNTED GUARD

Organized on September 3, 1859 as the Richmond Troop, and the Richmond Light Dragoons, this company became a part of the 4th Regiment of Cavalry, Virginia Militia, and was attached to the 19th Regiment of the line. Joseph R. Anderson of the Tredegar Iron Works was elected captain, and the company was to be equipped with sabres, revolvers, and lances. The fact that the last mentioned arm was to be issued led to the adoption of the name Richmond Lancers. However, lances were not issued, and in December 1859 the company was renamed the Governor's Mounted Guard. About April 1860, John Gratten Cabell succeeded Anderson as commander of the company.

On April 17, 1861 the company paraded in Richmond, and it was reported that "some fifty odd were in rank." With sixty-five men in the ranks, the company was mustered into State service on May 8, 1861 for one year; and on May 11 it was reported in camp at Ashland. By the end of May the company was encamped at Manassas Junction. On June 1 Captain Cabell was ordered to proceed to reinforce Colonel R. S. Ewell at Fairfax Court House. The company remained with Ewell's command and was reported with that command in the vicinity of Union Mills Ford at Bull Run on July 18, where it remained during the battle on the 21st. At that time, it was reported in Harrison's Battalion of Cavalry—an unbrigaded field organization—and apparently served as an independent company until assigned to the 6th Regiment Virginia Cavalry on September 12, 1861. Captain Cabell was promoted to major of the 6th Regiment, but the company did not join the regiment. Instead, it became Company I, 4th Regiment Virginia Cavalry, which was organized on September 19, 1861, and 1st Lieutenant Francis W. Chamberlayne was promoted to captain on September 21. The company remained in the vicinity of Manassas Junction until the spring of 1862. During this period the Governor's Mounted Guard spent the time drilling and on picket duty.

When General Joseph E. Johnston evacuated Manassas in March 1862, he directed General J. E. B. Stuart to protect the rear of the retreating army with the cavalry, which at that time consisted of only one brigade. General Johnston retired behind the Rappahannock River; and, after destroying the stores at Manassas Junction on March 10, General Stuart retired to the vicinity of Warrenton Junction. On March 18 General Johnston moved behind the Rapidan and General Stuart moved to the line of the Rappahannock and remained there, maintaining a line of pickets from the Blue Ridge to the vicinity of the Potomac. On March 27 the cavalry skirmished with the enemy at Bealeton, during which the 4th Regiment—under Colonel Beverly H. Robertson—charged the right flank of the enemy and drove him back. On the next day, about twenty-five prisoners were captured between Bealeton and Warrenton Junction.

On or about the 10th of April, the 4th Regiment with the main body of the army, began the march to Yorktown, arriving there about the middle of the month. While at Yorktown, the Governor's Mounted Guard was reorganized for the war on April 16, 1862. When General Johnston retired from Yorktown on May 3, the cavalry was directed to cover the retreat. Lieutenant Colonel Williams C. Wickham, commanding the 4th Regiment, occupied the left on the Telegraph Road from Yorktown to Williamsburg. Because of the slowness of the retreat and the rapid advance by the Federals, the cavalry was engaged throughout the 3rd and 4th. At Williamsburg on the evening of May 4 the 4th Regiment, in conjunction with the cavalry of the Wise Legion and the Hampton Legion, made a gallant charge upon the enemy near Fort Magruder, driving them from the field. The next day, May 5, the regiment was under fire but did not participate in the fight. From Williamsburg the route of the 4th Regiment led through New Kent County, where on May 9 a portion of the regiment was engaged at Slatersville, near New Kent Court House.

    From the time of arrival in the vicinity of Richmond until the Seven Days' Battles, the cavalry was employed in scouting, observing the enemy's movement, and protecting the flanks of the army. Colonel Robertson was ordered to reoccupy Mechanicsville on May 23 with the 4th Cavalry and two regiments of infantry. Accomplishing this, he sent his cavalry to scout the country. On May 27, 28 and 29 the cavalry was engaged at Hanover Court House, Taliaferro's Mill, and Ashland. On June 12-15, six companies of the 4th Regiment participated in General Stuart's ride around McClellan. In General Lee's order of battle for his initial move on McClellan's right, the main body of cavalry was ordered to remain in reserve while General Stuart—with the 1st, 4th and 9th Virginia Cavalry, the cavalry of Cobb's Legion, and the Jeff Davis Legion—was ordered to cross the Chickahominy River on the 25th and take position to the left of General Jackson's line of march. Following orders, Stuart moved to Ashland, where the Jeff Davis Legion and 4th Virginia Cavalry joined his command from an advanced position of observation on South Anna, where they had been screening Jackson's movements from the enemy. Stuart's command was on Jackson's left during the battle at Gaines' Mill, but was not engaged. On June 28 Stuart was ordered to cut the York River Railroad. After doing so, he moved on McClellan's supply depot at White House. Arriving near the landing at night, Stuart advanced and occupied the depot on the 29th. Although the Federals had evacuated the position and set fire to the stores, Stuart remained thoughout the 29th, while his troopers salvaged the undestroyed equipment and provisions. The next day, Stuart moved under orders to rejoin the army and did so by assuming a position on Jackson's left. With the exception of small skirmishes, the cavalry was not extensively engaged during the balance of the Seven Days'

    On July 28 the cavalry was reorganized into two brigades, and the 4th Virginia was assigned to the Second Brigade, under Brigadier General Fitzhugh Lee. The 4th Virginia had been stationed at the reserve camp of instruction at Hanover Court House since about July 10. General Stuart reported that during July and early August, his two brigades "alternated with each other on outpost duty before the enemy on the Charles City border and camp of instruction at Hanover Court House." On August 4 General Stuart moved Fitzhugh Lee's Brigade and the Stuart Horse Artillery toward Bowling Green. After routing a small Federal force at Port Royal on the 5th, Stuart moved toward Fredericksburg. On the 6th he moved up the Telegraph Road and attacked a Federal force at Massaponax Church. During this engagement, the 4th Virginia—under Colonel S. D. Lee—drove in the enemy rear guard and captured many prisoners and wagons. Encountering heavy enemy infantry, Stuart retired, and on the 7th his command returned to Hanover Court House.

Fitzhugh Lee's Brigade left Hanover on August 16 and was engaged throughout the campaign in Northern Virginia and Maryland. Marching by way of Raccoon Ford, the brigade was engaged on the 20th on the road from Madden's to Kelly's Ford. From there the route led by Brandy Station and the cavalry engaged the enemy while Jackson's force moved behind their screen. About 10 a.m. on the 22nd, General Stuart left Freeman's Ford with about 1500 cavalry (including the 4th Virginia), and marched to Catlett's Station where he captured General Pope's personal equipment and dispatch book. Efforts were made by the 4th Virginia to destroy the railroad bridge over Cedar Run, but rain and the enemy's presence in force prevented this. The next morning, Stuart marched into Jackson's line at Warrenton Springs.

Starting at 2 a.m. on the morning of the 26th of August, General Stuart followed General Jackson's line of march to Manassas Junction. Overtaking Jackson at Gainesville, he remained with that command. After posting some cavalry around Jackson's force, Stuart joined his main force on Jackson's right. On reaching the Orange and Alexandria Railroad south of Bristoe, Stuart's force fronted toward the main body of the enemy—still in the direction of the Rappahannock—and covered Jackson's operations at Bristoe. Rejoining Jackson, Stuart moved with a portion of his command and two regiments of infantry on Manassas Junction. Sending the 4th Virginia around "to gain the rear of Manassas," Stuart moved directly on the junction and captured the entire depot of stores on the night of August 26-27. On that same day, General Fitzhugh Lee was ordered to proceed with the 9th, 4th and 3rd Virginia Cavalry to the vicinity of Fairfax Court House to damage the enemy's communications. Proceeding to Burke's Station, General Fitzhugh Lee's detachment succeeded in capturing prisoners and supplies and in destroying that line of communication. On the 29th the detachment rejoined General Jackson's command, now engaged in the Battle of Second Manassas. On his arrival General Fitzhugh Lee was ordered to post his detachment on Jackson's left, where he remained throughout the battle.

Following the successful Confederate attack on Pope's army—which resulted in the Federal retreat to Centreville—Stuart was ordered to concentrate the cavalry on the left of the Army of Northern Virginia. Concentrating his command near Chantilly, Stuart moved to attack the enemy on the Centreville-Fairfax Court House pike. Succeeding in gaining some high ground overlooking the pike, Stuart shelled the long Federal column, but did not attack. During the night of August 31-September 1, Stuart withdrew his command to Ox Hill. When Jackson's command came up on the next day, Stuart left one brigade to cover Jackson's right flank while he took Fitzhugh Lee's Brigade. Following a demonstration toward Alexandria, Fitzhugh Lee's Brigade retired and joined the army in the vicinity of Leesburg.

On September 5 the brigade crossed the Potomac River and skirmished near Poolesville. During the Maryland Campaign the 4th Virginia was engaged in the usual work of screening, skirmishing, and serving as couriers. At Boonesboro, on the 16th, they were heavily engaged. At Sharpsburg they were on the left of Lee's army, but were not actively engaged. On the retreat from Sharpsburg, Fitzhugh Lee's Brigade covered the rear of the army and was the last to cross into Virginia on the morning of September 19.

After the Maryland Campaign, Lee's army received a much needed rest and went into camp near Winchester. During this time the cavalry had frequent skirmishes, and on October 9-12 the 4th Virginia participated in Stuart's second ride around McClellan. By October 22 the regiment was on outpost duty at Warrenton. When reports were received that McClellan had recrossed the Potomac, Lee ordered Stuart to scout east of the Blue Ridge to report the enemy's movements and delay him so that the Army of Northern Virginia could change its position. Stuart's cavalry skirmished with the Federal advance at Mountville and Aldie on October 31, at Philomont on November 1-2, and retired to Seaton's Hill on the evening of the 2nd. On November 3 Stuart was flanked out of Upperville after an all day skirmish. At Barbee's Cross Roads, on the 5th, the cavalry engaged the Federal advance until ordered to retire when information was received that the enemy was in Warrenton. Finding this information to be incorrect, Stuart sent a detachment to Warrenton while the main cavalry force moved south of the Rappahannock to form a protective screen in front of Longstreet's command, which had moved from the Valley to Culpeper Court House. The detachment sent to Warrenton rejoined Stuart's command after finding the town occupied by Federal forces. General Stuart described the general situation on November 6, 1862:

> The army of McClellan now occupied Warrenton and its vicinity, with strong infantry outposts on the Rappahannock, and Longstreet's corps occupied Culpeper County, with my cavalry interposed between him and the enemy, along the Rappahannock and in the forks of the Hazel and Westham Rivers.

On November 10, 1862 the cavalry of the Army of Northern Virginia was reorganized; however, the 4th Virginia remained in Brigadier General Fitzhugh Lee's Brigade. On the north side of the Rappahannock General A. E. Burnside replaced McClellan as commander of the Federal army and

Courtesy Confederate Museum

The Flag of the Governor's Mounted Guard

This flag, made of blue taffeta, is 37 1/2 inches square with gold braid border and fringe. The star above the lettering and floral design has dark red stones encased in gold thread or braid.

began moving his army to occupy Fredericksburg for his advance on Richmond. Lee used his cavalry to discover Burnside's intentions; and when the Federals arrived opposite Fredericksburg, Confederate infantry was in position while the balance of the army was moving up. When Lee was sure that Burnside intended to move on Richmond from Fredericksburg, Jackson's command was ordered to join the army at Fredericksburg. Using his cavalry to screen his own operations, Lee also employed it to obtain information of the enemy's moves. Prior to the battle at Fredericksburg the cavalry remained on the flanks of the army, picketing the fords over the Rappahannock and the roads in rear of the army. During the battle on December 13 the bulk of the cavalry was on the right of Lee's army. After the battle, in late December, Lee ordered Stuart to attack Burnside's communications. After attacking the enemy at Dumfries and moving as far as the vicinity of Fairfax Court House, Stuart withdrew to the south side of the Rappahannock. Going into winter quarters, small detachments of cavalry were sent to picket the crossings above and below the army at Fredericksburg. On January 26, 1863, the Governor's Mounted Guard—still officially serving as Company I, 4th Regiment Virginia Cavalry—was disbanded. The company officers were relieved from duty and the men were assigned to other cavalry companies.

Brigadier General Joseph R. Anderson (1813-1892), senior member of the firm of Joseph R. Anderson & Co., proprietors of the Tredegar Iron Works; Captain, Richmond Light Dragoons (later called Governor's Mounted Guard), 1859-1860; Major, Tredegar Bn., Local Defense Troops, 1861; Brigadier General, C. S. Army, 1861-1862; resigned to manage operations of the Tredegar Iron Works. Courtesy of the Library of Congress.

## GOVERNOR'S MOUNTED GUARD

### CAPTAINS

Cabell, John Grattan
Chamberlayne, Francis W.
Warwick, William B., Capt. A.C.S.

### LIEUTENANTS

Bossieux, Edmond, 1st Lieut.
Fisher, John P., 1st Lieut
George, John P., 2nd Lieut
Kennon, R. B., 1st Lieut.
Lea, David M., 3rd Lieut.
Lipscomb, C. B., 2nd Lieut.
Martin, Walter K., Adjutant
Parham, Benjamin M., 2nd Lieut.

### NON-COMMISSIONED OFFICERS AND PRIVATES

Allan, John, Pvt.
Alvey, John F., Pvt.
Atlee, Jacob S., Jr., Pvt.
Ball, J. T., Pvt.
Beard, J. A., Pvt.
Bell, R. F., Pvt.
Berry, Dorsey, Pvt.
Bierne, Patrick, Pvt.
Blankenship, S. R., Pvt.
Blanton, John S., Pvt.
Blanton, R. F., Pvt.
Bohmer, Henry, Pvt.
Carter, Julian M., Pvt.
Carter, William H., Pvt.
Chalk, R. W., Pvt.
Clopton, A. W., Pvt.
Clutter, L., Corpl.
Cole, George W., Pvt.
Cole, Joseph M., Pvt.
Day, John H., Pvt.
Deahl, C. L., Pvt.
Deane, Frank H., Pvt.
Duff, R. A., Pvt.
Duncan, C. B., Pvt.
Edmond, Walter, Pvt.
Edmonds, George, Pvt.
Ellis, John Leander, Pvt.
Ferguson, W. G., Pvt.
Filch, T. W.
Galt, John Allan, Pvt.
Galt, William, Pvt.
Gordon, John, Pvt.
Gough, Benjamin, Pvt.
Green, Samuel S., Pvt.
Hamilton, J. Heth, Pvt.
Hancock, W. F., Sergt.
Hanes, Walter, Sergt.
Hardy, Miles E., Pvt.
Harris, James H., Pvt.
Hatcher, Charles, Pvt.
Hatcher, Christopher J., Pvt.
Haxall, Philip, Sergt.
Hill, Frank D., Pvt.
Hobson, John W., Pvt.
James, R. D., Corpl.
Johnson, A., Pvt.
Johnson, David, Pvt.
Kavnaugh, John, Bugler
Kennon, W. D., Pvt.
Lewis, John, Pvt.
Little, Bethel, Pvt.
Loomis, E., Pvt.
Lorens, James P., Pvt.
MacMurdo, M. A., Pvt.
Marriott, C. H., Pvt.
Mayo, P. H., Pvt.
Mayo, W. S. P., Sergt.
Merrit, C. T., Pvt.
Messenger, Richard C., Pvt.
Mills, R. A., Pvt.
Mitchell, John R., Pvt.
Moore, George, Pvt.
Moore, T. J., Pvt.
Nichols, P.O., Pvt.
Norfleet, Nat. M., Pvt.
Parker, E. L., Pvt.
Payne, Thomas, Pvt.
Pool, J. J., Pvt.

Randolph, Allan, Pvt.
Ring, J. L., Pvt.
Rives, J. Henry, Pvt.
Royall, F. L., Pvt.
Samuels, A. S., Pvt.
Savage, J. H., Pvt.
Slingluff, John, Pvt.
Southall, R. P., Pvt.
Stewart, George, Pvt.
Storrs, Gervas, Pvt.
Stowe, William, Pvt.
Strother, Sidney, Pvt.
Stuart, Andrew, Pvt.
Sutherland, W. H., Pvt.
Talbott, C. H., Pvt.
Taling, M., Pvt.

Taylor, C. A., Pvt.
Taylor, J. Z., Pvt.
Taylor, Osborn B., Corpl.
Terrell, J. E., Pvt.
Walls, William, Pvt.
Warner, Alex, Pvt.
Warwick, Abraham Jr., Pvt.
Warwick, Clarence, Pvt.
Watson, Joseph, Pvt.
Wescott, P. C., Pvt.
White, C. B., Pvt.
Williams, W. D., Pvt.
Wilson, Nath M., 1st Sergt.
Woodbridge, George N., Pvt.
Worthing, W. A., Pvt.
Worthington, W. N., Pvt.

# HENRICO LIGHT DRAGOONS

Although a troop of Henrico Light Dragoons existed for many years before 1861, the troop by this name, which entered active service in 1861, was organized in May 1854 at Goddin's Tavern, with the election of Captain J. Lucius Davis. After graduating from the United States Military Academy in 1833, Davis served three years as a lieutenant in the 4th Regiment of Artillery. He resigned in 1836 and took up farming in the Valley of Virginia, but left in 1839 to serve as a captain of rangers in the service of the Republic of Texas. Davis was the author of *Light Artillery for Frontier Service*, published in 1839. In 1841 he returned to Virginia, and, after six years in Richmond County, moved to Henrico County in 1847.

The Henrico Troop belonged to the 4th Regiment of Cavalry, Virginia Militia, and was attached, for parade and administrative purposes, to the 33rd Regiment (Henrico County) of the line. On October 18, 1854 the Superintendent of the Public Armory was ordered to issue thirty-two cavalry sabres and pistols, with accoutrements, to Captain Davis' troop. By law, the State could only issue arms to companies that had provided themselves with uniforms. The troop, during the summer of 1854, had procured fatigue uniforms, in which they paraded for the first time on July 4, at Goddin's Tavern. Their dress uniforms were those worn by the former troop, which had ceased to exist by May 1850.

Throughout the seven years preceding the outbreak of war in 1861 the Henrico Light Dragoons regularly participated with other military organizations in public parades and ceremonies. In April 1860 the troop, under Captain Lawson H. Dance, paraded with other units at the dedication of the Henry Clay statue on Capitol Square, and, in November, was among the thirteen troops that attended the cavalry encampment held at the Fair Grounds.

Shortly before April 5, 1861 Dr. Zachariah S. McGruder was elected captain of the troop. He had long been a member of the company and represented Henrico County in the General Assembly. On May 10, 1861 the Henrico Troop, which had enrolled for service on the previous day, was mustered into State service at the Henrico County Court House for a period of twelve months. On the same day, the command, numbering three officers and fifty-two enlisted men, left Richmond and marched twenty-two miles to the camp of instruction at Ashland, a popular summer resort. By May 21, "Camp Ashland," under Colonel R. S. Ewell, was used exclusively for the training of cavalry. Also, during May, there was published in Richmond *The Trooper's Manual: or, Tactics for Light Dragoons and Mounted Riflemen*, compiled by Colonel J. Lucius Davis, the troop's former commander.

On June 11 at Camp Ashland, the officers and men of the Henrico Light Dragoons sent a petition to Colonel Davis, asking him to use his influence in having the troop assigned to the Wise Legion, then being raised by Brigadier General Henry A. Wise for service in western Virginia.

Colonel Davis, nominal commander of the 46th Regiment Virginia Infantry, was in Richmond at this time recruiting for the Wise Legion. The troop's request met with favor, and they soon left Ashland for the western part of the state.

The Henrico Troop apparently joined General Wise's command in late July, about the time of the retreat from Charleston and the Kanawha Valley, to White Sulphur Springs. General Wise reported on August 4 that Colonel Davis, with 500 cavalrymen, was guarding the passes from Fayetteville, Gauley, and Summerville.

In August, or possibly during late July, the cavalry was organized into the 1st Regiment of Cavalry, Wise Legion, under Colonel Davis. The Henrico Light Dragoons was designated as Company A in the regiment, which also included two other troops from Richmond.

On August 5 General John B. Floyd's command joined the Wise Legion at White Sulphur Springs. General Floyd, as senior in command, was soon determined to move into the Kanawha Valley against the Federals. The plan did not meet with Wise's approval, and opened a pronounced disharmony between the two. The offensive got underway, and on August 21, the commands of Wise and Floyd were at Gauley Mountain. In the advance toward Carnifax Ferry, on the Gauley River, Colonel Davis ordered the Henrico Light Dragoons to support a small cavalry force reported to be hard pressed by the enemy at Dogwood Gap. Upon arriving there, however, the fighting was over as well as the opportunity to pursue the enemy, and the troop occupied the tops of the nearby mountains. This incident, reported by Colonel Davis on August 25, is our first definite record of the Henrico Troop in Kanawha Valley. After the battle at Carnifax Ferry on September 10, Floyd and Wise fell back to Sewell Mountain, arriving there on the 14th. General Floyd, however, withdrew his forces twelve miles eastward to Meadow Bluff on the 16th. General Lee arrived at Meadow Bluff on September 21, and arrived at Sewell Mountain on the 24th with reinforcements for Wise, in whose front the enemy were advancing in force. On the preceding day, Captain McGruder, who had apparently just returned from a scouting mission, reported a decrease in the number of tents in the enemy's camps, and was of the opinion that Rosecrans was no longer with General Cox. The captain's report proved of little consequential value, but its inclusion in a letter to General Lee by Lieutenant Colonel Nat Tyler on September 23, left a permanent record of the presence and activities of the Henrico Troop at this time. During an enemy demonstration on September 25, General Wise was handed an order from the War Department directing him to hand over his command to General Floyd, and report to Richmond. On October 6 the Federals retired to the Gauley River, and General Floyd moved out against them, taking all troops with the exception of the Wise Legion, which he found "to be in such a state of insubordination and so ill-disciplined as to be for the moment unfit for military purposes." The Legion was sent to Meadow Bluff, where it guarded the road to Lewisburg. General Floyd's operations were soon abandoned, and General Lee left for Richmond on the 30th. The Kanawha Valley campaign, a failure, was over.

On December 4 the Wise Legion, under Colonel Davis, was ordered to Richmond, but the cavalry did not arrive there until almost two months later. On December 19, while en route from Lewisburg to White Sulphur Springs, the Henrico Troop was sent back to drive off an enemy force encamped on the Macfarland farm near Lewisburg. However, by the time the company arrived the Federals had left. On December 24-25 the troop was encamped at Jackson River, presumably near Covington. By January 28, 1862 the regimental headquarters had been established at Richmond.

In February 1862, four companies of Colonel Davis' regiment were encamped at the New Fair Grounds at Richmond; one company was at Lynchburg; another at Staunton; and Company A, the Henrico Troop, was at Petersburg. On February 12, Captain McGruder's company and the four companies at Richmond, were ordered to Garysburg, N. C. The Henrico Troop was located at Murfreesboro from about March 1 to May 6, and by May 14 had moved to Jackson. On May 16 General Huger, commanding the Department of North Carolina, with headquarters at Petersburg, was directed to send the companies in North Carolina to join the balance of Colonel Davis' regiment then serving on the lower Peninsula with General Johnston. The lines on the lower Peninsula had been evacuated on May 3, and on the 4th, at Williamsburg, Colonel Davis' command had won much praise for its charge and hand-to-hand battle with Federal cavalry near Saunders' Pond. Afterwards, the regiment moved with the army toward Richmond.

Shortly before May 24, 1862 Colonel Davis' regiment was detached from Wise's Brigade and ordered to report for duty with General J. E. B. Stuart's command. Later in the month, the regiment was organized as the 10th Regiment Virginia Cavalry, with Colonel Davis commanding. Captain McGruder, who had been re-elected captain of the Henrico Troop on May 8, was elected lieutenant colonel of the regiment on May 27. 1st Lieutenant George Hopkins was promoted to captain of the troop, which was designated Company I of the regiment.

During the Seven Days' Battles, the 10th Regiment, detached from Stuart's Brigade, served with General Magruder's command, guarding the right flank of the army, operating down the Williamsburg and Charles City roads. After the Seven Days', Stuart's command was reorganized into a division of two brigades. The 10th Regiment was assigned to Brigadier General Wade Hampton's First Brigade, which spent most of the summer of 1862 on outpost duty below Richmond, watching McClellan.

Hampton's Brigade joined Stuart in Fairfax County on September 2 after the Battle of Second Manassas, and crossed the Potomac River into Maryland on the 5th. Beyond the fact that the 10th Regiment served with Hampton during the campaign in Maryland, we know little about the regiment specifically, and next to nothing about the Henrico Light Dragoons. Records are equally vague on the history of the regiment at the time of Stuart's expedition into Maryland and Pennsylvania, October 9-12, 1862; however, General Hampton reported that one hundred and fifty men of the regiment participated in the expedition.

With the reorganization of the cavalry into four brigades on November 10, 1862, the 10th Regiment was assigned to the Third Brigade under the command of Brigadier General W. H. F. "Rooney" Lee. On November 18 the brigade was ordered to Fredericksburg to resist the advance of the enemy in that area. The regiment was on duty in the vicinity of Port Royal, Caroline County, in December and apparently during January 1863. At the end of February, the Henrico Troop was at Beaver Dam, in Orange County, and during April was with the brigade on picket duty along the Rappahannock River.

The Henrico Troop does not appear to have participated in a major action in 1863 until the opening of the Gettysburg Campaign. As Longstreet's and Ewell's corps were moving away from Fredericksburg, General Pleasonton's Federal cavalry made a surprise attack on Stuart at Brandy Station on June 9, the day after the grand review of the cavalry by General Lee. In this, one of the greatest cavalry battles of the war, the 10th Regiment saw their share of the fighting. The Henrico Troop, small in numbers, lost one killed and six wounded, one mortally. Battle casualties included General "Rooney" Lee, who was severely wounded.

The 10th Regiment moved with the brigade, now under the command of Colonel J. R. Chambliss, Jr., and crossed the Rappahannock on June 16. In the subsequent campaign the regiment was engaged in the actions at: Middleburg, Va., on June 19; near Upperville, on the 21st; and at Hanover, Pa., on June 30. On July 1 they were with Stuart at Carlisle, and participated in the cavalry battle at Gettysburg on the 3rd. On the return march to Virginia the regiment was engaged in the cavalry actions at Hagerstown on July 6, where Colonel Davis was captured, Williamsport, Funkstown, Beaver Creek Bridge near Boonsborough, and Shepherdstown.

In September 1863, with the reorganization of the cavalry into a corps of two divisions, the brigade, still under Colonel Chambliss, was assigned to Major General Fitzhugh Lee's Division. Sixteen months had passed since their entry into service when the Henrico Troop was encamped near Woodville in Rappahannock County on the 10th of September. Captain Hopkins, suffering from failing eyesight, had been absent since March 1863, as was 1st Lieutenant J. H. T. McDowell, who had been wounded. The troop, commanded by 2nd Lieutenant James T. Burton, had two officers and forty-two enlisted men present for duty. All seem to have been adequately clothed at this time, with gray jackets and pants; and were armed with carbines and Enfield rifles, probably of the short pattern model, which was popular in the Southern cavalry because of its range. On September 11, the troop's former captain, Lieutenant Colonel McGruder, resigned his commission following a long period of absence from the field.

The Bristoe Campaign opened on September 13, when Meade's cavalry crossed the Rappahannock into Culpeper County. Stuart drove them back, and then General Lee took the offensive. The 10th Regiment, with Chambliss's Brigade, participated in the Bristoe campaign, October 11-21, which took them north to the old battlegrounds near Manassas

Junction, and were engaged at Buckland on the 19th. Following this action the brigade recrossed the Rappahannock. After the Mine Run operations, November 28-December 1, the army went into winter quarters behind the Rapidan.

On May 7, 1864 the 10th Regiment, with Chambliss' Brigade, was engaged in the fighting at Todd's Tavern. While the infantry of the two armies were engaged at Spotsylvania Court House on May 9, General Sheridan's cavalry, about 12,000, started south toward Richmond, with the main purpose of drawing Stuart's cavalry away from the flanks of Grant's army. Within three hours, the Confederate cavalry had overtaken them. Clashes occurred along the way as Stuart tried to obstruct Sheridan's advance; and on May 11, in the battle at Yellow Tavern near Richmond, where Stuart was mortally wounded, Captain Hopkins was captured. Blind in his right eye, and with the sight of the other much impaired, Captain Hopkins had requested assignment to lighter duty in August 1863; however, he was back in the field with the Henrico Troop in the spring of 1864.

After the battles around Spotsylvania Court House, Grant moved east and southward toward Richmond. A frontal attack on Lee's positions at Cold Harbor, about eight miles east of Richmond, was repulsed with severe losses on June 3. The 10th Regiment, with W. H. F. Lee's Division, remained east of Richmond, when the cavalry under Hampton left on June 8 in pursuit of Sheridan, who had set out for Charlottesville to destroy the Virginia Central Railroad. After the fighting around Trevilian Station, in Louisa County, Sheridan, followed by the two divisions under Hampton, returned east. Chambliss' Brigade rejoined Hampton, and on June 24, at Samaria Church and Nance's Shop, attacked Gregg's Division of Cavalry. Among the 10th Regiment's dead at Samaria Church was Sergeant J. Lucius Davis, Jr., the 22-year-old son of the regiment's commander.

Hampton crossed the James, and on June 27 moved off to intercept Wilson's cavalry, returning from its raid to rejoin Grant's army. On the 28th, the 10th Regiment charged with Chambliss' Brigade against Wilson's raiders at Sappony Creek, a few miles west of Stony Creek Depot on the Weldon Railroad south of Petersburg. The Federals were driven back to Sappony Church, where they were again engaged by the brigade, fighting dismounted. After the rout of Wilson, the 10th Regiment was in no significant operations until August 14, when it was sent with W. H. F. Lee's Division to meet a Federal advance east of Richmond. On August 16 it was engaged at White Tavern, eight miles from the city on the Charles City Road, where General Chambliss was killed.

On August 25 Hampton's Divisions co-operated in the attack on the Federal II Corps at Reams Station, where they were engaged in destroying the Weldon Railroad. The 10th Regiment, with the brigade, now under Colonel Davis, was heavily engaged throughout the fighting. Captured on the return march from Gettysburg, Colonel Davis had been exchanged in March 1864; and after the death of Chambliss, commanded the brigade until his resignation from the army in February 1865.

In September, the Henrico Troop, under Lieutenant McDowell, participated in the "Beefsteak Raid," one of the most remarkable expeditions of the war. On the 14th, Hampton set out from Petersburg with W. H. F. Lee's Division, the brigades of Rosser and Dearing, and other attached troops, totaling about 4,000, to seize a large herd of cattle grazing near Coggins Point on the James River. Operating in the rear of the Federal army, Hampton returned on the 17th with over 2,400 head of cattle and more then 300 prisoners, while suffering only sixty-one casualties in the two engagements with Federal cavalry sent out to intercept him. Hampton's route, to and from his objective, covered about a hundred miles. On September 29 the 10th Regiment, with W. H. F. Lee's Division, co-operated with General Heth of Hill's Corps in the engagements fought along the Vaughn and Squirrel Level roads south of Petersburg, known as the Battle of Peebles' Farm. On October 27 the regiment was engaged in the fighting at Burgess' Mill, where the Boydton Plank Road crossed Hatcher's Run southwest of Petersburg.

On December 10, 1864 W. H. F. Lee's Division was engaged at Hicksford (now Emporia), where the Weldon railroad crossed the Meherrin River, and successfully prevented the further destruction of the railroad by Gregg's cavalry and elements of Warren's V Corps. On December 16, while encamped at Stony Creek above Hicksford, Lieutenant McDowell was promoted to captain of the Henrico Troop, replacing Captain Hopkins. After six months as a prisoner of war, Captain Hopkins was exchanged on December 13, 1864, and retired from active duty on the 16th.

The Henrico Troop remained with the regiment at Hicksford, and across the Meherrin at Belfield Depot, until March 13, 1865, when the division was sent to the right of the lines at Petersburg. On the fatal day April 1, at Five Forks, Lee's Division was on Pickett's right, and was heavily engaged against Custer's Division of Sheridan's cavalry. Pickett's forces were routed, and W. H. F. Lee's Division fell back toward the South Side Railroad. Petersburg was evacuated by General Lee's forces on April 2, and throughout the retreat westward, the division was constantly employed in scouting and screening the movements of the army. Their last fight was on April 9, near Appomattox Court House. Only two enlisted men of the Henrico Troop, and Captain Hopkins, who had, at an undetermined date, rejoined the troop, remained to be paroled at Appomattox. Captain McDowell, who had been absent for some time because of illness, was paroled at Ashland on April 16, 1865.

The Landing at Richmond from Harper's Weekly July 17, 1858

The Henrico Light Dragoons, wearing their dress uniforms with crested helmets, were among the troops present at the reception of Monroe's remains at Rocketts on July 5, 1858. The procession to Hollywood Cemetery was one of the most impressive military parades in Richmond's history.

Colonel J. Lucius Davis
1st Regiment of Cavalry,
Wise Legion
1861-1862
10th Regiment Virginia Cavalry
1862-1865

## HENRICO LIGHT DRAGOONS

### CAPTAINS

Hopkins, George
McDowell, James H. T.
McGruder, Z. S., Lt. Col.

### LIEUTENANTS

Belcher, James R., 3rd Lieut.
Burton, James T., 2nd Lieut.
Gunn, James M., 1st Lieut.
Smith, Marcellius, 2nd Lieut.
Toler, William G., 3rd Lieut.
Vaughan, James D., 2nd Lieut.

### NON-COMMISSIONED OFFICERS AND PRIVATES

Alley, Felix, Pvt.
Alley, Mosby, Pvt.
Amos, Berry B., Pvt.
Banks, Thomas Johnson, Pvt.
Barker, Robinson, Pvt.
Bond, Joseph, Pvt.
Bowles, Lyddall, Pvt.
Bowles, William Thomas, Pvt.
Brouddus, R. F., Pvt.
Burton, George, Pvt.
Carnagey, William A., Corpl.
Carter, Andrew T., Pvt.
Chandler, J. B., Pvt.
Chapman, G. H., Pvt.
Chapman, Samuel, Pvt.
Clark, James, Pvt.
Clarke, J. T., Pvt.
Coghill, S. G., Pvt.
Conway, P. H., Pvt.
Cord, C., Pvt.
Cottrell, Charles M., Pvt.
Cottrell, E. D., Pvt.
Cox, George H., Pvt.
Crafton, Thomas H., Sergt.
Cross, Joseph F., Pvt.
Cross, R. N., Pvt.
Curry, Joshua W., Pvt.
Dakenheart, Peter, Pvt.
Davis, B. T., Corpl.
Davis, J. N., Pvt.
Davis, J. R., Pvt.
Davis, Thomas Sandford, Pvt.
Dearheart, John C., Pvt.
Dodd, Robert, Pvt.
Duke, G. W., Pvt.
Duval, Benjamin J., Pvt.
Duvall, Mosby S., Pvt.
Duvall, S. A., Pvt.
Earnest, George L., Pvt.
Ellett, T. H., Pvt.
Elliott, Joseph, Pvt.
Ellis, Smith, Pvt.
Ellyson, Thomas J., Pvt.
English, John, Pvt.
Exall, Henry, Pvt.
Falley, J., Pvt.
Fincham, H. L., Pvt.
Ford, Edgar, Pvt.
Ford, John, Pvt.
Ford, Marcus, Pvt.
Ford, Robert A., Sergt.
Ford, William, Pvt.
Francis, O. A., Pvt.
Freeman, Lewis, Corpl.
French, R. E., Pvt.
Fussell, George W., Pvt.
Gardner, James M., Pvt.
Gentry, James Dallas, Pvt.
Gilman, James Henry, Pvt.
Goodson, J. R., Pvt.
Grant, Charles S., Corpl.
Gray, James W., Pvt.
Gregory, William H., Pvt.
Griffin, S., Pvt.
Happer, George D. W., Pvt.
Hardin, Henry M., Pvt.
Harris, G. H., Pvt.
Harris, John L., Pvt.
Hicks, Major, Pvt.
Howlett, Edwin J., Corpl.

Hudson, J. C., Pvt.
Huffman, J. T., Pvt.
Huffman, P. H., Pvt.
Huffman, W. T., Pvt.
Hughes, T. W., Pvt.
Jennings, R. F., Pvt.
Keessee, Samuel H., Pvt.
Kelley, John Ashton, Corpl.
Kerr, J. Lucius, Pvt.
Kholer, Charles, Pvt.
King, Carver, Pvt.
Kuper, Frederick A., 1st Sergt.
Lewis, T. F., Pvt.
Mann, Joseph C., Corpl.
McGruder, C. B., Pvt.
McGruder, Joseph L., Sergt.
Meisch, John, Pvt.
Miles, L. M., Pvt.
Mitchell, William F., Corpl.
Neurohr, Henry, Pvt.
Oephin, George, Pvt.
Ottenburg, Louis, Pvt.
Perkins, A. B., Pvt.
Perkins, B. R., Pvt.
Porterwig, C. J., Pvt.
Poterwig, Henry, Corpl.
Priddy, Henry B., Pvt.
Priddy, R. C., Pvt.
Pruit, Walter, Pvt.
Rae, John J., Pvt.
Redd, E. T., Pvt.
Rhynhardt, Mike, Pvt.
Riddell, Charles, Pvt.

Roper, Robert A., Hosp. Steward
Ross, John, Pvt.
Sanderson, W. G., Pvt.
Schermerharn, Egmond P., Pvt.
Schermerhorn, John P., Pvt.
Scott, James S., Pvt.
Shaw, Jacob, Pvt.
Sheppard, Thomas R., 1st Sergt.
Shultz, John T., Pvt.
Sizer, W. H., Pvt.
Sneed, James W., Pvt.
Snyder, Frederick, Pvt.
Soutter, Philip, Pvt.
Stacy, E. C., Pvt.
St. Clair, L. W., Pvt.
Swan, S. E., Pvt.
Thomas, Walker, Pvt.
Thomas, W. L., Pvt.
Thornton, J. T., Pvt.
Waldrop, George H., Pvt.
Walton, Archer Thomas, Pvt.
Walton, George Washington, Pvt.
Watford, David A., Corpl.
Watson, John, Pvt.
White, John H., Pvt.
Wicks, J. T., Pvt.
Wilkins, D. T., Pvt.
Wilson, J. W., Pvt.
Winston, H. Clay, Sergt.
Woodson, J. L., Pvt.
Wright, J. C., Pvt.
Wuyne, William, Jr., Pvt.

## HENRICO MOUNTED GUARD

## COMPANY A

The Henrico Mounted Guard was organized on March 17, 1862 under Captain John F. Wren at Westham House on the plank road in Sidney, which was then a community on the western outskirts of Richmond. Captain Wren had for many years served as an officer in the Henrico Light Dragoons, and in 1861 was serving as adjutant of the 4th Regiment of Cavalry, Virginia Militia. Beginning March 19, 1862, the company was accepted into the Provisional Army of the Confederate States for a period of three years — unless sooner discharged — exclusively for local service in and around the city of Richmond. The Richmond Daily Dispatch announced that the company paraded in front of the City Hall on March 24 for the purpose of being mustered into service, which is some indication that March 19 was the date on which the company enrolled for service. At the time of their acceptance into service, the Henrico Mounted Guard numbered four officers and ninety-nine enlisted men. On April 4 the Daily Dispatch reported that the company was on picket duty in and around the city. The organization of the company does not appear to have been completed until July 24, when the first and fifth sergeants and four corporals were elected.

During the summer of 1862 the Henrico Mounted Guard established itself at Camp Maynard, near the city, where they remained for about a year. At the end of August 1862 the company was reported as being well clothed, accoutred with cartridge boxes and cap pouches, and armed with 104 sabres and 20 shotguns.

On September 8, 1862 the Henrico Mounted Guard was divided into two companies to form a battalion under Captain Wren, who was promoted to major on November 11, 1862. The command was designated the 31st Battalion of Virginia Cavalry, and the original company was denominated as Company A, of which 1st Lieutenant B. W. Green, Jr., was promoted to captain.

The 31st Battalion was included in the forces of the Department of Richmond under Major General Arnold Elzey, which was established on April 1, 1863, with geographical limits defined as "all north of the James River," with headquarters in Richmond. On April 23 the limits were extended to include Drewry's Bluff and Manchester. Presumably, the battalion could be legally employed as "local defense" troops at any point within the department. On May 22 Wren's Battalion was ordered to proceed westward in "the direction of Lynchburg," to guard the passes of the James River. A muster roll of Company B, dated "Near Scottsville," in Fluvanna County, June 30, 1863, is evidence that at least part of the battalion went on this mission.

In late June 1863, while Lee's army was moving into Pennsylvania, Federal landings on the Peninsula created no little concern for the safety of Richmond. Local defense organizations were called out to reinforce the troops of the department in manning the defenses of the city. Wren's Battalion was reported on July 5 as being on the outer line, just north of Emmanuel Church on Brooke Turnpike. The danger subsided within a short time, and the local defense troops were relieved on July 6; the militia and departmental troops, however, were kept on duty.

The 31st Battalion moved into Camp Elzey, near Richmond, about the first of July 1863. On July 16 four companies were added to the battalion, and the command was redesignated as the 40th Battalion of Virginia Cavalry. Lieutenant Colonel William T. Robins, formerly a captain and Assistant Adjutant General in the Department of Richmond, was appointed to command the new organization, in which Captain Green's company retained its designation as Company A. At this time the battalion seems to have been largely engaged in scouting and picket duty in Hanover County. By late August, the battalion had been assigned to the cavalry forces attached to the brigade of Brigadier General Henry A. Wise, then serving in the Department of Richmond.

On the night of August 27 the battalion moved with General Wise's command to meet an enemy force reported advancing toward Bottom's Bridge on the Chickahominy. The battalion continued on the march beyond the bridge and on the 28th, at New Kent Court House, engaged elements of the 1st New York Mounted Rifles and the 5th Pennsylvania Cavalry. Afterwards the battalion fell back and rejoined General Wise at Bottom's Bridge, remaining there until the evening of the 30th when they returned to Camp Elzey.

On September 24, 1863 the 40th Battalion and Major John R. Robertson's 32nd Battalion were consolidated to form the 42nd Battalion under the command of Lieutenant Colonel Robins. Major Wren was no longer with the command, having resigned on August 28, 1863. In September, Wise's Brigade was sent to South Carolina, and for the remainder of the year the 42nd Battalion served as departmental "Detached Cavalry," and apparently saw much service in Charles City County.

In January 1864 the 42nd Battalion was attached to Brigadier General Eppa Hunton's Brigade, which had been assigned to the Department of Richmond. From March 1-4 the battalion was engaged in operations against General Judson Kilpatrick, who, finding the defenses of Richmond too strong, had turned eastward across the Chickahominy. A portion of the battalion, under Captain McGruder, was included in the ambush in King and Queen County, on March 2, in which Colonel Ulric Dahlgren was killed, but there is no evidence to show that any members of Company A were present. On March 10, while encamped at Carlton's Store, near King and Queen Court House, the 42nd Battalion fought its old adversaries the 1st New York Mounted Rifles, and the 11th Pennsylvania Cavalry. In reprisal for the shooting of Dahlgren, commands had been sent out to burn the public buildings at King and Queen Court House. Kilpatrick ordered the capture of the 42nd Battalion, but was successful only in the destruction of their camp.

A portion of the battalion was engaged in a skirmish on May 17 with the 9th New York Cavalry, Devin's Brigade, which was moving on the Varina road toward Chaffin's Bluff. On May 30, as Grant's army was nearing Cold Harbor, the 42nd Battalion engaged the 9th New York and other elements of Devin's Brigade, at Matadequin Creek in the vicinity of Old Church.

On June 8, 1864 two additional companies were assigned to the 42nd Battalion, which was redesignated the 24th Regiment of Virginia Cavalry. Lieutenant Colonel Robins' commission as colonel commanding the regiment, was approved on June 14, the day after the regiment engaged the 3rd Indiana and 8th New York cavalry regiments at Riddell's Shop. At this time the 24th Regiment was brigaded with the Hampton Legion and the 7th Regiment of South Carolina Cavalry, under Brigadier General Martin W. Gary. On June 24 the regiment participated in the attack on Gregg's Division, Sheridan's Cavalry, at Samaria Church.

On July 23 1st Lieutenant James W. Dabney was promoted to captain of Company A, replacing Captain Green who resigned on the same day. On the 27th the company, with the regiment, took part in an engagement with elements of Kautz's cavalry division near Deep Bottom. Their next major fight occurred August 13-20 at Fussell's Mill on the Darbytown Road, where Colonel Robins was wounded while leading a dismounted charge. Gary's Brigade remained in the vicinity of Deep Bottom throughout September, and, about the first of October, went on picket duty at White Oak Swamp where it was engaged on the 7th, 13th, and 27th.

In February 1865 the 24th Regiment was transferred, with Gary's Brigade, into Fitzhugh Lee's cavalry division. The division was ordered to the right of the army at Petersburg in March; but Gary's Brigade remained on the north side of the James River employed in picket duty and scouting in the vicinity of Bottom's Bridge, White Oak Swamp, and Deep Bottom. Gary's Brigade followed the retreating Confederates over Mayo's Bridge at Richmond on the morning of April 3, being the last troops to evacuate the city. The brigade moved with the wagon train to Tomahawk Church, and crossed the Appomattox River at Clementon Bridge. Most of the wagons were destroyed near Paineville; and the brigade, en route to Amelia Springs, was engaged in a running fight with Davies' Brigade of Sheridan's cavalry. Gary's Brigade moved westward with the army to Appomattox Court House, where it surrendered. Of the 157 members of the 24th Regiment who were paroled on April 10, 1865, eleven — including Captain Dabney — were from Company A.

## HENRICO MOUNTED GUARD

### MAJOR

Wren, John

### CAPTAIN

Green, Benjamin W., Jr.

### LIEUTENANTS

Dabney, James W., Jr., 2nd Lieut.
Gardner, William N., 1st Lieut.
Powers, Lemuel, 2nd Lieut.
Saunders, William O., 2nd Lieut.

### NON-COMMISSIONED OFFICERS AND PRIVATES

Adams, John T., Pvt.
Alexander, William J., Pvt.
Allen, Robert H., Sergt.
Allen, Williamson W., Pvt.
Alley, Ira W., Pvt.
Anderson, Henry T., Pvt.
Barker, William N., Pvt.
Baugh, Edward J., Pvt.
Bazzarea, Alexander, Pvt.
Blackburn, David A., Pvt.
Bradley, Littleberry D., Pvt.
Brill, Casper, Pvt.
Brock, Robert H., Pvt.
Burging, Christian, Pvt.
Burton, George, Pvt.
Carter, George P., Pvt.
Carter, Richard, Pvt.
Carter, William G., Pvt.
Christian, Horace B., Corpl.
Cook, William H., Pvt.
Corker, William H., Pvt.
Cornett, Jesse M., Pvt.
Cosby, James J., Pvt.
Cosby, Phillip L., Pvt.
Cottrell, Benjamin, 1st Sergt.
Cottrell, George, Pvt.
Cottrell, Henry A., Pvt.
Cottrell, Richard H., Sergt.
Davis, Hugh L., Pvt.
Dearheart, John C., Pvt.
Dicken, Thomas N., Pvt.
Dickinson, Russell J., Pvt.
Dixon, William H., Pvt.

Drumheller, Leonard T., Pvt.
Drumheller, William L., Pvt.
Ellis, John A., Pvt.
Farrar, Micanus C., Pvt.
Finkie, Henry, Pvt.
Ford, Joseph H., Pvt.
Ford, William P., Pvt.
Ford, William T., Pvt.
Franklin, James F., Pvt.
Franklin, William A., Pvt.
Frick, Guthold, Pvt.
Gatewood, Jackson D., Pvt.
Gathright, Miles, Pvt.
Gathright, Robert C., Pvt.
Gathright, W. A., Pvt.
Gauldin, Ellison, Pvt.
Gordon, George M., Pvt.
Gordon, Obediah, Pvt.
Gordon, William B., Pvt.
Grant, J. Randolph, Pvt.
Green, Andrew, Pvt.
Green, Eugene A., Pvt.
Griffin, Robert S., Pvt.
Hall, William G., Pvt.
Haynes, John R., Sergt
Hendrick, L. D., Pvt.
Hendrick, William J., Pvt.
Henly, John A., Pvt.
Hutchinson, Hugh M., Pvt.
Hutchinson, Joseph, Pvt.
Johnson, Henry, Pvt.
Johnson, Jesse L., Pvt.
Johnson, John T., Pvt.

Keck, Frederick, Pvt.
Landrum, Ed. S., Pvt.
Lawrence, Alex M., Pvt.
Lawrence, J. R., Pvt.
Livsay, George M., Pvt.
Mander, Alexander, Pvt.
Maurray, P. M., Pvt.
Mayo, James E., Pvt.
McGee, William H., Pvt.
Meredith, John H., Pvt.
Miller, Edward R., Pvt.
Miller, William L., Pvt.
Mitchell, Henry C., Pvt.
Moore, Pleasant D., Pvt.
Morris, John, Pvt.
Muller, Andrew, Pvt.
Nelson, Olonzo J., Pvt.
O'Neil, Dennis, Pvt.
Padget, James H., Pvt.
Padgett, Robert R., Pvt.
Patman, William R., Pvt.
Pfeiffer, William, Musician
Phillips, Richard, Pvt.
Pitts, David O., Pvt.
Pitts, William H., Pvt.
Pleasants, John H., Pvt.
Poindexter, Edward H., Pvt.
Powell, Charles S., Pvt.
Powell, Richard, Pvt.
Robinson, Willis W., Corpl.
Saunders, John S., Sergt.
Senton, Joseph, Pvt.
Shaw, Thomas H., Pvt.
Shelton, Edward B., Corpl.
Shoemaker, William, Pvt.
Smith, Andrew K., Pvt.
Smith, Burwell, Pvt.

Smoot, Thomas B., Pvt.
Snead, C. F., Pvt.
Snead, John B., Pvt.
Stevens, John B., Corpl.
Sundberg, John V., Pvt.
Swartz, Samuel, Pvt.
Taylor, John B., Pvt.
Taylor, Martin S., Pvt.
Thompson, John, Pvt.
Timberlake, Alpheus R., Sergt.
Timberlake, Edward T., Pvt.
Timberlake, John H., Pvt.
Timberlake, Ro W., Pvt.
Timberlake, William A., Pvt.
Tinsley, Adolphus, Pvt.
Toler, Callum, Pvt.
Traylor, John B., Pvt.
Turner, John J., Pvt.
Turner, Richard M., Pvt.
Tyler, Henry C., Pvt.
Tyler, William H., Pvt.
Wade, Joseph D., Pvt.
Wade, Thomas, Pvt.
Wade, William D., Pvt.
Wagner, Lewis, Pvt.
Walbour, Fred, Pvt.
Waldrop, Patrick, Pvt.
Waller, Joseph, Pvt.
Walton, Isham C., Pvt.
White, James E., Pvt.
Wilkerson, George, Pvt.
Woodson, Thomas M., Pvt.
Woodward, David H., Pvt.
Woodward, John R., Pvt.
Wren, W. H. F., Pvt.
Wright, Alfred J., Pvt.

## HENRICO MOUNTED GUARD

## COMPANY B

On September 8, 1862 Captain John F. Wren's cavalry company, the Henrico Mounted Guard, was divided into two companies to form the 31st Battalion of Virginia Cavalry. 2nd Lieutenant William H. McGruder of the original company was promoted to captain of the new company, designated Company B. Captain Wren, commanding the battalion, was appointed major on November 11, 1862. The original company had been accepted into Confederate States service on March 19, 1862, exclusively for local service in and around Richmond.

The two companies of Henrico Mounted Guards were stationed at Camp Maynard when the battalion was organized, and remained there throughout 1862. On October 31, 1862 Company B was reported with four officers, five sergeants, four corporals, and seventy-four privates present for duty. Their clothing at this time was rated as "Very Good" by the inspecting officer, but their arms seem to have consisted of only fifty-nine sabres.

The battalion, comprising part of the forces of the Department of Richmond, created on April 1, 1863, was ordered on May 22, 1863 to proceed westward to guard the passes of the James River. On June 30 Company B was reported as being "Near Scottsville," in Fluvanna County. They were, apparently, soon back in Richmond for on July 5, 1863 Wren's Battalion was reported as being on duty on the outer defenses, just north of Emmanuel Church on Brooke Turnpike.

About the first of July 1863 the battalion moved to Camp Elzey, where on July 16 four companies were added and the command, under Lieutenant Colonel William T. Robins, was redesignated as the 40th Battalion of Virginia Cavalry. Captain McGruder's company was retained in the new organization as Company B. In late August the battalion was assigned to the cavalry attached to Wise's Brigade, which then comprised a part of the forces of the Department of Richmond.

On the night of August 27 the 40th Battalion moved with General Wise's command to meet an enemy force reported nearing Bottom's Bridge, on the Williamsburg Road. Upon finding no enemy troops at the bridge, the battalion moved on to New Kent Court House, where it encountered Federal cavalry. After a brief encounter, the battalion fell back and rejoined General Wise at Bottom's Bridge. On the evening of the 30th they returned to Camp Elzey.

On September 24, 1863 the 40th and 32nd cavalry battalions were consolidated to form the 42nd Battalion of Virginia Cavalry under Lieutenant Colonel Robins. In September Wise's Brigade was sent to South Carolina, and for the remainder of the year the 42nd Battalion served as departmental "Detached Cavalry," and apparently saw much service in Charles City County. In September, 1863 Company B was comprised of two officers, seven noncommissioned officers, and about eighty-two privates present for duty.

In January 1864 the 42nd Battalion was attached to Brigadier General Eppa Hunton's Brigade, which had been assigned to the Department of Richmond. Captain McGruder was reported in February 1864 as commanding the 2nd Squadron of the battalion. From March 1-4 the battalion was engaged in operations against General Judson Kilpatrick, who, finding the defenses of Richmond too strong, had turned eastward across the Chickahominy. Seventy men of Captain McGruder's command took part in the ambush in King and Queen County on March 2 in which Colonel Ulric Dahlgren was killed, but it is not certain if any members of Company B were present. While encamped near Carlton's Store near King and Queen Court House on March 10, the 42nd Battalion engaged Federal cavalry which had been sent out to avenge the shooting of Colonel Dahlgren.

On May 30 as Grant's army was approaching Cold Harbor, the 42nd Battalion fought the 9th New York Cavalry and other elements of Devins' Brigade at Matadequin Creek, in the vicinity of Old Church. Company B had five men wounded in this engagement.

Two additional companies were assigned to the 42nd Battalion on June 8, 1864, whereupon the command was reorganized as the 24th Regiment of Virginia Cavalry, with Colonel Robins commanding. On June 13 the regiment was brigaded with the Hampton Legion and the 7th South Carolina Cavalry, under Brigadier General Martin W. Gary. The 24th Regiment was engaged at Riddell's Shop on the 13th, and on June 24 participated with Gary's Brigade in the battle at Samaria Church in Charles City County, where Company B had two wounded.

The 24th Regiment engaged elements of Kautz's cavalry division at Deep Bottom on July 27, where Company B had one killed and three wounded. Their next engagement was at Fussell's Mill, sometime between August 13-20. At the end of August Company B was posted at New Market Heights, a few miles south of the mill. Through September Gary's Brigade was on duty in the vicinity of Deep Bottom and about the first of October went on picket duty at White Oak Swamp, where it engaged the enemy on the 7th, 13th and 27th.

The 24th Regiment, with Gary's Brigade, was transferred to Fitzhugh Lee's cavalry division in February 1865. The division was ordered to the right of the army at Petersburg in March, but Gary's Brigade remained on the north side of the James River, where it was employed on picket duty and scouting in the vicinity of Bottom's Bridge, White Oak Swamp and Deep Bottom. Gary's Brigade followed the retreating Confederates over Mayo's Bridge at Richmond on the morning of April 3, being the last troops to evacuate the city. The brigade moved with the wagon train to Tomahawk Church and crossed the Appomattox River at Clementon Bridge. Most of the wagons were destroyed near Paineville, and the brigade, en route to Amelia Springs, was engaged in a running fight with Davies' Brigade of Sheridan's cavalry. Gary's Brigade moved westward with the army to Appomattox Court House where it surrendered. Of the 157 members of the 24th Regiment who were paroled on April 10, 1865, fifteen were from Company B.

# HENRICO MOUNTED GUARD

## COMPANY B

### CAPTAIN

McGruder, William M.

### LIEUTENANTS

Alvis, John S., Jr., 2nd Lieut.
Cottrell, Albert B., 2nd Lieut.

Deitrick, Thomas, M., 1st Lieut

### NON-COMMISSIONED OFFICERS AND PRIVATES

Alvis, George H., Pvt.
Alvis, S. A., Pvt.
Alvis, William W., Sergt.
Amos, George W., Pvt.
Armstrong, L. W., Pvt.
Atkins, A., C., Pvt.
Atkinson, P. T., Pvt.
Barker, Benjamin, Pvt.
Barker, David, Pvt.
Barker, Jordon, Pvt.
Barker, Leander, Pvt.
Bennett, Randolph, Pvt.
Bennett, T. C., Pvt.
Blackburn, Paulin A., Pvt.
Blake, E. B., Pvt.
Bowles, Joseph H., Pvt.
Bowles, Thomas H., Pvt.
Bowles, William S., Pvt.
Boze, R. P., Pvt.
Brill, Henry, Pvt.
Buhl, Christian E., Pvt.
Burnett, James E., Pvt.
Burnett, William P., Pvt.
Callahan, Patrick, Pvt.
Carter, Andrew B., Corpl.
Carver, Thomas P., Pvt.
Champion, Z., Pvt.
Christian, William, Pvt.
Clark, James, Pvt.
Clark, Thomas E., Pvt.
Cook, John M., Pvt.
Corbell, A. B., Pvt.
Cottrell, Peter, Corpl.
Crenshaw, J. W., Pvt.
Crouch, B. S., Pvt.

Crouch, John E., Pvt.
Davis, Ed. F., Pvt.
Davis, Samuel T., Pvt.
Depriest, William F., Pvt.
Dickman, Frank, Pvt.
Eacho, Thornton, Pvt.
Ellett, Thomas C., Pvt.
Ellis, John T., Pvt.
Ellis, Joseph, Pvt.
Erhardt, John F., Pvt.
Euker, Edward J., Sergt.
Ferguson, W. J., Pvt.
Fleshman, Fielding Z., Pvt.
Ford, E. A., Pvt.
Ford, Jacob, Pvt.
French, Thomas J., Pvt.
Frommer, Charles, Pvt.
Gardner, John B., Sergt.
Gatewood, George W., Pvt.
Gauldin, L., Pvt.
Grant, Clinton, Pvt.
Gravin, John B., Pvt.
Green, William C., Pvt.
Haley, Joseph C., Pvt.
Harden, George W., Pvt.
Harrison, William F., Pvt.
Hart, James R., Pvt.
Harwood, Otis A., Pvt.
Hawkins, William W., Corpl.
Henley, Robert A., Pvt.
Higgins, Thaddeus, Pvt.
Holt, Sterling F., Pvt.
Hooper, Richard H., Pvt.
Hudgins, Robert M., Sergt
Hudson, Edwin T., Pvt.

Jennings, William J., Pvt.
Johnson, James M., Pvt.
Jones, Andrew J., Pvt.
Jude, Joseph, Pvt.
Kellum, W. P., Pvt.
King, Robert L., Pvt.
Lawrence, M. W., Pvt.
Lawrence, William F., Pvt.
Leadbetter, H. L., Pvt.
Lewis, Archer B., Pvt.
Lipscomb, Newton, Pvt.
Livsey, William, Pvt.
Loughnane, Martin, Pvt.
Lubbs, John P., Pvt.
Lumsden, John M., Pvt.
Lynham, William J., Jr., A.Q.M.
Maisch, Gottlieb, Pvt.
Martin, Berry
Martin, J. T., Pvt.
Maxwell, John W., Pvt.
McAllister, Daniel, Pvt.
McAllister, Joseph, Pvt.
McCloy, William W., Pvt.
Meyers, Henry G., Pvt.
Miller, Augustus, Pvt.
Miller, Benjamin, Pvt.
Mitchell, Henry C., Pvt.
Mitchell, Joseph, Pvt.
Moore, Richard, Pvt.
Moran, George N., Pvt.
Nash, L. N., Pvt.
Nuckols, Joseph W., Pvt.
Nuckols, Thomas R., Pvt.
Nuckols, William P., Pvt.
Oakley, James, Pvt.
Oakley, Thomas, Pvt.
Patram, John H., Pvt.
Pearce, Oscar F., Pvt.
Pendleton, Virginius, Pvt.
Phillips, Whitfield W., Pvt.
Picot, John T., Pvt.

Pleasants, John H., Pvt.
Poindexter, James D., Pvt.
Saunders, Charles H., Pvt.
Saunderson, John T., Pvt.
Shepperson, William, Pvt.
Shurm, John H., Pvt.
Shurm, Joseph H., Pvt.
Sitman, Joseph O., Pvt.
Slaughter, R. J., Pvt.
Smither, Joseph A., Pvt.
Spruiel, Bailey, Pvt.
Starke, Gideon, Pvt.
Stern, Daniel, Corpl.
Sulivant, Richard, Pvt.
Swalm, George, Pvt.
Tate, Henry, Pvt.
Throckmorton, T. N., Pvt.
Tinsley, Joseph, Pvt.
Toler, James W., Pvt.
Toler, Robert T. L., Pvt.
Tuck, George W., Pvt.
Turpin, Elisha S., Pvt.
Turpin, Horace, Pvt.
Tyler, John A., Pvt.
Tyler, Joseph F., Pvt.
Tyler, Reuben A., Pvt.
Vaughan, George M., 1st Sergt.
Vaughan, J. D., Pvt.
Vaughan, Robert, Corpl.
Vaughan, Edward B., Pvt.
Wade, John A., Pvt.
Weimer, August, Pvt.
Weymack, William H., Pvt.
Whitford, Thomas H., Pvt.
Whittle, Adam, Pvt.
Wickham, John, Pvt.
Williams, George H., Pvt.
Winston, P. H., Pvt.
Woodall, Jacob H., Pvt.
Woodard, George B., Pvt.
Wooldridge, J. C., Pvt.

# HENRICO MOUNTED RANGERS

The Henrico Mounted Rangers were organized on January 31, 1861 at the home of Ronald Mills near Varina. As required by law, commissioned officers of the militia presided over the organizational meeting. Colonel John P. Harrison was named chairman and Dr. Z. S. McGruder, of the Henrico Light Dragoons, was elected secretary. Fifty-seven members were enrolled in the troop, after which Captain Mills and the other commissioned and noncommissioned officers were elected.

Membership in the troop apparently was not confined to the lower end of the county, or District No. 1, for members residing in Districts No. 2 and No. 3 were notified by 2nd Lieutenant J. P. Schermerhorn to attend a meeting on February 14 at Frank's Grocery, just above the toll gates on the Mechanicsville Turnpike.

On February 22, 1861 the Varina Troop, as it was called by this time, numbered sixty-seven men and paraded in Richmond with other companies. The troop wore undress uniforms and according to the Richmond Daily Dispatch, made a "creditable display for its first appearance." By March 16 the troop, which had increased to eighty, had been issued sabres by the State. The troop applied for Colt revolvers, but had not received them—"the only weapon now lacking to make the company a most effective military organization."

By April 2, Albert M. Akin, quartermaster of the troop, had been elected as its new captain. Regular meetings and drills were held by the troop throughout April and May at Rockett's Old Field, on the eastern edge of Richmond. On May 26 General Lee informed Colonel Magruder, commanding at Yorktown, that the Varina Troop had been ordered to him. A notice appeared in the Dispatch that the troop would be mustered into service at Rockett's Old Field on May 27, but for some undetermined cause they were not mustered in on that date. On May 29 members were again advised that the troop was to be mustered into service, this time on the 30th. Again the Varina Troop failed to be mustered into service, and by June 5 the troop had reorganized as an artillery company and elected Colonel John P. Harrison as captain. The Varina Artillery enlisted on June 6, and was assigned to Archer's Battalion, Virginia Volunteers.

However, the company again changed its branch of service to infantry. For its subsequent history, see the historical sketch of the Varina Artillery in the Infantry section.

## TEXAS RANGERS

This company, known originally as the Virginia Mounted Rangers, was organized on April 27, 1861 "in Colonel Rosser's office, in the Law Building." The organization was completed June 1, 1861 and the company enrolled for one year's service with J. Travis Rosser as captain, and became known as Rosser's Mounted Rangers. Captain Rosser was a graduate of law from the University of Virginia, a native Virginian who had served for four years as Territorial Secretary of Minnesota Territory and was a resident of Minnesota when the Southern States began to secede. He returned to Virginia early in 1861. Many of the original members of the company had returned from the western states and territories at the same time. Advertisements described the company as being composed of "Californians and Texas Rangers," thus the name of Texas Rangers was adopted.

The company was mustered into Confederate States service at Richmond on July 1, 1861 for one year's service, with eighty-five men rank and file. After muster-in, the company was stationed at Howard's Grove, just east of the city. Here it remained until August 13, when it was ordered to proceed to White Sulphur Springs to "join the army under Brigadier General H. A. Wise." Upon its arrival it was assigned as Company H, 1st Cavalry Regiment, Wise Legion, under Colonel J. Lucius Davis. However, the records show that another company also served as Company H, so the designation of the Texas Rangers within the regiment was probably changed. Because of the loose organization of the 1st Cavalry Regiment, Wise Legion, records do not indicate when the change was made or what letter designation the company was later assigned.

The company arrived at White Sulphur Springs after General John B. Floyd had assumed command over the forces operating in the Kanawha Valley area. General Floyd decided to advance and moved to Meadow Bluff on August 10. General Wise was ordered to join the force at Meadow Bluff on the 14th. Crossing the Gauley River at Carnifax Ferry, Floyd defeated a Federal force at Cross Lanes on August 26. After this action, Floyd remained inactive at Carnifax Ferry, waiting for reinforcements. Moving as if to join Floyd, Wise started conducting his own campaign against Federal positions at Hawk's Nest. Failing to drive the Federals, Wise took a position at Dickersons, covering Miller's Ferry, some fifteen miles southwest of Floyd's position. After the battle at Carnifax Ferry on September 10, Floyd and Wise fell back to Sewell Mountain, arriving there on the 14th. General Floyd, however, withdrew his forces twelve miles eastward to Meadow Bluff on the 16th. The records do not indicate the specific movements of the Texas Rangers during these moves, but vouchers indicate the company was at White Sulphur Springs on August 25 and September 16, 1861. A letter by Captain Rosser indicates that the company was "engaged on the Big Coal River (near Charleston on the Kanawha) in September 1861."

General Lee arrived at Meadow Bluff on September 21, and arrived at Sewell Mountain on the 24th with reinforcements for Wise, in whose front the enemy were advancing in force. During an enemy demonstration on September 25, General Wise was handed an order from the War Department directing him to hand over his command to General Floyd, and report to Richmond. On October 6 the Federals retired to the Gauley River, and General Floyd moved out against them, taking all troops with the exception of the Wise Legion, which he found "to be in such a state of insubordination and so ill-disciplined as to be for the moment unfit for military purposes." The Legion was sent to Meadow Bluff, where they guarded the road to Lewisburg. General Floyd's operations were soon abandoned, and General Lee left for Richmond on the 30th. The Kanawha Valley campaign, a failure, was over.

On December 4 the Wise Legion, under Colonel Davis, was ordered to Richmond; but the cavalry did not arrive there until almost two months later. On December 10 Colonel Davis was ordered to proceed to Lynchburg with the Legion; and, on the 21st of that month, to proceed to Richmond. On January 3, 1862 the Texas Rangers were at Abingdon. By January 28, 1862 the regimental headquarters had been established at Richmond.

In early February 1862 four companies of Colonel Davis' regiment were encamped at the New Fair Grounds at Richmond, one company was at Lynchburg, one at Staunton, and one at Petersburg. On February 12 five companies of the regiment, including Captain Rosser's Company, were ordered to Garysburg, N. C. By Special Orders No. 72, Adjutant and Inspector General's Office, March 29, 1862, Colonel Davis was officially assigned to command the Wise Legion Cavalry and ordered to proceed with four companies of the Legion Cavalry, and two independent companies, to report to General Magruder at Yorktown. The Texas Rangers remained in North Carolina, and were located at Murfreesboro from about March 1 to May 6 and by May 14 moved to Jackson. On May 16, the day before the company was reorganized for the war, General Huger, commanding the Department of North Carolina with headquarters at Petersburg, was directed to send the companies in North Carolina to join the balance of Colonel Davis' regiment then serving on the lower Peninsula with General Johnston. The lines on the lower Peninsula had been evacuated on May 3 and on the 5th, at Williamsburg, Colonel Davis' command had won much praise for their charge and hand-to-hand battle with Federal cavalry near Saunders' Pond. After this engagement, the army had retired up the Peninsula toward Richmond, where the companies from North Carolina rejoined the regiment. Colonel Davis' Regiment had been assigned to General Wise's newly formed brigade on May 10 but on May 28 it was placed under the command of Brigadier General J. E. B. Stuart. The regiment was officially designated the 10th Regiment Virginia Cavalry, and Captain Rosser's Company was designated Company K. Captain Rosser was promoted to major on July 16, 1862 and 1st Lieutenant James L. Dickson was promoted to captain of the Texas Rangers.

During the Seven Days' Battles the 10th Regiment, detached from Stuart's Brigade, served with General Magruder's command, guarding the right flank of the army, and operating down the Williamsburg and Charles City roads. After the Seven Days', Stuart's command was reorganized into a division of two brigades. The 10th Regiment was assigned to Brigadier General Wade Hampton's First Brigade, which spent most of the summer of 1862 on outpost duty below Richmond watching McClellan. The regiment remained on outpost duty until Hampton's Brigade was ordered to rejoin the army in Northern Virginia.

Hampton's Brigade joined Stuart in Fairfax County on September 2 after the Battle of Second Manassas, and crossed the Potomac River into Maryland on the 5th. Beyond the fact that the 10th Regiment served with Hampton during the campaign in Maryland, we know little about the regiment specifically and next to nothing about the activities of the Texas Rangers. Records are equally vague on the history of the regiment at the time of Stuart's expedition into Maryland and Pennsylvania, October 9-12, 1862; however, General Hampton reported that one hundred and fifty men of the regiment participated in the expedition.

With the reorganization of the cavalry on November 10, 1862 into four brigades, the 10th Regiment was assigned to the Third Brigade under the command of Brigadier General W. H. F. "Rooney" Lee. On November 18 the brigade was ordered to Fredericksburg to resist the advance of the enemy in that area. The regiment was on duty in the vicinity of Port Royal, Caroline County, in December and, apparently, in January 1863.

The Texas Rangers did not participate in any major action in 1863 until the opening of the Gettysburg Campaign. As Longstreet's and Ewell's troops were moving away from Fredericksburg, General Pleasanton's Federal cavalry made a surprise attack on Stuart at Brandy Station on June 9, the day after the grand review of the cavalry by General Lee. In this, one of the greatest cavalry battles of the war, the 10th Regiment saw their share of the fighting. Battle casualties included "Rooney" Lee, who was severely wounded.

The 10th Regiment moved with the brigade, now under the command of Colonel J. R. Chambliss, Jr., and crossed the Rappahannock on June 16. In the subsequent campaign the regiment was engaged in the actions at Middleburg, Va. on June 19, near Upperville on the 21st and Hanover, Pa. on June 30. It was at Hanover that Captain Dickinson was killed while leading a charge down one of the streets in the town. 1st Lieutenant William L. Graham was promoted to captain, effective June 30, 1863. On July 1 the company was with Stuart at Carlisle, and participated in the cavalry battle at Gettysburg on the 3rd. On the return march to Virginia the regiment was engaged in the cavalry actions at Hagerstown on July 6, where Colonel Davis was captured, at Williamsport, Funkstown, Beaver Creek Bridge near Boonsborough, and Shepherdstown.

In September 1863, with the reorganization of the cavalry into a corps of two divisions, the brigade, still under Colonel Chambliss, was assigned to Major General Fitzhugh Lee's Division. The company clerk reported the company station as Woodville, Rappahannock County, on the July-August 1863 muster roll. The Bristoe Campaign opened on September 13, when Meade's cavalry crossed the Rappahannock into Culpeper County. Stuart drove them back, and then General Lee took the offensive The 10th Regiment, with Chambliss' Brigade, participated in the Bristoe Campaign, October 11-21, which took them north to the old battlegrounds near Manassas Junction, and were engaged at Buckland on the 19th. Following this action, the brigade recrossed the Rappahannock. After the Mine Run operations, November 28-December 1, the army went into winter quarters behind the Rapidan. The November-December 1863 company muster roll, dated January 22, 1864, shows the company was stationed at Ivy Depot, Virginia Central Railroad.

On May 7, 1864 the 10th Regiment, with Chambliss' Brigade, was engaged in the fighting at Todd's Tavern. While the infantry of the two armies were engaged at Spotsylvania Court House on May 9, General Sheridan's cavalry, about 12,000, started south toward Richmond, with the main purpose of drawing Stuart's cavalry away from the flanks of Grant's army. Within three hours, the Confederate cavalry had overtaken them. Clashes occurred along the way as Stuart tried to obstruct Sheridan's advance; and on May 11, in the battle at Yellow Tavern near Richmond, where Stuart was mortally wounded, the Confederate cavalry defeated Sheridan, forcing him to discontinue his move southward.

After the battles around Spotsylvania Court House, Grant moved east and southward toward Richmond. A frontal attack on Lee's positions at Cold Harbor, about eight miles east of Richmond, was repulsed with severe losses on June 3. The 10th Regiment, with W. H. F. Lee's Division, remained east of Richmond when the cavalry under Hampton left on June 8 in pursuit of Sheridan, who had set out for Charlottesville to destroy the Virginia Central Railroad. After the fighting around Trevilian Station, in Louisa County, Sheridan, followed by the two divisions under Hampton, returned east. Chambliss' Brigade rejoined Hampton and on June 24, at Samaria Church and Nance's Shop, attacked Gregg's Division of Cavalry. Among the 10th Regiment's dead at Samaria Church was Sergeant J. Lucius Davis, Jr., the 22-year-old son of the regiment's commander.

Hampton crossed the James River and on June 27 moved off to intercept Wilson's cavalry, returning from the raid to rejoin Grant's army. On the 28th, the 10th Regiment charged with Chambliss' Brigade against Wilson's raiders at Sappony Creek, a few miles west of Stony Creek Depot on the Weldon Railroad south of Petersburg. The Federals were driven back to Sappony Church, where they were again engaged by the brigade, fighting dismounted. After the rout of Wilson, the 10th Regiment was in no significant operations until August 14, when they were sent with W. H. F. Lee's Division to meet a Federal advance east of Richmond. On August 16 they were engaged at White Tavern, eight miles from the city on the Charles City road, where General Chambliss was killed.

This sketch, found in Captain Rosser's records in the National Archives, may have been his design for a Ranger guidon.

On August 25, Hampton's Division cooperated in the attack on the Federal II Corps at Reams Station where they were engaged in destroying the Weldon Railroad. The 10th Regiment, with the brigade, now under Colonel Davis, was heavily engaged throughout the fighting. Captured on the return march from Gettysburg, Colonel Davis had been exchanged in March 1864 and after the death of Chambliss, commanded the brigade until his resignation from the army in February 1865. The 10th Regiment with W. H. F. Lee's Division, cooperated with General Heth of Hill's Corps in the engagements fought along the Vaughn and Squirrel Level roads south of Petersburg on September 29, in what is known as the Battle of Peebles' Farm. Again, on October 27, the regiment was engaged in the fighting at Burgess' Mill, where the Boydton Plank Road crossed Hatcher's Run southwest of Petersburg. Remaining on the right of Lee's army, W. H. F. Lee's Division was engaged at Hicksford (now Emporia) where the Weldon Railroad crossed the Meherrin River, and successfully prevented the further destruction of the railroad by Gregg's cavalry and elements of Warren's V Corps.

The regiment remained in the vicinity of Hicksford until March 1865, when the division was sent to the right of the lines at Petersburg. On March 28, 1865 Captain Graham resigned and the company was commanded by 1st Lieutenant James H. Turner after that date. On the fatal day April 1 at Five Forks, Lee's Division was on Pickett's right and was heavily engaged against Custer's Division of Sheridan's cavalry. Pickett's forces were routed, and W. H. F. Lee's Division fell back toward the South Side Railroad. Petersburg was evacuated by Lee's forces on April 2 and throughout the retreat westward, the division was constantly employed in scouting and screening the movements of the army. Their last fight was on April 9, near Appomattox Court House. When the army was paroled at that place only one man, Private E. H. Poindexter, was recorded on the parole roll under Company K, 10th Regiment Virginia Cavalry.

## TEXAS RANGERS

### MAJOR

Rosser, J. Travis

### CAPTAINS

Dickinson, James L.
Graham, William L.

| SURGEON | ASST. SURGEON |
|---|---|
| Williams, Benjamin | Hairston, William |

### LIEUTENANTS

Burwell, William A., 2nd Lieut.
Hatcher, Thomas F., 1st Lieut.
Phillips, Hopestill R., 2nd Lieut.
Roome, Charles, 3rd Lieut.
Turner, James H., Jr., 2nd Lieut.
Williams, George T., 3rd Lieut.

### NON-COMMISSIONED OFFICERS AND PRIVATES

Anderson, A. S., Pvt.
Anderson, Thomas, Pvt.
Armstrong, John R., Pvt.
Arrington, John C., Pvt.
Arrington, William S., Corpl.
Ashworth, John H., Pvt.
Barber, Jeremiah
Beech, James T., Pvt.
Bennett, A. C., Pvt.
Bennett, Thomas F., Pvt.
Bennett, William D., Pvt.
Bennett, Z. P., Pvt.
Bernard, McH., Pvt.
Bernard, Robert C., Pvt.
Bernard, Walter A., Pvt.
Bird, Samuel W., Pvt.
Bird, Silas J., Pvt.
Bird, Silas W., Pvt.
Blunt, Henry C., Pvt.
Bondurant, J. S., Pvt.
Bondurant, Robert W., Pvt.
Bowles, Jabel, Pvt.
Bowles, John, Pvt.
Brooks, A. J., Pvt.
Brooks, David S., Pvt.
Brooks, John M., Pvt.
Brooks, Peter H., Pvt
Brooks, Robinson L., Pvt.
Brooks, William E., Corpl.
Brooks, Z., Pvt.
Brown, S. P. G., Pvt.
Bryant, James S., Pvt.
Bryant, Robert, Pvt.
Burchett, H. H., Pvt.
Burnett, John W., Pvt.
Burwell, Edward W., Pvt.
Burwell, James H., Pvt.
Campbell, John, Pvt.
Campbell, W. A., Pvt.
Carvell, Jacob, Pvt.
Chitwood, John H., Pvt.
Clement, Charles J., Pvt.
Cooper, James D., Pvt.
Copeland, William W.
Craghead, John, Pvt.
Craghead, John M., Pvt.
Craghead, Thomas L., Pvt.
Dandridge, H. Clay, Pvt.
Dandridge, Thomas W., Pvt.
Davidson, David, C., Pvt.
Davis, J. W., Pvt.
Dean, G. G., Pvt.
Dent, J. J., Pvt.
Dent, S. F., Pvt.
Dickinson, W., Pvt.
Dickinson, W. H., Pvt.
Dillard, William C., Pvt.
Dillon, S., Pvt.

Divers, D. C., Pvt.
Doss, L. P., Pvt.
Dudley, Guynne T., Pvt.
Dudley, J. T., Pvt.
Ferguson, Patrick H., Pvt.
Frith, C. R., Pvt.
Frith, William H., Corpl.
Gilbert, A. C., Pvt.
Gilbert, Samuel R., Pvt.
Giles, S. S., Pvt.
Gilfoyle, Patrick, Pvt.
Grante, James R., Pvt.
Gravely, C. B., Pvt.
Griffin, John P., Pvt.
Griffin, Robert V., Pvt.
Haines, E. A., Pvt.
Hancock, C. R., Pvt.
Harbour, Joshua W., Corpl.
Harris, Benjamin B., Pvt.
Harrison, James P., Pvt.
Hatcher, Edwin C., Pvt.
Hatcher, Judson N., Pvt.
Hatcher, R. B., Pvt.
Hatcher, T. M., Pvt.
Hempstead, J. A., Pvt.
Holland, E. M., Pvt.
Holland, H. J., Pvt.
Holland, J. H., Pvt.
Holland, John H., Pvt.
Holland, Mark D., Pvt.
Holland, P. A., Pvt.
Holland, R. E., Pvt.
Holland, Thomas S., 1st Sergt.
Holland, W. A., Pvt.
Houseman, William R.
James, Bruce A., Pvt.
James, R. C., Pvt.
Jefferson, O. S., Pvt.
Jones, W. H.
Kesler, George P., Pvt.
Keyser, J. W., Pvt.
Landcaster, L. P., Pvt.
Law, S. G., Pvt.
Lovell, James M., Pvt.
Lovell, John P., Pvt.
Martin, S.H., Pvt.
Mason, Charles F., Pvt.
Mattox, E. D., Pvt.
Mattox, Gabriel T., Pvt.
Mattox, Harmon C., Pvt.
Mattox, William G., Sergt.
McAlexander, Peter, Pvt.
McGhee, John W., Pvt.
Meagher, Andrew, Pvt.
Miller, C. D., Pvt.
Mills, G. W., Pvt.
Mitchell, J. H., Pvt.
Montrief, William, Pvt.
Moore, Andrew, Pvt.
Morris, Daniel F., Pvt.
Muse, D. S., Pvt.
Myers, A., Pvt.
Ottey, Willis, Pvt.
Pannill, William H., Pvt.
Pelter, S. D., Pvt.
Penn, P. L., Pvt.
Penn, S. A., Pvt.
Philpot, Charles, Pvt.
Pinkard, John, Pvt.
Poe, W. P., Pvt.
Poindexter, E. H., Pvt.
Potter, J. D., Pvt.
Powell, William, Corpl.
Preston, C. P., Pvt.
Preston, Stephen B., Sergt.
Rice, George W.
Rives, Robert B., Pvt.
Rives, William W., Pvt.
Robbins, Thomas J., Pvt.
Robertson, Daniel A.
Robertson, Samuel T., Pvt.
Rogers, W., Pvt.
Satterfield, Edward R., Pvt.
Schermerhorn, John P., Pvt.
Seay, C. T., Pvt.
Semones, B. T., Pvt.
Semones, Benjamin M., Sergt.
Semones, J. A., Q.M. Sergt.
Semones, J. S., Pvt.
Semones, J. T., Pvt.
Shelton, J., D., Pvt.
Showalter, Jabez, Pvt.
Simmons, Joel, Pvt.
Smith, Calvin W., Pvt.
Smith, J. D., Pvt.
Smith, Samuel J., Pvt.
Smith, W. H., Pvt.
Starky, John C., Pvt.
Stegall, T. W., Pvt.
Street, John A., Pvt.

Thomas, Pleasant, Pvt.
Turner, A. E., Pvt.
Turner, G. A., Sergt.
Turner, John A., Pvt.
Turner, John P., Pvt.
Tyree, Meridith G., Pvt.
Via, W. B., Pvt.
Wade, J. E., Pvt.
Wade, John H., Corpl.
Walker, Jacob B., Pvt.
Weaver, Josiah, Pvt.
White, A. E., Pvt.

White, William P., Corpl.
Wigginton, Henry H., Pvt.
Williams, Creed T., Pvt.
Williams, Wiley, Pvt.
Wills, Henry H., Pvt.
Wills, Lindsey T., Pvt.
Wills, Nat. T., Pvt.
Wills, William L., Pvt.
Witcher, J. L., Pvt.
Woods, John S., Sergt.
Woody, Samuel
Ziegler, C. N., Sergt.

# Infantry
## 1ST REGIMENT VIRGINIA INFANTRY

The 1st Regiment of Virginia Volunteers was created on May 1, 1851 by General Orders No. 1, issued by Adjutant General William H. Richardson, which provided for the organization of a regiment to be formed from the volunteer militia companies of the city of Richmond and the counties of Chesterfield and Henrico. The officers of the various companies met on May 2 to elect the regiment's field officers. Walter Gwynn, Chief Engineer of the James River and Kanawha Canal Company, was elected colonel. After graduating from West Point in 1822, Gwynn served in the army until his resignation as first lieutenant in 1832. Later he was appointed a major in the militia of North Carolina; and after his removal to Virginia, served as captain of the Richmond Light Dragoons, 1846-1849. Captain Christopher Quarles Tompkins, of the Richmond Light Dragoons, a West Point graduate of 1836 and veteran of the Seminole and Mexican wars, was elected lieutenant colonel. A prominent Richmond lawyer, Thomas P. August, was elected major. During the Mexican War, he had served as adjutant of the State's regiment of volunteers.

On May 29, 1851 the 1st Regiment held its first formation, on Broad Street opposite the City Hall, and marched to a nearby field for drill. The original companies of the regiment were: the Richmond Light Infantry Blues, Richmond Light Dragoons, Richmond Fayette Artillery, Richmond Grays, Montgomery Guard, Eagle Infantry, German Rifles, Young Guards, and the Caledonian Guards.

Throughout the decade before secession, the 1st Regiment was a familiar part of the Richmond scene. Public observances of national patriotic anniversaries were largely dependent upon a parade by the regiment. Rarely did the regiment fail to parade on January 8, the anniversary of the Battle of New Orleans; Washington's birthday anniversary; Fourth of July; and October 19, the anniversary of the surrender at Yorktown. The arrival of visiting dignitaries, dedications of monuments, funerals, and other civic-military events, were other occasions for the appearance of the 1st Regiment. In addition, there were meetings held for the instruction of officers and non-commissioned officers. Until 1856 these meetings were held at Lafayette Hall on Ninth Street, between Main and Franklin. After the building was razed to make way for the Mechanics Institute, the meetings took place at Military Hall, above the First Market, at Main and 17th streets. The companies of the regiment maintained their own armories or drill halls, met regularly for drill, and sponsored frequent social gatherings, which usually provided good copy for the local newspapers.

The composition of the 1st Regiment underwent considerable change from 1851 to 1861. In 1853 Colonel Gwynn resigned, and Major

August was elected colonel, a post he held until 1860. During the decade preceding the war, some of the companies were short-lived, and were disbanded because of a lack of interest, which failed to keep them up to the strength required by law. The first lettered designations for companies appear in 1856, when the regiment was organized as follows:

Co. A, Richmond Grays
Co. B, Young Guard (detached and reassigned 1857)
Co. C, Montgomery Guard
Co. D, Eagle Infantry (disbanded November 1856)
Co. E, Richmond Light Infantry Blues
Co. F, Richmond Fayette Artillery
Co. G, Continental Guard (disbanded 1857)
Co. H, Mechanics Guard (disbanded 1857)
Co. I, National Guard (disbanded 1858)
Co. K, Virginia Rifles (formerly German Rifles)

The regiment was comprised of seven companies when it turned out with other local militia units on July 5, 1858 to honor the reception of former President James Monroe's remains, which arrived in Richmond that day for reburial.

The year 1859 was one of significant changes in the regiment. Richmonders had marveled at the sight of the neat and uniform appearance of the 7th New York, which had visited the city on July 5, 1858 as an escort to Monroe's remains. Before the end of the month, a regimental uniform for the 1st Regiment was suggested, but the matter was dropped as the companies were "reluctant to give up their favorite and long established styles," which included gray, blue, and green uniforms. The 7th New York made quite an impression on Richmond, and the Daily Dispatch seldon missed an opportunity to cite the New Yorkers as the ideal pattern for the city's military. By the end of July 1859 two new companies had been added to the regiment, Captain Cary's Company F, and Captain English's Company G.

In October 1859, when the news of John Brown's raid reached Richmond, the Grays, Montgomery Guard, and the Young Guard (then attached to the 179th Regiment of Militia), were ordered by Governor Wise to leave on the 18th for Harpers Ferry. Captain Cary's Company F had accompanied the Governor to Harpers Ferry on the 17th. These companies, however, were soon returned to Richmond. Rumors of an attempt to free the prisoners at Charlestown became widespread; and on the evening of November 19, the following companies of the 1st Regiment left Richmond for duty at Charlestown: Richmond Grays, Richmond Light Infantry Blues, Company F, Montgomery Guard, the newly formed Howitzer company, and the Virginia Rifles. Company D, the Rocky Ridge Rifles, which was attached to the regiment in 1858, and the Fayette Artillery, were on the verge of disbandment, and were not included in the Richmond contingent. The immediate result of the John Brown episode, in Richmond, was the organization of new companies for the 1st Regiment, and the revival of the Fayette Artillery and the Rocky Ridge Rifles. The latter company, however, in late December 1859, was detached and assigned to the 23rd Regiment of Militia from Chesterfield County.

On April 19, 1860 at the dedication of the Henry Clay statue on Capitol Square, the regiment turned out with eight companies, totaling 439 men. The Fayette Artillery, which had just been reorganized, and Captain Randolph's Howitzers, were not fully uniformed and equipped so they did not parade. In April 1860, James B. Smith's Armory Band which had provided music for the regiment since 1853, was regularly enlisted in the 1st Regiment; and Sergeant Pohle of Company K was appointed regimental drum major, with instructions to form the musicians of the various companies into a regimental drum corps.

In September 1860, Captain Patrick T. Moore, of the Montgomery Guard, was elected to succeed Thomas P. August as colonel of the regiment. Colonel August had resigned following his appointment as brigadier general of the Second Brigade, Fourth Division, State Militia.

On the eve of Virginia's secession from the Union, the 1st Regiment was comprised of eleven companies, a band, and a drum corps. All companies were armed, and uniformed in gray. Four years previously, no two of the regiment's companies were dressed alike. By April 1, 1861 the 1st Regiment consisted of the following organizations:

    Co. A, Richmond Grays
    Co. B, Richmond City Guard
    Co. C, Montgomery Guard
    Co. D, Old Dominion Guard
    Co. E, Richmond Light Infantry Blues
    Co. F, Captain R. M. Cary's "F Company"
    Co. G, Captain William H. Gordon's company
    Co. H, Howitzer Company
    Co. I, Captain Robert Morris' company
    Co. K, Virginia Rifles
    Richmond Fayette Artillery
    1st Regiment Band
    Drum Corps

On April 19, 1861 Company A, Richmond Grays, enrolled for active service; and on the 21st, it left for Norfolk, where it was later assigned to the 12th Regiment Virginia Infantry as Company G. Companies B through K and the regiment's field officers enrolled for service on April 21. The Fayette Artillery, which was attached to the regiment without a lettered designation, was enrolled on April 25. This company was detached from the regiment, and was stationed at the Richmond College artillery barracks in May. Captain Randolph's Howitzers, Company H, went into quarters at the Spotswood Hotel on April 19, but soon moved to Richmond College, where they were detached from the 1st Regiment and reorganized into an artillery battalion. On April 24, Company E, the Richmond Light

Infantry Blues, and Captain Cary's Company F left Richmond for Fredericksburg, and were never returned to the 1st Regiment.

The ordinance passed by the State Convention on April 17 provided that all volunteer organizations would be mustered into State service by companies. Thus, the commissions of field officers in the 1st Regiment, and in the several other volunteer battalions and regiments that then existed, were vacated. Field officers were to be appointed by the Governor, rather than, as in the past, elected by the officers of the regiment or battalion. An exception, however, was made in the case of the 1st Regiment, when the Advisory Council of Virginia was warned that such a course of action would lead to the total disorganization of the regiment. In spite of this decision by the Council, the companies of the 1st Regiment were mustered into service separately, and the field officers were appointed by Governor Letcher. Colonel Moore was retained as regimental commander, and was commissioned on May 2.

On April 27 the regiment was assembled and marched to the Camp of Instruction at the New Fair Grounds (Camp Lee), on the western edge of Richmond. About May 4, Captain Francis J. Boggs' Richmond Grays No. 2, was assigned to the regiment, replacing the Howitzers as Company H. The long expected day arrived on May 25, when the 1st Regiment boarded the train to join the forces being assembled at Camp Pickens, Manassas Junction.

From the 2nd until the 21st of June, Companies B, D, G and K were on outpost duty at Fairfax Court House. On the 22nd, Captain Charles K. Sherman's company of volunteers, from the District of Columbia, was assigned to the regiment and designated as Company E, bringing the 1st Regiment up to eight companies present, and one, the Richmond Grays, on detached service.

The regiment experienced its baptism of fire at Blackburn's Ford on July 18, by which time it had been attached to Longstreet's Brigade. Colonel Moore was severely wounded, and the command of the regiment fell to Major Frederick G. Skinner, Lieutenant Colonel William H. Fry having left the field earlier because of sunstroke. At the battle of First Manassas, on July 21, the regiment was exposed to severe artillery fire, losing six men wounded, including Major Skinner. The 1st Regiment on July 18 and 21 had a total of nine killed and thirty-three wounded.

On July 23, Captain Frank B. Schaeffer's Beauregard Rifles, composed of Maryland volunteers, was assigned to the regiment, and designated as Company F. This brought the 1st Regiment up to the normal complement of ten companies; but after the Richmond Grays were attached to the 12th Regiment in August, the 1st Regiment became a nine-company unit. On September 7 the "Maryland Company" was detached and the 1st Regiment was reduced to eight companies.

The 1st Regiment went into winter quarters at Centreville on October 16, and remained there until March 8, 1862 when it moved with Ewell's Brigade, Longstreet's Division, to Warrenton. A month later the command left Louisa Court House; and on April 16 it marched through

Richmond, en route to join General Magruder's forces on the lower Peninsula. The 1st Regiment marched to Rocketts, the wharf in the east end of Richmond beyond the foot of 30th Street, where it embarked on the steamer Glen Cove, which took it down the James River to King's Mill Wharf, arriving there at 2:00 a.m. on the 17th. At 9:00 a.m., the regiment started on the march to the Yorktown lines, where on the 18th it was posted at Wynn's Mill. Here the regiment, exposed to heavy shelling, was occupied with picket duty and strengthening the fortifications.

On April 27, while near Yorktown, the 1st Regiment was reorganized, following the conclusion of its first term of enlistment on April 21. Lewis B. Williams was elected colonel, replacing Colonel Moore, who declined re-election; Lieutenant Colonel Frederick G. Skinner was re-elected; and 1st Lieutenant William P. Palmer was elected major, replacing Major John Dooley who, because of ill health, declined re-election. Company E was transferred to the 7th Regiment, and was disbanded shortly thereafter. Company K, the Virginia Rifles, was also disbanded. Thus the 1st Regiment was now reduced to six companies.

Yorktown was evacuated on May 3, and on the 5th, the regiment participated in the battle near Williamsburg. The regiment, posted on the right of Fort Magruder, captured an enemy battery of six guns. Colonel Williams was wounded and captured; and eight men were killed and thirty wounded. Early on May 6 the regiment left Williamsburg, reaching the Chickahominy at Long Bridge on the 9th. Here the regiment rested for six days. On April 27 the 1st Regiment was encamped near Howard's Grove, on the eastern outskirts of Richmond.

On May 31 the 1st Regiment, greatly reduced by absentees, fought with the brigade, then under Brigadier General James L. Kemper, in the Battle of Seven Pines. With fifteen killed and between thirty-five and fifty-four wounded, and many of the men absent, the 1st Regiment, after Seven Pines, virtually ceased to exist as an organization. About June 9, Captain James W. Tabb, of Company I, undertook the revivification of the regiment, which reported for duty with the brigade on June 27. The regiment was held in reserve during the Seven Days' fighting until June 30, when it crossed the Chickahominy and engaged the enemy at Frayser's Farm. The regiment was in reserve at Malvern Hill on July 1, and shortly afterwards, with only about thirty-nine men, went into camp near Richmond. On August 1, Major Palmer, who had been absent since he was wounded at Williamsburg, took charge of the regiment, which by the middle of August numbered only about 141 present for duty.

The regiment left Richmond on August 10 for Gordonsville, where it arrived that evening. Moving against Pope's army, the regiment, with Kemper's Brigade, commanded by Colonel Montgomery D. Corse, Longstreet's Corps, crossed the Rapidan; and on August 29 it was engaged at Groveton. On the 30th the regiment participated in the severe fighting of that day, when Colonel Skinner was wounded while sabering three of the enemy, receiving a bullet from each. He afterwards stated: "I hated to kill those brave men. How splendidly they stood by their guns." Colonel

Skinner's wounds were so severe that he was unfit for further service in the field. The regiment's casualties for the 29th and 30th of August totaled four killed and twenty-six wounded. Lee's army crossed the Potomac into Maryland, and on the 14th, the brigade was ordered to support Hill's Division at South Mountain, where the regiment had four wounded and two captured. On September 17 the regiment was engaged in the battle at Sharpsburg.

After Sharpsburg, the army recrossed the Potomac and went into camp near Winchester, where they remained for a month. On November 2 the regiment went into camp at Culpeper Court House and remained there until December 1, when it moved to the vicinity of Fredericksburg. On December 13, the day of Burnside's assault, the regiment was held in reserve until late in the afternoon when it was hurried to the support of troops in front of Marye's Heights. On December 25 the regiment went into winter quarters near Guiney's Station, on the Richmond Fredericksburg and Potomac Railroad, below Fredericksburg.

On February 14, 1863 it was learned that transports bearing Federal troops, suspected to be Burnside's IX Corps, were steaming down the Potomac. There was the probability that their destination was southeastern Virginia, with Richmond as the objective. Also, there was the possibility that the Federals might undertake an attack on the exposed Petersburg & Weldon Railroad, a vital supply line leading from North Carolina into Virginia. Kemper's Brigade, with Pickett's Division, was started for Richmond on February 15. They were soon followed by Hood's Division, and on February 17 General Longstreet was ordered south to command the two divisions.

On March 1, the 1st Regiment left Chester Station in Chesterfield County, marched through Petersburg, and went into camp near Prince George County Court House. The regiment was sent to Fort Powhatan on March 13 and on the 20th it marched to Petersburg, where the brigade entrained for Goldsboro, N. C., to strengthen Major General D. H. Hill's command. After reaching Goldsboro, the brigade was sent to Kinston, where it remained on guard while Hill moved out with the brigades of Garnett, Pettigrew and Daniel against Washington on the Pamlico River.

While General Hill was investing Washington, Kemper's Brigade was recalled by General Longstreet, who was planning a move against Suffolk. On April 4 the 1st Regiment left Kinston with the brigade, which proceeded by rail to Franklin Station, Virginia, where they arrived on the 9th. On April 11 the brigade marched to join Hood's Division in front of Suffolk, where they were engaged in constructing earthworks and picket duty until May 3, when Longstreet withdrew to join Lee's army on the Rappahannock. After a long and weary march, the 1st Regiment went into camp near Richmond on May 8, and remained there until the 13th, when it left for Taylorsville on the Richmond, Fredericksburg and Potomac Railroad in Hanover County.

The regiment, under Colonel Williams, who had been exchanged as a prisoner of war in August 1862, left Taylorsville on June 8 for Culpeper Court House, where it arrived on the 11th. On June 15, with Pickett's Division, it started on the march into Maryland and Pennsylvania. Crossing the Potomac on June 25, the regiment reached Chambersburg on the 27th. Here General Longstreet halted the corps for several days rest. Pickett's Division was left as a rear guard on the morning of June 30th when the corps resumed its march. On the morning of July 2, the division started for Gettysburg, and encamped near the town late that night. Pickett moved his command on to the battlefield on the morning of the 3rd.

At about 3:00 p.m., following the cannonading which had continued for about an hour and a half, the division was ordered to advance. Pickett's three brigades formed the right of the close lines of battle, which moved steadily toward the Federals on Cemetery Hill in the assault that came to be known as "Pickett's Charge." Kemper's Brigade was on the division's left, with the 1st Regiment forming its center. Colonel Williams, like most of the other field officers, was mounted, and rode in front of his regiment, presenting a conspicious target for enemy sharpshooters. Under the withering fire which met them on the slope of Cemetery Hill, the alignment of the brigades was lost. Two of Pickett's brigade commanders, Garnett and Armistead, were killed and the other, Kemper, was seriously wounded. Twelve of the fifteen regimental commanders were either killed or mortally wounded. Colonel Williams was struck down with a spinal wound from which he died four or five days later, after intense suffering. The regiment's remaining field officers, Lieutenant Colonel Frank H. Langley and Major George F. Norton, were wounded. Of the approximately 4,800 men and officers who went into action with the division, 2,800 were killed, wounded, missing or captured. The 1st Regiment suffered 120 casualties out of the 155 with which it entered the battle. The regiment lost all of its officers, killed or wounded, and only one, who was captured, survived the battle without injury. On July 4 the remnants of the 1st Regiment, under Sergeant Major R. McC. Jones, took charge of prisoners taken during the battle, and escorted them on the return march with the brigade to Williamsport, Md., where they were handed over to Brigadier General John D. Imboden of the cavalry on the 9th. Late on the evening of July 10 the 1st Regiment, with the 3rd and 24th regiments, crossed the Potomac River into Virginia.

On July 15, Kemper's Brigade, under the command of Colonel Joseph Mayo, Jr. of the 3rd Regiment, arrived at Bunker Hill, twelve miles north of Winchester, where it remained in camp until the 19th. The brigade marched through Culpeper Court House on July 24, and on August 3 went into camp near Mountain Run in Orange County. On September 8 the regiment left camp with the brigade, and marching through Gordonsville and Richmond, reached Chaffin's Farm east of the city on the 13th.

On September 23 the shattered division was detached from Longstreet's Corps to recuperate and recruit in the Department of North Carolina, of which General Pickett was made departmental commander with headquarters at Petersburg. Kemper's Brigade, under Colonel William R. Terry, was detached for duty with the Department of Richmond. On September 25 the 1st Regiment marched with the brigade to Richmond and boarded the train for Taylorsville, where it arrived the next day.

The regiment, with the brigade, left Taylorsville by rail on January 8, 1864 for Weldon, N. C., where it encamped for several days before leaving for Goldsboro. On January 29 the brigade left for Kinston, and from January 30 through February 3, participated in General Pickett's unsuccessful expedition against New Bern. In response to an appeal for re-enforcements by Major General William H. C. Whiting, commanding the Department of Cape Fear, the brigade left Goldsboro for Smithville (now Southport) on March 4. However, the brigade was soon recalled; and on March 23 the brigade was back in Goldsboro. On April 15 the brigade marched for Plymouth and from April 18-20, participated in Major General Robert F. Hoke's investment and capture of the town.

The regiment, under Major Norton, left Greenville, N. C., with the brigade on May 2 and boarded the train at Kinston for Virginia on the 9th. On May 16, Terry's Brigade, attached to Ransom's Division, participated in the Battle of Drewry's Bluff, in which the 1st Regiment lost ten killed and about twenty wounded. Two days later, the regiment was on duty at the battery near the Howlett House, where it was subjected to severe shelling by the enemy's gunboats in the James River. On the 19th the regiment was in position near the Clay House, and late in the evening it marched toward Richmond, reaching the city at dawn on the 20th. As the brigade marched through the streets, each regiment carried one of the flags captured during the previous fighting near Drewry's Bluff.

During the evening of May 20, part of the brigade, including a portion of the 1st Regiment, under Major Norton, boarded a train which took them to Milford Depot on the Richmond, Fredericksburg and Potomac Railroad above Hanover Junction (now Doswell). Here, on the 21st, the command engaged Torbert's cavalry, the advance of Grant's army moving from Spotsylvania Court House. The skirmish delayed the enemy long enough for Lee to reach Hanover Junction first. Major Norton's command fell in with the rear guard of Lee's forces on the morning of May 22, and marched to Hanover Junction, where they rejoined the brigade. After an absence of about eight months, the 1st Regiment, with the brigade and Pickett's Division, was back with Longstreet's Corps. Since May 6, when General Longstreet was wounded, the corps had been under Major General Richard H. Anderson.

On May 30 Pickett's Division moved toward Cold Harbor in support of Early's Corps, but soon abandoned the movement and went into position on Early's left. The division moved about two miles to the right on the 31st and remained there about a mile north of Gaines' Mill Pond, throughout the bitter fighting at Cold Harbor of June 1-3, which was on the division's right. On June 7 the 1st Regiment was engaged in skirmishing, and on the 12th was exposed to a severe enfilading fire from the enemy's artillery.

When it was discovered on the morning of June 13 that the Federals had left the Cold Harbor front, Longstreet's (Anderson's) Corps was put in motion. After crossing the Chickahominy at McClellan's Bridge, it marched by Seven Pines, and went into bivouac near the battlefield at Frayser's Farm. On June 16 the corps marched to Chaffin's Bluff and crossed the James River by pontoon bridge. Passing over the Drewry's Bluff battlegrounds, it moved in the direction of Petersburg. Near Port Walthall Junction the troops halted and formed a line of battle. During the ensuing fighting, the 1st Regiment had four wounded in the charge near the Clay House. The 1st Regiment remained with Pickett's Division on the lines near Swift Creek from June 19 until the 30th, doing guard and picket duty, and constructing earthworks. At this time most of Lee's forces, including two of the three divisions of Longstreet's (Anderson's) Corps, were in the lines at Petersburg.

On August 16 the 1st Regiment, with the 11th and 19th regiments, under Colonel Langley, moved out, crossed the James River and went into camp near Chaffin's Farm. Late on August 18 they relieved Wright's Brigade at Fussell's Mill, about eight miles east of Richmond on the Darbytown Road. Here part of the command worked on the fortifications, while the remainder stood guard. A small enemy force was discovered the next morning on the other side of the mill pond. Much to the astonishment of some militia held in reserve nearby, the opposing forces began an exchange of newspapers, coffee, and tobacco. The Federals were gone by the next morning, and Colonel Langley started his command on the return march to their camp near Port Walthall, which was reached late on the 20th. On September 14 the regiment moved to the rear, into a new line of works, erected huts, and went into winter quarters.

On January 8, 1865 the regiment moved to the left of the line near the Howlett House, remaining there until February 24 when they were sent to the right of the line near Swift Creek. While here the regiment received about eighty recruits. Of these, about twenty-eight were organized as Company K, under the command of Lieutenant William M. Lawson who, as color sergeant, had lost an arm at Gettysburg.

With the exception of a few skirmishes, all was quiet with the 1st Regiment until March 5, when the division, relieved by General Mahone's, was put into the field for active duty. A division review was held at Chester Station on March 8, and on the following day it marched to Manchester. On the 10th the division marched through Richmond to the outer line of works on Brook Road and then along the works to Nine Mile Road east of the city. On the following day, it returned to the defenses on Brook Road.

General Longstreet reviewed Pickett's Division on March 23 and on the 25th it marched to Richmond, where it took the train for Dunlop's Station above Petersburg. On March 29 the division was ordered to the right of the lines, west and beyond Petersburg. After crossing the Appomattox River on a pontoon bridge about five miles above Petersburg, the division proceeded to Sutherland's Tavern on the Cox Road. The division was again on the march by daybreak on March 30; and upon reaching Five Forks, via the Claiborne and White Oak roads, the 1st and 7th regiments were thrown out to drive off the advance elements of Sheridan's cavalry. On the morning of March 31 the division marched from Five Forks toward Dinwiddie Court House. Pickett moved his command across Chamberlayne's Bed, and drove a portion of Sheridan's forces back to within a mile of the court house. When Pickett learned that the Federal force concentrated in the area far outnumbered his own, he ordered the division back to Five Forks, where the night and most of the next day was spent in defense preparations.

On April 1 the first indication that Sheridan was nearing Five Forks was late in the afternoon, when skirmishers rushed back with the news that nearly all of Company C of the 1st Regiment had been captured. Sheridan launched his attack about 4:00 p.m., and by dark, Pickett's command had been overwhelmed. The 1st Regiment lost about eighty-five captured, one killed, and ten wounded. The remnants of the division fell back to the Southside Railroad, and early on the morning of April 2 marched about twelve miles to Exeter Mill on the Appomattox River, where they halted. During the night of April 2, the Confederates evacuated Richmond and Petersburg, retreating to Amelia Court House, which had been designated as the rendezvous for the troops from both cities.

The regiment, under Colonel Langley, reached Sayler's Creek with Pickett's command late during the night of April 5. In the battle of the next day, the division, with Ewell's forces, fought desperately against the overwhelming numbers of the enemy until they were surrounded and captured. Some of the division, including General Pickett, managed to escape. Of the 1st Regiment, only seventeen remained to be paroled with the army at Appomattox Court House.

Colonel Walter Gwynn
1st Regiment Virginia Volunteers
1851-1856

Commissioned as major general in Virginia's volunteer forces, Colonel Gwynn was in command of state troops at Norfolk from April 26, 1861 to May 23, 1861. He resigned from the Virginia service and served as brigadier general in North Carolina army until August 1861. Afterwards, as a civilian, he was employed as an engineer by the Confederate Bureau of Engineers.

From oil painting in Confederate Museum

Col. Lewis B. Williams, Jr.
1st Regiment Virginia Infantry
1862-1863

Mortally wounded at Gettysburg
July 3, 1863

Courtesy Confederate Museum

Col. Frederick Gustavus Skinner
1st Regiment Virginia Infantry

Colonel Skinner was promoted from major to lieutenant colonel November 1861, and colonel of the regiment August 25, 1863. Severe wounds received at the Battle of Second Manassas disabled him for service in the field.

From De Leon's Belles, Beaux and Brains of the 60's. Courtesy of the Virginia State Library.

## 1ST REGIMENT VIRGINIA INFANTRY

### FIELD AND STAFF

Colonel
Moore, Patrick T.
Skinner, Frederick G.
Williams, Louis B., Jr.

Lieutenant Colonel
Fry, William H.
Langley, Frank H., Co. G.

Major
Dooley, John, Co. C.
Mumford, William P.
Norton, George F., Co. D.
Offutt, George W., Co. E.
Palmer, William H., Co. D.

Adjutant
Fry, William T.
Stockton, John N. C.

Cadet
Mercer, Thomas H.

Assistant Quartermaster
Allan, William G.

Surgeon
Cullen, J. S. D.
Grigsby, A. S.
Hinton, John R.

Assistant Surgeon
Butler, M. A.
Matthews, Thomas P.
Maury, Thomas F.
Sergeant, Henry H.

Sergeant Major
Harvie, William O.
Jones, Robert McC., Cos.C&D
Polak, Jacob, Co. I.
Simpson, Andrew J., Co. D.

Quartermaster Sergeant
Dean, William H.Co. B.
Grohnwald, Charles E.
Haake, Gerhard J., Co. K.

Ordinance Sergeant
Hudgins, Elias P., Co. G.

Assistant Commissary of Subsistence

Harney, Henry

Chaplain

Aldridge, W. A.
Harrold, J. R.
Martin, J. Edward

# 1ST REGIMENT VIRGINIA INFANTRY

## COMPANY B

### RICHMOND CITY GUARD

Organized in December 1860 as the "Fireside Protectors," this company of light infantry under Captain T. J. Cropper, was designated in the 1st Regiment as Company B by January 2, 1861, replacing Company B which had ceased to exist by the end of 1860. The new Company B held its drills at the Mechanics Institute; and about January 20 the company name was changed to the Richmond City Guard. In early February, James K. Lee was elected captain. Lee's Riflemen, as the company was sometimes called, was enrolled for active service on April 21, and was mustered into State service on the 24th for twelve months. The company, although mustered into service as riflemen, was armed at this time with Springfield .69 calibre smoothbore muskets.

1st Lieutenant Samuel P. Mitchell was appointed adjutant of the 1st Regiment on April 27; and from June 1-21, when Companies B, D, G, and K were at Fairfax Court House, 2nd Lieutenant William Wirt Harrison served as adjutant of the provisional battalion. At the end of June, the company had four officers, four sergeants, four corporals, and fifty-three privates, present for duty. On July 18, at Blackburn's Ford, Captain Lee was mortally wounded, one private was killed and Lieutenant Harrison and three others were wounded. The company suffered no casualties on July 21.

Captain Randolph Harrison, formerly a lieutenant in the Richmond Grays, was in command of Company B from August 5, 1861 until his resignation on April 27, 1862. He was subsequently commissioned as captain of cavalry, and served as an aide on the staff of Brigadier General Montgomery D. Corse. 1st Lieutenant Mitchell was promoted to captain and appointed as division quartermaster. 2nd Lieutenant James W. Archer was elected first lieutenant, and on October 14, 1861 was transferred to the regular army of the Confederate States. 2nd Lieutenant Harrison was elected first lieutenant to replace Lieutenant Mitchell. At the end of October 1861, Company B had three officers and forty-seven enlisted men present for duty.

At Williamsburg on May 5, 1862, Company B had three killed and four wounded, one mortally. On May 31, 1862, at Seven Pines, the company lost one killed and nine wounded, one of whom, 2nd Lieutenant Francis M. Mann, later died. Among the wounded was Captain T. Herbert Davis, who had been elected to replace Captain Harrison. 1st Lieutenant Logan S. Robins was wounded at Malvern Hill, and on July 22, 1862, the company had only one officer and twenty-four enlisted men present for duty. Company B, under Captain Davis, went into battle at Second Manassas on August 30, 1862 with a total strength of only fourteen, and lost two killed and six wounded.

Captain Davis was wounded and captured at Gettysburg on July 3, 1863. After six months imprisonment on Johnson's Island, he escaped and rejoined his company in 1864. During his absence, the company was commanded by Lieutenant Robins. At the end of August 1864 the company, under Lieutenant Robins, had three officers and twenty-three enlisted men present for duty. Two men were on detached service, two were prisoners of war, seven were sick, and eleven were absent without leave.

Captain Davis and seven members of Company B were captured at Sayler's Creek on April 6. Only four men of the company were paroled at Appomattox Court House.

Courtesy Confederate Museum

Pickett's Charge at Gettysburg
By A. R. Waud

# RICHMOND CITY GUARD

## CAPTAINS

Davis, Thomas H.  Harrison, Randolph  Lee, James K.

## LIEUTENANTS

Archer, James W., 1st Lieut.
Cobb, James H., 2nd Lieut.
Harrison, William Wirt, 1st Lieut.
Mann, Frances M., 2nd Lieut.
Mitchell, Samuel P., Adj.1st Lieut.
Payne, Jesse Armistead, 2nd Lieut.
Robins, Logan S., 1st Lieut.

## NON-COMMISSIONED OFFICERS AND PRIVATES

Acre, Thomas Drummer
Allen, John E., Pvt.
Armstrong, J.,
Austin, William G., Pvt.
Bacon, W. E., Pvt.
Beale, Charles D. Pvt.
Beale, John H., Pvt.
Blankship, William H.
Bodeker, George H., Pvt.
Bohannan, William A., Pvt.
Boltz, Augustus, Pvt.
Boltz, Henry, Pvt.
Boyden, James J., Pvt.
Brooks, Lafayette, Pvt.
Brown, Theophilus, Pvt.
Buchannan, Mungo P., Corpl.
Burnett, John W., Pvt.
Byron, John, Pvt.
Carson, Thomas
Carter, C. C., Pvt.
Carter, William Irvin, Corpl.
Cawthorn, W. J., Pvt.
Charles, John H., Pvt.
Childrey, John H., Pvt.
Clarke, John T., Sgt.
Conroy, John, Pvt.
Crigger, William H., Pvt.
Crow, Benjamin M., Sgt.
Dandridge, William H., Pvt.
Daniels, J. H., Pvt.
Daniels, J. R., Pvt.
Davis, Bengal T., Pvt.
Davis, Richard T., Pvt.
Dean, William H., Q.M.Sgt.,F&S
Delmonti, Louis, Pvt.
Doll, John, Pvt.
Dove, W.A., Pvt.
Drinkwater, R. C., Pvt.
Duffner, Joseph, Pvt.
Duncan, William M., Pvt.
Earnest, George, Pvt.
Earnest, Nathaniel T., 2nd Corpl.
Embry, David M.
Emory, D. M., Pvt.
Euker, Charles, Pvt.
Evans, Henry J., Pvt.
Ferslew, William Eugene, Sgt.
Figg, John Q., Sgt.
Ford, Fkenubg, Pvt.
Francis, Thomas, Pvt.
Frankenthall, Simon, Pvt.
Franklin, Fendall, Pvt.
Garrett, John R., Pvt.
Goddin, Gustavus Giles, Corpl.
Goodwin, J. E., Pvt.
Gotze, Ernst Augst, Pvt.
Gravett, William J., Pvt.
Gray, Howard, Pvt.
Gray, W. M., Pvt.
Green, James A., Pvt.
Guy, John H., Pvt.
Hancock, G. C., Pvt.
Hankins, James F., Pvt.
Harlow, T. G., Pvt.
Harris, Porter W., Pvt.
Hartman, Fred W., Pvt.
Hay, Hampden Pleasants, Pvt.
Hazelwood, John, Pvt.
Heath, George R., Pvt.
Hitchcock, Robert F., Pvt.
Hoch, A., Pvt.
Hudgins, J. A., Pvt.
Jacob, John Jr., Pvt.
Jones, William A., Pvt.

Jordan, Pleasants, Pvt.
Kayton, Herman H., Pvt.
Kessler, J., Pvt.
Kessler, Nathaniel, Pvt.
Lakeman, Richard, Pvt.
Littlepage, John L., 1st Sgt.
Loehr, Fred, Pvt.
Lumpkin, William J., Jr., Pvt.
Lutz, Frederick, Pvt.
Lyneman, Anthony H., Pvt.
Lytle, William A., Pvt.
Mallory, William J., Pvt.
Martin, R. M., Pvt.
Matthews, J., Pvt.
Matthews, John C., Pvt.
McDaniel, J., Pvt.
Melton, P. W., Sgt.
Mesco, John, Pvt.
Meyer, Max, Pvt.
Mills, Robert N., Pvt.
Mitchell, Charles, Corpl.
Morrisson, R., Pvt.
Moss, Peter, Pvt.
Mountcastle, Oliver, Pvt.
Mountjoy, John, Pvt.
Mullen, William H., Corpl
Noel, B. D., Pvt.
O'Brien, Patrick, Pvt.
Ogden, Lewis W., Sgt.
Otey, Edward T., Pvt.
Overstreet, John P., Pvt.
Parler, William H., Sgt.
Pinchbeck, T. W., Pvt.
Pledge, Joseph W., Pvt.
Pollard, Robert J., Pvt.
Pool, J. A., Pvt.
Ratcliffe, John W., Pvt.
Reid, Robert, Pvt.
Richards, Charles E., Pvt.
Roberts, Philip S., Pvt.
Rooney, Arthur J., Pvt.
Saunders, J. W., Pvt.
Schadd, Adam, Pvt.

Schernborn, Charles E., Pvt.
Shiflett, J. T.
Silver, Henry, Pvt.
Simms, R., Pvt.
Smith, Adam, Pvt.
Smith, J. R., Pvt.
Smith, J. S., Pvt.
Smith, J. W., Pvt.
Smith, Thomas, Pvt.
Snyder, John F., Pvt.
Spickard, H. L., Pvt.
Spratley, J. M., Pvt.
Stagg, James, Pvt.
Stoaber, William A., Corpl.
Storie, W., Pvt.
Stratton, Thomas E., Pvt.
Straus, Robert, Pvt.
Street, Richard H., Pvt.
Strom, Lewis H., Corpl.
Sullings, G. L., Pvt.
Sutliffe, James, Pvt.
Tate, James, Pvt.
Taylor, James, Pvt.
Terry, John, Pvt.
Tilghman, George M., Pvt.
Toomey, Jerry, Pvt.
Totty, Robert T., Pvt.
Tower, Isaac S., Pvt.
Turner, G. M., Pvt.
Tyler, W. E., Pvt.
Vermillera, Philip J., Pvt.
Weinburg, Matthew J., Pvt.
Wells, J. P., Pvt.
West, Francis A., Pvt.
West, George L., Pvt.
Whiting, Levin A., Pvt.
Willey, John, Pvt.
Wilson, John
Wilson, John W., Pvt.
Wolfe, Henry, Pvt.
Wong, Wendel, Pvt.
Wright, John T., Pvt.

# 1ST REGIMENT VIRGINIA INFANTRY

## COMPANY C

## MONTGOMERY GUARD

The Montgomery Guard, recruited from the Irish citizenry of Richmond, is reputed to have been organized in September 1849; however, the company observed its anniversary in January of each year. The company, originally attached to the 179th Regiment of Militia, was one of the original companies that were organized into the 1st Regiment of Virginia Volunteers in May 1851.

Commissioned on July 10, 1850, Captain Patrick T. Moore commanded the Montgomery Guard throughout the decade preceding the outbreak of the Civil War. The company was one of the most active in the regiment, and, unlike others, it seems to have never been threatened with disbandment through lack of interest. It always made a good showing at regimental parades, and on other occasions when the city's military was called out.

Each year the Montgomery Guard held a civic-military ball to commemorate the anniversary of the company's organization. After the annual parade on the Fourth, the Guards customarily adjourned to some secluded spot for a dinner and entertainment. In 1856 they went to Griffin's Springs on Chimborazo Heights. The company engaged for this occasion Winston's Black Band, the "only one in the city." Dinner was served, innumerable toasts were drunk, speeches were made, songs were sung, and the <u>Daily Dispatch</u> reported that the Guards "had a fine time of it."

In 1850 the company adopted a uniform consisting of a single-breasted green coatee with three rows of brass Virginia buttons down the front, and a buff cassimere collar and cuff slashings, ornamented with buttons and gold lace. Sky-blue pantaloons, with a buff stripe down the outer seam, were worn with the winter dress and plain white pantaloons were worn in the summer. The company had a green cloth-covered cap with a buff cassimere band. The brass letters "M.G." encircled by a wreath of shamrock and both surmounted by an eagle, were worn on front of the cap. The cock's feathers plume was white tipped with green, and the pompons, which were worn on occasions, were buff worsted with a green upper half. The company's accoutrements were comprised of a white patent leather waist belt fastened in front with a gilt clasp bearing the letters "M. G."; bayonet scabbards with gilt tops; cap boxes, presumably white; and white musket slings. This distinctive dress was worn until July 5, 1859 when the company, for the first time, appeared in their new gray uniforms.

The company, numbering about fifty, was among the Richmond troops sent to Harpers Ferry and Charlestown in October and November

1859. The <u>Richmond</u> <u>Whig</u>, on December 6, noted that many members of the company returned to the city with John Brown pikes as souvenirs. On January 11, 1860 Lieutenant John Dooley, an officer in the company since at least 1852, was elected captain, replacing Captain Moore, who had been elected colonel of the 1st Regiment. In March 1861 the Montgomery Guard celebrated Saint Patrick's Day for the last time in Richmond. Preceded by the regiment's band, the company marched to Hattorff's garden, where "the day was spent most pleasantly."

On April 21, 1861 the company, totaling about ninety-eight officers and men, enrolled for active service and was mustered into state service on the 25th as a light infantry company for a term of twelve months. In age, the company's officers were apparently among the oldest line officers of the regiment. Captain Dooley was fifty; 1st Lieutenant David King, thirty-five; 2nd Lieutenant William English, forty-two; and 2nd Lieutenant Michael Seagers, forty-four. All of them were merchants in civilian life.

At the outset, the company had their own uniforms and accoutrements; but with the increase in strength, a supply of cartridge boxes, cap pouches, bayonet scabbards, and knapsacks were issued to them by the state. By the end of June 1861 the company was in need of new uniforms.

Company C was engaged with the regiment at Blackburn's Ford on July 18, 1861, and had seven, including Lieutenant English, wounded, and of these, one died a few days later. One member of the company was wounded on July 21.

In November 1861, Captain Dooley was elected major of the regiment, and Lieutenant English was elected as his successor. When the company reorganized on April 27, 1862, Lieutenant James Mitchell was elected captain. The company at the end of April 1862 had four officers and twenty-one enlisted men present for duty. Forty-three men were carried on the muster roll for this period as absent without leave. Captain Mitchell was later transferred to Gordon's Brigade as assistant adjutant general.

The company had five men, including Lieutenant James Hollinan, wounded and one killed at Williamsburg on May 5, 1862; and at Seven Pines on May 31, lost one killed and one wounded. At the end of June 1862 the company was reduced to two officers and nine enlisted men present for duty; sixty-two enlisted men were carried on the muster roll for this period as absent without leave. Lieutenant Hollinan was promoted to captain in August 1862 and served until July 3 when he was mortally wounded and captured at Gettysburg. The company lost sixteen wounded and captured in the attack of the 3rd. Captain Hollinan died a few days after the battle and 1st Lieutenant John Dooley, son of Major Dooley, who had retired because of ill health in April 1862, was elected captain, although at the time he was among the captured.

On July 9, 1863, Sergeant R. McC. Jones, regimental sergeant major, and formerly of Company D, was promoted to 2nd lieutenant of

Company C for gallantry displayed on the field at Gettysburg. Lieutenant Jones was in command of the company until the end. Captain Dooley was released on parole in March 1865 and visited his old command at Petersburg; but as a paroled prisoner, he could not take up arms until after his exchange, which was prevented by the surrender in April. Only one man of Company C, Private J. N. Johnson, was present among those that were paroled at Appomattox Court House.

Courtesy Library of Congress
Brigadier General Patrick T. Moore

Served as captain of Montgomery Guard 1850-1860. Elected colonel of 1st Regiment Virginia Volunteers in 1860. Severely wounded at First Manassas, he declined re-election as colonel of the regiment in 1862. In 1864 he was appointed brigadier general and at the close of the war was in command of a brigade of local defense troops at Richmond.

# MONTGOMERY GUARD

## CAPTAINS

Dooley, John E.
English, Willian

Hallinan, James
Mitchell, James.

## LIEUTENANTS

Donahue, John H., Bvt. 2nd Lieut.
Jones, Robert McC., 2nd Lieut. Co D,& F&S
King, David, 1st Lieut.

Seagers, Michael, 2nd Lieut.
Sullivan, John, 1st Lieut.

## NON-COMMISSIONED OFFICERS AND PRIVATES

Ahern, Cornelius, Pvt.
Akens, William, Pvt.
Bell, Jeremiah, Pvt.
Bernstein, Nathaniel, Pvt.
Boland, John, Pvt.
Bondurant, William, Pvt.
Bresnaham, Mathew, Pvt. Co H.
Brock, William H., Pvt.
Buckley, William, Pvt.
Burke, William J., Corpl.
Burns, Thomas, Pvt.
Burns, Timothy C., Sgt.
Burton, William G., Pvt.
Byrnes, Edward, Sgt.
Carey, Miles H., Pvt.
Carr, Thomas V., Pvt.
Carroll, Lawrence, Corpl.
Casey, Martin, Pvt.
Casey, Patrick, Pvt.
Clark, J. D., Pvt.
Clark, Willis, Pvt.
Clarke, James D., Pvt.
Clifford, Thomas C., Pvt.
Collins, Hillery W., Pvt.
Collins, Thomas, Pvt.
Collins, William G., Pvt.
Conley, William, Pvt.
Connor, James, Pvt.
Consadine, Michael, Pvt.
Corcoran, James W., Pvt.
Costello, Timothy, Corpl.
Creamer, Patrick, Pvt.
Crenshaw, William H., Pvt.

Cummings, Patrick, Pvt.
Dailey, Michael, Pvt.
Davis, Eli M., Pvt.
Dennis, James, Pvt.
Deskin, William H., Pvt.
Dooley, James, H., Pvt.
Dornin, Michael B., Sgt.
Dove, John C., Pvt.
Driscoll, James W., Pvt.
Duffy, Patrick, Pvt.
Dunn, James, Pvt.
Edwards, James, Pvt.
Enright, Michael, Pvt.
Ewell, Robert, Pvt.
Fagan, James, Pvt.
Farrar, Thomas E., Pvt.
Fenton, Roger, Pvt.
Finnerty, John, Pvt.
Fitzgerald, Edward, Pvt.
Fleming, Michael, Pvt.
Forsythe, Andrew W., Pvt.
Frawlwy, John, Pvt.
Gaffney, Lawrence, Pvt.
Gannon, Alfred, Pvt.
Gentry, William H., Pvt.
Giblin, James, Pvt.
Giles, Richard, Pvt.
Gillespie, Samuel H., Pvt.
Goulder, John H., Pvt.
Gravely, Jabez M., Pvt.
Griffin, John, Pvt.
Haley, John, Pvt.
Haley, Patrick, Pvt.

Hallowell, William H., Pvt.
Hamilton, John, Pvt.
Hargraves, Benjamin L., Pvt.
Harrington, Patrick, Pvt.
Hassett, Patrick, Pvt.
Higgins, Daniel, Pvt.
Hoare, James, Pvt.
Hollingsworth, R. P., Pvt.
Hughes, Michael, Pvt.
Hutchison, William, Pvt.
Ingram, William P., Pvt.
Johnson, George A., Pvt.
Johnson, John N., Pvt.
Jones, Abram, Pvt.
Joyce, John, Corpl.
Kavanagh, John, Pvt.
Kean, Charles, Sgt.
Kearney, Michael, Pvt.
Keating, Patrick, Pvt.
Kehoe, Michael, Pvt.
Keiley, John D., Pvt.
Kenney, Joseph, Pvt.
Kieley, John D., Pvt.
Landers, Richard, Pvt.
Larkins, Martin, Pvt.
Lisofke, Otto, Pvt.
Mahoney, Martin, Pvt.
Maideon, E. R., Pvt.
Marooney, Patrick, Pvt.
McArdle, George, Pvt.
McCabe, Lawrence, Pvt.
McCarthy, Daniel, Pvt.
McCary, Benjamin J., Pvt.
McCauley, Peter, Corpl.
McCrossen, James, Pvt.
McDonald, John, 1st Sgt.
McGee, Patrick, Pvt.
McGowan, John, Pvt.
McGrady, William E., Pvt.
McMahan, John, Pvt.
McMahon, Stephen, Pvt.
McMullen, James, Pvt.
McNanara, Francis, Pvt.
McRickards, Samuel, Pvt.
Miles, W. D., Pvt.
Miller, Charles E., Pvt.
Moore, William, Pvt.
Moriarty, John, Sgt.
Murphy, James, Pvt.
Murphy, John, Pvt.
Murphy, Michael, Pvt.
Murphy, Thomas, Pvt.
Neagle, Thomas, Pvt.

Nobles, Benjamin R., Pvt.
Noel, F. R., Pvt.
Nolan, Michael, Pvt.
Noonan, Patrick, Pvt.
Nottin, L., Pvt.
OBryan, Patrick, Pvt.
O'Gorman, Owen, Pvt.
O'Keefe, Arthur, Pvt.
O'Keefe, John, Pvt.
Pinnell, George A. J., Pvt.
Plunkett, Hugh, Pvt.
Pollard, George W., Pvt.
Potts, Francis, 1st Sgt.
Powell, Alex E., Pvt.
Price, Richard C., Corpl.
Prince, George W., Pvt.
Purcell, Timothy, Pvt.
Rainey, Calvin, Pvt.
Rankin, James, Pvt.
Rankin, Patrick, Sgt.
Rankin, Timothy, Corpl.
Redmond, Michael, Pvt.
Ryan, Thomas, 1st Sgt.
Ryan, William, Corpl.
Schammel, John H., Pvt.
Seay, A. G., Pvt.
Self, George R., Pvt.
Shortell, Michael, Pvt.
Sloan, Samuel H., Pvt.
Smeltzer, J. H., Pvt.
Stack, Garrett, Pvt.
Sullivan, Daniel, Pvt.
Sullivan, Henry, Sgt.
Sullivan, Patrick, Pvt.
Thomas, James, Pvt.
Thorpe, James A., Pvt.
Tillman, James, Pvt.
Tompkins, John, Pvt.
Trueman, Jackson, Pvt.
Tyrell, Patrick, Pvt.
Walter, Robert P., Pvt.
Warrolow, Joseph, Pvt.
White, E. L., Pvt.
Whittaker, Joseph L., Pvt.
Williams, A. L., Pvt.
Williams, Abram J., Pvt.
Woods, Joseph, Pvt.
Woods, Patrick, Sgt.
Wormack, Castine
Worrell, William J. G., Pvt.
Wright, E. A., Pvt.
Youell, Robert, Pvt.

1ST REGIMENT VIRGINIA INFANTRY

COMPANY D

OLD DOMINION GUARD

Organized in March 1861, the Old Dominion Guard, under Captain Joseph W. Griswold, a 26-year old Richmond lawyer, was designated in the 1st Regiment as Company D, replacing the Guard of the Metropolis, which had dissolved by February 1861.

Captain Griswold's company enrolled for active service on April 27, at which time the company was only partially uniformed and equipped. The Alexandria, Va., Gazette, on April 29, reported that the company had been mustered into service and appointed as the "Governor's Body Guard." Details, however, on this designation are not clear; presumably, it was purely honorary. The company's roll at this time included Sergeant Edwin H. Chamberlayne, Jr., author of a series of pamphlets containing rosters of Richmond and Henrico companies, which were published in 1879; and 18-year old Private Charles T. Loehr, author of the War History of the Old First Virginia, published in 1884.

On June 30, 1861 when the regiment was at Camp Pickens, the Old Dominion Guard numbered three officers and fifty-four enlisted men present for duty. Uniformed in gray caps, jackets, and pants, the company was armed with Springfield percussion muskets.

When Company D reorganized at the expiration of its term of enlistment on April 26, 1862, 2nd Lieutenant George F. Norton was elected captain. The company's first lieutenant, William H. Palmer, who had served as adjutant of the 1st Regiment, was elected major on April 27, 1862.

Near the end of December 1862, when they were at Fredericksburg, the company had three officers and its ranks had dwindled down to twenty-one privates present for duty. About eleven men were away on detached service, ten were absent without leave and eleven were absent sick.

At Gettysburg on July 3, Company D had ten wounded, including all four of its officers, and nine captured. Effective on the same date, were the promotions of the company's officers. Captain Norton was promoted to major of the 1st Regiment, 1st Lieutenant E. P. Reeve was made captain of Company D, and 2nd Lieutenant William H. Kenningham was promoted to 1st Lieutenant.

On April 30, 1864 the company, under Captain Reeve, numbered one officer and twenty-seven enlisted men present for duty. There was no drastic reduction in Company D's strength until March 31, 1865, when ten men were captured near Dinwiddie Court House. Only four of the company were present for the surrender at Appomattox Court House.

Charles T. Loehr
1st Regiment Virginia Infantry
1861-1865   Company D

Wounded twice in 1864, he was a sergeant when the war ended. After the war, Loehr served as the secretary and treasurer, 1st Va. Infantry Association and wrote the War History of the Old First Virginia. Died 1915.

Springfield Hall

Located at M & 26th Streets in Richmond, the hall was built in 1850 by Springfield Lodge, Sons of Temperance. It is the only known surviving meeting place of antebellum military companies in the area. Used as a hospital during the war, it now serves as a church.

## OLD DOMINION GUARD

### CAPTAINS

Dooley, John E., Co. C. F&S
Griswold, Joseph G.
Norton, George F., F&S
Reeve, Edward P.

### LIEUTENANTS

Blair, Adolphus, 2nd Lieut.
Blanton, Lee M., 2nd Lieut.
Harney, Henry, 2nd Lieut. F&S.
Keiningham, William H., 1st Lieut.
Palmer, William H., 1st Lieut. F&S

### NON-COMMISSIONED OFFICERS AND PRIVATES

Andrews, J. N., Pvt.
Angle, James, B., Pvt.
Armstrong, William J., Pvt.
Bass, William U., Pvt.
Bates, Joseph W., Pvt.
Beasley, R., Pvt.
Belesario, E., Pvt.
Blankenship, Reuben, Pvt.
Bottoms, Samuel D., Pvt.
Boucher, Henry, Pvt.
Bowe, H. C., Pvt.
Bowe, N. W., Pvt.
Braton, J. G., Musician
Breeden, William F., Pvt.
Brown, Valentine, Jr., Pvt.
Bryant, J. B., Pvt.
Burton, Harrison W., Pvt.
Burton, Robert C., Pvt.
Cardoza, Julian C., Pvt.
Chamberlayne, Edwin H., 1st Sgt.
Chockley, William E., Pvt.
Collier, Edward J., Pvt.
Costican, J. M., Pvt.
Craig, George E., Sgt.
Crenshaw, Thomas E., Pvt.
Crowe, George W., Sgt.
Dabney, Virginius, Corpl.
Davis, T. S., Pvt.
Denigri, John B., Pvt.
Doyle, Benjamin H., Drummer
Draper, Jackson, Pvt.
Edwards, David S., Pvt.
Farmer, John T., Pvt.
Ferneyhough, Edward M., Corpl.
Ferneyhough, Edward S., Pvt.
Finn, James M., Sgt.
Foushee, D. R., Pvt.
Fox, A., Pvt.
Freeman, J. W., Pvt.
Frith, Joseph A., Pvt.
Fuqua, Peter, Pvt.
Furcron, Henry W., Pvt.
Gallagher, James B., Pvt.
Garrett, Benjamin K., Pvt.
Gianini, F. W., Pvt.
Govan, Archy, Pvt.
Hackman, B. F., Pvt.
Haley, T. H., Pvt.
Harris, Hezekiah, Pvt.
Hendrick, J. P., Pvt.
Howard, Joseph W., Pvt.
Howard, Thomas A., Pvt.
Howry, John W., Pvt.
Jarvis, D. A., Pvt.
Jennings, John C., Sgt.
Johnson, George W., Pvt.
Jones, Edris B., Pvt.
Jones, Robert McC., Co. C, F&S
Keiningham, J. C., Pvt.
Keplar, John H., 1st Sgt.
King, Edward H., Pvt.
Lechler, A. F., Pvt.
Lee, George W., Pvt.
Lee, John W., Pvt.
Lewis, J. A., Pvt.
Lipscomb, John T., Pvt.
Logan, George, Pvt.
Loher, Charles T., Corpl.

Mahane, W. P., Pvt.
Mayo, David C., Pvt.
McMillan, Thomas, Pvt.
McMinn, Delaware, Pvt.
Meanley, George L., Pvt.
Melson, Charles, L., Pvt.
Meyer, Louis V., Pvt.
Miles, Marion, Pvt.
Miller, Edward R., Pvt.
Mitchel, William, Pvt.
Mitchell, George W., Pvt.
Mitchell, J. H.,
Morris, William A., 1st Sgt.
Morton, Tazewell S., Pvt.
Moss, Alexander, Pvt.
Moss, R., Pvt.
O'Hare, T., Pvt.
Peachy, Thomas G., Pvt.
Peake, William, Pvt.
Pearman, R. A., Pvt.
Perrin, J. P., Sgt.
Perrin, John H., Pvt.
Pettit, Corbin L., Pvt.
Pizzini, Andrew, Pvt.
Porter, Isaac T., Pvt.
Porter, William L., Pvt.
Prendergast, E. M., Pvt.
Priddy, E., Pvt.
Quarles, John T., Pvt.
Redman, Robert H., Pvt.
Richeson, William, Pvt.
Roberts, T. B., Pvt.
Robertson, Theoderick J., Pvt.
Robinson, William, Pvt.
Ross, J. R., Pvt.

Samanni, Francis R., Pvt.
Saunders, J., Pvt.
Simpson, Andrew J., Pvt. F&S.
Smith, L. R., Pvt.
Smither, Joseph W., Pvt.
Steger, A. G. Jr., Pvt.
Steger, J. R., Pvt.
Stewart, C., Pvt.
Stewart, William H., Pvt.
Strausburdger, Henry, Pvt.
Sublett, Chasteen M., Pvt.
Traylor, Thomas, Pvt.
Turner, William W., Pvt.
Vanatter, J., Pvt.
Van Riper, John, Pvt.
Waddy, George T., Pvt.
Wagoner, D. B., Pvt.
Walthall, Howard M., Pvt.
Watson, H. W., Pvt.
Westmoreland, W. A., Pvt.
Wheat, N. F., Pvt.
Wheeler, C. H., Pvt.
Wheely, John F., Pvt.
White, John, Pvt.
Wilkes, W. C., Pvt.
Wilkins, W. R., Pvt.
Williams, C. C., Pvt.
Wingfield, L. R., Pvt.
Wingfield, M. J., Pvt.
Wingfield, S. L., Pvt.
Wingo, Charles E., Pvt.
Womack, J. T., Pvt.
Word, B. H., Pvt. Co I
Wren, Powhattan S., Pvt.

## 1ST REGIMENT VIRGINIA INFANTRY

## COMPANY G

Organized at Springfield Hall, at M and 26th Streets, in July 1859, this company was comprised of volunteer militiamen from Church and Union Hills. Within a week or so after its organization, the company, under Captain Joseph J. English, was designated in the 1st Regiment as Company G. The company was not among the Richmond units sent to Harpers Ferry and Charlestown in 1859, presumably because it had not been fully organized and equipped. On April 19, 1860 the company, numbering forty-three men uniformed in gray, paraded with the regiment at the dedication of the Henry Clay statue on Capitol Square. By January 1861, William H. Gordon, a 32-year-old Richmond merchant, had been elected as captain of the company. On April 21, 1861 the company enrolled for active service and was mustered into State service on the 27th for a period of twelve months.

On June 30, 1861, when the regiment was at Camp Pickens, Company G had four officers and eighty enlisted men present for duty. The company, on July 18, lost 2nd Lieutenant Humphrey H. Miles and two privates killed, and five others wounded.

When Company G reorganized near Yorktown on April 26, 1862, 1st Lieutenant Frank H. Langley was elected captain and 2nd Lieutenant Eldridge Morris was promoted to 1st Lieutenant. The company, at the end of April 1862, had three officers and sixty-eight enlisted men present for duty.

In June 1863, Captain Langley was promoted as major of the 1st Regiment; and in July, 1st Lieutenant Morris was promoted as captain of the company. Major Langley was promoted to lieutenant colonel in July 1863 and, after the death of Colonel Williams, commanded the regiment until the end of the war.

Company G, at the end of February 1864, had two officers and twenty-nine enlisted men present for duty. The rolls show that at this time four men were on extra duty, five were on detached service, nine were absent sick, one was absent with leave, and nine were prisoners of war.

There was no appreciable decrease in company strength until near the surrender, when the company disintegrated. Six members of the company are recorded as being captured at Sayler's Creek on April 6. There were no members of Company G among the few who were paroled from the regiment at Appomattox Court House.

# COMPANY G

## CAPTAINS

Gordon, William H.    Langley, Frank H., F&S.    Morris, Eldridge

## LIEUTENANTS

McDonald, John, 2nd Lieut.
Miles, Humphrey H., 2nd Lieut.
Riddick, James E., 1st Lieut.
Shell, Leonidas R., 2nd Lieut.

Tucker, Atticus J., 2nd Lieut.
Tucker, Sylvester J., 1st Lieut.
Woody, William T., 1st Lieut.

## NON-COMMISSIONED OFFICERS AND PRIVATES

Aderson, William, Pvt.
Albertson, Abraham E., Pvt.
Allen, George W. Jr., Pvt.
Allen, John, Sgt.
Allen, Richard P., Pvt.
Allport, John F., Pvt.
Armstrong, John H., Pvt.
Armstrong, William R., Pvt.
Ashby, Benjamin F., Pvt.
Ashby, Henry C., Pvt.
Ashby, Robert, Pvt.
Atkins, Edward C., Pvt.
Atkinson, James Rosser, Corpl.
Atkinson, John J., Pvt.
Ball, George W., 1st Sgt.
Bell, Charles W., Pvt.
Birmingham, Thomas, Pvt.
Black, Robert, Pvt.
Brimmer, Henry F., Pvt.
Bryant, James E., Pvt.
Butler, Robert L., Pvt.
Chaney, A. C., Pvt.
Chapman, Gustavus A., Pvt.
Childress, Thaddeus K., Pvt.
Cook, Thomas, Pvt.
Cook, William F., Pvt.
Craddock, Robert B., Pvt.
Crump, Robert A., Sgt.
Cullingsworth, William H., Pvt.
Dansey, John A., Pvt.
Dean, William H., Pvt.
Doss, Gehu, Pvt.
Durham, Thomas H., Sgt.
England, George W.,
Epps, J. Ryland, Pvt.
Farrar, James, Pvt.

Fergusson, Henry C., Pvt.
Fergusson, Robert A., Pvt.
Fergusson, William J., Pvt.
Foley, John, Pvt.
Folkes, Canellem C., Pvt.
Fuller, James R., Pvt.
Furbush, Robert A., Pvt.
Gary, Edwin J., Pvt.
Gary, Hezekiah B., Pvt.
Gentry, Charles W., Pvt.
Gregory, George, Pvt.
Gunn, Thomas H., Pvt.
Hamilton, Theodore, Pvt.
Hart, John
Harvey, Thomas P., Pvt.
Haskins, Augustus L., Pvt.
Haskins, George W., Pvt.
Hay, Thomas W., Pvt.
Hodges, Vernon E., Pvt.
Hoffman, Charles C., Pvt.
Hord, Benjamin H., Pvt.
Hord, William F., Pvt.
Hudgins, Elias P., Pvt.
Hudnut, Edgar A., Pvt.
Jackson, John D., Pvt.
Jones, Thomas R., Pvt.
Jordan, Richard D., Corpl.
Kendrick, William F., Pvt.
Knauff, George F., Pvt.
Lambert, George W., Pvt.
Layard, William S., Pvt.
Leidey, Samuel, Pvt.
Ligon, John L., Jr., Pvt.
Lindsey, John J., Pvt.
Lord, John R., Pvt.
Lowler, Thomas, Pvt.

Lumpkin, Gilmer A., Pvt.
Mahone, James R., Pvt.
Mahone, Marcellus R., Pvt.
Mallory, J. Scott, Pvt.
Martin, William H., Pvt.
Miles, Thomas W., Pvt.
Miller, William T., Corpl.
Mitchell, James C., Pvt.
Montgomery, Joseph, Pvt.
Moore, Harper C., Pvt.
Nobles, Nehemiah, Pvt.
O'Keeffe, James, Musician.
Parker, James, Pvt.
Patrick, Henry Clay, Pvt.
Patterson, William, Pvt.
Payne, Pleasant H., Pvt.
Pollard, Fielding, Pvt.
Prease, Charles W., Pvt.
Pritchard, John T., Pvt.
Pryor, Junius B., Pvt.
Puryear, John W., Pvt.
Redford, Cornelius A., Pvt.
Reynolds, Stephen W., Pvt.
Riley, John, Pvt.
Robinson, Edwin, Pvt.
Rogers, Thomas S., Pvt.
Royster, James A., Pvt.
Royster, Norborne L., Pvt.
Schener, Philip V., Pvt.
Schliescher, George, Pvt.
Seager, Joseph Jr., Pvt.
Sharp, James P., Pvt.
Sharp, Thomas L., Pvt.

Smith, Savage, Pvt.
Snead, Alfred J., Pvt.
Spraggins, John O., Pvt.
Spraggins, William S., Sgt.
Stewart, James R. F., Pvt.
Stuart, Robert G., Pvt.
Taliaferro, Charles C., Pvt.
Tucker, Robert L., Pvt.
Tyree, Robert F., Sgt.
Underwood, William L., Pvt.
Vaughan, Alfred J., Pvt.
Vaughan, John M., Pvt.
Vaughan, Robert P., Pvt.
Via, James T., Pvt.
Voigler, Henry, Pvt.
Walker, Alexander, Pvt.
Walker, Daniel M., Pvt.
Walthall, Robert R., Pvt.
Walthus, George, Pvt.
Ware, William S., Pvt.
Watkins, Thomas, Pvt.
Wells, Henry, Pvt.
White, George W., Pvt.
Wilkinson, George A., Pvt.
Wilkinson, John K., Pvt.
Wilkinson, Southey S., Pvt.
Wilson, James R., Pvt.
Wilson, William H., Pvt.
Winckler, William T., Pvt.
Winfree, John M., Sgt.
Wood, Patrick H., Pvt.
Wood, William A., Pvt.
Wright, Elijah, Sgt.

# 1ST REGIMENT VIRGINIA INFANTRY

## COMPANY H

## RICHMOND GRAYS, NO. 2

The second company of Richmond Grays was organized in late April 1861, under Captain William Ira Smith. The <u>Daily Dispatch</u>, on April 26, reported that it had taken only twenty-four hours to raise this company of seventy men. By May 4, when the company was enrolled and mustered into State service, the 38-year-old Rev. Francis J. Boggs, of the Methodist Church, had succeeded Captain Smith as company commander. The Grays replaced Captain Randolph's Howitzers as Company H in the regiment. Captain Boggs, who had for a number of years been chaplain to the Seamen's Bethel in Richmond, was appointed chaplain of the 1st Regiment about April 21, 1861, but relinquished this office to become captain of the second company of Richmond Grays.

On June 30, 1861 Company H had three officers and sixty-nine enlisted men present for duty. The company was well clothed, with a dress uniform, and was armed with Springfield rifled muskets.

Captain Boggs resigned on September 6, 1861, and on October 19 1st Lieutenant John H. Greaner was elected to succeed him. Captain Greaner served until April 26, 1862, when the company reorganized and elected 2nd Lieutenant William E. Tysinger as captain.

Captain Tysinger, one sergeant, and four privates, were wounded at Williamsburg on May 5, 1862; and at Seven Pines, on May 31, the company's orderly sergeant was killed, and five privates were wounded. The company had eight men wounded at Second Manassas on August 31; and of these, three, including Captain Tysinger, were mortally wounded. After the death of Captain Tysinger, 1st Lieutenant Abner J. Watkins was promoted to captain and served until the end of the war.

Twenty-nine men, rank and file, went into battle with the regiment at Gettysburg on July 3, 1863. All but one, a private, were wounded and twenty were captured. The ranks so dwindled that by the end of October 1863, when they were in camp at Taylorsville, Company H, under 1st Lieutenant E. W. Martin, had only twelve enlisted men present for duty.

On April 29, 1864, when Company H was at Greenville, N. C., it numbered three officers and twenty enlisted men present for duty. The company's strength remained about the same until near the close of the war in Virginia. Only one enlisted man, Private R. E. Womack, was among the seventeen men of the 1st Regiment paroled at Appomattox Court House.

## RICHMOND GRAYS, NO. 2

### CAPTAINS

Boggs, Francis J.
Greaner, John H.

Tysinger, William E.
Watkins, Abner J.

### LIEUTENANTS

Allan, William G., Jr., 2nd Lieut. F&S
Cabell, Paul Carrington, 2nd Lieut.
Hough, Oscar R., 2nd Lieut.

Lawson, William M., 2nd Lieut.
Martin, Ellison W., 1st Lieut.
Vaughan, James T., 1st Lieut.

### NON-COMMISSIONED OFFICERS AND PRIVATES

Anderson, William N., Pvt.
Armstrong, Richard E., Sgt.
Asher, Lewis, Pvt.
Balentine, James W., Pvt.
Ball, William W., Pvt.
Banks, Solomon, Pvt.
Barnes, Milton H., Pvt.
Belcher, I., Pvt.
Belcher, W. M., Pvt.
Betts, Russell S., Corpl., Hosp. St.
Bishop, F. M., Pvt.
Bitzel, Adam, Pvt.
Bonn, George E., Pvt.
Bonn, Henry R., Pvt.
Bonn, Joseph, Corpl.
Bray, James L., Pvt.
Bresnaham, Mathew, Pvt. Co. C.
Brotherton, David H. Pvt.
Brown, Josiah T., Pvt.
Burchell, W. D., Pvt.
Burton, M. H.
Camp, James W., Pvt.
Carter, John, Pvt.
Casey, Thomas, Pvt.
Chadick, John J., Pvt.
Chadick, Richard, Pvt.
Chaplinger, H., Pvt.
Claggett, Morris, Pvt.
Clarke, Henry C., Pvt.
Clash, Cornelius V., Pvt.
Clayton, Allen O., Pvt.
Clayton, Robert J., Pvt.
Copenhaver, G. E., Sgt.
Cox, Augustus G., Pvt.
Crow, David, Pvt.

Daniel, John H., Pvt.
Davidson, E. F., Pvt.
Davis, John R., Pvt.
Davis, William A., Pvt.
Delaway, William H., Pvt.
Dennis, Samuel C., Pvt.
Dignum, Robert E., Pvt.
Doland, James T., Pvt.
Duerson, William H., Pvt.
Dunn, Robert N., Corpl.
East, George, Pvt.
Eggleston, Walter B., Pvt.
Estress, William C., Pvt.
Farson, Stephen, Pvt.
Fisher, E. C., Pvt.
Flowers, David, Pvt.
Ford, Fleming H., Pvt.
Ford, James A., Pvt.
Fowlkes, P. A., Pvt.
Fuller, James R., Pvt.
Gentry, James A., Pvt.
Giles, G., Pvt.
Gilman, Edwin, Pvt.
Gilman, James D., Pvt.
Hammell, Robert T., Pvt.
Hammill, Henry J., Pvt.
Hansford, Calvin P., Sgt.
Hart, Robert, Pvt.
Hartman, John H., Pvt.
Hennicke, Frederic A., Pvt.
Hite, H. C., Pvt.
Hodges, J., Pvt.
Horner, James E., Pvt.
Hymiller, Herman, Pvt.
Jackson, Andrew, Pvt.

Jackson, Thomas E., Pvt.
Jackson, William M., Pvt.
Jacobs, Joseph, Pvt.
James, Edwin, Pvt.
Jordan, Edgar, Pvt.
Jordan, Richard D., Corpl.
Joseph, Wilson B., Pvt.
Justice, John, Pvt.
Kilby, Walter R., Pvt.
Kingsy, James, Pvt.
Kuhn, Lilburn P., Pvt.
Lafong, Edward, Pvt.
Lawrence, James F., Pvt.
Lawson, Marcus Cicero, Pvt.
Lentz, J., Pvt.
Lichtenstein, Isadore, Pvt.
Mahoney, James E., Pvt.
Martin, Richard W. S., Pvt.
Martin, Theodore R., Pvt.
McCabe, Hugh D., Pvt.
McDonald, Patrick, Pvt.
McGee, Joseph S., Pvt.
Meanly, John A., Pvt.
Micholl, Abraham, Pvt.
Miller, James P., Pvt.
Mills, Robert, Pvt.
Montague, John A., Pvt.
Morgan, A. B., Pvt.
Morgan, John H., Pvt.
Morris, R. H., Pvt.
Mosby, William B., Pvt.
Mouring, Thomas, Pvt.
Moyers, Henry, Pvt.
New, Charles R., Corpl.
Nolting, George A., Pvt.
Norvell, Ryland H., Sgt.
Nuckols, E. G., Pvt.
Pairo, Charles H., Pvt.
Patton, J. Houston, Pvt.
Paul, George W., Pvt.
Payne, James William, Pvt.
Peddle, Benjamin, Pvt.
Phrami, L., Pvt.

Potee, Thomas, Pvt.
Pratt, Joshua, Pvt.
Pumphrey, William F., Pvt.
Rea, George A., Pvt.
Read, J. H., Pvt.
Redford, George E., Pvt.
Richards, George H., Pvt.
Riddick, Thomas S., Sgt.
Rose, Marcus A., Pvt.
Roy, A. A., Pvt.
Shepherd, Lewis, Pvt.
Sims, Charles F., Pvt.
Sinnott, John J., Pvt.
Smith, F. M., Corpl.
Smith, J. P., Pvt.
Smith, William H. C., Pvt.
Stacy, Charles, Pvt.
St. Clair, B. S., Pvt.
Stratton, James L. R., Pvt.
Swords, Robert D., Pvt.
Thomas, Lawrence Ringgold, Pvt.
Thorpe, John N., Pvt.
Toler, H. H., Pvt.
Tompkins, G. G., Pvt.
Towers, James E., Pvt.
Vaughan, N., Pvt.
Via, James Archibald, Corpl.
Viar, Jesse W., Pvt.
Waddell, W. D., Pvt.
Watson, T. M., Pvt.
Weller, Joseph, Pvt.
West, A., Pvt.
Weston, George E., Pvt.
Wight, William M., Pvt.
Williams, Oliver, Pvt.
Williams, Thomas J., Pvt.
Wilson, Robert B., Pvt.
Wilzinski, Lewis, Pvt.
Winn, John W., Pvt.
Wittig, George, Pvt.
Womack, R. E., Pvt.
Woods, W. T., Pvt.
Wynne, John W., 1st Sgt.

## 1ST REGIMENT VIRGINIA INFANTRY

## COMPANY I

Organized on November 19, 1859 under Captain Samuel T. Bayley, this company was designated in the 1st Regiment as Company I by January 12, 1860. The company, apparently not fully uniformed or equipped, did not parade with the regiment at the dedication of the Henry Clay statue on April 19, 1860. By November 15, 1860, the company, then under Captain Robert F. Morris, seems to have been well organized, uniformed, and equipped. The company was enrolled and mustered into the service of the State on April 21, 1861 for a period of twelve months. On May 1 Captain Morris resigned; and on May 8, William O. Taylor was elected captain.

At the end of June 1861, the aggregate strength of Company I was forty-seven. The company, rated as being poorly uniformed and equipped, was armed with altered smoothbore percussion muskets, which were considered as being "very unreliable." In the fall of 1861, however, the company was rearmed with Springfield muskets "in good order." Also, by this time an adequate supply of clothing had been procured.

Captain Taylor resigned on September 7, 1861, and 2nd Lieutenant James W. Tabb was elected captain. On September 28, Sergeant Benjamin F. Howard was elected first lieutenant to replace Lt. J. T. Rogers, who resigned on the 27th. At the end of October, Company I had three officers and forty enlisted men present for duty.

At the battle near Williamsburg on May 5, 1862, the company lost one killed and two wounded. Casualties were slightly higher on May 31 at Seven Pines, where three were killed, and Lt. Howard and two others were wounded.

Captain Tabb, who had been responsible for the revivification of the 1st Regiment in June 1862, was among the three from Company I mortally wounded at Second Manassas on August 30, 1862. After Captain Tabb's death, at the Warrenton hospital on September 13, 1st Lieutenant Howard was promoted to captain of the company.

The muster roll for Company I dated June 30, 1863, near Chambersburg, Pa., shows that three officers and twenty-seven enlisted men were present for duty. Thirteen of the company were absent sick, and sixteen were absent without leave. The company emerged from the fighting at Gettysburg, on July 3, with nineteen casualties, including killed, wounded and missing. The roll dated October 13, 1863, shows the company reduced to two officers and fifteen enlisted men present for duty. Eleven members were prisoners of war, thirteen were absent sick, sixteen were absent without leave, three were on detached service, two were under arrest, and five were on extra duty.

By April 30, 1864, when it was encamped near Greenville, N. C., the company's strength had increased to two officers and thirty-four enlisted men present for duty. On May 16, at the Battle of Drewry's

"CARRY ME BACK TO OLE VIRGINNY."

Allen C. Redwood

Bluff, the company had one killed, one mortally wounded, and several slightly wounded; and on the 19th, in the fighting along the Howlett Line, the company lost one killed and another mortally wounded. By the end of June 1864, Company I had been reduced to two officers and nineteen enlisted men present for duty.

The company was greatly depleted in strength during the final days of the fighting in April 1865, and only three enlisted men were paroled at Appomattox Court House.

Source:   Collection of William A. Albaugh III.

In this 1859 ambrotype John Tyler of Company F is standing on the far right. Seated in front of him is a member of the Greys. The soldier in blue is presumably of the Virginia Rifles.

## COMPANY I

### CAPTAINS

### LIEUTENANTS

Ballow, Henry C., 1st Lieut.
Caho, William A., 2nd Lieut.
Fore, Lee, 2nd Lieut.

McKaig, W. W., 2nd Lieut.
Rogers, John Tait, 1st Lieut.
Tyree, John A., 2nd Lieut.

### NON-COMMISSIONED OFFICERS AND PRIVATES

Ainsko, James, Pvt.
Ainsko, John, Pvt.
Ainsko, Joseph, Pvt.
Allen, James L., Pvt.
Anderson, Henry T., Pvt.
Ashby, Richard A., Pvt.
Ashworth, J. L., Pvt.
Ayres, John T., Corpl.
Ballow, Thomas W., Pvt.
Ballow, William T., Pvt.
Boler, George W., Pvt.
Bonay, H., Pvt.
Boucher, John, Pvt. F&S
Brooks, Hezekiah
Buckley, Joseph, Pvt.
Burgess, Armisteadt A., Pvt.
Button, James, Pvt.
Carter, R. L., Pvt.
Chaiffens, A., Pvt.
Chaiffens, Moses, Pvt.
Chappell, Alonzo A., Pvt.
Chappell, C. H., Pvt.
Chappell, John F., Pvt.
Chappell, William T., Pvt.
Clark, Samuel, Pvt.
Collins, Cornelius, Pvt.
Collins, M., Pvt.
Cordle, R. E., Pvt.
Cornick, George C., Pvt.
Crew, John T., Sgt.
Dabney, James E., Pvt.
Devaux, Julius F., Pvt.
Duke, Henry, Pvt.
Ellett, Lemuel O., Corpl.
Ellig, John, Pvt., Band, F&S
Emerson, Richard, Pvt., Band, F&S
Eubank, George W., Pvt.
Evans, Dudley, Pvt.

Figner, Alphonzo A., Pvt.
Ford, John, Pvt.
Fox, Frederick, Pvt., Band, F&S
Frayser, Donald, Pvt.
Fremmer, William, Pvt.
Gerhardt, Charles C., Pvt.
Glinn, Germain R., Pvt.
Godwin, Wright, Pvt.
Goodall, John M., Pvt.
Goodson, Edwin C., Sgt.
Grammar, John G., Pvt.
Green, John F., Pvt.
Green, William C., Pvt.
Griffin, E. J., Pvt.
Grill, George Jr., Pvt.
Hahn, Philip, Pvt.
Head, John C., Pvt.
Hodges, Martin, Pvt.
Hogsett, J. Mc., Pvt.
Holsman, Simon, Pvt.
Hooker, John G., Pvt.
Huffman, Thomas R., Pvt.
Hugel, Louis M., Pvt.
Hundley, J. C., Pvt.
Hurshberger, Joseph, Pvt., Band, F&S
Ish, Milton A., Hosp. Stew.
James, J. Henry, Pvt.
James, Robert W., Sgt.
Jenkins, Charles H., Pvt.
Jones, Richard M., Sgt.
Joy, George, Pvt.
Kahn, Martin, Pvt.
Kelley, John C., Pvt.
Kelley, Robert T., Pvt.
Kennedy, John A. B., Pvt.
Lacy, Theophilus A., Pvt.
Lamb, George, Pvt.
Lester, Thomas, Pvt.

Lipscomb, William H., Pvt.
Loving, Edwin B., Corpl.
Loyd, J. G., Pvt.
Mackey, John, Pvt.
Matthews, Nath G., Pvt.
McGrail, Paul, Pvt.
McGuigan, E. Pvt.
McLaughlan, Hugh, Pvt.
McLear, James M., Pvt.
Melton, James M., Pvt.
Meredith, Richard O., Pvt.
Minor, Andrew T., Pvt.
Moore, William H., Pvt.
Morrisett, Robert C., Pvt.
Moss, Robert J., Corpl.
Mouring, Thomas, Pvt.
Murrell, George W., Pvt.
Neal, S. S., Pvt.
Oeters, Martin, Pvt., Co.. K.
Parker, Calvin L., Corpl.
Pendleton, E., Pvt.
Pike, Henry C., Pvt.
Pleasants, John, Pvt.
Polak, Jacob, Pvt., F&S
Pugh, Fred R., Pvt.
Pulling, John, Pvt.
Quinn, Patrick, Pvt.
Raynes, A. G., Pvt.
Regan, John, Pvt.
Robey, William B., Pvt.
Robinson, Henry R., Pvt.
Robinson, James E., Pvt.
Rosenberger, John A., Pvt., F&S, Band
Rosenberger, Lawrence, Pvt., F&S, Band
Rosenberger, Philip, Pvt., F&S, Band
Rudd, Aurelius, Pvt.

Rudd, Benjamin, Pvt.
Rudd, William, Pvt.
Schuman, Charles, Pvt., Band
Senior, Thomas, Pvt.
Shoemaker, George W., Pvt.
Smith, Jacob H., Pvt.
Smith, James, B., 1st Sgt., F&S Band
Smith, William P., Pvt.
Snow, Joseph R., Pvt.
Stern, George, Pvt.
Stransbudger, John
Strasburger, John, Pvt.
Sweeny, (unknown), Pvt.
Tabb, Robert L., Pvt.
Taliaferro, Edwin, Pvt.
Taliaferro, William C. Jr., Pvt.
Tallard, Charles F., Pvt.
Terry, William F., Sgt.
Tinsley, Clement C., Pvt.
Traylor, Thomas E., Sgt.
Tyree, James T., Pvt.
Vanderventer, Edward E., Pvt.
Walker, John, Pvt.
Wallace, James B., Pvt.
Welsh, John, Pvt.
Wesley, J. R., Pvt.
White, William T., Sgt.
Wildt, Lewis, Drummer
Wills, Charles A., Pvt.
Wills, S. S., Pvt.
Wilson, J. B., Pvt.
Wingo, William W., Pvt.
Wood, R., Pvt.
Word, B. H., Pvt. Co. D.
Yancey, James K., Pvt.

# 1ST REGIMENT VIRGINIA INFANTRY

## COMPANY K

## VIRGINIA RIFLES

The Virginia Rifles was organized as the Richmond German Rifles, under Captain Augustus Bodeker, about January 31, 1850; and was one of the original companies of the 1st Regiment. In early 1853 the company was being called the Virginia Rifles, and by the end of the year, the name German Rifles had disappeared. Captain Bodeker resigned on May 12, 1853, and John Hartz was elected to succeed him.

Like most of the other military companies in the city, the Virginia Rifles held an annual "Civic and Military Ball," and on the evening of January 31, 1853, at Lafayette Hall, thirty-six couples attended the company's third annual ball, which broke up at about five o'clock in the morning. In August 1853, the company, which soon became known for its socialities, conducted a "Military and Civic Excursion" to Slash Cottage, the popular resort which was to become Ashland. Almost every year, after the regiment's parade on July 4, the Rifles, as was common with most other companies, would retire to some spot and hold their own celebration of the day, usually in the form of a sumptuous dinner accompanied by "large quantities of liquid compounds."

Captain Hartz resigned in 1856, and on September 25, 1856 the company assembled at its regular meeting place, Schad's Hall, and elected Albert Lybrook as its new captain. By July 1859, when the company celebrated the Fourth at Kraus' Garden, Florence Miller had replaced Lybrook as captain.

On November 19, 1859 the Virginia Rifles, numbering thirty-five, left with other Richmond companies for Charlestown where they remained until after the execution of John Brown.

At a monthly meeting held at Schad's Hall on February 23, 1860, the Virginia Rifles voted to replace their blue uniforms with the gray uniforms then being adopted by most of the companies in the regiment. On April 12 the company made its first appearance in new gray uniforms, with "black cross belts and shoulder straps."

On April 21, 1861, the Virginia Rifles, under Captain Miller, enrolled for active service. The company was mustered into State service as a light infantry company on the 26th for a term of twelve months. On June 30, 1861 the company had two officers, six noncommissioned officers, and sixty-seven privates present for duty. The company, adequately uniformed, was reported at this time as being armed with Harpers Ferry rifles, presumably the Model 1855 with sabre bayonets. On July 18 1861 at Blackburn's Ford, the company lost one killed and three wounded.

Captain Miller, who had been absent on sick furlough for much of the time since the company was mustered into service, resigned on December 14, 1861. On December 24, 2nd Lieutenant Frederick W. Hagemeyer was promoted to captain.

Upon the expiration of their term of enlistment in April 1862, the Virginia Rifles did not re-enlist, and Company K was disbanded. Rolls show that forty-four enlisted men of the company were discharged on April 26, 1862.

Old print showing 1st Regiment Virginia Volunteers. Colonel T. P. August, Camp Robinson, Hanover County, May 22, 1858. Companies from left to right: Grays, Blues, National Guard, Montgomery Guard, Rocky Ridge Rifles, Virginia Rifles. In foreground, right and left, Artillery.

Reproduced from Miller's
Photographic History of the Civil War
Members of the Richmond Grays

This photograph showing members of the Richmond Grays was apparently made in 1859 when the company was called into active service for duty at Charlestown. The bearded soldier in the blue uniform and wearing the cap with a plume, was Julian Alluisi of the Virginia Rifles. The ambrotype from which this photograph was originally made is now in the possession of Alluisi's grandson, Mr. Philip Colevita, Jr. of Richmond.

# VIRGINIA RIFLES

## CAPTAINS

Chambers, George W.   Hagemeyer, Friedrich W.   Miller, Florence

## LIEUTENANTS

Avis, John, 1st Lieut.
Baumann, Cletus, 2nd Lieut.
Engle, William T., 2nd Lieut.
Linkhauer, Henry, 3rd Lieut.

Lohmann, Frederick W.E., 1st Lieut.
Paul, Hermann, 1st Lieut.
Pfaff, William, 2nd Lieut.

## NON-COMMISSIONED OFFICERS AND PRIVATES

Alluisi, Julian, Pvt.
Amey, William, Pvt.
Arsberger, Charles, Pvt.
Barnickel, Henry, Pvt.
Barnickel, John W., Pvt.
Beier, Friedrich, Pvt.
Bergmeyer, Bernhard, Pvt.
Bitzel, Adam, Pvt.
Blenkner, Gottfried, Pvt.
Blenkner, Julius, Pvt.
Botzen, Louis, Pvt.
Brau, John, Pvt.
Breisacher, Charles, Pvt.
Brunner, Richard, Pvt.
Buchnan, Conrad, Corpl.
Buchnan, Henry, Pvt.
Bumgarner, J. W., Pvt.
Burkart, Henry, Corpl.
Catron, A. B.
Catron, Ephriam, Pvt.
Catron, P. E., Pvt.
Cock, George, Pvt.
Crecelius, Charles A., Pvt.
Cree, William E., Pvt.
Deboer, Dietrich, Pvt.
Deckmann, George J., Sgt.
Degenhardt, Philip, Pvt.
Diacant, Adam, Pvt.
Diacont, Philip, Pvt.
Diacont, Wolfgang, Pvt.
Dick, John, Pvt.
Dilger, Joseph, Pvt.
Dubel, Henry, Pvt.
Elsasser, Henry, 1st Sgt.
Emmenhauser, John, Sgt.
Fahrenbruch, August

Ferguson, Robert, Pvt.
Fink, John, Pvt.
Fleckenstein, Herman, Pvt.
Gehring, Joseph, Pvt.
Gelhausen, Leonhard, Pvt.
Gentry, James, Pvt.
Gentry, John D., Pvt.
Gerhardt, Frederick J., Pvt.
Gersdorfer, George, Pvt.
Glass, George, Pvt.
Grossmann, Ernst, Pvt.
Gutbier, Friedrich, Pvt.
Haake, Gerhard J., Sgt., F&S
Habermehl, Gustav, Pvt.
Hach, Friedrich, Pvt.
Hach, John, Pvt.
Hadermann, Henry, Pvt.
Hattke, Andreas, Pvt.
Hebring, Frederick, Sgt.
Heinemann, Henry, Pvt.
Helwig, Louis, Pvt.
Herzog, Edward, Pvt.
Hetke, Andrew, Pvt.
Hoch, Andreas, Pvt.
Hoffman, John Ph., Pvt.
Honner, Xavier, Pvt.
Hufner, Edward, Pvt.
Koch, George, Pvt.
Krutop, Henry, Pvt.
Lauterbach, Frederick, Pvt.
Lehmkuhl, Frederick, Pvt.
Lindner, Charles, Pvt.
Lucke, Bernhard, Pvt.
McCarthy, Edward, Pvt.
Merkel, Tobias, Pvt.
Meyer, Felix, Pvt.

Mullins, John, Pvt.
Musser, Washington, Pvt.
Nagelsmann, Joseph, Pvt.
Newland, Preston N., Pvt.
Niedemayer, Francis E., Pvt.
Nolte, David, Pvt.
Nolte, Henry, Pvt.
Nolte, Hermann, Pvt.
Ocker, Joseph, Pvt.
Oeters, Martin, Pvt., Co. I.
Paul, William H., Corpl.
Perri, Otto, Pvt.
Peters, Louis, Pvt.
Raymann, Louis, Pvt.
Reidt, Peter, Pvt.
Repass, Gordon, Pvt.
Richter, Robert, Pvt.
Rcik, John, Pvt.
Roduis, John, Pvt.
Rommel, John A., Pvt.

Rosenbaum, Alfred J., Pvt.
Schaptoch, Simeon, Pvt.
Schmidt, Jacob, Pvt.
Smith, Jacob, Pvt.
Staab, Philip, Pvt.
Stadelhofer, Maxmilian, Pvt.
Stephan, Charles, Sgt.
Thiebes, Wilhelm, Pvt.
Thomas, P. M., Pvt.
Tolger, Gerhardt, Pvt.
Umbarger, Stephen, Pvt.
Viereck, John, Pvt.
Wachter, Jacob, Pvt.
Wagner, John, Pvt.
Ward, Ballard E., Pvt.
Weidenhahn, August F., Corpl.
Werner, Adam, Pvt.
Winter, John, Pvt.
Witzleben, Theodore A., Pvt.

## 1ST REGIMENT VIRGINIA INFANTRY

## BAND

In November 1859, the Governor authorized the discharge of members of the Public Guard, which included James B. Smith's Armory Band, provided members could find substitutes to fill their places in the Guard. On the 15th the *Daily Dispatch* announced that Richmond would still have a fine band and that the band contemplated attaching themselves to the 1st Regiment.

James B. Smith's Armory Band was composed of members of the Public Guard; and since 1845 it had provided music for military parades in the city, in addition to its regular duties of protecting public property. The Public Guard, Virginia's "standing army" of a company of light infantry, was quartered at the State Armory; hence the name "Armory Band." Concerts were given during the summer evenings on Capitol Square, and on July 25, 1853 the program included selections from *Norma* and *La Fille du Regiment*, marches, waltzes, quicksteps and instrumental solos. The *Daily Dispatch* reported that "no concert ever given in this city could boast of so large an audience," but it further noted, however, that "some of the pieces played were excellent, but then again there were some of very ordinary character." On January 19, 1854 the Armory Band gave a concert at Metropolitan Hall. The proceeds went to their leader, James B. Smith, whose family barely escaped when their home was destroyed by fire. The band was frequently called upon to provide music for the regiment's companies on local excursions and on out-of-town trips. In February 1855 the band accompanied the Richmond Light Infantry Blues to Philadelphia, where the two organizations paraded on the 22nd as guests of the Washington Greys of that city. En route home, they were entertained in Baltimore by the Law Greys. The Baltimore *Clipper* complimented the Blues on their uniforms and drill, and stated that the company was "accompanied by the Armory Band, which can be excelled in the execution of music by but few bands in the country." The members and instruments comprising the band at this time were: James B. Smith (leader), bugle; James M. Melton, first cornet; William Tremer, second cornet; Frederick Fox, alto horn; Michael Gardons, first trombone; William Karrer, second trombone; R. Emerson, baritone; John Boucher, first tuba; J. H. Koop, second tuba; Edward Felvey, side drum; A. Heffron, bass drum; and W. Totty, cymbals. Under the leadership of Smith, the band continued to enjoy great popularity throughout the eighteen fifties. In late 1859, an increase in the duties required of the Public Guard threatened to break up the band; however, Governor Wise, after consultation with Smith and Captain R. Milton Cary of the 1st Regiment's Company F, agreed to discharge members from the Public Guard if they could find substitutes to replace them in the company. Inability on the part of the members to find substitutes prevented the band from immediately withdrawing from the Guard. In December 1859, an increase in the number of guards at the State Penitentiary compelled the band to suspend its activities, which, however, were resumed in January 1860 when they performed at the Mechanics Institute at the banquet given to the delegates to the Military Convention.

The separation of the band from the Public Guard was accomplished by April 13, 1860, when it was announced that the band had attached itself to the 1st Regiment. Six days later the band paraded with the regiment at the dedication of the Henry Clay statue on Capitol Square. In April, 1860 Smith's Band was regularly enlisted in the regiment and from then on was known as the 1st Regiment Band. The <u>Dispatch</u> announced on July 7 that friends and admirers were making efforts to purchase a silver bugle for Smith as a token of appreciation of his efforts to keep the band together. The <u>Dispatch</u> stated that the bugle for Smith would complete the number of silver instruments in the band, which had begun to acquire them in 1855.

On July 31, the band left Richmond with Company F for a visit to White Sulphur Springs, where they had been invited to spend a week or two. Governor Letcher was reported to have been with them, as was the 1st Regiment's drum major and a portion of the drum corps.

No legal provision seems to have been made for the mustering of the band into active service as an organization in 1861, but the matter was circumvented on April 21 when members were enrolled for service as privates of Company I, and mustered in with the company on April 27. Afterwards they were detached from the company as musicians by order of Colonel Moore. In addition to Sergeant James B. Smith, the band was comprised at this time of the following: James Buckley, John Boucher (discharged April 23, 1861), Richard Emerson (discharged April 23, 1861), John Ellig, Joseph Hirschberg, James M. Melton, Philip Rosenberger, Lawrence Rosenberger, J. A. Rosenberger, Charles Schuman, and William Trimmer.

On May 25, 1861 the 1st Regiment, accompanied by the music of the band, boarded the train for Manassas Junction. When the regiment was encamped at Centreville, the band acquired a splendid reputation among the troops in the area. Charles Loehr, historian for the regiment for many years after the war, wrote: "One of the features of our camp life was our regimental dress parades, the regiment making a splendid appearance...and then our fine band and drum corps added to the display." William Miller Owen, first lieutenant and adjutant of the famous battalion Washington Artillery from New Orleans, which was encamped beside the 1st Regiment, recorded in his history of the battalion published in 1885:

> He [Colonel Moore] had an excellent band, better, I think, than ours, and each gave excellent music at guard-mounting and dress parade. "Listen to the Mockingbird" was the favorite air of the Virginians.

In August 1861, the monotony of the daily camp routine was broken by the arrival of Prince Jerome Bonaparte, who had passed through

Members of the Young Guard pictured on the cover of "The Young Guard Quick Step" composed by the Armory Band and published in 1855.

the lines from Alexandria to visit General Beauregard. A grand review was ordered, and five brigades were drawn up for the singular honor of being reviewed by the Prince, who was accompanied by General Beauregard John Esten Cooke, who was present with the 1st Company, Richmond Howitzers, described the review as follows:

> The First Virginia regiment was seen in motion, and advancing; reaching the centre of the field, it went through all the evolutions of infantry for the Prince's inspection; and while the movements were going on, the band of the regiment—that same old band!—played the "Mocking Bird," and all the well known tunes, impressing itself upon the memory of everybody present, as an inseparable "feature" of the occasion!
>
> ...And if Prince Jerome ever sees this page, and is led to recall what he looked upon that day, I think he will remember the band of the First Virginia, playing the "Mocking Bird" and the "Happy Land of Dixie."

The above is quoted from the chapter, "The Band of the First Virginia," in Cooke's <u>Wearing of the Grey</u>, published in 1867. His pages on the band are largely eulogistic and contain few historical facts. However, from Cooke's and other accounts written after the war, we can surmise that Smith's musicians were better than average. Certainly they leave little doubt as to the popularity of "Listen to the Mocking Bird."

When the 1st Regiment was reorganized in April 1862, after its term of enlistment for twelve months had expired, either the members of the band did not re-enlist or no provision was made for the band's continuance. At an undetermined date before August 31, the five musicians then comprising the band were discharged by order of the Secretary of War.

## FIRST REGIMENT BAND

Smith, James B., Leader
Boucher, John, Pvt.
Buckley, James, Pvt.
Buckley, William, Pvt.
Ellig, John, Pvt.
Emerson, Richard, Pvt.
Fox, Frederick, Pvt.

Hurshberger, Joseph, Pvt.
Melton, James M., Pvt.
Rosenberger, John A., Pvt.
Rosenberger, Lawrence, Pvt.
Rosenberger, Philip, Pvt.
Schuman, Charles, Pvt.
Tremmer, William, Pvt.

## 1ST REGIMENT VIRGINIA INFANTRY

## DRUM CORPS

The order which enlisted Smith's Armory Band in the 1st Regiment, dated May 3, 1860, also provided for the formation of a regimental drum corps. Sergeant Charles R. M. Pohle of Company K, the Virginia Rifles, was named drum major. The order specified that he was to organize the musicians of the companies into a drum corps and instruct them in their duties as field music for the regiment.

The drum corps was apparently first started in November 1859, for on the 14th of that month the <u>Daily Dispatch</u> reported that "...a drum corps has at length been formed for the Regiment, consisting of fifteen drummers, with Mr. Chas. R. M. Pohle as drum major." Presumably, these drummers were the musicians of the companies of the 1st Regiment, as the organization of volunteer militia companies usually included two musicians, drummers and fifers. On May 3, 1860 the <u>Dispatch</u> announced that a drum corps, consisting of from fourteen to ten boys under Pohle, would make its appearance with the 1st Regiment. On July 31 the Dispatch reported that the regimental drum major and a portion of the corps accompanied Captain R. Milton Cary's F Company on a visit to White Sulphur Springs.

The 1st Regiment's drum major, Sergeant Charles Rudolph Maximillian Pohle was born in the city of Delitzsch, near Leipzig, Prussia, on April 17, 1821. He was the only son of General Carl Gotlieb von Pohle, military governor of Mayence. Pohle emigrated to the United States in 1844, and for a while was an actor with a German theatre, Palm's Opera House, in New York City. In May 1846 he enlisted as a private in Captain William H. Duff's troop of hussars, New York State Artillery, attached to the Sixth Brigade, First Division of Artillery, State Militia. Later he served as a musician in the United States Navy, and on August 12, 1852 was discharged from the <u>Pennsylvania</u>. He was later connected with the Medical College in Richmond; and in 1856 he was employed as a painter at the Tredegar Locomotive Works. For a number of years, Pohle was a member of the Richmond Cornet Band which often paraded with the militia companies of the city.

Most of the original members of the drum corps were apparently too young to enter active military service in 1861, for in April of that year the <u>Dispatch</u> announced that twelve boys over sixteen years were wanted for the corps. On April 21, 1861 members of the drum corps enrolled for active service; and on May 25, the day the regiment left for Manassas Junction, the corps was mustered into service for one year. The members of the corps and their ages at this time were as follows: Sergeant Major C. R. M. Pohle, 40; Frank Brannon, 16; Alexander Berry, 17; William Bleton, 15; George Burch, 17; Thomas McDonough, 16; George Eubank, 16; Frederick Harris, 17; Henry Hardester (with the Richmond Grays at Norfolk), 17; James W. Johnson, 16; Joseph R. Shoe-

Sergeant Charles R. M. Pohle
Drum Major
1st Regiment Virginia Infantry
1860-1862

Sergeant Pohle was also a violinist and an inventor. His final years were spent in the Confederate Soldiers Home in Richmond, where he died on April 21, 1889.

maker, 17; George W. Strang, 17; Willie Street, 15; Henry Solomons, 15; and William F. Sweeney, 17.

Charles Loehr, in his history of the 1st Regiment, recalled that "our fine band and drum corps added to the display," when the regiment appeared on dress parade. The drum corps, however, at least in October 1861, does not seem to have measured up to the standards of the regiment's band. Muster rolls for this period rated the discipline and military appearance of the corps as "not very good." Also, at this time, the drum corps was reported as being "in want of jackets & pants."

In the summer of 1862, the nine musicians then comprising the 1st Regiment's drum corps, were discharged by order of the Secretary of War.

## DRUM CORPS

Pohle, Carl R. M., Drum Major
Berry, Alexander, Pvt.
Burch, George, Pvt.
Bolton, William, Pvt.
Brannon, Frank, Pvt.
Eubank, George, Pvt.
Hardester, Henry, Pvt.
Harris, Frederick, Pvt.

Johnson, James, W., Pvt.
McDonough, Thomas, Pvt.
Shoemaker, Joseph R., Pvt.
Solomons, Henry, Pvt.
Strang, George W., Pvt.
Street, Willis, Pvt.
Sweeney, William F., Pvt.

## 1ST REGIMENT VIRGINIA INFANTRY

### Miscellaneous

Allstadt, Thomas, Pvt.
Arvin, Thomas E., Pvt.
Ashby, William F., Pvt.
Baker, James, Pvt.
Barr, Thomas S., Pvt.
Baugher, Isaac N., Pvt.
Blanchfield, Owen, Pvt.
Bobett, James, Pvt.
Boyd, Frederick, Pvt.
Bremmerman, John L., Pvt.
Brooks, F. I., Pvt.
Brown, H. R., Pvt.
Brown, John A., Pvt.
Bumpers, George D., Pvt.
Burke, John R., Corpl.
Burke, Mathew P., Pvt.
Burnum, H. F., Pvt.
Buzzard, Albert, Pvt.
Buzzard, George W., Pvt.
Calan, Owen, Pvt.
Carr, William, Pvt.
Colbert, Richard W., Pvt.
Collis, Joseph W., Pvt.
Corkley, John, Pvt.
Dailey, William, Pvt.
Davis, John, Sgt.
Decker, Palatine, Sgt.
Doyle, Garrett, Pvt.
Emerson, Ridgeley, Pvt.
Fishach, George, Pvt.
Flemming, Jesse A., Corpl.
Foley, John, Pvt.
Forsythe, Henry H., Corpl.
Furr, John E., Pvt.
Furth, John
Gompf, Marcellus C., Corpl.
Hamilton, Edwin R
Hays, William, Pvt.
Higgins, Andrew, Pvt.
Hudson, Samuel, Pvt.
Kennedy, William, Pvt.
Leavitt, Charles P., Pvt.
Legg, John N., Corpl.
Loutz, Nicholas, Pvt.
Mackin, Patrick, Pvt.
McArdle, Owen, Pvt.
McCabe, James, Pvt.
McCormick, Philip J., Pvt.
Payne, James F., Pvt.
Pegram, R., Sgt.
Pope, Charles W., 1st Sgt.
Rector, William, Pvt.
Rogers, John W., Pvt.
Ruben, W. L., Pvt.
Saunders, John P., Pvt.
Scott, Michael, Pvt.
Skinner, Willis, Pvt.
Slaughtery, John, Pvt.
Smith, Daniel C., Pvt.
Stewart, Charles H., 2nd Lieut.
Stillerson, James K.
Strider, John S., Pvt.
Sturdy, John W., Sgt.
Trail, Charles H., Pvt.
Trainer, Bernard, Pvt.
Troy, Larry, Pvt.
Waters, Benjamin, Pvt.
Williams, John, Pvt.
Williamson, C. P., Pvt.
Willis, William
Zane, Noah, Pvt.

## 15TH REGIMENT VIRGINIA INFANTRY

The 15th Regiment Virginia Infantry is reported to have been organized on May 17, 1861; however, its organization apparently was not completed until May 27, the date of Colonel Thomas P. August's appointment. Colonel August was a lawyer by profession, but had seen previous military service. During the Mexican War he was Adjutant of the regiment of volunteers raised by the State. He served in the 1st Regiment of Virginia Volunteers as major from 1851 to 1853, and was colonel of the regiment from 1853 to 1860. In 1860-1861 he was a brigadier general in the State Militia and commanded the Second Brigade of the Fourth Division.

Originally designated as the 3rd Regiment Virginia Infantry, the regiment was officially designated the 15th Regiment Virginia Infantry on June 1, 1861. When accepted into Confederate State service on July 1, 1861 the regiment consisted of ten companies. Seven of the original companies were from the City of Richmond and Henrico County. The other three were from Hanover County.

When Colonel (later Major General) John B. Magruder was assigned to command on the lower Peninsula on May 21, 1861 the 15th Regiment was ordered to proceed to join his command on the same day. Leaving Richmond on May 24, the regiment arrived at Williamsburg on the 25th where it was ordered to remain. On May 27 the regiment was moved to Grove Wharf. When General Benjamin Butler advanced a force up the Peninsula, Companies B, G and H were placed under Lieutenant Colonel William D. Stuart and joined Colonel (later Major General) D. H. Hill's command at Big Bethel. Arriving on the field, the companies were placed on the right of Hill's line, where they were engaged during the Battle of Big Bethel on June 10. During the battle Lieutenant Colonel Stuart was forced to withdraw his command to a second line. Reinforced by Company A, which arrived on the field during the engagement, Lieutenant Colonel Stuart reoccupied his original line.

Following the battle, the four companies of the 15th Regiment rejoined the regiment. Magruder reported the regiment scattered as follows on June 16: "I have stationed four companies of Colonel August's regiment at Grove Wharf, with one piece of artillery, with orders to fortify (breastwork and an intrenchment for one gun) immediately. Same at King's Mill. Also one company on the King's Mill road, at Tetter's Neck, and another on Spratley's farm." Regimental headquarters were maintained at Williamsburg until June 27, when Colonel (later Major General) Lafayette McLaws was assigned to command the forces at and in the vicinity of Williamsburg. On that date, Colonel August was ordered to move his headquarters to "King's Mill or Grove Landing, at his option." Regimental headquarters were established at Camp Deas, Young's Mill, Deep Creek, Warwick County, where the regiment was encamped for the rest of the year.

On October 3, 1861 the 15th Regiment was brigaded with the 14th

Regiment Virginia Infantry to form the 3rd Brigade, Army of the Peninsula. Colonel August was assigned to command the brigade, which occupied the left of the King's Mill-Deep Creek line, commanded by McLaws. However, the companies of the regiment did not remain stationary for the balance of 1861. The company muster roll of Company B for September-October 1861, reported the movements as follows:

> On 5th September, 1861—Broke up camp at King's Mill. Marched to Yorktown that evening. 6th September—Marched to Cockle Town and encamped near there at Camp DeSota. 14th-Left that camp, marched to Warwick Court House and there camped. 16th September-Broke up camp. Marched to Young's Mills. Camped near Mesanda Mills in a field. On 19th moved the camp into the woods near Mesanda Mills. 23rd September-Broke up camp and came to Camp Deas near Young's Mill. On the 13th October the company, with the regiment, laid in ambush all day near Lee's Store. On 21st, three men from the company with a detachment from the regiments—15th Virginia, 2nd and 5th Louisiana, 10th Georgia, and Montague's Virginia Battalion--in all 100 men, being a scouting party, took one prisoner and killed one, wounded one. The afternoon of the 21st the company, with three others of the regiment, marched to Smith's Store to reinforce the scouting party and returned to camp same day. On 22nd October the whole regiment, with 2nd Florida and 10th Louisiana, detachment of 2nd Louisiana and two guns of Sand's Battery, under command of Colonel August, marched to Smith's Store and next day laid in ambush without success and returned to camp at night. Owing to exposure to bad weather and dampness of camping grounds, the health of the company has been unusually bad during the past two months. Have been engaged the whole of October on earth works, strengthening the position at Young's Mill."

The movements of Company B were typical of the other companies in the regiment. When they were not out scouting, the men were constructing fortifications. The captain of Company C reported on December 31, 1861 that "military exercise and instruction have been mostly intermitted." On January 31, 1862 the regiment was reported at Mulberry Point Battery, Land's End, Mulberry Island, and by the end of February it was back at Young's Mills.

On April 5, 1862 a Federal army under General George B. McClellan began advancing up the Peninsula toward Magruder's line. Concentrating his army in front of Magruder's position, McClellan began to lay siege to the Confederate line which extended across the Peninsula along the Warwick River to Yorktown. The 15th Virginia did not see any action until April 16, when ordered up as reserves for the forces at Lee's Mill

(Dam No. 1) which had come under attack. However, the Federals did not continue the attack, and the regiment was not engaged. On April 25 the 15th Virginia was reorganized for the war with only eight companies; Companies F and K, having refused to reorganize, were soon afterwards disbanded by order of the Secretary of War.

General Joseph E. Johnston, having arrived with his army from northern Virginia, was now in command of all Confederate forces, and on April 28 Brigadier General Paul J. Semmes was assigned to command the brigade composed of the 15th Virginia, 10th Georgia, 10th Louisiana, and Noland's Louisiana Battalion. The brigade, remaining in McLaws' Division, began the retreat from the lower Peninsula on May 3. On the 4th it was ordered by General Johnston to reoccupy Fort Magruder at Williamsburg. Finding the enemy advancing and in close proximity, Johnston had ordered the closest body of troops forward. Holding the enemy in check, the brigade was withdrawn during the night of May 4-5 and ordered to continue its march to the rear. It was not engaged at Williamsburg on the 5th of May. Following this rear guard action, Johnston continued his retreat toward Richmond, where he established a defensive position just east of the city. McClellan followed and began to lay siege to Johnston's line. At Seven Pines, on May 31, Johnston tried to defeat a portion of McClellan's army. During this unsuccessful attack, McLaws' Division was held in general reserve.

Within the Confederate defensive line, Magruder's command occupied the Williamsburg road front. When General Lee moved with a portion of his army to join with Jackson to turn McClellan's right, he left Magruder's command south of the Chickahominy River to defend the approaches to Richmond. With Huger on his right, Magruder's troops occupied the lines while the remainder of the army engaged McClellan's right at Mechanicsville. Magruder's troops were not engaged during the first days of the Seven Days'; however, as McClellan began withdrawing his army to the south side of the Chickahominy, Lee ordered Magruder to advance. At Savage Station, on June 29, McLaws' Division engaged the enemy with Kershaw's and Semmes' brigades. During the engagement the 15th Virginia was held in reserve by General Semmes. Not engaged at Frayser's Farm (Glendale) on the 30th, the 15th Virginia saw action at Crew's Farm during the engagement at Malvern Hill on July 1. Although General Semmes reported the 15th Virginia as being in reserve, it lost one officer killed, and one officer and seven enlisted men wounded. The wounded officer was Colonel August, who had received a disabling wound in the hip. When sufficiently recovered, Colonel August was placed at the head of the Conscript Bureau in Richmond, and never returned to the regiment.

Following the Seven Days' Battles, Lee reorganized the Army of Northern Virginia, and McLaws' Division was assigned to Longstreet's command. When Lee moved to oppose General John Pope's army in northern Virginia, McLaws' Division remained in the Richmond defenses, and did not rejoin the Army of Northern Virginia until after the Battle of Second Manassas.

Advancing into Maryland, Lee's army encamped at Frederick. On September 9 General Lee issued orders for the movement of the army, which included the capture of Harpers Ferry. While Longstreet's troops were to continue the march toward Hagerstown, Jackson was ordered to move to take Harpers Ferry from the west. General McLaws' Division, reinforced by General R. H. Anderson's Division, was ordered to occupy Maryland Heights across the Potomac from Harpers Ferry while General John G. Walker's Division was ordered to occupy Loudoun Heights opposite Harpers Ferry. Jackson, McLaws, and Walker were to act in conjunction to capture Harpers Ferry.

Leaving Frederick on September 10, McLaws moved to capture Maryland Heights. Posting Semmes' and Mahone's brigades in the northern end of Pleasant Valley, McLaws occupied the Heights on the 13th. On that day, General Semmes ordered the 15th Virginia and the 32nd Virginia to defend Brownsville Gap just south of Crampton's Gap. It was necessary to hold both these passes to prevent the Federals from entering Pleasant Valley and taking McLaws' force from the rear. However, on the 14th the Federals began driving the Confederate cavalry force at Crampton's Gap in McLaws' rear. Reinforcements from Mahone's and Semmes' brigades did not prevent the Federals from capturing Crampton's Gap. However, no move was made against Brownsville Gap. During the night of the 14th-15th, McLaws concentrated his forces at the foot of Crampton's Gap, and when Harpers Ferry surrendered on the 15th he moved toward that place.

Leaving Harpers Ferry on the 16th, McLaws moved to join the army at Sharpsburg, arriving on the morning of the 17th. After a brief rest, McLaws' Division was ordered to reinforce the army's left under Jackson. This portion of the army had successfully withstood two Federal assaults, and was engaged in holding its own against a third assault when McLaws arrived. Under orders from Jackson, McLaws deployed his division, with Semmes' brigade on the left, and advanced through the West Wood, drove the Federals back, and re-established the line. McLaws' men were forced to give up the pursuit of the Federals because of the heavy Federal artillery, and retired to the edge of the West Wood. Here they remained for the balance of the battle.

In this charge, the 15th Virginia, commanded by Captain E. M. Morrison, Company C, was on the left of Semmes Brigade, and went into action with fourteen officers and one hundred and fourteen men. During the battle, the regiment suffered fifty-eight percent casualties, losing one officer and ten men killed and six officers and fifty-eight men wounded. In his report, Captain Edward J. Willis of Company A, commanding the regiment, reported: "The unusual loss, from our ranks, of men and officers has naturally cast a feeling of depression over those who now constitute the regiment."

Following the Battle of Sharpsburg, Lee withdrew his army and retired to Virginia, where the army received a much needed rest. When McClellan moved across the Potomac, Lee moved Longstreet's Corps east of the mountains to Culpeper Court House. On November 26 the 15th

Virginia was transferred to form a brigade of Virginia regiments under Brigadier General Montgomery D. Corse. This new brigade was assigned to Major General George E. Pickett's Division, Longstreet's Corps. When the Federal army, now under General A. E. Burnside, began moving toward Fredericksburg, Lee moved Longstreet's Corps to that town. Occupying the heights west of Fredericksburg, Longstreet placed Pickett's Division to the right of Marye's Heights. Here it remained during the Battle of Fredericksburg, December 13th, subjected to Federal artillery, but not actively engaged in the fight. In late December the army went into winter quarters.

On February 15, 1863 Pickett's Division marched under orders to proceed to Richmond. Increased Federal activity in the Hampton Roads area required the dispatch of forces from the army, should the Federals advance from that area on Richmond. Hood's Division followed, and on the 18th of February General Longstreet was ordered to assume command of the two divisions at Richmond. In March-April Longstreet moved his command toward Suffolk. Halting before that place, Longstreet began siege operations while portions of his command were detailed to collect provisions. Longstreet's siege of Suffolk was lifted when he was ordered to rejoin the army on April 29. However, he could not move at once, and as his troops were passing through Richmond word was received of the victory at Chancellorsville.

As Lee's army began the move into Pennsylvania which was to terminate at Gettysburg, President Davis ordered that General Corse's Brigade be retained at Hanover Junction. There the brigade remained until June 25, when it moved to Gordonsville. Here it remained until July 7, when it was ordered to proceed to Winchester to join the army returning from Pennsylvania.

When the army returned to Virginia, Lee intended moving into Loudoun County, but the high waters of the Shenandoah River prevented any immediate move. Before Lee could execute his plan, the enemy crossed the Potomac and occupied the mountain passes, closing the routes into Loudoun. Fearing the enemy would try to interpose a force between Richmond and the army, Lee ordered Longstreet to move his troops to Culpeper Court House on July 19. Elements of Corse's Brigade crossed the river and occupied Manassas and Chester Gaps, after skirmishing with Federal cavalry. Longstreet's troops crossed the river and moved through the gaps to Culpeper Court House, arriving on the 24th. During this move, elements of Corse's Brigade saw action at Manassas Gap. On August 3, Lee moved his army, and on the 4th the army occupied the line of the Rapidan.

In September, Pickett's Division was sent to Petersburg to recuperate and recruit its ranks. With headquarters at Petersburg, Pickett was placed in command of the Department of North Carolina. However, Corse's Brigade did not remain with Pickett long. Ordered to Southwestern Virginia to reinforce General Sam Jones, Corse reported his brigade at Bonsack's on September 16. By the end of September, Corse was ordered to return with his brigade to Petersburg. His stay was short; on October 15 Pickett ordered Corse to return to Southwestern Virginia. Arriving with three regiments of his brigade (15th, 29th, and 30th Virginia regiments), Corse joined General Sam Jones' small army and was attached to General Robert Ransom's Division, Army of Western Virginia and East Tennessee. The 15th Virginia was reported near Bristol on November 30, and on December 15 Corse's Brigade was ordered to New River Bridge as the Federals moved on Salem. Although Ransom's Division was part of the Department of Western Virginia and East Tennessee, they operated under General Longstreet in east Tennessee. Corse's Brigade was engaged at Dandridge, Tenn., January 16-17, 1864, but did not see any heavy fighting during their stay in the department. On January 21, 1864 Longstreet received orders to send Corse's Brigade to Pickett at Petersburg.

At Petersburg orders awaited which were to take the brigade into another of the numerous departments. General Pickett had been chosen to command an expedition against New Bern, North Carolina. The brigade proceeded to Kinston where Pickett's force was concentrating. General Pickett divided his command into three columns, and on the morning of January 30 moved in the direction of New Bern. Later in the day General Pickett ordered the 15th and 17th Virginia regiments of Corse's Brigade to report to Colonel James A. Dearing, commanding the column moving on Fort Anderson, north of New Bern. The remainder of Corse's Brigade constituted a portion of the column under General Pickett moving on New Bern from the west, while the other two columns moved on the town from north and south. On February 1, Pickett's column drove in the Federals at Batchelder's Creek and advanced to within a mile of New Bern. However, Pickett was forced to withdraw when his two converging columns failed to gain their objectives and get into position. Colonel Dearing reported that he found Fort Anderson too strong to attack. The troops returned to Kinston. Pickett returned to Virginia and General Robert F. Hoke was placed in command of the troops at Kinston. General Hoke moved on Plymouth on April 19, and, with the help of the <u>Albemarle</u>, forced the Federal commander to surrender on the 21st. Hoke then turned his attention to New Bern, and was advancing on the town when orders arrived for him to return to Virginia with his troops.

As Corse's Brigade was now in Hoke's Division, the brigade returned to Virginia. The movements of the 15th Virginia for May-June 1864 were recorded on the Field and Staff muster roll as follows:

> May 3 and 4, 1864—Marched from Kinston, N.C., distance thirty-eight miles. 6th and 7th—Returned to Kinston. May 8th—Took train for Petersburg, Va., at which place arrived on 10th. From thence marched to Halfway House, distance eleven miles. May 14—Engaged in skirmish near Drewry's Bluff in which Major C. H. Clarke, commanding skirmish line, was wounded in thigh. Behaved gallantly in action at Drewry's Bluff. On 16th charged the enemy behind dirt works from a distance of 1,200 or 1,300 yards; Adjutant J. A. August severely wounded. 20th—

Marched to Richmond, Va. 21st—Took cars for Penola Station, R. F. & P. Railroad. 22nd—Marched back to Hanover Junction, distance fifteen miles, lay in line of battle. 25th—Marched to Atlee's, on Virginia Central Railroad, distance twelve miles. June 3rd—In skirmish near Cold Harbor. 13th—Marched to Malvern Hill, distance thirteen miles. 16th—Marched to south side [of James River], engaged in skirmish near Howlett's House. Division complemented by General Lee."

The last action mentioned was the securing of the Bermuda Hundred line, which had been vacated by Beauregard in his move to Petersburg. Lee now moved his army to Petersburg, and Corse's Brigade returned to Pickett's Division, which was placed in the Bermuda Hundred line. Although portions of Pickett's Division were moved north of the James, muster rolls indicate that the 15th Virginia remained in the trenches near the Howlett House through December 1864.

In March 1865 Pickett's Division was ordered to Petersburg to support the attack on Fort Stedman, but did not arrive in time to take part in the attack. Increased Federal activity on the right of Lee's line necessitated the dispatching of troops to prevent a Federal column from turning his lines and cutting his lines of communications. Lee ordered Pickett, with Corse's, Terry's and Stewart's brigades of his division, to the right to drive back Sheridan's cavalry. Reinforced with Ransom's and Wallace's brigades of Johnson's Division, Pickett moved to Five Forks. Here he met Fitz Lee's Division of cavalry, and on the 31st moved against Sheridan's cavalry. After driving the Federals to Dinwiddie Court House, Pickett withdrew his force, now reinforced by W. H. F. Lee's and Rosser's divisions of cavalry.

At Five Forks, Pickett deployed his infantry in a defensive line with Corse's Brigade on the right and cavalry on both flanks. Sheridan, reinforced by General G. K. Warren's Corps of infantry, advanced against Pickett's line and launched an attack late on the 1st of April. Warren's infantry drove in the Confederate left and began advancing westward down the Confederate line. Corse's Brigade, holding Sheridan's cavalry in front, was ordered to form a line facing eastward. The men of Corse's Brigade held the Federal infantry momentarily, but were soon overpowered and forced to retreat. Pickett's entire force was routed from the field and did not rejoin the army, now retreating westward from Petersburg, until April 3. On April 6 the remnants of Pickett's Division were engaged at Sayler's Creek, where General Corse was captured. Following this battle, the remnants of Pickett's Division were assigned to Gordon's Corps. On April 9, at Appomattox Court House, ten officers and fifty-nine men of the 15th Virginia were present when the Army of Northern Virginia surrendered.

## 15TH REGIMENT VIRGINIA INFANTRY

### FIELD AND STAFF

Colonel
August, Thomas P.

Lieutenant Colonel
Crenshaw, James R.
Morrison, Emmett M., Co. C.
Peyton, Thomas G.
Stuart, William D.
Tucker, St. George, Co. E.

Major
Clarke, Charles H., Co. G.
Walker, John S., Co. B.

Adjutant
August, James A.
Harrison, Randolp
Lyon, Arthur L., Co. B.

Ensign
Parrish, John Edward, Co. A.

Assistant Quartermaster
Carr, Wilson C. N.
West, James F.

Assistant Commissary of Subsistence
Mayo, J. H. F.

Chaplain
August, Philip F.

Surgeon
Ghent, Henry C.
Harris, Alexander
Todd, George K.

Assistant Surgeon
Bagnall, J. H.
Benson, D. B., Co. D.
Brock, Charles W. P.
Fields, H.
Morris, H. M.
Morris, William

Sergeant Major
Briggs, William H., Co. B.
Scott, M. P.

Quartermaster Sergeant
Corbin, John G., Co. I.

Hospital Steward
Swank, Luther L., Co. B.

Drummer
Lipscomb, Thomas, Cos. C & A.

Private
Burch, Edward T., Co. I.

## 15TH REGIMENT VIRGINIA INFANTRY

## COMPANY A

## HENRICO GRAYS

The Henrico Grays, first known as the Henrico Rifles, were organized on Church Hill in December 1860 with John Wilder Atkinson as captain. The company, designated as Company A, 33rd Regiment (Henrico County), State Militia, was mustered into State service on April 23, 1861 for one year. It was assigned to Colonel August's 3rd Regiment Virginia Volunteers in May. The 3rd Regiment was redesignated the 15th Regiment Virginia Infantry on June 1, 1861, and the Henrico Grays became Company A of the regiment.

On April 25, 1862 the company was reorganized for the war. After the reorganization, Captain Atkinson was dropped, when Edward J. Willis was elected captain. Captain Willis resigned on February 20, 1864, and 1st Lieutenant Martin W. Hazelwood commanded the company for the balance of the war.

Colonel Thomas P. August

Colonel August was colonel, 1st Regiment Virginia Volunteers from 1853 to 1860; brigadier general, Second Brigade, Fourth Division, Virginia Militia, wounded at Malvern Hill July 1, 1862; afterwards assigned to the Bureau of Conscription in Richmond and retired December 31, by reason of disability.

# HENRICO GRAYS

## CAPTAINS

Atkinson, John Wilder
Hazlewood, Martin W.
Willis, Edward J.

## LIEUTENANTS

Acree, William O., 2nd Lieut.
Atkinson, James C., 2nd Lieut.
Bradley, John E., 1st Lieut.
Bradley, John R., 1st Lieut.

Cooke, Benjamin F., 1st Lieut.
Dabney, James W., 2nd Lieut.
Hall, Patrick H., 2nd Lieut.
Smith, William L., 1st Lieut.

## NON-COMMISSIONED OFFICERS AND PRIVATES

Alley, D. H., Pvt.
Alvis, Charles W., Pvt.
Atkins, Henry C., Pvt.
Atkinson, Archilaus M., Pvt.
Atkinson, William R., Pvt.
Bailey, Parks D., Pvt.
Baker, William J., Corpl.
Barlow, James M., Pvt.
Bethel, John C., Corpl.
Birchett, J. W., Pvt.
Blankenship, Wiley A., Sgt.
Blunt, Thomas G., Pvt.
Boswell, James H., Pvt.
Bradley, John W., Pvt.
Brooke, Christopher C., Pvt.
Brooke, George W., Pvt.
Brown, William A., Pvt.
Brown, William D., Pvt.
Brown, William J., Pvt.
Burch, James H., Corpl.
Burch, R. O., Pvt.
Burley, James, Pvt.
Bush, James R., Pvt.
Bush, John W., Pvt.
Catlett, George T., Pvt.
Chalk, Arthur P., Pvt.
Chamberlayne, Thomas B., Pvt.
Cherry, Christopher C., 1st Sgt.
Childrey, Stephen J., Pvt.
Clayton, Robert H., Pvt.
Crabbin, Thomas J., Pvt.
Day, Robert A., Pvt.

Denny, Richard S., Pvt.
Dodd, John B., Sgt.
Dugar, A. J., Pvt.
Duke, Alonzo M., Pvt.
Duke, Thomas, Pvt.
Ellington, A. C., Pvt.
Fox, James, Sgt.
Garthright, Joseph B., Pvt.
Gainier, Francis, Pvt.
Gally, Foster P., 1st Sgt.
Gentry, James T., Pvt.
Gill, John Henry, Pvt.
Gill, Joseph A., Pvt.
Gill, Theophilus P., Pvt.
Goddin, George E., Pvt.
Goodman, Thomas N., Pvt.
Gregory, William J., Pvt.
Grubbs, John T., Pvt.
Hagan, John H., Sgt.
Hall, Thomas F., Pvt.
Harden, Thomas, Pvt.
Hardie, James A., Pvt.
Heath, Joseph P., Pvt.
Hedgeman, C. G., Pvt.
Herbert, Julius W., Pvt.
Hibble, Christopher A., Pvt.
Hobson, Christopher C., Pvt.
Howard, George H., Pvt.
Howard, Joseph A., Pvt.
Hudson, L. L. Pvt.
Jackson, T. B., Pvt.
Johnson, John W., Pvt.

Jones, A. Otey, Pvt.
Jude, Alvin L., Pvt.
Jude, Frederick A., Pvt.
Kane, John, Pvt.
Keppler, Charles, Pvt.
Lockett, Charles Thomas, Pvt.
Lowrey, G. T., Pvt.
Lipscomb, Thomas, Musician, F&S.
Manning, George W., Pvt.
Manning, William H., Pvt.
Mason, William H. H., Pvt.
Mays, Stephen B., Pvt.
Meredith, Newton M., Pvt.
Michaels, Hugh, Pvt.
Michaels, Samuel, Sgt.
Miller, William M., Pvt.
Morris, Anderson L., Pvt.
Morriss, Gideon W., Pvt.
Mountcastle, Albert W., Pvt.
Mountcastle, Andrew H., Pvt.
Otey, George W., Pvt.
Otey, Jones A.
Parrish, John Edward, Pvt.
Pearman, Albert W., Pvt.
Pearman, W. H., Pvt.
Richardson, B. F., Pvt.
Richardson, George W., Pvt.
Robinson, William Booker, Corpl.
Savage, C. W., Pvt.
Scherrer, Henry T., Pvt.
Schwalmeyer, Henry, Pvt.
Schwalmeyer, J. T., Pvt.
Siegle, Jacob, F., Pvt.
Simon, James Alonzo
Simon, John A., Pvt.
Smith, Daniel, Pvt.
Smith, Robert R., Corpl.
Smith, W. R., Pvt.
Smithers, George W., Pvt.
Spraggins, Richard N., Pvt.
Taliaferro, James L, Pvt.
Taylor, William S., Pvt.
Tiller, Thomas M., Pvt.
Trainum, Edward C., Pvt.
Trueheart, J. H., Pvt.
Valentine, Thomas E., Pvt.
Waters, John W., Pvt.
Waters, William S., Pvt.
Watkins, Charles B., Pvt.
Willis, E. B., Pvt.
Willis, E. H., Pvt.
Willis, James S., Sgt.
Willis, John V., Pvt.
Wise, William H., Pvt.
Withey, William, Pvt.
Woodward, Patrick H., Pvt.
Woodward, R. A., Pvt.
Wright, P. H., Pvt.
Wyatt, John R., Pvt.

## 15TH REGIMENT VIRGINIA INFANTRY

## COMPANY B

## VIRGINIA LIFE GUARD

The Virginia Life Guard was organized in January 1861 as a uniformed company of the line. As such, the company was not required to parade "except when necessity demands." In February, John Stewart Walker was elected captain. The company's uniform, manufactured by the Crenshaw Woolen Mills of Richmond, consisted of blue flannel cloth hunting shirts with blue fringe and Virginia buttons, blue cloth caps, black pants, and white gloves. In April the company numbered seventy-one and was equipped with Enfield rifles.

The company was mustered into State service on May 14, 1861 for one year, and left Richmond on May 24 in Colonel August's 3rd Regiment Virginia Volunteers. The 3rd Regiment was redesignated the 15th Regiment Virginia Infantry on June 1, and the Virginia Life Guard became Company B of the regiment. The company was reorganized for the war on April 25, 1862. On April 29, 1862 Captain Walker was promoted to major, and 1st Lieutenant Norman S. Walker was promoted to captain. When Captain Walker resigned on September 26, 1862, 1st Lieutenant Allen M. Lyon was promoted to command the company. Captain Lyon commanded the company for the balance of the war.

## VIRGINIA LIFE GUARD

### CAPTAINS

Lyon, Allen M.     Walker, John S., F&S     Walker, Norman S.

### LIEUTENANTS

Bates, Benjamin, 1st Lieut.
Lumsden, Arthur L., 2nd Lieut.
Parker, William W., 3rd Lieut.
Rady, Charles P., 1st Lieut. Co. H.
Willis, Joseph Melville, 1st Lieut.

### NON-COMMISSIONED OFFICERS AND PRIVATES

Adam, Henry, Pvt.
Alfriend, Thomas L., Pvt.
Allen, Charles P., Pvt.
Allen, Joseph T., Pvt.
Alsop, John T., Pvt.
Alsop, Richard B., Pvt.
Antohny, John L., Pvt.
Baldwin, Lucius H., Pvt.
Baldwin, William W., Pvt.
Benson, Richard H., Pvt.
Bidgood, Robert W., Pvt.
Bourn, David N., Pvt.
Bowen, Charles H., Pvt.
Briggs, Robert T., Pvt.
Briggs, William H., Pvt., F&S
Brondeecker, Henry, Pvt.
Burns, Thomas, Pvt.
Butler, Edward P., Pvt.
Butler, William F. Jr., Pvt.
Carter, John W., Pvt.
Catlin, William N., Pvt.
Corbett, Bartholomew, Pvt.
Crew, John H., Sgt.
Crew, William H., Corpl.
Cronin, Thomas, Pvt.
Crump, George, Pvt.
Daly, William H., Pvt.
Davis, Howard, Pvt.
Denny, Douglass P., Pvt.
Denson, Richard H., Pvt.
Devlin, Patrick, Pvt.
Fenwick, Charles C., Pvt.
Fischer, Frederick A., Pvt.
Foster, Eldridge M., Ord. Sgt.
Garey, George M., Pvt.
Garey, William W., Corpl.
Gates, Erasmus W., Pvt.
Gates, Sidney R., Corpl.
Gates, William J., Pvt.
Gibbs, Edward S., Pvt.
Goode, John C., Pvt.
Goode, Silas S., Pvt.
Hall, David C., Pvt.
Hall, David S., Pvt.
Hall, Elijah F., Pvt.
Hardie, Robert Jr., Pvt.
Harvey, Samuel H., Pvt.
Hayes, William C., Pvt.
Hill, John G., Pvt.
Holland, George W. L., Pvt.
Hopkins, Joseph V., Pvt.
Huff, Charles H., Pvt.
Jarvis, William H., Jr., Pvt.
Joyner, Matthew S., Pvt.
Keesee, George F., Pvt.
King, John C., Pvt.
Leigh, Richard H., Pvt.
Long, Laton N., Pvt.
Lyon, Thomas T., Sgt.
Marshall, William M., Pvt.
Mason, Robert A., Pvt.
Matthews, Miles T., Pvt.
Matthews, Samuel D., Pvt.
McKim, William A., Pvt.
McKinney, William, Pvt.
McWilliam, John, Corpl.
Meredith, James D., Pvt.
Moore, Josiah S., Pvt.
Morris, John R., Pvt.
New, Josiah S., Pvt.
Nimmo, Thomas E., Sgt.
Parr, James, Pvt.
Parr, John L., Pvt.
Pearce, John T., Pvt.

Perkins, William R., Pvt.
Pollard, Chapman T., Pvt.
Powell, George D., Sgt.
Purdy, Thomas B., Pvt.
Pate, John B., Pvt.
Reed, William M., Pvt.
Richardson, Charles A., Pvt.
Richardson, James A., Sgt.
Robertson, Daniel H., Sgt.
Roy, James C., Pvt.
Rudd, Frederick J., Pvt.
Samuel, Archibald, Pvt.
Seelan, John H., Pvt.
Shea, Thomas, Pvt.
Sinton, Charles H., Corpl.
Stunderfor, John N., Pvt.
Swank, Luther L., Pvt., F&S.
Taylor, James Curtis, Corpl.
Taylor, John W., S., Pvt.

Taylor, Richardson, W., O. Sgt.
Thompson, Charles C. S., Pvt.
Turner, William T., Pvt.
Tyler, Sylvester N., Corpl.
Walker, Charles B., Pvt.
Walker, John W., Pvt.
Webster, Archibald, Pvt.
Wells, Henry Lee, Sgt.
West, Thomas J. Jr., Pvt.
Whitlock, John E., Pvt.
Whitlock, Robert H., Pvt.
Whitlock, William B., Pvt.
Wilks, John W., Pvt.
Williams, Robert A., Pvt.
Willis, J. P., Pvt.
Willis, Samuel P., Pvt.
Winston, Philip P., Pvt.
Yates, Samuel R., Pvt.

## COMPANY D

## HENRICO GUARD

Organized in January 1861 as the Sidney Guard, this company was a volunteer company raised in the Oregon Hill and Sidney Hill districts, then on the western suburbs of Richmond. In February 1861 the company numbered seventy-five men and was commanded by Captain Lawson H. Dance. At this time the company was known as the Henrico Guard, and was mustered into State service on May 13, 1861 for one year. On May 24 the company left Richmond in Colonel August's 3rd Regiment Virginia Volunteers. The 3rd Regiment was redesignated the 15th Regiment Virginia Infantry on June 1, and the Henrico Guard became Company D of the regiment.

The company was reorganized on April 25, 1862. Captain Dance was dropped on April 26, following the election of Abner V. England as captain. Captain England was killed at Sharpsburg on September 17, 1862 and 1st Lieutenant D. B. Benson was promoted to captain. Following Captain Benson's resignation on November 21, 1862, 1st Lieutenant Jonathan F. Vannerson was promoted to captain and commanded the company for the balance of the war.

# HENRICO GUARD

## CAPTAINS

Benson, D. B.  
Dance, Lawson H.

England, Abner V., Co. H.  
Vannerson, John T., Co. H.

## LIEUTENANTS

Dunnavant, Edmond M., 1st Lieut.  
McCloy, William J., 1st Lieut.

Phillips, Alonzo L., 2nd Lieut.  
Rowe, William W., 2nd Lieut.

## NON-COMMISSIONED OFFICERS AND PRIVATES

Alley, William A., Pvt.
Anthony, Arthur, Pvt.
Anthony, James T., Pvt.
Armentrout, James M., Pvt.
Baker, John W., Corpl.
Beauchamp, Samuel, Pvt.
Bell, John C., Pvt.
Bernard, Carlos F. W., Pvt.
Bernard, Fleming W., Sgt.
Bland, Edward P., Pvt.
Butler, George W., Pvt.
Carnell, Hiram, Pvt.
Carwiles, Jacob W., Pvt.
Clark, James H., Pvt.
Dunn, Thomas H., Pvt.
Dunnavant, William H., Pvt.
Eubank, George, Pvt.
Eubank, James, Pvt.
Faudree, Benjamin, Pvt.
Fick, Peter G., Pvt.
Fletcher, William F., Pvt.
Gardner, Cornelius W., Pvt.
Gordon, Thomas, Pvt.
Gray, William T., Pvt.
Griffiths, John, Pvt.
Grimsley, Simeon U., Pvt.
Grubbs, William A., Pvt.
Guest, James M., Pvt.
Guest, Joseph M., Pvt.
Ham, Robert, Pvt.
Hancock, Benjamin A., Sgt.
Harris, August, Pvt.
Hendrick, George S., Corpl.
Hendrick, James T., Sgt.
Hoback, William A., Pvt.
Holloway, William, Pvt.
Howell, John T., Pvt.

Jacob, Joseph C., Pvt.
Jenkins, Henry, Pvt.
Jennings, Alexander, Pvt.
Jones, Franklin, Pvt.
Jones, Thaddeus, Pvt.
Journey, Nicholas J., Pvt.
Kersey, William M., Pvt.
Kreigle, John, Pvt.
Lapine, Charles E., Pvt.
Lepreux, Augustus, Drummer
Lewellen, John, Pvt.
Martin, George T., Pvt.
Meeks, Peter, Pvt.
Milstead, John T., Pvt.
Minter, Henry T., Pvt.
Montague, Robert A., Corpl.
Moore, James, Pvt.
Mundin, James E., Pvt.
Noar, George, Pvt.
Oliver, George W., Pvt.
Oliver, William E., Pvt.
Pae, William, Pvt.
Pitts, John W., Corpl.
Pratt, James A., Pvt.
Prosser, John J., Pvt.
Rice, Robert F., Pvt.
Roach, James, Drummer
Roach, Mineweather, Pvt.
Roundtree, Robert B., Pvt.
Ryan, James, Pvt.
Ryan, John H., Pvt.
Saunders, John W., Pvt.
Shelley, William H., Pvt.
Shepperson, Elijah, Sgt.
Shipe, John W., Pvt.
Stephens, Hezekiah, D., Pvt.
Stubbs, Wilber F., Pvt.

Swartley, Valentine, Pvt.
Thomas, John H., Pvt.
Tindal, Matthew A., Pvt.
Totty, Thomas W., Pvt.
Tyler, Jacob S., Pvt.
Tyler, John J., Pvt.

Walker, George M., Pvt.
Walker, Richard B., Pvt.
Willis, Bernard
Willis, John, Pvt.
Wills, John C., 1st Sgt.
Wood, John A., Pvt.

## 15TH REGIMENT VIRGINIA INFANTRY

## COMPANY F

## EMMETT GUARD

This company, known as the Emmett Guard, was formed about May 1, 1861 with William Lloyd as captain. The company was largely Irish and numbered eighty men when mustered into State service on May 1, 1861 for one year. On May 24 the company left Richmond in Colonel August's 3rd Regiment Virginia Volunteers. The 3rd Regiment was redesignated the 15th Regiment Virginia Infantry on June 1, and the Emmett Guard became Company F of the regiment.

The company refused to reorganize for the war in April 1862, claiming exemption from service under the clause of the Conscript Act of April 16, 1862 discharging from service nondomiciled residents. The officers left the company, and the enlisted men who remained were temporarily assigned to other companies of the regiment. Captain Lloyd was dropped from the rolls on May 10, 1862, and on June 20, 1862 the company was ordered to be "immediately disbanded and mustered out of service" by Special Orders No. 142, Adjutant and Inspector General's Office. A few of the men enlisted in the companies to which they had been attached and remained with the regiment.

## EMMETT GUARD

### CAPTAIN

Lloyd, William

### LIEUTENANTS

Adams, John H., 1st Lieut.
Coen, Fin, 2nd Lieut.

Collins, James, 2nd Lieut.
Mason, Jeffrey, 1st Lieut.

### NON-COMMISSIONED OFFICERS AND PRIVATES

Bayne, Thomas, Pvt.
Bolan, John, Pvt.
Burk, Anthony, Pvt.
Burk, William, Pvt.
Burns, James, Pvt.
Burns, Patrick, Pvt.
Burrows, Charles A., Pvt.
Byrnes, James, Pvt.
Byrnes, Patrick, Pvt.
Clary, Denis, Pvt.
Cole, John, Pvt.
Collins, Henry, Sgt.
Connor, Michael O., Sgt.
Costello, Patrick, Pvt.
Cronin, John, Pvt.
Danahy, Daniel, Pvt.
Disney, John, Pvt.
Dorain, Philip, Sgt.
Driscol, Daniel, 1st Pvt.
Driscol, Daniel, 2nd Pvt.
Dugan, Michael, Pvt.
Farley, Patrick, Pvt.
Feeny, Michael, Pvt.
Finton, Joseph, Pvt.
Flaherty, John, Pvt.
Flaherty, Peter, Pvt.
Ford, John, Pvt.
Freeney, Michael, Pvt.
Galvin, John, Pvt.
Gillespie, Andrew, Pvt.
Glancy, John, Corpl.
Graham, Cornelius, Pvt.
Griffin, Parrick, Pvt.
Haden, John, Pvt.
Harrington, John, Corpl.
Harrington, Michael, Pvt.
Heffey, Patrick, Pvt.
Hurley, Daniel, Corpl.
Hurley, William, Pvt.
James, George C., Corp., Co. H.
Keenan, James, Pvt.
Kelley, Daniel, Pvt.
Kelley, John, Pvt.
Kelley, William, Pvt.
Keyton, Patrick, Pvt.
Kirk, Nicholas, Pvt.
Lillis, John, Sgt.
Logan, James, Pvt., Musician
Lynch, John, Pvt.
Mahony, James, Pvt.
Manning, Denis, Pvt.
Martin, Maurice, Pvt.
Maughan, Patrick, Pvt.
McCave, John, Corpl.
McDonald, James, Pvt.
McDonough, Michael, Pvt.
McBuire, Bryan, Pvt.
McGuire, John, Pvt.
Murphy, Daniel, Pvt.
Murphy, John, 1st, Pvt.
Murphy, John, 2nd Pvt.
O'Callahan, James, Sgt.
O'Neill, John, Pvt.
Parke, George, Pvt.
Phillips, John, Pvt.
Russell, James F., Pvt.
Sculley, Bartley, Pvt.
Slattery, Michael, Pvt.
Sullivan, John, Pvt.
Sullivan, Michael, Pvt.
Sullivan, Owen, Pvt.
Teirney, Edward P., Pvt.
Tracy, Michael, Pvt.
Walker, Charles, Pvt.
Williams, James, Pvt.
Williams, Patrick, Pvt.
Williams, Robert A., Pvt.

# COMPANY G

## SOUTHERN GUARD

The Southern Guard was organized about January 1860 with Jackson F. Childrey as captain. Mustered into State service in May 1861 for one year, the company left Richmond on May 24 in Colonel August's 3rd Regiment Virginia Volunteers. The 3rd Regiment was redesignated the 15th Regiment Virginia Infantry on June 1, and the Southern Guard became Company G of the regiment.

Captain Childrey resigned on September 11, 1861, and 1st Lieutenant John D. Warren was promoted to captain. When the company reorganized for the war on April 25, 1862, Charles H. Clarke was elected captain and Captain Warren was dropped from the rolls. Upon the promotion of Captain Clarke to major of the regiment, 1st Lieutenant Josiah M. Gunn succeeded to command of the company. Captain Gunn commanded for the balance of the war.

## SOUTHERN GUARD

### CAPTAINS

Childrey, Jackson F.
Clarke, Charles H., F&S
Gunn, Josiah M.
Warren, John D.

### LIEUTENANTS

Allen, John H., 2nd Lieut.
Fussell, John K., 1st Lieut.
Garthright, John R., Jr. 2nd Lieut.
Gunn, William F., 1st Lieut.
Hanes, Garland Jr., 2nd Lieut.
Shook, Jacob, 2nd Lieut.

### NON-COMMISSIONED OFFICERS AND PRIVATES

Adams, P. F., Pvt.
Adams, Richard J., Pvt.
Ball, Carter, Pvt.
Basnight, R., Pvt.
Bass, S. C., Pvt.
Brackett, Henry L., Pvt.
Brackett, Robert N., Pvt.
Bullington, Robert J., Sgt.
Carter, Hill, Pvt.
Chappell, F. B., Pvt.
Childrey, Malchias, Pvt.
Childrey, Thomas J., Pvt.
Clark, Almoran S., Pvt.
Clarke, J. F., Pvt.
Clarke, W. A., Pvt.
Collins, Nathan, Pvt.
Cosby, N. D., Pvt.
Cradoe, James E., Pvt.
Crittenden, John J., Pvt.
Crittenden, William C., Pvt.
Easley, William H., Corpl.
English, Charles L., Pvt.
English, Richard H. B., Pvt.
Eppes, John E., Corpl.
Evans, James B., Pvt.
Fisher, George, Pvt.
Folkes, William A., Pvt.
Francis, William B., Pvt.
Frayser, William J., Pvt.
Fuqua, Edward C., Pvt.
Garthright, Alpheus C., Pvt.
Garthright, Fuller M., Pvt.
Garthright, John, Pvt.
Garthright, John, Pvt.
Garthright, William D., Corpl.
Gatewood, Liston Temple, Pvt.
Gay, William H., Pvt.
Goodman, James, Pvt.
Gunn, John H., Pvt.
Hanvey, John R., Pvt.
Hendrick, John W., Pvt.
Hobson, A. Owen, Pvt.
Hobson, Nicholas, Pvt.
Hobson, Robert, Pvt.
Hobson, Samuel, Pvt.
Hobson, Thomas F., Pvt.
Hobson, William L., Pvt.
Hughes, James, Pvt.
Johnson, John D., Corpl.
Jones, Alexander P., Pvt.
Jordan, Daniel B., Pvt.
Landrum, Samuel, Pvt.
Lawrence, Samuel R., Pvt.
Lewis, Thomas, Pvt.
Lipscomb, Thomas
Maridd, Peter, Pvt.
Miller, John, Pvt.
Minson, John C., Pvt.
Minter, George F., Pvt.
Morgan, Albert, Drummer
Newman, R. L., Pvt.
Night, James M., Pvt.
Pearman, Christopher, Pvt.
Pearman, Warren C., Pvt.
Pearman, William, Pvt.
Pearman, William H., Pvt.
Pearman, Zachariah, Pvt.
Perkins, Edwin J., Pvt.
Pinchback, E. F., Pvt.
Pleasants, Robert T., 1st Sgt.
Ragland, Thomas F., Pvt.
Redford, Andrew J., Pvt.

Redford, Benjamin, Pvt.
Riley, John, Pvt.
Robinson, Charles H., Pvt.
Robinson, Jervace W., Pvt.
Robinson, M. B., Pvt.
Rock, John, H., Pvt.
Rock, Phillip H., Pvt.
Rock, William N., Pvt. Co. H.
Sanders, William T., Pvt.
Stansbury, James E., Pvt.
Stansbury, R., Pvt.
Stunk, William B., Sgt.
Sweeney, Charles H., Pvt.
Sweeney, Stephen B., Pvt.
Taylor, Jefferson Monroe, Pvt.
Taylor, R. J., Pvt.
Throgmorton, A. Christian, Pvt.
Throgmorton, Atheleus, Pvt.
Throgmorton, Henry, Pvt.
Throgmorton, Jesse P., Pvt.
Throgmorton, Thomas, Pvt.
Towles, George R., Pvt.
Turner, George, Pvt.
Warefield, John, Pvt.
Warriner, Carson T., Pvt.
Warriner, John W., Sgt.
Warriner, Josiah C., Pvt.
Watkins, Benjamin C., Pvt.
Watkins, Charles H., Pvt.
Watkins, D. G., Pvt.
Waymack, Shadrach W., Sgt.
Whitlock, John T., Pvt.
Whitlock, William G., Pvt.
Williams, Burwell, Pvt.
Wills, E. E., Pvt.
Winfree, A. F., Pvt.
Winfree, W. A., Pvt.
Woodfin, Josiah B., Pvt.
Wright, Thomas, Pvt.
Yarbrough, Thomas J., Pvt.

## 15TH REGIMENT VIRGINIA INFANTRY

### COMPANY H

### YOUNG GUARD

Organized April 13, 1850 the Young Guard, then under Captain John H. Richardson, was one of the original companies of the 1st Regiment of Virginia Volunteers organized on May 1, 1851. About 1857, the Young Guard left the 1st Regiment, expanded into a battalion of two companies, and was attached to the 179th Regiment of Militia. In January 1858 the Young Guard Light Battalion, under Colonel John Richardson, consisted of Company A, Captain Hugh W. Fry, Jr., and Company B, Captain Samuel P. Mitchell. The new company commanders that appear in the battalion by July 1858 were: Company A, Captain W. L. Satterwhite; Company B, Captain John S. Rady.

The Young Guard ceased to exist as a battalion in November 1859. The battalion had dwindled to a company of forty men under Captain Rady when it, with other Richmond companies, left for Charlestown in November 1859 for the John Brown trial and hanging. Members of the Young Guard agreed to rejoin the 1st Regiment of Virginia Volunteers in January 1860 on the condition that they would not be required to change their uniforms of red and blue. This proposal occurred at the time when the companies of the 1st Regiment were adopting the gray uniform, and it is likely that the regiment was not inclined to make an exception to the Young Guard. The Daily Dispatch commented that the Young Guard was composed chiefly of working men who were not always able to afford purchasing a new uniform.

On April 27, 1861 the Young Guard was mustered into State service for one year with William A. Charters as captain. On May 24 the company left Richmond in Colonel August's 3rd Regiment Virginia Volunteers. The 3rd Regiment was redesignated the 15th Regiment Virginia Infantry on June 1, and the Young Guard became Company H of the regiment. Captain Charters resigned on October 16, 1861, and 1st Lieutenant Charles P. Rady of Company B, 15th Regiment Virginia Infantry, was elected captain of the Young Guard on October 19, 1861. Captain Rady resigned on January 23, 1862 and 1st Lieutenant Campbell G. Lawson was elected captain. When the company was reorganized for the war on April 25, 1862 Captain Lawson was re-elected. Captain Lawson served as commander of the Young Guard until he retired from active service on December 20, 1864. 1st Lieutenant George A. Charters was then promoted to captain and commanded the company for the balance of the war.

# YOUNG GUARD

## CAPTAINS

Charters, George A.
Charters, William A.
Lawson, Campbell G.

Rady, Charles P., Co. B.
Richardson, John H.

## LIEUTENANTS

Bailey, Charles, 2nd Lieut.
Berry, George W., 2nd Lieut.
Dabney, Henry W., 1st Lieut.
England, Abner V., 1st Lieut., Co. D.

Lindsay, Albert L., 2nd Lieut.
Smith, Lewis L., 1st Lieut.
Vannerson, John T., 2nd Lieut.

## NON-COMMISSIONED OFFICERS AND PRIVATES

Acree, James S., Pvt.
Allen, James R., Sgt.
Allen, Lawrence, Corpl.
Allen, William B., Pvt.
Anthony, Albert G., Pvt.
Askew, Joseph, Pvt.
Barnes, Edwin F., Pvt.
Batkins, Benjamin M., Corpl.
Bell, John J., Pvt.
Bendall, John J., Pvt.
Bethell, Elisha, Corpl.
Betts, Lewis, Pvt.
Bird, Charles M., Pvt.
Blankenship, Marcellus J., Pvt.
Bowman, A. P., Pvt.
Breeden, James O., Pvt.
Broaddus, Muscoe W., Pvt.
Brower, John J., Pvt.
Brown, William A., Pvt.
Buchannan, William, Pvt.
Burnett, John H., Pvt.
Burns, George W., Pvt.
Burns, John B., Pvt.
Butler, Andrew J., Pvt.
Calhoun, George A.
Carnell, John G., Pvt.
Carroll, John C., Pvt.
Chapman, William C., Sgt.
Clash, John H., Pvt.
Croy, C. L., Pvt.
Croy, Michael, Pvt.
Curtin, Edward B., Pvt.
Dabney, Arthur C., Pvt.

Davis, John, Pvt.
Dean, William H., Pvt.
Edwards, George H., Pvt.
Ellison, John, Pvt.
Emory, Edward, Pvt.
England (unknown), Pvt.
England, Richard W., Corpl.
Eppling, Henry, Pvt.
Evans, Joel S., Pvt.
Evans, Osborne, Pvt.
Evans, William, Pvt.
Fandre, George W., Pvt.
Fox, Richard H., Pvt.
Froman, John F., Pvt.
Gill, James A., Pvt.
Gillespie, James, Pvt.
Griffin, Patrick, Pvt.
Harper, Henry P., Pvt.
Hayden, William R., Pvt.
Hazlegrove, Henry C., Pvt.
Hermans, Charles A., Pvt.
Hodges, Henry, Pvt.
Holland, Richard, Pvt.
Hollis, Edward, Pvt.
Holmes, William H., Pvt.
Holt, Robert L., Pvt.
Hopkins, Andrew J., Pvt.
Hopkins, Edward R., Corpl.
Howell, John H., Pvt.
Jackson, Levi M., Pvt.
James, George C., Corp., Co. F.
Jennings, Elijah, Pvt.
Johnson, Chund, Pvt.

Johnson, Edward L., Sgt.
Johnson, Joseph, Pvt.
Jones, Benjamin, Pvt.
Jones, Edward W., Sgt.
Kerr, George W., Sgt.
Lacy, James B., Pvt.
Lambert, Philip, Pvt.
Lambert, William A., Pvt.
Lane, John, Pvt.
Lawson, Peter R., Pvt.
Lee, William E., Pvt.
Lux, George, Pvt.
Lyle, James D., Pvt.
Lynham, Edward N., Pvt.
McCormack, Samuel S., Pvt.
McCormack, William H., Pvt.
Meredith, Lucius F., Sgt.
Minor, Thomas J., Pvt.
Mitchel, J. E., Pvt.
Moore, Martin, Pvt.
Moore, R. E., Pvt.
Morrisay, Patrick, Pvt.
Murray, Daniel F., Pvt.
Napier, James P., Pvt.
Neurohr, Peter, Drummer
Odekirk, James F., Pvt.
Owens, Thomas T., Pvt.
Padgett, Charles W., Pvt.
Peatross, Richard D., Pvt.
Phelps, John, Pvt.
Pittman, Frank W., Pvt.

Pollard, Robert C., Corpl.
Pollard, Thomas, Pvt.
Puckett, Chiffney,I., Pvt.
Puller, James E., Pvt.
Rink, Lewis S., Pvt.
Robinson, William Thomas,1st Sgt.
Rock, William N.,Pvt., Co. G.
Rogers, Henry C., Pvt.
Schwalmeyer, William C., Pvt.
Shaner, Jacob, Pvt.
Smith, Charles N., Pvt.
Smith, George T., Pvt.
Smith, Richard T., Pvt.
Smith, William C., Pvt.
Steinam, Isaac L., Pvt.
Stevenson, John, Pvt.
Stidham, Martin, Pvt.
Stopher, H. G., Pvt.
Swabacker, Simon, Pvt.
Taylor, Pleasant S., Pvt.
Tennant, William W., Pvt.
Thayer, M. G., Pvt.
Timberlake, James L., Pvt.
Trueheart, Adolphus H., Pvt.
Tucker, Allen J., Pvt.
Wade, William H.
Walker, Philip H., Pvt.
Watkins, William C., Pvt.
Wells, James D., Pvt.
Wilson, James T., Pvt.
Young, Charles P., Pvt.

# 15TH REGIMENT VIRGINIA INFANTRY

## COMPANY K

## MARION RIFLES

    This company, known as the Marion Rifles and the Marion Riflemen, was in existence in April 1861 under Captain Albert Lybrock. The company was largely German and numbered seventy-five when mustered into State service on May 16, 1861 for one year. On May 24 the company left Richmond in Colonel August's 3rd Regiment Virginia Volunteers. The 3rd Regiment was redesignated the 15th Regiment Virginia Infantry on June 1, and the Marion Rifles became Company K of the regiment.

    The company refused to reorganize for the war in April 1862, claiming exemption from service under the clause of the Conscript Act of April 16, 1862 discharging from service nondomiciled residents. The officers left the company, and the enlisted men who remained were temporarily assigned to other companies of the regiment. Captain Lybrock submitted his resignation on August 3, 1862. Endorsements on his resignation indicate that the company had just been mustered out of the service. Captain Lybrock's resignation was accepted on August 16, 1862. A few of the men enlisted in the companies to which they had been attached and remained with the regiment.

## MARION RIFLES

### CAPTAIN

Lybrock, Albert

### LIEUTENANTS

Eucker, Edward, 2nd Lieut.
Fischer, Jul C., Jr. 2nd Lieut.
Fisher, George, 2nd Lieut.

Schad, August, 1st Lieut.
Schnabele, Henry, 2nd Lieut.

### NON-COMMISSIONED OFFICERS AND PRIVATES

Altschuh, Martin, Pvt.
Beckman, Henry, Pvt.
Bell, Edward, Pvt.
Bierschenck, Frederick, Pvt.
Blantz, George, Pvt.
Blenner, August, Pvt.
Bockelman, Henry, Pvt.
Brill, Philip, Pvt.
Brown, August, Pvt.
Brown, Charles B., Pvt.
Dill, Fred, Pvt.
Doel, William, Pvt.
Drescher, Adolph, Pvt.
Eckenbush, Charles, Pvt.
Eggling, William, Pvt.
Eucker, Charles, Sgt.
Faulhaber, August, Pvt.
Fiedler, August F., Pvt.
Fillman, Emil, Pvt.
Frank, Adolph, Pvt.
Geese, Fred, Pvt.
Grimmel, Henry, Pvt.
Haas, Charles, Pvt.
Halem, August V., Pvt.
Halem, Ernst V., Pvt.
Halem, Henry V., Pvt.
Hasenohr, George, Corpl.
Hecht, Coleman, Pvt.
Heirsch, Frederick, Corpl
Heitmuller, William, Pvt.
Heninghausen, Charles, Pvt.
Johnson, John, Pvt.
Kempf, William, Pvt.
Keppler, Jacob, Pvt.
Klein, George, Pvt.
Kolbe, John, Pvt.

Krebs, Charles, Pvt.
Kroedel, Henry, Pvt.
Krohne, Theodore, Pvt.
Lehman, Henry E., Pvt.
Leiss, Edward, Pvt.
Lentz, William, Pvt.
Lieberman, Lewis, Pvt.
Marxhausen, John, Pvt.
Meister, Otto, Pvt.
Merkel, Frank, Pvt.
Miller, John, Pvt.
Neutzel, William, Pvt.
Noswith, Lewis, Pvt.
Otto, Fred, Pvt.
Paul, George F., Sgt.
Peasley, James, Drummer
Pflugfelder, Charles, Sgt.
Rees, Fred, Pvt.
Reidt, Henry, Pvt.
Reinhardt, Lewis, Pvt.
Roeth, Conrad, Pvt.
Runge, Gustav, Pvt.
Runkwitz, Otto, Pvt.
Schmitt, Fred, Pvt.
Schneider, Frederick, Pvt.
Schneider, Henry, Pvt.
Schurman, Henry, Corpl.
Schwartz, Jacob, Pvt.
Schwartz, , Valentine, Corpl.
Seeger, Fred, Pvt.
Sevin, John, 1st Sgt.
Simmons, Charles, Pvt.
Simon, Benedict, Pvt.
Stecker, Philip, Pvt.
Tannbald, Charles, Pvt.
Teske, John, Pvt.

Thiele, Robert, Pvt.
Valck, Charles, Pvt.
Wagner, Charles, Pvt.
Walcker, Emil, Pvt.

Walker, (unknown), Pvt.
Walter, John, Pvt.
Walter, John L., Pvt.
Wurtemburg, Lewis, Pvt.

## 15TH REGIMENT VIRGINIA INFANTRY

### Miscellaneous

Allen, J. H., Pvt.
Allen, John, Pvt.
Bethel, Thomas, Pvt.

Duncan, William, Conscript.
Garretts, Wm., Conscript.
Goodwyn, M., Conscript.

# F COMPANY

The organization of F Company, or Company F, as it was variously called, was completed on June 23, 1859 with the election of Captain R. Milton Cary. Captain Cary, a successful Richmond attorney, had served as adjutant of the 1st Regiment of Virginia Volunteers, 1855-1856, and as lieutenant colonel of the regiment from 1856 until 1859, when he resigned to organize a volunteer militia company of light infantry. Soon after its organization, the company entered the 1st Regiment and was designated as Company F.

Details of the uniform adopted by the company were published in the Constitution and By-Laws of F Company, First Regiment Volunteers. Adopted June 30, 1859, a copy of which is now in the library of the Confederate Museum in Richmond. The uniform consisted of a single-breasted cadet gray frock coat, trimmed in black, with a row of ten brass Virginia seal buttons down the front. Gray pants, with a two-inch black stripe down the outer seams, were prescribed for winter dress, while plain white pants were worn in the summer. Officers wore the same uniform, except for a gold braid trim on the coat collar and a gold stripe on the pants. For dress, the company wore a black felt and patent leather cap, with a white pompon. The company also had a gray fatigue jacket and a forage cap with a brass letter F on the front. It was a handsome uniform, and other companies in the city soon adopted it for their own. John H. Worsham, who enlisted to the company in April 1861, recalled in his One of Jackson's Foot Cavalry, published in 1912, that F Company also had red and white calfskin knapsacks imported from Paris, imported canteens, and black overcoats with Virginia seal buttons.

When the news of John Brown's raid reached Richmond on October 17, 1859, F Company, numbering seventy men, left the city that evening to accompany Governor Wise to Harpers Ferry. The company arrived there five hours after the raiders had taken the engine house. The other Richmond companies left on the morning of October 18. They got as far as Washington, where they received orders to return to Richmond, the raiders having in the meanwhile been captured. All companies were back in Richmond by the evening of October 19. Rumors of attempts to free the prisoners at Charlestown became widespread, and on the evening of November 19 F Company with six other Richmond companies left for Charlestown, where they remained until after the execution of Brown.

On July 31, 1860 the company, under Captain Cary, with the 1st Regiment Band and a portion of the drum corps, left the city for a visit to White Sulphur Springs. The Daily Dispatch reported that it was believed that Governor Wise would accompany them. Aside from participation in regimental parades, this was probably the most significant event in the history of F Company during 1860.

F Company was among the companies called out on April 21, 1861, when it was believed that the Federal gunboat Pawnee was steaming up the James River to shell Richmond. At sunset, F Company reached Wilton, about ten miles down the river, where they were joined by the Howitzers. The <u>Pawnee</u> never appeared, and on the next day the companies returned to the city on barges which had been sent down for them.

News was received on April 24 that the Federals were landing at Aquia Creek, the terminus of the Richmond Fredericksburg and Potomac Railroad. F Company and the Richmond Light Infantry Blues were ordered there at once. Upon reaching Fredericksburg it was learned that the enemy had not landed, and the two companies were sent to the Fair Grounds, where Camp Mercer was established. About three weeks later F Company was ordered to Aquia Creek, where the company received its baptism of fire when enemy gunboats shelled the area on June 7. While the company was at Aquia Creek it was drilled almost daily, perfecting the skirmish drill and bayonet exercises.

While at Fredericksburg and Aquia Creek, a number of changes occurred in F Company. When it left Richmond the company was comprised of three officers, seven noncommissioned officers, 123 privates, one surgeon, and an assistant surgeon. A number of men left the company afterwards to join other commands. Notable among them was William R. J. Pegram, who was assigned to the Purcell Battery, and subsequently became one of the Confederacy's most eminent artillerists. Captain Cary was given command of a battalion, and was appointed colonel of the 30th Regiment Virginia Infantry on June 15. 1st Lieutenant Richard H. Cunningham was elected to replace Cary as captain of F Company.

F Company was ordered to Richmond on June 14, and was sent to Camp Lee upon reaching the city. On June 28 the company was mustered into State service for one year, effective from April 21, the date on which it was enrolled for active service. Near the end of June the 21st Regiment Virginia Infantry was organized and Captain Cunningham's company was assigned to it as Company F. The regiment, under Colonel William Gilham of the Virginia Military Institute, was comprised of ten companies, totaling about 850 rank and file.

On July 18 the regiment left for Staunton, arriving there on the next day. The regiment resumed its march on the 21st into western Virginia to join the command of General Loring, arriving at Huntersville, Pocahontas County, on July 26. Here the 21st was joined by several regiments of infantry and some cavalry and artillery. An epidemic of measles and typhoid fever broke out, and by August 3, when they left Huntersville, at least a third of the regiment was hospitalized.

Loring's command continued on the march, and on August 6 went into camp at Valley Mountain. Here they were joined by General Lee, who had arrived to co-ordinate operations in the western part of the State. On September 9 the regiment was ordered forward, and engaged the enemy at Conrad's Mill on the 11th. The Federals retired, and the 21st Regiment fell back to Valley Mountain, where they remained until September 24, when Lee left to join General Floyd at Sewell Mountain. Lee took with him all troops except the 21st Regiment, 1st Battalion (Irish) Virginia Infantry, a battery of artillery, and a company of cavalry. Colonel Gilham was placed in command of these troops, and soon moved them two miles back to Middle Mountain. On September 28, Gilham moved his command to Elk Mountain, remaining there until October 9, when they left for Edray. Remaining at Edray until October 14, Gilham moved his troops to the Greenbrier River, where they were encamped for about a month. After marches and encampments at Warm Springs, Bath Alum Springs, and Milboro, Gilham's command left for Staunton on December 4. On December 10 the regiment left for Winchester to join General Jackson. At Winchester the Irish Battalion, and the 48th, 42nd and 21st regiments were formed into the Second Brigade, Jackson's Division.

The first real fight in which F Company participated occurred on January 3, 1862, when Jackson's forces were about five miles from Bath in Morgan County. When contact was made with the enemy F Company was moved to the front and deployed as skirmishers. Heavily engaged until dark, the company lost Private William Exall, killed, and Lieutenant James B. Payne, seriously wounded. On the next morning, Jackson moved against the enemy at Bath, the Second Brigade marching with F Company as the advance guard. The Federals were driven from Bath and crossed the Potomac during the night.

Colonel Gilham and Major Scott Shipp left the regiment on January 9, 1862 to resume their duties at the Virginia Military Institute. As a token of respect for Colonel Gilham, F Company presented him with a fine horse, with the company's letter F attached to the bridle.

On January 14, Jackson moved into Romney, where F Company established its quarters in the bank building. Jackson then returned to Winchester with his original force, leaving Loring's command at Romney. Romney was evacuated on February 3, and Loring moved his command to rejoin Jackson at Winchester. On March 22, Jackson marched twenty-seven miles from Rude's Hill, and bivouacked that night near Fisher's Hill. On the 23rd, near Kernstown, the regiment was heavily engaged in the battle there, in which Jackson was defeated. This was the first "regular" battle experienced by F Company, which had six wounded.

After Kernstown, Jackson retired up the valley, and went into camp near Swift Run Gap on April 19. Here, with the reorganization of the army, the 21st Regiment elected John M. Patton, colonel; Richard H. Cunningham, Jr., lieutenant colonel; and John B. Moseley, major; and F Company elected William H. Morgan, captain.

On May 2 Jackson was at Port Republic, and on the 4th reached Staunton. Leaving Staunton early on May 6, Jackson joined General Edward Johnson's command about noon. The two forces moved westward, and on May 8 defeated Milroy near McDowell. Jackson abandoned his pursuit of the enemy on May 13 and marched back through McDowell toward Harrisonburg, which he reached on the 20th. Jackson's army marched down the valley, and on May 22 it was joined by General Ewell's command. Three days later Jackson drove Banks from Winchester and advanced beyond Winchester to threaten Harpers Ferry. On May 28 the 21st Regiment, numbering about 250 men, returned to Winchester to take charge of about 3,000 prisoners, which they guarded until June 18, when they were turned over to the guard at Lynchburg. The regiment then proceeded by rail to Charlottesville and rejoined the brigade on June 21, as Jackson's army was moving to join Lee's forces at Richmond against McClellan.

On June 27 the 21st Regiment, with the Second Brigade, under the command of Colonel Cunningham, was heavily engaged at Gaines' Mill, where the Federals held "the strongest point I saw occupied by either army during the war," wrote John Worsham of F Company. Jackson's men spent the night on the hard-won field, and after rebuilding the bridge at the Chickahominy, crossed over on the morning of June 30. Passing the Savage farm, Jackson moved into White Oak Swamp, and later found the enemy in position at Malvern Hill. The Second Brigade received a terrific shelling on July 1, but did not become engaged. On July 11, Jackson's troops went into camp at the Morris farm on the Mechanicsville Turnpike, remaining there until July 16, when they left for Louisa Court House.

On August 7, Jackson moved from Gordonsville, and defeated Pope's advance at Cedar Mountain on the 9th. Nearly half of Jackson's losses in the battle were with the Second Brigade. Lieutenant Colonel Richard H. Cunningham, formerly captain of F Company, and then in command of the brigade, was among the dead. F Company, which went into battle with only eighteen men, had six killed and six wounded.

After Longstreet's Corps had joined General Jackson, the army broke camp on August 20 to move against Pope. Crossing the Rapidan and Rappahannock rivers, they were beyond Gainesville in Prince William County on August 26. The Second Brigade, commanded by Colonel Bradley T. Johnson, was sent with the division into Manassas Junction, where vast quantities of stores were seized. After setting fire to the depot, the division moved across the old Manassas battlefield of 1861 to a ridge near Groveton. The 21st Regiment, with the brigade, was engaged in the ensuing Battle of Second Manassas, from the very beginning until the end. On the 30th, Lieutenant Edward G. Rawlings, commanding F Company, was killed in the fighting along the railroad cut. F Company had been greatly depleted in strength by the time of Second Manassas, and when the army crossed the Potomac into Maryland, there were only three present for duty in the company: Malcolm L. Hudgins, Reuben J. Jordan, and John H. Worsham. These men were permitted to march, camp and fight anywhere within the regiment they might choose. During the Maryland Campaign they were known as the "guerrillas of the 21st."

In January 1863 the few men comprising F Company were sent to Camp Lee, near Richmond, to recruit and rebuild the company. A few men were enlisted as soon as the company reached camp, some old members rejoined, and by June 22 when they left for Staunton, the company, under Captain William A. Pegram, had three officers and forty-nine enlisted men. Upon reaching Staunton, the company was placed in charge of about a hundred stragglers and ordered to deliver them to the provost guard of the army, which at the time was about to invade Maryland and Pennsylvania. Because of the trouble given by the prisoners, the column traveled only during the day. On July 5 the company turned the men over to the provost guard and crossed the Potomac at Williamsport. Here, they received news of the battle at Gettysburg, and were ordered to halt and rejoin the army as it fell back into Virginia. On July 6 Federal cavalry attacked F Company while it was on picket duty outside Williamsport. Captain Pegram, rather than just defending his position, ordered a charge, in which he and three members of the company were killed. Afterwards the company marched to Hagerstown and rejoined the regiment on July 8, which was encamped two miles beyond the town.

The 21st Regiment marched with Ewell's Corps, to which they now belonged, into Orange County, joined General Lee there on August 1 and went into camp at Montpelier, the old home of President Madison. On August 20 the Second Brigade was drawn up in line for the presentation of a new battleflag to the 21st Regiment, which was presented to the color bearer, who had lost an arm at Chancellorsville. This flag was carried until the surrender. At Montpelier the company enjoyed their longest rest of the war. After a grand review of the division, which now was under Major General Edward Johnson, the rest was disturbed only by regular drills and the usual camp duties. On September 16 the army commenced a series of marches and engagements which included the Bristoe campaign and ended with the Mine Run operations of November 26-December 2. The division spent much of the winter of 1863-1864 in quarters near Mount Pisgah Church in Orange County.

On May 2, 1864 winter quarters were broken up and the brigade, with Ewell's Corps, marched ten miles to Bartley's Mill. On the 4th they proceeded to Locust Grove, and on May 5 marched but a short distance, formed a line of battle, and soon became engaged in the Battle of the Wilderness. The brigade's losses here were very severe and nearly all of one regiment, the 25th, was captured. F Company lost three killed and two wounded.

Ewell's Corps, with the Second Brigade in advance, moved from Lee's left to his right on May 8. Marching by Todd's Tavern, the troops were moved into the line of battle at Spotsylvania Court House at sunset, but were not engaged. Early on the morning of May 9 the brigade was moved further to the right of the line. The brigade occupied the salient, with the 21st Regiment near the toe of the "horseshoe" as it was called. The men worked hard constructing works especially designed for protection against fire from all directions. The regiment had scarcely finished when orders came to report to General Stewart about three quarters of a mile to the front. The night was spent on the line, in advance as skirmishers. Heavy fighting occurred along the front during the 10th. Soon after dark on the 11th, the enemy began to move in front of the skirmish line held by the 21st Regiment, and at daybreak on May 12, General Hancock launched his attack, one such as had never before been witnessed. The 21st Regiment, as skirmishers, was driven in; and, after making a circuit to the left, passed through the line. The regiment moved to the rear and reported to General Ewell, who informed them that the division had been captured and that he had believed the 21st was among them. The regiment was immediately ordered back into the line and was heavily engaged for the remainder of the day, during which F Company had two wounded. The regiment fell back and remained in the rear until the morning of May 15, when they were again committed to action. On May 16 the regiment was engaged in skirmishing, and on the 17, with skirmishers from Rodes' Division, the 21st Regiment drove back an enemy attack with heavy losses. On May 19 Ewell's Corps marched in pursuit of the enemy and engaged them until late in the night before returning to their old positions in the breastworks.

After the capture of Johnson's Division, the Virginia stragglers and others who escaped capture, about six hundred, were organized into a brigade to which William Terry, of the Stonewall Brigade, was assigned to command. Terry's Brigade, and the brigades of Evans and York, were formed into a division, to which Major General John B. Gordon was appointed to command.

On May 21 Gordon's Division marched to Hanover Junction ahead of Grant, who was marching for the same point. The operations of the two armies moved to the south, east of Richmond. On May 29 Gordon's Division was in line of battle at Bethesda Church ready for Grant, who after some skirmishing, withdrew. On the 30th Gordon attacked and drove back the Federals for about a mile and a half. The division moved to the right on the 31st, and on June 1 the Second Corps moved out to attack, but only became engaged in skirmishing. On June 2 the division captured three lines of the enemy's fortifications and took about seven hundred prisoners. While occupying these works during the 3rd, they repulsed several attempts by the enemy to retake them. One enlisted man of F Company and Captain Jordan were severely wounded during the fighting. John Worsham remembered that in the midst of the fighting on the 3rd, the enemy's artillery fired over two rammers, both of which stuck in the ground a little to the rear of the positions held by the 21st Regiment.

On June 9 the Second Corps, after being on active duty for thirty-five days, moved to the rear and went into camp. Ewell was sick and General Early was assigned to command the corps, which was then comprised of the divisions of Rodes, Gordon, and Ramseur. Early was ordered to move his command on June 13 to Lynchburg, then being threatened by the advance of the Federals under Hunter. Marching to a point just north of Keswick Depot in Albemarle County, which was reached on June 17, Early's men boarded a train which took them to Lynchburg. Hunter, who was at the time only two miles from Lynchburg, turned away towards the valley. Early followed, and on June 23 passed over Natural Bridge, where he halted his command to rest. On the next day, Early marched to Lexington, where the whole corps marched past Jackson's grave. Staunton was reached on June 27. On July 3, Early arrived at Martinsburg, where a large quantity of stores were taken, and on the 4th F Company celebrated the day with a keg of lager beer. On July 6 Gordon's Division was before Harpers Ferry and, after driving the enemy back into their fortifications, they turned east, marched by Antietam, Boonsboro, through South Mountain at Fox Gap, and into Frederick.

At the Monocacy River east of Frederick, on July 9, Early crossed the river, flanked the Federals and drove them back. As the two advance divisions of the corps were hurried forward, it appeared as if Gordon's men could sit this one out; and they prepared themselves to do just that, on an open hill under blankets and oilcloths stretched out by a fence to shelter them from the sun. They comfortably watched the opening phase of the battle, but within a short time Gordon rode up and ordered his men to move at once. Crossing the river, the brigade moved forward in line of battle through a cornfield to a field surrounded by a fence. Gordon directed some of the men to pull down part of the fence so that the brigade could pass through. This was no sooner done than one of F Company passed through, and without waiting for orders, the brigade rushed through into the battle. The losses in Early's command at Monocacy were largely confined to Gordon's Division. F Company had one killed and one wounded.

Two days after Monocacy, Early passed through Rockville, Md., and in the afternoon came within sight of Washington. They were shelled and Rodes drove back skirmishers, which had been sent out from the defenses. Early had been instructed to "threaten Washington" only, and on the night of July 12 left Washington and recrossed the Potomac, and went into camp near Leesburg.

General Early remained in the lower valley until the second week of August 1864, when Sheridan forced him to withdraw to Fisher's Hill. Early, however, received re-enforcements from Lee, and by August 17, had pushed Sheridan back across the Potomac. The Confederates were once again in the lower valley, where they remained for a month. Sheridan moved against Winchester on September 19, forcing Early to retreat as far as Fisher's Hill, where he made a stand. F Company had three wounded in the battle fought there on September 22. After Fisher's Hill, Early retired up the valley to Mt. Jackson. On October 19 he attacked Sheridan at Cedar Creek, but what was initially a Confederate victory turned into a defeat at the close of the day. Early was driven from the field, losing most of his artillery and many of his men as prisoners. F Company lost one killed, and three wounded, including Lieutenant Hudgins, who was captured. Cedar Creek virtually ended the 1864 Valley Campaign. On December 6, Gordon's Division marched from New Market to Waynesboro, where they boarded a train for Petersburg on the 7th.

On their arrival at Petersburg the division was sent into trenches on the right of Lee's defense line. On February 5, 1865 the 21st Regiment participated in the battle at Hatcher's Run. Here, Captain Jordan, after the brigade had been thrown back, rallied seven men, including one from F Company, and stopped an advance of the enemy. The incident did not escape the attention of General Gordon, who complimented them on the spot, "in that peculiar way of his," wrote John Worsham, "which bound those men to him forever."

Early on the morning of March 25, Gordon's command attacked and captured Fort Stedman, on the lines east of Petersburg. A considerable portion of the Federal works were captured, but by 8:00 a.m. the enemy had counterattacked and driven the Confederates back. Gordon's losses were more than 4,000 killed, wounded and captured. In the struggle, the last offensive that Lee would launch at Petersburg, Captain Jordan was wounded and three others of the company were wounded and captured.

Petersburg was evacuated on April 2, and the army moved westward toward Lynchburg. When it was evident that they were to surrender at Appomattox Court House on April 9, the flag of the 21st Regiment was torn into pieces and distributed among the regiment's survivors. A corporal and three privates were the only members of F Company paroled, and none of these had been members of the company when it left Richmond in 1861.

Colonel R. Milton Cary

Captain Reuben J. Jordan

Colonel Cary held the rank of lieutenant colonel, 1st Regiment Virginia Volunteers, 1856-1859; captain, F Company, 1st Regiment Virginia Volunteers, 1859-1861; colonel, 30th Regiment Virginia Infantry, 1861-1862. assigned to Bellona Arsenal in 1862 to supervise the manufacture of cannon. Captain Jordan was with F Company, 21st Regiment Virginia Infantry, from 1864-1865.

## F COMPANY

### CAPTAINS

Cary, R. Milton
Cunningham, Richard H.
Jordan, Reuben J.

Morgan, William H.
Pegram, William A.

### LIEUTENANTS

Gray, William G., 1st Lieut.
Hudgins, Malcolm, 1st Lieut.
Mayo, Edward P., 1st Lieut.
Miller, Henry T., 2nd Lieut.

Payne, James B., 2nd Lieut.
Peterkin, George W., 2nd Lieut.
Rawlings, Edward G., 2nd Lieut.
Wellford, Phillip A., 1st Lieut.

### NON-COMMISSIONED OFFICERS AND PRIVATES

Anderson, Archer, Pvt.
Anderson, Henry V., Pvt.
Anderson, Junius H., Pvt.
Archer, William S. Jr., O. Sgt.
Barber, N., Pvt.
Barker, William C., Pvt.
Bates, Edward, Pvt.
Bates, W., Pvt.
Baughan, R. S., Pvt.
Baughman, Charles C., Pvt.
Baughman, George Jr., Pvt.
Baughman, Greer H., Pvt.
Beers, Henry H., Pvt.
Bell, Henry E., Pvt.
Bell, Michael, Pvt.
Billeade, E., Pvt.
Binford, James M., Pvt.
Binford, Robert E., Pvt.
Blunt, Ira W., Hosp. Steward
Bottom, B., Pvt.
Bowles, A. J.,
Bridges, David Jr., Pvt.
Bridges, Richard M., Pvt.
Brock, Robert A., Corpl.
Brown, A. D., Pvt.
Brown, A. H., Pvt.
Brown, G. W., Pvt.
Brown, H., Pvt.
Brown, J. R., Pvt.
Bullington, Henry N., Pvt.
Callis, G., Pvt.
Chamberlayne, John H., Pvt.

Chapman, Isaac W., Pvt.
Chapman, John C., Corpl.
Child, Jesse, Pvt.
Clarke, Maxwell T., Pvt.
Clopton, John, Pvt.
Cocke, Lorenzo G., Pvt.
Coldman, J. C., Pvt.
Cole, Addison C., Pvt.
Coleman, N., Pvt.
Couch, L. M., Pvt.
Craig, John A., Pvt.
Cumbie, W. E., Pvt.
Cumbie, W. S., Pvt.
Danforth, Henry D., Pvt.
Dill, Adolph Jr., Pvt.
Dillard, R. H., Pvt.
Divers, W. H., Pvt.
Doggett, Frances W., Pvt.
Dowden, John, Pvt.
Edds, Hawkins, Pvt.
Edmunds, William B., Pvt.
Ellerson, John H., Pvt.
Ellett, Robert, Pvt.
Ellett, Thomas, 1st Sgt.
English, J. C., Pvt.
Etting, Samuel M., Pvt.
Exall, Charles H., Pvt.
Exall, William, Pvt.
Floyd, G. J., Pvt.
Fontaine, Richard M., Pvt.
Fox, H. C., Pvt.
Funk, O., Pvt.

Gentry, John W., Corpl.
Gentry, M. G., Pvt.
Gibson, William T., Sgt.
Gilbert, B., Pvt.
Gilliam, Robert H., Pvt.
Gouldman, E., Sgt.
Grady, J. J., Pvt.
Gray, Somerville, Pvt.
Green, J. C., Pvt.
Green, John W., Pvt.
Green, Thomas R., Pvt.
Griffin, Jesse, Pvt.
Harrison, Thomas R., Pvt.
Hawkins, L. A., Pvt.
Haynes, George A., Pvt.
Henry, Patrick, Pvt.
Hobson, Deane, Pvt.
Holley, J. E., Pvt.
Holley, J. W., Pvt.
Houston, G. W., Pvt.
Jenkins, William S., Pvt.
Johnson, J. W., Corpl.
Johnson, William, Pvt.
Jones, David B., Pvt.
Jones, Philip B. Jr., Pvt.
Kayton, P. W., Pvt.
Kellogg, Timothy H., Pvt.
Kidd, J. A., Pvt.
King, M., Pvt.
King, Otho, Pvt.
King, Shirley, Qm. Mr. Sgt.
Legg, A. C., Pvt.
Lindsay, Roswell S., Pvt.
Macmurdo, Richard C., Pvt.
Marion, R., Pvt.
Mason, J. M., Pvt.
Mayo, Joseph E., Pvt.
McEvoy, Charles A., Pvt.
Meade, Everard B., Pvt.
Mebane, James A., Pvt.
Meredith, John F., Pvt.
Merriman, J. T., Pvt.
Mitchell, Samuel D., Pvt.
Mittledorfer, Charles, Pvt.
Morris, Walter H. P., Pvt.
Mountcastle, John R., Pvt.
Munt, H. F., Corpl
Nance, J. L., Pvt.
Nash, T. C., Pvt.
Norwood, William Jr., Pvt.
Nunnally, Joseph N., Pvt.
Oliver, John W., Pvt.
Oliver, William M., Pvt.
Pace, George R., Corpl.
Pace, Theodore A., Pvt.
Page, Mann, Pvt.
Peaster, Henry, Pvt.
Phillips, H. A., Pvt.
Picot, Henry V., Pvt.
Piet, William E., Corpl.
Pizzinini, John A., Sgt.
Pollard, William G., Pvt.
Powell, John G., Pvt.
Randolph, Merewether L., Pvt.
Randolph, Tucker, 1st Sgt.
Redd, Clarence M., Pvt.
Reeve, David, J. B., Pvt.
Reeve, John J., Sgt.
Rennie, George H., Sgt.
Richeson, P. S., Pvt.
Richeson, W. R., Pvt.
Roberts, R., Pvt.
Robertson, Christopher A., Pvt.
Robertson, William S., Sgt.
Robinson, Richard F., Pvt.
Rutledge, William, Pvt.
Searles, S., Pvt.
Seay, M., Pvt.
Seay, W. C., Pvt.
Simpson, F. J., Pvt.
Singleton, Andrew J., Pvt.
Sizer, Milton D., Pvt.
Skinker, Charles R., Pvt.
Smith, Edwin H., Pvt.
Smith, Horace, Pvt.
Smith, J. T., Pvt.
Smith, R. S., Pvt.
Smith, Thomas, Pvt.
Smith, W. A., Sgt.
Soles, P. D., Pvt.
Sublett, Peter A., Pvt.
Tabb, Robert M., Sgt.
Talley, Daniel D., Pvt.
Tatum, Augustus R., Pvt.
Tatum, Vivian H., Pvt.
Taylor, Charles E., Pvt.
Taylor, Clarence E., Pvt.
Taylor, Edward B., Pvt.
Taylor, Robert T., Pvt.
Tinney, W. C., Corpl.
Tompkins, Edmond G., Pvt.
Trainum, Charles, Pvt.

Tyler, James E., Pvt.
Tyler, John, Sgt.
Tyler, Robert E., Pvt.
Tyree, H. C., Corpl.
Van Buren, Benjamin B., Pvt.
Waldrop, Richard W., Pvt.
Walker, T. B., Sgt.
Wallace, R. H., Pvt.
Watkins, Aurelius S., Pvt.
Watkins, Henry H., Pvt.

White, Robert C., Pvt.
Wilkins, J. M., Pvt.
Willis, Joseph N., Pvt.
Witt, William, Pvt.
Wood, S. E., Pvt.
Worsham, John H., O., Sgt.
Worsham, Thomas R., Pvt.
Wren, Joseph P., Sgt.
Young, Charles, Pvt.
Young, James, Pvt.

## JACKSON GUARD

The organization of the Jackson Guard was begun by Captain Hiram B. Dickinson about May 27, 1861. Headquarters for the company were established at the St. Charles Hotel in Richmond, at Main and 15th streets. The company was named for James T. Jackson, the keeper of the Marshall House in Alexandria, who was killed after he had shot Colonel Elmer E. Ellsworth. The Richmond Whig on June 20, 1861 noted:

> ...The Yankees are raising companies and regiments of "Ellsworth Avengers," why cannot we of Virginia enlist companies in honor of Jackson, the first martyr in the cause of the South.

On July 3 it was announced that the company, still in need of a few more recruits, was to be attached to the Wise Legion and would leave Richmond in a few days. The Jackson Guard enlisted on July 19, and on the 23rd left Richmond for Lewisburg to join the Legion of former Governor Henry A. Wise. By August 10 the Jackson Guard, numbering about forty-two rank and file, was at White Sulphur Springs where they were attached to the 2nd Regiment of Infantry, Wise Legion, as Company I and shortly afterwards redesignated as Company E. The regiment was also designated as the 59th Regiment Virginia Infantry.

General John B. Floyd, near Lewisburg on August 11, assumed command of all forces, including the Wise Legion, and "intended to operate against the enemy now occupying the Kanawha Valley." On August 16 the Wise Legion reached Big Sewell Mountain where Colonel Charles Frederick Henningsen was assigned to command the 2nd Regiment of Infantry. General Wise advanced to Dogwood Gap, while Floyd occupied Summersville. On August 21 the Wise Legion united with General Floyd's command at the foot of Gauley Mountain. General Wise, on the 22nd, marched to Carnifax Ferry at the junction of the Gauley and Meadow rivers; but, finding no enemy force there, returned to Dogwood Gap on the next day. After the battle at Carnifax Ferry on September 10, Floyd's command and the Wise Legion, which did not participate in the battle, fell back to Sewell Mountain, arriving there on the 14th. On the 16th General Floyd withdrew his forces twelve miles eastward to Meadow Bluff. General Wise, on September 25, received orders to report to Richmond and Colonel J. Lucius Davis was placed in command of the Legion. On October 6 the Federals retired from their positions in front of Sewell Mountain to the Gauley River. General Floyd moved out against the Federals, but did not take the Wise Legion as he considered them unfit for further field operations. The Legion was sent to Meadow Bluff, where they guarded the road to Lewisburg. Floyd's offensive was soon abandoned and, by the end of October, the campaign in the Kanawha Valley was over.

On December 21 General Wise was assigned to the command of the forces in the military district composed of that part of North Carolina east of the Chowan River, and the counties of Washington and Tyrrell, which were designated as the Fourth Brigade, Department of Norfolk. At General Wise's request, the War Department had agreed earlier to send his Legion to whatever location he might be assigned. Immediately after receiving his new assignment on the 21st, Wise ordered Colonel Davis to proceed to Richmond with the Legion, which was still in western Virginia. Colonel Henningsen's regiment, if not the others, had arrived by December 24 for records indicate that on that date—at Richmond—the Jackson Guard was issued overcoats, articles which would have doubtless been much appreciated earlier while they were in the western part of the State. The 1st Regiment (46th Virginia Infantry) under Colonel Richardson left Richmond by railroad for Norfolk and the North Carolina coast on January 14, but the 2nd Regiment (59th Virginia Infantry) did not depart until a week later. On January 28 Colonel Henningsen reached Norfolk with his regiment and three batteries of the Wise Legion artillery. From Norfolk, on February 1, the command proceeded southward to Roanoke Island, N. C.

When the Jackson Guard was engaged in the battle at Roanoke Island, February 7-8, 1862, the company was comprised of about four officers, seven noncommissioned officers, two musicians (drummers), and fifty-four privates. The two musicians had enlisted in the company during January. One private, John L. Turpin, was killed and Lieutenant William Dickinson was wounded. After the surrender Wise's command was held as prisoners of war until February 18 when they were released on parole. Following their arrival in Richmond on February 25, members of the Jackson Guard, still on parole, were sent to their homes until they could be exchanged.

For some time after Roanoke Island, General Wise was without a command. On May 10, 1862 the remnants of the 46th and 59th regiments, together with the 26th and 34th regiments, were formed into an infantry brigade to which General Wise was assigned to command. Brigade headquarters were established at Chaffin's Farm, and the command served east of Richmond, guarding the batteries on Chaffin's Bluff, performing outpost duty and participating in harassing expeditions against the enemy until the fall of 1863. The organizations within the brigade were greatly reduced by desertions and absentees. By the end of December 1862 the Jackson Guard was exceptionally low in strength, with only three officers and eleven enlisted men present for duty. The roll for this period shows that thirty-five men, including one of the drummers, were absent without leave; twelve were carried on the rolls as deserters and twenty were listed as having never reported since their exchange as paroled prisoners of war after Roanoke Island. Efforts by Captain Dickinson to collect the missing men met with little success.

In January 1863 about thirty-eight conscripts were assigned to the Jackson Guard. By the end of February the company had about fifty-two rank and file present for duty. The new men had received Springfield muskets and a full supply of accoutrements on January 12. In March the company's discipline, instruction, military appearance, arms, accoutrements and clothing were all rated as "good" by the inspecting officer.

Throughout January, February and March 1863, the 59th Regiment which had been under Colonel William B. Tabb since November 1, 1862, was apparently posted at Diascund Bridge on the Williamsburg Road where it crossed the Chickahominy. The Jackson Guard, which had been redesignated as Company D, was detached from the regiment during this time and was presumably in the main camp at Chaffin's Farm recuperating its strength and efficiency. By April 7 the company had rejoined the regiment at Diascund Bridge. General Wise was ordered to move his command down the peninsula, doing as much damage as possible, so as to prevent the enemy from sending reinforcements against General Longstreet, who was operating against Suffolk. On April 11 the 59th Regiment burned the Federal headquarters and stores of provisions and munitions at Whitaker's Mill, five miles to rear of the enemy's positions at Williamsburg. On April 12 the command was back at Diascund Bridge.

On May 6 the regiment marched from Riddell's Shop, Henrico County, and crossing the Chickahominy at Turner's Bridge, proceeded to Tunstall's Station, New Kent County. By May 8 the regiment was encamped at Mechanicsville. The Jackson Guard was back at Chaffin's Farm on July 6, and at the end of August was posted at Bottom's Bridge, at which time the company had one officer and twenty-seven enlisted men present for duty.

In September 1863 Wise's Brigade was sent to South Carolina, where it was almost constantly engaged in guard duty and in the construction of fortifications between the Ashley and Edisto rivers. By the end of October Captain Dickinson's company was with the regiment at Camp Wappoo, near Charleston. The regiment, by December 6, was located at Church Flat on the Stono River in St. Paul's Parish, where they were engaged in the construction of earthworks. The company was stationed at Battery William Washington in St. Andrews' Parish by the end of December 1863, and reported three officers and thirty-three enlisted men present for duty. On February 9, 1864 the regiment left Church Flat for John's Island, Stono River, where they reinforced Major Jenkins' command, which was under attack. The regiment took part in a skirmish there on the 10th and remained on the island after the retirement of the Federals on the 12th. On February 18 the regiment was ordered to Adams Run and arrived there on the 20th.

The regiment's stay at Adams Run was indeed brief for on February 21 they were ordered to Florida where on the 29th Colonel Tabb reported to Major General Patton Anderson, commanding the District of Florida at Camp Milton, near Baldwin. On April 17 the regiment was ordered to Savannah and by the 30th was on duty near Green Pond, S. C. The regiment had just reported for service at Charleston on May 3 when it was ordered to Virginia.

The brigade proceeded by rail to Virginia on May 5 with the 59th Regiment in advance. On May 8 at Nottoway Bridge, the regiment drove back an attack by Kautz' cavalry. After its arrival at Petersburg, Wise's Brigade was assigned to General Whiting's command. The regiment participated in the fighting on May 17 at Port Walthall Junction, where company E had two men killed. On May 18-19 the brigade was heavily engaged along the Howlett line, bottling up Butler's army.

The regiment remained north of the Appomattox River until June 15, when they were hurried down into the lines at Petersburg, which was then under attack. On July 30 the regiment was engaged in the fighting at the Crater and served in the trenches east of Petersburg until March 1865. By the end of February 1865 the company had only three officers and nineteen enlisted men present for duty.

Early in March 1865, Wise's Brigade was ordered to Hatcher's Run on the extreme right of the lines. On March 29 the brigade formed in line of battle at Burgess' Mill and advanced toward Gravelly Run but were driven back to their former positions on Hatcher's Run. The regiment did not, however, participate with the brigade in the attack on the 31st, being left behind to guard the trenches. On the night of the 31st the brigade fell back to Sutherland Station on the Southside Railroad, and from there it was intended to march to the assistance of General Pickett at Five Forks. When it was learned on Sunday morning April 2 that Pickett had been overrun, the brigade fell back to Namozine Creek. Petersburg was evacuated on the night of the 2nd, and the army moved westward. On April 6 the 59th Regiment was engaged in the fighting at Sayler's Creek; and on April 9 only Captain Dickinson, 1st Lieutenant William Lewis, 2nd Lieutenant E. W. Harvey, and eight enlisted men of the Jackson Guard remained with the surrendered army.

Charles Frederick Henningsen, colonel of the 2nd Regiment of Infantry, Wise Legion (59th Regiment Virginia Infantry) 1861-1862. As a captain of lancers, he served with the Carlists in Spain, and was knighted in 1835. He subsequently served with the Hungarians against Austria, and as a brigadier general with William Walker in Nicaragua, 1856-1857.

## JACKSON GUARD

### CAPTAIN

Dickinson, Hiram B.

### LIEUTENANTS

Dickinson, William B., 1st Lieut.
Fisher, William, 2nd Lieut.
Hart, George, 2nd Lieut.
Harvey, Elijah W., 2nd Lieut.

Lewis, William, 1st Lieut.
Miller, Edgar A., 1st Lieut.
Walker, William L., 2nd Lieut.

### NON-COMMISSIONED OFFICERS AND PRIVATES

Acree, James E., Pvt.
Adams, George S., Sgt.
Akehurst, Charles, Pvt.
Allen, Richard J., Pvt.
Allen, William P., Pvt.
Andrews, John, Pvt.
Ashby, James, Pvt.
Baker, Andrew C., Pvt.
Beasley, Edwin T., Pvt.
Beasley, John T., Pvt.
Berry, Sylvester A., Pvt.
Bohannon, Abner G., Sgt.
Bond, Francis L., Pvt.
Briggs, Fountain R., Pvt.
Brightwell, Lemuel, Pvt.
Browder, Robert H., Pvt.
Brown, P. C., Pvt.
Bryant, William H., Corp.
Burns, Thomas H., Pvt.
Butler, Michael, Pvt.
Chandler, Robert J., Pvt.
Clarke, Marcus, Pvt.
Cooper, William A., Pvt.
Cullingsworth, William H., Pvt.
Devallen, William T., Pvt.
Develin, Patrick, Pvt.
Dickens, John, Sgt.
Dickinson, R. L., Pvt.
Dillon, Henry T., Pvt.
Donovan, James, Pvt.
Duffey, William, Pvt.
Duffy, James, Pvt.
Edwards, John, Pvt.
Eheart, Robert W., Pvt.

Estes, William T., Corp.
Evans, Maurice F., Corp.
Farley, Richard A., Pvt.
Farrell, John W., Pvt.
Fields, William A., Pvt.
Firschkom, Henry, Pvt.
Fleming, A. J., Pvt.
Foley, John, Pvt.
Ford, Fleming, Pvt.
Franklin, John T., Pvt.
Franklin, William, Pvt.
Garber, G., Pvt.
Gill, John L., Pvt.
Goode, Samuel, Pvt.
Goodman, R. T., Pvt.
Harrington, Patrick, Pvt.
Harris, William H., Pvt.
Hazelwood, Dunreath H., Pvt.
Henderson, William, Pvt.
Hendrick, Fabius H., Pvt.
Hinton, Nelson J., Pvt.
Hudgens, Ellsworth C., Pvt.
Hundley, C. B., Pvt.
Hyman, Louis, Pvt.
Iconium, Alfred Z., Pvt.
Jones, George T., Pvt.
Jones, James T., Pvt.
Kennedy, John, Pvt.
Lappin, William J., Pvt.
Leake, Josiah, Pvt.
Leitch, Adolphus T., Pvt.
Leitch, George B., Pvt.
Leitch, James H., Pvt.
Leitch, John F, Pvt.

Macke, James, Pvt.
Maguire, Owen, Pvt.
Marks, James, Pvt.
Martin, Joseph H., Pvt.
McCue, C. W., Pvt.
McDowell, Olin F., Pvt.
McGuire, John, Pvt.
McKuskee, John, Pvt.
McMahan, Timothy, Pvt.
Melton, David G., Pvt.
Merritt, James, Pvt.
Mettert, William H., Pvt.
Millard, W. H., Pvt.
Miller, David M., Pvt.
Mills, John N., Pvt.
Mills, William T., Pvt.
Mitchell, Charles J., Pvt.
Mitchell, John D., Sgt.
Monk, C. L., Sgt.
Moore, Richard H., Pvt.
Mulligan, John J., Pvt.
Mulligin, Ro, Pvt.
Nash, William, Pvt.
Newman, James, Pvt.
Noland, John, Pvt.
Nugen, Lorenzo, Pvt.
O'Conner, John, Pvt.
O'Donald, John, Pvt.
Page, Joseph F., Pvt.
Parley, Richard, Pvt.
Pearce, Richard, Pvt.
Petross, James M., Pvt.
Phelps, James E., Pvt.
Pleasants, James, Pvt.
Raymond, Joseph, Pvt.
Russell, Nicholas, Pvt.
Salmon, Robert, Pvt.

Seamster, Timothy, Pvt.
Sizer, James L., Sgt.
Sizer, William T., Pvt.
Smith, John, Pvt.
Smith, John, Pvt.
Smith, Louis, Pvt.
Spencer, Charles W., Pvt.
Spencer, Lewellen, Pvt.
Starke, Preston, Pvt.
Starke, William H., Pvt.
Stevenson, John, Pvt.
Street, Samuel G., Pvt.
Thomas, R. S., Pvt.
Tinsley, Wallace H., Sgt.
Toler, Callum J., 1st Sgt.
Toombs, Thomas L., Pvt.
Trautman, William, Pvt.
Traynor, John, Pvt.
Turpin, John S., Pvt.
Turpin, Thomas L., Pvt.
Tyler, John H., Pvt.
Vest, George W., Pvt.
Voland, John, Pvt.
Wade, John T., Pvt.
Wade, Miles P., Pvt.
Wade, Mitchel A., Pvt.
Warthen, John E., Pvt.
Wash, Edward T., Pvt.
White, Lafayette A., Pvt.
Williams, George D., Sgt.
Williams, Thomas, Pvt.
Wilson, Elisha D., Sgt.
Wilson, Thomas R., Pvt.
Winfree, Jerome, Pvt.
Wyatt, Doctor J., Pvt.
Young, M. R., Pvt.

## RICHMOND GRAYS

The Richmond Grays organized on January 29, 1844 with the election of Charles Dimmock as captain. A few months later Captain Dimmock was appointed captain of the Public Guard, Virginia's "standing army" of one infantry company, which protected State property in Richmond. In 1859, the Grays dated their organization from June 12, 1844, when Henry L. Brook was elected captain of the company. On July 4, 1844 the Grays, numbering thirty-six uniformed men, paraded for the first time. Lieutenant Robert G. Scott, Jr. was elected captain of the company on June 18, 1845. On May 22, 1846 the company held a meeting and offered their services for the Mexican War. Although the company was not accepted into active service, Captain Scott was successful in raising a company of Richmond Grays, which, under his command, saw service in Mexico with the volunteer regiment furnished by the State. Thus at the time of the Mexican War there were two companies known as the Richmond Grays.

The Grays, formerly attached to the 19th Regiment of Militia, was one of the original companies of the 1st Regiment of Virginia Volunteers created on May 1, 1851. When the companies of the regiment were given lettered designations in 1856, the Grays were denominated as Company A.

In 1844 the Grays adopted a uniform almost identical to that which was then worn by the famous 7th Regiment of New York, with coatee of the style worn at West Point. About 1851, however, the Grays replaced the coatee with a short-skirted gray frock coat and procured new caps of the style worn by the French infantry. By 1859 the company had an undress uniform consisting of a gray jacket trimmed with black, which was worn with gray trousers in the winter and white during the summer. Gray cloth forage caps were worn with the undress uniform. Black varnished knapsacks with the letters of the company on them were used, and, in July 1859, brasses (company initials) for cartridge boxes were procured. New gray frock coats of the long-skirt pattern were procured by the company in early 1861.

Throughout the decade preceding the Civil War, the Richmond Grays under Captain Wyatt M. Elliott turned out regularly for regimental parades, in addition to their own company drills and meetings. A native of Buckingham County, Elliott graduated from the Virginia Military Institute in 1842. He later studied law at the University of Virginia and was practicing in Richmond at the time of his election as captain of the company.

When the news of John Brown's raid reached Richmond, the Grays with other city companies were ordered to Harper's Ferry on October 18, 1859. The companies got as far as Washington, where they were ordered to return to Richmond. Rumors of an attempt to free the prisoners at Charlestown became widespread and on the evening of November 19, the Grays, numbering eighty under the command of Lieutenant Louis J. Bossieux, and six other companies, totaling a little over 400, left for

Brady-Handy Collection
Library of Congress

John Wilkes Booth, who was in Richmond at the time, accompanied the Richmond Grays to Charlestown in November 1859. A correspondent for the Petersburg Daily Express reported that Booth, ". . . who, though not a member, as soon as he heard the tap of the drum, threw down the sock and buskin, and shouldered his musket and marched with the Grays to the reported scene of deadly conflict."

Courtesy Confederate Museum

This photograph of members of the Richmond Grays was apparently taken about the same time as the one which is reproduced in Miller's Photographic History of the Civil War.

Courtesy Virginia State Library

Charles Dimmock (1800-1863); captain, Richmond Grays, 1844, captain, commanding, Public Guard, 1844-1861; superintendent, Virginia State Armory; appointed colonel, Virginia Ordnance Department March 26, 1861; appointed brevet general, April 4, 1862. From an oil portrait by William Garl Brown.

Charlestown where they remained until after the execution of Brown. As Colonel August—commanding the 1st Regiment—was ill, Captain Elliott was placed in command of the contingent which left the city.

The Grays enrolled for active service on April 21, 1861, and on the same day the company, numbering over one hundred rank and file, left for Norfolk. It was at first quartered in the Virginia Hotel on Commerce Street, but within a few days was transferred to the Norfolk Academy Building on Bank Street. On May 9 the Richmond Grays was mustered into State service for a period of twelve months. It was at this time still designated as Company A of the 1st Regiment of Virginia Volunteers. At the end of June 1861 the company had four officers and eighty-seven enlisted men present for duty.

On July 12, 1861 the Grays was attached to Colonel David A. Weisiger's 12th Infantry Regiment and designated as Company G. Regimental headquarters were at the "Intrenched Camp," located on the Harrison Farm east of Norfolk, where also Companies A-E were stationed. Companies F and G were stationed in Norfolk, Companies H and I were at Boush's Bluff, and Company K was on Craney Island. In September the Grays joined the regiment at the "Intrenched Camp." From December 1861 through the end of April 1862, the 12th Regiment was stationed at the "Cockade Barracks," which was presumably at the same location as the "Intrenched Camp."

In October 1861 the 12th Regiment was assigned to the Second Brigade of the forces of General Huger, commanding at Norfolk. Colonel William Mahone of the 6th Regiment was assigned to the command of the brigade, and was commissioned a brigadier general in November.

Captain Elliott and 1st Lieutenant Louis J. Bossieux resigned on May 1, 1862, and 2nd Lieutenant Jacob Crawford was promoted as captain of the company. In August 1862 Elliott was appointed major, commanding the 25th Battalion Virginia Volunteers (Richmond City Battalion), Local Defense Troops. When the battalion was increased Major Elliott was promoted to lieutenant colonel. Bossieux was captain of Company B, 25th Battalion in 1862 and was later promoted to major.

When Norfolk was evacuated on May 10, 1862, Mahone's Brigade proceeded by rail to Petersburg, from where they were sent to construct defenses at Drewry's Bluff and Chaffin's Bluff on the James River.

On May 31 and June 1, Mahone's Brigade, Huger's Division, participated in the Battle of Seven Pines, in which the Richmond Grays had two killed. The brigade, going to the relief of Major General D. H. Hill's command, was instrumental in the repulse of the enemy. Throughout most of June Mahone's Brigade was in position on the Charles City Road. On June 25 the brigade took part in the engagement at French's Farm, between the Charles City and Williamsburg roads, and in the ensuing engagement at Oak Grove. In the battle at Malvern Hill on July 1, Mahone's Brigade had a conspicuous part, with casualties in the 12th Regiment amounting to nine enlisted men killed, four officers wounded, thirty enlisted men wounded, and fifty-three missing. The Grays had one killed and another mortally wounded.

With the reorganization of the Army of Northern Virginia in July 1862, Mahone's Brigade was assigned to Major General Richard H. Anderson's Division of Longstreet's Corps. The brigade was composed of the 6th, 12th, 16th, 41st and 49th regiments of Virginia infantry. In early August, Mahone's Brigade was in the vicinity of Rhea's Bluff on the James River.

Captain Crawford, who had been absent on sick leave since June 1, resigned on August 15, 1862, leaving 1st Lieutenant Edwin White Branch in command of the company. Lieutenant Branch had long been a member of the Grays and was first sergeant when the Company was mustered into service. He was promoted to second lieutenant on September 27, 1861 and on May 1, 1862 was promoted to first lieutenant.

Mahone's Brigade left Richmond for Gordonsville on August 16, to participate in Lee's operations against General Pope. Jackson's Corps started off first, moving into Pope's rear. When it became evident that the Federals were turning away from the Rappahannock to find Jackson, Longstreet crossed on August 26; and on the 29th, after passing through Thoroughfare Gap, arrived on Jackson's right near Groveton. In the ensuing Battle of Second Manassas, August 30, Mahone's Brigade had 37 killed and 190 wounded. General Mahone was among the wounded and Colonel Weisiger, who was also wounded in the fighting, assumed command of the brigade. The 12th Regiment had about eight killed and fourteen wounded, and Company G had two killed, one of them being the regiment's color bearer, George Nicholas, and seven wounded. Among the regiment's wounded was Adjutant William E. Cameron, who was to serve as governor of Virginia, 1882-1886.

Lee's army crossed the Potomac into Maryland and on September 14 the 6th and 12th regiments of Mahone's Brigade, under Colonel William A. Parham, fought in the battle at Crampton's Gap, in which the 12th Regiment had about three killed a little over nineteen wounded, and six captured. The regiment was not engaged at Sharpsburg on September 17.

After the Maryland Campaign, the army recrossed the Potomac and went into camp near Winchester where they remained for a month. At the end of October 1862, Company G, under Lieutenant Branch, was at Front Royal with two officers and twenty-seven enlisted men present for duty. Thirty-four enlisted men were carried on the rolls as absent, sick and wounded.

On December 1 Longstreet's Corps moved to Fredericksburg, and on the 12th, Mahone's Brigade was in line near the Stansbury House on the extreme left, which was not attacked by Burnside on December 13. While the regiment was encamped near Fredericksburg in December 1862, 1st Lieutenant Branch, by special order of General Mahone, was promoted to captain to rank from August 15, 1862.

April 29, 1863 found Mahone's Brigade in position near the Chancellor House on the plank road which ran east to Fredericksburg. When it was learned that an enemy force was advancing on the road from Ely's

Ford, Mahone withdrew his command eastward along the road to Tabernacle Church, moving with the 12th Regiment deployed as skirmishers to cover the rear. The brigade went into position at the church at about 10 a.m. on April 30. The enemy moved up to within sight, but the day passed with little firing. On the next morning, May 1, Mahone's Brigade, with McLaws' Division behind them, moved forward and was soon engaged with the advance of Sykes' regulars. In the day's fighting, which resulted in the Federals withdrawing to Chancellorsville, the 12th Regiment, deployed as skirmishers, lost heavily and with some of its finest officers killed. Late in the afternoon the regiment fell back to rejoin the brigade, which moved into position in front of the Chancellor House. On the evening of the 2nd the 12th Regiment was brought up into position with the brigade to the support of McLaws' artillery, of which one of the batteries was the 1st Company, Richmond Howitzers. Later in the day the brigade moved up to the skirmish line, with the 12th in reserve. On May 3, Mahone's Brigade was ordered to Salem Church, on the plank road about five miles west of Fredericksburg, where they helped turn back Sedgwick who was moving to aid Hooker. Figures on the casualties suffered by the 12th Regiment at Chancellorsville vary, but there were about five killed and eighty-one wounded. Company G had one officer and five enlisted men wounded.

After Chancellorsville Lee's army moved on its second invasion of the North. Mahone's Brigade with Anderson's Division, which had been transferred from Longstreet's to Hill's Corps, marched from Fredericksburg through Culpeper Court House, Berryville, Hagerstown, Chambersburg, and on July 2-3 participated in the battle at Gettysburg. The brigade was placed in support of Pegram's batteries, and its skirmishers in front were almost constantly engaged throughout the two days. Exposed to severe shell fire, the brigade suffered 102 casualties: killed, wounded and missing. Captain Branch's company had three wounded.

The army fell back from Pennsylvania, and on July 14 Mahone's Brigade recrossed the Potomac at Falling Waters, passed through Martinsville, and on the 15th went into camp near Bunker Hill, north of Winchester. On the 21st they marched to Winchester and on July 25 went into camp at Culpeper Court House. On August 1 the brigade was ordered out and drove back an enemy force which had advanced from Brandy Station. In this action, Captain Branch was killed and 2nd Lieutenant James E. Phillips assumed command of the company. On August 3 the regiment resumed its march and on the 4th went into camp near Orange County Court House.

On October 9 Lee began a series of maneuvers which forced Meade almost back to Washington. Mahone's Brigade participated in this campaign and on October 14 the 12th Regiment was present at Bristoe Station, but took no active part in the battle. Lee, finding that he could not subsist the army in northern Virginia, fell back to his old positions south of the Rapidan. Meade then took the offensive and on November 25 moved on Lee's right. Lee, however, established a strong defense line on Mine Run, from which Meade withdrew without battle. At the end of December 1863 the 12th Regiment was encamped with the brigade near Rapidan Station. Company G was at this time under Captain Robert Mayo, Jr., who had received his promotion from first lieutenant on November 6. The company had two officers and twenty-four enlisted men present for duty and nineteen absent on detached service.

Grant's army moved across the Rapidan on May 3-4 1864, and on May 5-6 occurred the Battle of the Wilderness. Mahone's Brigade, which had been near Madison Run Station, broke camp on the 4th and on the evening of the next day, joined Anderson's Division. On the morning of the 6th, the brigade went into position on Longstreet's front, but was soon ordered to co-operate with the brigades of Wofford and G. T. Anderson in an attack on the enemy's left, which proved a great success, sweeping the enemy from an advantageous position and from the plank road. In following up the attack Longstreet was wounded, and General Anderson was temporarily relieved from duty with Hill's Corps and assigned to command Longstreet's Corps. At the same time General Mahone was assigned to command Anderson's Division. From the Wilderness the division, under Mahone, moved to Spotsylvania, where, during the attacks of May 9-10, they were on the left of the line near Blockhouse Bridge. On May 12 the brigade was shifted over to the right of the line to attack the Federal left with the intention of relieving the pressure against Ewell's front. General Grant, failing to strike a decisive blow against Lee at Spotsylvania, began a series of "sliding movements" designed to interpose his army between the Army of Northern Virginia and Richmond. Both armies moved eastward and southward toward Richmond. After suffering severe losses in the attacks on Lee at Cold Harbor, June 1-3, Grant moved his forces south across the James River to capture Petersburg, twenty-three miles south of Richmond. This city was a road and rail center of utmost importance to the Confederacy, and a gateway to the capital city. After the failure of his first assault on Petersburg, June 15-18, Grant began a series of movements south and westward to encircle the city. The first drive—to cut the Weldon Railroad, June 22-23—was turned back by the divisions of Wilcox and Mahone.

By means of a mine tunnel 511 feet long, an explosion of four tons of powder on the morning of July 30 blew up a Confederate battery and a portion of the line at Elliott's Salient on the lines east of Petersburg. The explosion left a crater 170 feet long, 60 feet wide and 30 feet deep. The Federals easily occupied the crater but the attack failed and resulted in much confusion. Confederate batteries and South Carolina infantrymen pinned down the enemy in the breech in the line until reinforcements under General Mahone were brought up. In the early afternoon attacks by Mahone's old brigade under Colonel Weisiger, Wright's Georgia brigade, and Saunder's Alabama brigade, drove back the enemy and regained the lost portion of the line. Federal casualties were estimated at over 4,000 in killed, wounded and captured, while Confederate casualties were about 1,500. The 12th Regiment had about twelve killed and twenty-six wounded, with Company G losing two killed and two wounded.

From August 19 to 21 the 12th Regiment, with Hill's Corps, fought a desperate but unsuccessful battle to drive back Federal troops under Warren, which had reached the Weldon Railroad at Globe Tavern, three miles south of Petersburg. On August 25 the regiment participated in Hill's attack on Reams Station, about five miles below Globe Tavern, and on October 27 they fought in the battle at Burgess' Mill, twenty-seven miles southwest of Petersburg. The defense here temporarily checked Grant's encircling movement. At the end of October 1864, the Richmond Grays had one officer, 1st Lieutenant Phillips, and nineteen enlisted men present for duty. Lieutenant Phillips had assumed command of the company after the retirement of Captain Mayo by the Medical Examiner's Board at Richmond in October 1864. In November Mahone's Division constructed winter quarters on the lines southwest of Petersburg.

On February 5-7, 1865 Mahone's Division fought back another Federal drive westward at Hatcher's Run, and on March 5 relieved Pickett's Division on the Howlett Line, between Petersburg and Richmond. The situation along the division's front was relatively quiet throughout the remainder of the month. In co-ordination with the general assault on the Petersburg defenses on the morning of April 2, Hartsuff's troops attacked Mahone's front, but were only able to carry the picket lines.

On the night of April 2 the lines at Petersburg and Richmond were evacuated. Mahone's Division was at Chesterfield Court House the next morning, and on the morning of April 4 reached Amelia Court House. Lee's army marched westward and on April 7 the division repulsed an enemy attack at Farmville. Mahone's Division remained intact until the very end, and at Appomattox Court House on April 9 was apparently in better fighting trim than any other division of the army. Consisting of five brigades, the division numbered 3,537 officers and men. In the 12th Regiment 174 members were paroled, and of this number one sergeant and three privates were from the Richmond Grays.

# RICHMOND GRAYS

## CAPTAINS

Branch, Edwin W.
Crawford, Jacob V.
Elliott, Wyatt M.

Mayo, Robert Jr.
Tyler, James E.

## LIEUTENANTS

Boseieux, Louis J., 1st Lieut.
Crawford, Zachary L., 2nd Lieut.
Harrison, Randolph, 2nd Lieut.

Kelley, Patrick H., 2nd Lieut.
Phillips, James E., 1st Lieut.

## NON-COMMISSIONED OFFICERS AND PRIVATES

Allegree, W. R., Pvt.
Allen, Lorenzo D., Pvt.
Askew, John H., Pvt.
Baker, Dabney G., Pvt.
Baughn, Stephen D., Pvt.
Beck, Alexander, Pvt.
Bennett, John, Pvt.
Blackwell, James G., Pvt.
Bolling, Andrew W., Pvt.
Booth, Charles E., Pvt.
Booth, Robert S., Pvt.
Bossieux, Cyrus, Sgt.
Bossieux, Virginius, Pvt.
Bowers, Marcus M., Sgt.
Brett, William P., Ord. Sergt.
Burke, Edward, Pvt.
Clarke, Charles D., Pvt.
Clarke, Samuel S., Pvt.
Clements, James M., Pvt.
Collier, John E., Pvt.
Crump, Albert K., Pvt.
Crump, William W., Pvt.
Curtis, Henry, Pvt.
Curtis, John F., Pvt.
Daniel, John H., Pvt.
Daniel, John W., Pvt.
Davis, Francis J., Pvt.
Dickerson, Joseph C., Pvt.
Dickerson, Little J., Pvt.
Dowden, William, Pvt.
Duval, Francis, Pvt.
Edwards, P. D., Pvt.
Ellyson, Richard, Pvt.
Everett, William C., Pvt.
Ezekiel, E. M., Pvt.

Figg, James P., Pvt.
Fischer, Charles, Pvt.
Fiske, William H., Pvt.
Forde, William H., Pvt.
Gaines, Harry B., Pvt.
Gathright, Urias A., Pvt.
Gibson, George K., Corpl.
Gibson, Jed, Pvt.
Gibson, John Jr., Pvt.
Gibson, William, Pvt.
Goddard, Isaac, Pvt.
Grame, James, Pvt.
Grame, Thomas, Pvt.
Granger, Charles W., Corpl.
Grattan, George G., Pvt.
Grattan, James F., Pvt.
Griffin, Thomas, Pvt.
Gunn, Eugene K., Pvt.
Gunn, Richard B., Pvt.
Hankins, James F., Pvt.
Hardester, Henry, Pvt.
Hardgrove, James H., Pvt.
Hardgrove, John S., Pvt.
Harris, Abner T., Pvt.
Harrison, James R., Pvt.
Hawkins, Benjamin, Pvt.
Hawkins, Frank, Pvt.
Hazlewood, Robert, Pvt.
Heath, Robert T., Pvt.
Heth, Robert, Pvt.
Hill, George W., Pvt.
Hill, John A., Pvt.
Hirsh, Herman, Pvt.
Hollingsworth, James, Pvt.
Hunter, John G., Pvt.

James, George H., Pvt.
James, Thomas, Pvt.
Jennings, Robert F., Pvt.
Johns, William R., Pvt.
Johnson, William H., Corpl.
Kayton, John, Pvt.
Keesee, Jesse M., Pvt.
Keesee, Josiah T., Pvt.
Kelly, John, Pvt.
Kelly, Oscar R., Sgt.
Knowles, John A., Pvt.
Laughton, John E., Sgt.
Laughton, Lyman J., Pvt.
Learmont, John, Pvt.
Lee, William H., Pvt.
Libby, George W., Sgt.
Lovenstein, Isadore, Sgt.
Maben, John C., Pvt.
Mayo, William C., Sgt.
McConnochie, David, Corpl.
Meadows, Samuel J., Pvt.
Miller, Charles E., Pvt.
Mills, James H., Pvt.
Mills, Josiah, Pvt.
Mills, William O., Pvt.
Morganstein, Otto, Pvt.
Morse, Thomas, Pvt.
Mull, Oscar O., Pvt.
Mundy, J. H., Pvt.
Munford, Robert B., Corpl.
Myers, Marx, Pvt.
Nesbitt, William O., Pvt.
Nicholas, George O., Pvt.
Nimmo, Edward E., Pvt.
Old, Jacob B., Pvt.
Old, Philip W., Pvt.
Perdue, James, Pvt.
Phillips, Miles T., Pvt.
Phillips, Robert L., Sgt.
Pickett, Robert B., Pvt.
Pitt, John, Pvt.
Redford, Channing E., Corpl.

Richards, G. H., Pvt.
Richardson, D. A., Pvt.
Robins, Albert H., Pvt.
Rogers, Augustus F., Pvt.
Rogers, Winston, Pvt.
Rosenfels, Simon, Pvt.
Royster, Lawrence, Pvt.
Sacrey, Joseph B., Pvt.
Saunders, Christopher W., Pvt.
Shanks, John, Pvt.
Shipp, Josiah P., Pvt.
Siddons, James M., Pvt.
Smith, Harvey M., Pvt.
Smith, Samuel J., Corpl.
Smith, William Ira, Pvt.
Spence, E. Leslie, Pvt.
Stevenson, James Y., Pvt.
Sublet, Benjamin T., Pvt.
Swan, John, Pvt.
Symington, John B., Pvt.
Teel, Josiah, Pvt.
Teel, Nicholas, Pvt.
Teller, William R., Pvt.
Toms, Richard H., Pvt.
Turner, John A., Pvt.
Tyler, Sylvester N., Pvt.
Vaughan, John B., Sgt.
Walsh, Thomas C., Pvt.
Walton, Christ, Pvt.
Warden, William R., Pvt.
Warwick, Samuel, Pvt.
Weller, Joseph, Pvt.
West, John T., Pvt.
Whitlock, Philip, Pvt.
Williams, Evan, Pvt.
Williams, James, Pvt.
Williams, John W., Pvt.
Williams, Thomas B., Pvt.
Wilson, David, Pvt.
Wilson, John H., Pvt.
Wood, J. M., Sgt.
Woodson, William S., Pvt.

## RICHMOND LIGHT GUARD

The Richmond Light Guard, a company of infantry, was organized with over sixty-four men on July 19, 1861, with the election of Captain Gustavus A. Wallace, 1st Lieutenant James W. Spalding, and 2nd Lieutenant A. B. Shepperson. Captain Wallace began recruiting the company early in July and at his own expense provided the men with uniforms, board, and lodging. Headquarters for the company was located on 13th Street, between Main and Cary; presumably this was Captain Wallace's office. Lieutenant Spalding was the first colonel of the 179th Regiment of Militia, organized in 1848. The company enrolled for active duty on July 20, and by the 27th was encamped on Vauxhaul's Island in the James River. By August 3, however, the company was stationed at the New Fair Grounds on the western edge of Richmond.

On August 8 the Richmond Light Guard, under Lieutenant Spalding, left Richmond for White Sulphur Springs, where they joined the Wise Legion. Captain Wallace remained in Richmond to procure additional supplies of clothing for the company and to bring up the few members which had been left behind. By August 13 the Wise Legion was permanently organized. Lieutenant Spalding was appointed lieutenant colonel of the 3rd Regiment of Infantry, Wise Legion, in which the Richmond Light Guard was assigned as Company H. The regiment was also designated the 60th Regiment Virginia Infantry. On August 20 the Richmond Light Guard was mustered into Confederate States service.

The forces of Generals John B. Floyd and Henry A. Wise moved in the direction of the Kanawha Valley, and on August 21 were united at Gauley Mountain. Wise moved to Carnifax Ferry on the 22nd, but on the next day marched to Dogwood Gap. From August 24-31 the Richmond Light Guard is known to have been with the regiment at Camp Dogwood. After the battle at Carnifax Ferry on September 10, Floyd and Wise fell back to Sewell Mountain, arriving there on the 14th. General Floyd, on September 16, withdrew his command twelve miles eastward to Meadow Bluff. General Wise was ordered to Richmond on September 25 and Colonel J. Lucius Davis was placed in command of the Legion. Two days later, Lieutenant Colonel Spalding, commanding the regiment, died and Lieutenant Colonel James L. Corley, who later served as Quartermaster on General Lee's staff, was appointed as Spalding's successor. At the same time, Colonel William E. Starke was assigned to command the regiment. The Federals retired to the Gauley River on October 6 and General Floyd moved out against them. The Wise Legion, however, was detained and sent to Meadow Bluff where they guarded the road leading to Lewisburg. General Floyd's operations were abandoned, and by the end of October the Kanawha Valley Campaign was over.

When the 60th Regiment Virginia Infantry was reorganized in November 1861, to exclude the four companies raised in eastern Virginia the Richmond Light Guard was transferred to Colonel Charles F. Henningsen's

59th Regiment Virginia Infantry (2nd Regiment of Infantry, Wise Legion), in which organization they were designated as Company L. The 60th Regiment was transferred out of the Wise Legion.

General Wise, on December 21, 1861, was assigned to command the forces in the district composed of that part of North Carolina east of the Chowan River and the counties of Washington and Tyrrell, which were designated the Fourth Brigade, Department of Norfolk. At his request the War Department consented to assign the Legion to General Wise's new command and on December 21, Colonel Davis was ordered to proceed immediately to Richmond with the Legion, which was still in the western part of the State. The 1st Regiment of Infantry, Wise Legion, left Richmond on January 14 for Norfolk and the North Carolina coast. Colonel Henningsen's regiment left about a week later and was in Petersburg on January 21, when four men of the Richmond Light Guard were shot for mutiny. On January 28 Henningsen's command, which included three batteries of the Wise Legion artillery, arrived in Norfolk, and departed for North Carolina on the 1st of February.

Captain Wallace, a second lieutenant, and forty-five enlisted men of the Richmond Light Guard, were engaged in the battle of Roanoke Island on February 7-8, 1862. The officers and forty-two enlisted men were among the troops surrendered to the forces of General Burnside. Three men made their escape from the island, and three of the company who were held as prisoners were not released on parole. The company lost all arms, accoutrements and clothing, save that which they wore. On February 18 the regiment was released on parole and placed on a steamer which took them up the Albemarle Sound where they were transferred to another vessel. The regiment arrived in Richmond on February 25. On March 19 the Richmond Light Guard was ordered to be mustered out of service, but on May 13 the order was revoked and the company was reassigned to the 59th Regiment, in which it was designated as Company L.

For some time after the Roanoke Island disaster, General Wise was without a command. Through the influence of General Lee, however, on May 10, 1862 the remnants of the 46th and 59th regiments, which formerly belonged to the Wise Legion, and the 26th and 34th regiments, were formed into an infantry brigade to which Wise was assigned to command. The brigade was stationed at Chaffin's Farm and for the next sixteen months performed outpost duty and participated in various expeditions east of Richmond.

In September 1862 the 59th Regiment was apparently ordered to western Virginia, whereupon the Richmond Light Guard was transferred to the 46th Regiment Virginia Infantry, and was reported on the regiment's returns for September and October as Company L. In November the Richmond Light Guard was returned to the 59th Regiment, which had been reorganized under Colonel William B. Tabb and designated as Company F. The company was stationed at Varina, Henrico County, from October through November 16; and during this period lost twelve men by desertion. By November 23 the company was back in camp at Chaffin's Farm.

On March 29, 1863 the Richmond Light Guard participated in Colonel Tabb's expedition which captured Williamsburg. The company was also among Captain Wallace's forces in the unsuccessful attempt to seize Fort Magruder, about two miles outside the town. On March 30, Tabb's command was back at Diascund Bridge. Three men from the company were captured in the skirmishing at Williamsburg.

Early in April of 1863, General Wise was ordered to proceed as far as practicable in the direction of Fort Monroe, threaten the enemy, and do as much damage as possible. This move was intended to prevent the Federals from sending reinforcements against General Longstreet, who was operating around Suffolk. The 59th Regiment was ordered to attack the headquarters of the enemy at Whitaker's Mill, five miles in rear of the Federal positions at Williamsburg. On April 11, Colonel Tabb's regiment successfully burned the headquarters and stores of provisions and munitions at the mill. About nine men from the Richmond Light Guard were captured during the expedition.

The regiment was at Riddell's Shop in Henrico County on May 5, and on the 6th marched for Turner's Bridge and toward Tunstall's Station on the York River Railroad in New Kent County. On May 8 the regiment was encamped at Mechanicsville, and by the end of June the Richmond Light Guard was posted at Long Bridge, on the Chickahominy. The company at this time had three officers and thirty-nine enlisted men present for duty; sixteen were absent without leave, and nineteen were carried on the rolls as deserters.

In September 1863 Wise's Brigade was sent to South Carolina for duty in the Sixth Military District of the Department of South Carolina, Georgia and Florida. There the brigade was almost constantly engaged in guard duty and in the construction of fortifications between the Ashley and Edisto rivers.

On January 15, 1864 while the Richmond Light Guard was at Camp Stono on the Stono River, near Wilkes, Captain Wallace tendered his resignation, following a quarrel with Colonel Tabb which had apparently been going on for some time. 1st Lieutenant Robert C. Nicholas was promoted to captain on February 20, succeeding Captain Wallace, whose resignation was accepted on the same day.

On February 9 the 59th Regiment, then constructing earthworks down the Stono River at Church Flat, was ordered out with other elements of the brigade against a Federal force which had occupied John's Island further up the river. After the retirement of the enemy on the 12th, the regiment was kept on the island for the purpose of erecting defenses.

In late February the regiment was transferred to Florida for duty with Major General Patton Anderson's command at Camp Milton, near Baldwin. On April 17 the regiment was ordered to Savannah; however, by April 30 they were in camp near Green Pond, S. C. The regiment had just reported for service in the Charleston defenses when, on May 3, they were ordered to Virginia.

Wise's Brigade proceeded by rail to Virginia, with the 59th Regiment in advance. At Nottoway Bridge the regiment engaged Kautz's cavalry, and succeeded in driving them back, although they failed to prevent the destruction of the bridge. The brigade reached Petersburg and was assigned to General W. H. C. Whiting's command. Although they did not arrive in time to reinforce General Beauregard at the Battle of Drewry's Bluff, the brigade was heavily engaged on May 18-28 on the Howlett line, bottling up Butler's army.

The 59th Regiment remained north of the Appomattox River until June 15 when they were hurried down to Petersburg, then under attack. The regiment saw much hard fighting in the repulse of the Federal assaults east of Petersburg, June 15-18, and throughout the remainder of the month. On July 30 at the Battle of the Crater, the brigade was located east of the breech in the lines caused by the explosion. The 59th was brought into a position from which it could assist others in delivering a deadly fire at the crater, holding the enemy until the arrival of reinforcements under General Mahone. Following the Battle of the Crater, the company remained in the Petersburg line.

The Richmond Light Guard, by the end of February 1865, had dwindled down to one officer, 1st Lieutenant Charles Volk, and seven enlisted men present for duty. Captain Nicholas and others were absent on sick leave, eleven were absent without leave, and five were in Federal prison camps.

Early in March, Wise's Brigade was ordered from the lines east of Petersburg, to the extreme right at Hatcher's Run. On March 29 the brigade was ordered into line of battle near Burgess' Mill, from where they advanced toward Gravelly Run, with the 59th Regiment on the right flank. The enemy was soon encountered and the brigade was forced back to Hatcher's Run. On the night of March 31st the brigade fell back to Sutherland's on the Southside Railroad, and proceeded to reinforce General Pickett at Five Forks. News of Pickett's defeat was learned on the morning of the 2nd, and the brigade fell back to Namozine Creek. Petersburg was evacuated that night and the army began its march westward. On April 6 the brigade was engaged in the fighting around Sayler's Creek. None of the officers and only six enlisted men of the Richmond Light Guard received their paroles at Appomattox Court House on April 10.

## RICHMOND LIGHT GUARD

### CAPTAINS

Wallace, Gustavus A.
Nicholas, Robert C.

### LIEUTENANTS

Aitchison, William A., 2nd Lieut.
Little, John Chapman, 2nd Lieut.
Pearce, James H., 2nd Lieut.
Shepperson, Alfred B., 1st Lieut.
Spalding, James W., 1st Lieut.
Trehen, John R., 2nd Lieut.
Valk, Charles, 1st Lieut.

### NON-COMMISSIONED OFFICERS AND PRIVATES

Adams, John B., Pvt.
Armstrong, John, Pvt.
Baber, William S., Pvt.
Bailey, Daniel, Pvt.
Bailey, John, Pvt.
Baker, William H., Pvt.
Baker, William M., Pvt.
Bardell, John P., Pvt.
Bassford, William, Pvt.
Bower, Michael, Pvt.
Bradfield, John E., Pvt.
Breen, Michael, Pvt.
Brown, Charles, Pvt.
Brown, James, Pvt.
Brunson, Albert, Pvt.
Bryant, J. A., Pvt.
Bryant, J. H., Pvt.
Burke, James, Corp.
Burton, Robert, Pvt.
Cain, Richard, Pvt.
Campbell, Frederick, Corp.
Campbell, James, Pvt.
Carpenter, Peter, Pvt.
Chambers, C. G., Pvt.
Coghill, John E., Pvt.
Conner, Samuel, Pvt.
Conners, Andrew, Sgt.
Conners, Christopher, Pvt.
Cromwell, Solomon M., Pvt.
Crumley, John, Pvt.
Cullen, Patrick, Pvt.
Cusick, Dennis, Pvt.
Cutter, George F., Pvt.
Daily, Peter, Pvt.
Davis, William J., Pvt.
Dawson, John G., Sgt.
Day, Henry, Pvt.
Deary, Robert, Pvt.
Dewitt, William, Pvt.
Douglass, George, Pvt.
Edwards, James, Pvt.
Edwards, John, Pvt.
Eghart, J., Pvt.
Eudailey, C. H., Sgt.
Evans, Richard M., Pvt.
Fisher, Benjamin, Pvt.
Fitzgerald, Michael, Pvt.
Flinn, James, Pvt.
Foster, William T., Pvt.
French, Samuel, Pvt.
Fuller, Moses D., Pvt.
Galvin, James, Pvt.
George, John, Pvt.
Glover, R. B., Pvt.
Golden, Patrick, Pvt.
Grainer, John, Pvt.
Hall, William, Pvt.
Harris, William, Pvt.
Hart, John L., Pvt.
Hartless, L., Pvt.
Hartnall, Jerry, Pvt.
Hinston, Edwin J., Pvt.
Hodges, Thomas R., Pvt.
Hudnall, P. P., Pvt.
Hulschbacker, Joseph, Pvt.
Hurley, John, Pvt.
Ingraham, Nath. P., Pvt.
Irvine, William, Pvt.

Jackson, Joseph, Pvt.
Johnson, Hiram P., Pvt.
Johnstone, Thomas, Pvt.
Jones, Charles, Pvt.
Jones, J. M., Pvt.
Keating, John, Pvt.
Kelly, Robert W., Pvt.
Kenney, Edward, Sgt.
Kestler, William, Pvt.
King, A. S., Pvt.
Kinston, Edgar J., Pvt.
Knight, T. A., Pvt.
Kraus, William, 1st Sgt.
Larkin, Joseph, Pvt.
Leffew, John R., Pvt.
Linder, Edward, Pvt.
Long, Madison, Pvt.
Loran, Michael, Pvt.
Loving, Peter, Pvt.
Maloney, Robert R., Pvt.
Martin, Reuben, Pvt.
Mason, William, Pvt.
Maupin, C. W., Pvt.
Maxwell, John, Pvt.
McCarty, John, Pvt.
McCraw, J. T., Pvt.
McDonald, John, Pvt.
McDuffy, Michael, Pvt.
McGary, John, Pvt.
McGowan, Patrick, Pvt.
McMahon, John, Pvt.
McNeil, Stephen, Pvt.
Mears, George Thomas, Pvt.
Merideth, Jasper, Pvt.
Miller, Augustus, Pvt.
Miller, R. S., Pvt.
Miller, William M., Pvt.
Miller, W. M., Pvt.
Montgomery, James, Pvt.
Moore, Patrick, Pvt.
Morarity, Michael, Pvt.
Murphy, Edward J., Pvt.
Murphy, Patrick, Pvt.
Newman, L. P., Pvt.
Nichols, John W., Pvt.
Nowlan, J., Pvt.
O'Brien, Eustace, Pvt.
Odot, Vincent N., Pvt.
Oniel, Joseph, Pvt.
Orr, H. V., Pvt.
Owens, Richard, Pvt.
Puller, A. B., Corp.
Quinn, Michael, Pvt.
Reynolds, Thomas, Pvt.
Robinson, C. T., Pvt.
Rogers, William H., Pvt.
Rogers, William T., Pvt.
Ryan, William, Pvt.
Saunders, John, Pvt.
Saunders, William R., Pvt.
Schneider, Frederick, Pvt.
Scott, George W., Pvt.
Sellers, Calvin, Pvt.
Shide, James H., Pvt.
Smith, P., Pvt.
Smith, R., Pvt.
Snell, James A., Pvt.
Somers, Charles, Pvt.
Starke, A. J., Pvt.
Steele, George, Pvt.
Talman, William A., Pvt.
Tarrant, John T., Pvt.
Tensor, Charles, Pvt.
Thomas, J. J., Corp.
Thomas, John S., Pvt.
Thompson, George W., Pvt.
Thompson, R., Pvt.
Towers, William, Pvt.
Tuck, William Thomas, Pvt.
Tutwiler, C. H., Pvt.
Valentine, William, Pvt.
Vick, James, Pvt.
Waller, Charles, Pvt.
Walls, E. B., Pvt.
Walsh, John, Pvt.
Walter, John, Pvt.
Ward, Frank, Pvt.
White, Charles H., Corp.
Whorton, S. G., Pvt.
Wilson, Henry, Corp.
Wright, Thomas N., Pvt.

# RICHMOND LIGHT INFANTRY BLUES

The exact date of the organization of the Richmond Light Infantry Blues is not known. In 1788 John Willis was reported as captain of a company known as the Richmond Light Infantry. However, it appears that Captain Willis' company failed to complete its organization, as he was not commissioned by the State. In 1789 William Richardson raised a company, also known as the Richmond Light Infantry, and was elected its captain. In its early days the company wore a uniform of scarlet. The unpopularity of the color contributed to the waning interest in the company prior to 1793.

In 1793 the company was reorganized and adopted a blue uniform trimmed with white. The officers resigned and an election was held on May 1, 1793. Captain Richardson was re-elected and commissioned on May 10. John A. Cutchins wrote in *A Famous Command The Richmond Light Infantry Blues*, published in 1934, that because of the new blue uniform "the company came to be spoken of generally as the Blues. Apparently the word Blues ultimately was incorporated in the official designation by common consent and from usage, and since that time the company has been known as the Richmond Light Infantry Blues." When Congress passed the act establishing the Militia on May 8, 1792, the Militia of Richmond was formed into a regiment and designated the 19th Regiment of Militia. The Blues became a light infantry company of one of the battalions of the 19th Regiment of Militia.

On August 30, 1800 the news of a slave insurrection caused Governor James Monroe to order the 19th and 33rd Regiments of Militia to hold themselves in readiness for service. "General" Gabriel's insurrection failed to materialize when his plans were disclosed, but the troops remained in service until October 18. The company did not see service again until 1807, when it was ordered to Norfolk to defend against a threatened invasion by the British squadron in Hampton Roads. Leaving Richmond on July 8, the company reached Portsmouth on the 15th. When the threatened invasion did not materialize the troops were ordered back, and the company returned to Richmond on July 28.

During the War of 1812, the company, now commanded by Captain William Murphy, was called into active service on two occasions. From March 18, 1813 to March 27, 1813 the company was on duty every other day. On August 14, 1814 the British entered Washington. Rumor spread that they were moving on Richmond, and on August 25 the Blues were called into service. They remained on active duty until October 5, 1814. Following these brief tours, the company remained on inactive duty, participating in local events and celebrations.

When the 1st Regiment of Virginia Volunteers was organized in May 1851, the Richmond Light Infantry Blues were assigned to the regiment. At first the companies of the regiment were not given letter designation; but in 1856 they were, and the Blues were designated Company E. The Blues were at drill in their armory on the night of October 18, 1859

**Brigadier General Henry A. Wise**

He was Governor of Virginia 1856-1860; commissioned as brigadier general, Provisional Army, Confederate States, on June 5, 1861.

Courtesy Virginia State Library

**O. Jennings Wise**

Son of former Governor and Brigadier General Henry A. Wise, Jennings Wise was elected captain Richmond Light Infantry Blues, January 1861. He was killed at Roanoke Island February 9, 1862 while in command of the Blues (Company A, 46th Regiment Virginia Infantry) which company was serving in his father's brigade.

Courtesy Virginia State Library

when word was received of John Brown's attack on Harpers Ferry. Orders came to prepare to leave the next morning for Harpers Ferry. The company entrained as ordered, but was turned back en route. On November 19 the entire 1st Regiment was ordered to Charlestown, when rumors spread that an attempt would be made to release the prisoners. As the regiment moved to Charlestown, the company was left at Harpers Ferry and moved to Martinsburg, where it remained until it returned to Richmond on the 7th.

On January 21, 1861 O. Jennings Wise was elected captain, and seven days later the men of the company amended their by-laws to direct that "each member shall provide himself with a grey uniform as prescribed by the requirements of the First Virginia Regiment of Volunteers, to be used on regimental parades or whenever the company may be ordered into the service by the Governor of Virginia." However, there was a growing dissatisfaction by members of the company over their assignment to the 1st Regiment Virginia Volunteers. When war came, the company responded to the Governor's call, and was encamped near the city at the reservoir on April 21. On the 23rd of April the company voted unanimously to attach itself "to some new regiment to be placed under the command of a former United States officer who is a tactician and a disciplinarian." Thus the company voted to withdraw from the 1st Regiment. On that same day, a detachment of the Blues was ordered to Rocketts, in the lower part of the city, when the alarm was given that the U. S. ship Pawnee was ascending the James. The detachment returned to camp when the Pawnee failed to appear.

The company left for Fredericksburg on April 24 with F Company. Upon their arrival, on the same day, the companies went into camp at the fair grounds. On May 14 the Blues moved to Aquia Creek to repel a reported Federal landing. Finding the report to be false, the company moved to Marlboro Point, where it remained until June 10. During this period, the company was engaged in supporting the batteries along the river; and whenever a Federal steamer appeared, the company was moved to support the threatened battery. On June 7, Captain Wise informed the company that this father, ex-Governor Henry A. Wise, had been appointed a Brigadier General, and that he was going to western Virginia. Considering it his duty to be with his father, Captain Wise left it to the company to decide whether it would stay or request a transfer. The company voted to follow Captain Wise; and upon receipt of authorization to transfer to General Wise's command, the company entrained for Richmond on June 10.

After three days in Richmond, the company entrained on June 13 for western Virginia. Arriving at Lewisburg, Greenbrier County, on the 14th, the company went into camp on the fair grounds. On June 17 the company was mustered into Confederate States service for the duration of the war. At this time it was apparently assigned to the 59th Regiment Virginia Infantry (2nd Regiment of Infantry, Wise Legion) as Company A. The next day, the company moved to Gauley Bridge, where it remained until the 25th. On that day, Wise moved his command to the Kanawha

River. Boarding a steamer, the command moved to Charleston, arriving on the 26th. From Charleston, the company moved to Ripley, Jackson County, on the 29th. Here it remained, scouting the surrounding country, until relieved and ordered back to Charleston on July 9.

With the defeat of the Confederate forces in northwestern Virginia, General Wise determined to retire eastward. Leaving Charleston on the 24th of July, Wise's command crossed Gauley Bridge on the 27th. Closely pursued, Wise retired to Lewisburg. Before departing from Gauley Bridge on the 27th, the Blues were assigned to the 46th Regiment Virginia Infantry (1st Regiment of Infantry, Wise Legion) as Company A. The movements of the company were recorded in the company record book as follows:

> We arrived at Boyd's Mills, 5 miles from Lewisburg, and remained there until August 2nd, when we took up the line of march for the White Sulphur Springs, and reached there on Saturday, August 3rd, resting, recruiting and drilling until Thursday, 15th. By command of Brigadier General J. B. Floyd, the Wise Legion, with the Blues at their head, took the line of march again for the west and went as far as Sewell Mountain, from thence to Dogwood Gap, 16 miles from Gauley Bridge. Thursday, 25th August. Was ordered to Carnifax Ferry to meet the enemy, but as usual they had left.
>
> From the 1st of August to the 20th of the same month, remained principally at Dogwood Gap, and about the 1st of September had a slight skirmish near the Hawk's Nest. Went with a flag of truce to the Hawk's Nest next day.

On August 5 General Floyd had been ordered to join Wise at White Sulphur Springs. Uniting forces, Floyd determined to march against the advancing Federals. With his command, Floyd crossed the Gauley and defeated a Federal force at Cross Lanes on the 26th. Wise had moved his command to Dogwood Gap. Floyd retired to Carnifax Ferry and Wise moved on Hawk's Nest on the 2nd of September. Finding the enemy reinforced, Wise retired to Hamilton. On September 10 Floyd retired from Carnifax Ferry after withstanding a determined Federal attack. After a conference, both Wise and Floyd withdrew to Big Sewell Mountain on the 14th of September. Floyd withdrew his command on the night of the 16th to Meadow Bluff. Wise refused to follow, and continued entrenching his position on Little Sewell Mountain.

General Lee arrived at Meadow Bluff and moved forward to Wise's position. After examining the terrain, he ordered Floyd's command to reinforce Wise. On the 23rd of September the Federals began driving in Wise's pickets. On the 25th, General Wise received orders to report to Richmond, and on that day Floyd's command arrived at Little Sewell. Lee hoped the Federals would assault his strong position, but on October 6 the Federal commander withdrew westward. Lee ordered Floyd to pursue the enemy. Leaving the Wise Legion at Little Sewell, Floyd attempted to organize his advance; but the terrain, bad weather, and the condition of his command delayed the execution of his plan, and the Federals retired without being molested.

The Wise Legion remained at Little Sewell until October 20, when it was moved to Meadow Bluff. On December 10 the Blues moved to Lewisburg, and to Red Sweet Springs on the 13th. On the 15th the company moved to Salem, where it entrained for Lynchburg. On December 22 the company started for Richmond, arriving on the 23rd. Here it remained until January 14, 1862.

General Wise had been assigned to command "that part of North Carolina east of the Chowan River, together with the counties of Washington and Tyrrell" on December 21, 1861. He assumed command on January 7, 1862 and requested that the Wise Legion be ordered to him. Portions of the infantry regiments were ordered to do so, and on January 14, 1862 the Blues left Richmond for Petersburg. From Petersburg the company moved to Nags Head, North Carolina, by way of Norfolk. Arriving at Nags Head on January 21, the company received a brief rest before moving to Roanoke Island. Here, on February 8, the company was heavily engaged in the unsuccessful defense of the island against a numerically superior Federal force. Captain Wise was mortally wounded during the fighting; and as the company tried to regroup, it was learned that the island had been surrendered. Marching into the Federal camp, the Blues surrendered their arms. The company losses were: three mortally wounded, seven wounded, and fifty-one captured. On February 12 the men signed paroles and boarded boats on the 19th and 20th for the trip to the James. They arrived in Richmond on February 25.

Steps were immediately taken to reorganize the company. A recruiting office was set up and all members not on parole were ordered into camp near the reservoir. Those on parole could not rejoin the company until they were exchanged on August 16, 1862. The company's next captain, Fred Carter, was a paroled prisoner and could not join the company until after his exchange. Until that time, the company was commanded by Lieutenant Richard I. Sanxay. With the remnants of the 46th Regiment, the Blues remained in camp until the regiment was ordered to Yorktown on March 30, 1862. Companies A, B, C, E and H, 46th Regiment, left Richmond on the next day. On April 5 the company manned the redoubts near Fort Magruder, and was subjected to artillery fire without casualty. On the morning of April 16 the regiment crossed the York River to reinforce the garrison at Gloucester Point.

On May 3, General Johnston began withdrawing his troops up the Peninsula, and the forces at Gloucester Point were ordered to retire. During the night of May 3-4, the 46th Regiment marched to Gloucester Court House, where it received orders to move to Centreville. Arriving late on the 4th, the regiment moved to King and Queen Court House on the 5th. On May 10 General Wise was assigned to command a brigade consisting of the 46th and 59th Regiments, two of his old Legion regiments.

Later the 4th Regiment Virginia Heavy Artillery and the 20th and 26th Regiments Virginia Infantry were added to the brigade.

After several long marches, the company was encamped on Roper's Farm, near Richmond, on May 18. By May 29, Wise's Brigade was moved to Chaffin's Bluff, on the right of the Confederate line around Richmond. During the Seven Days', a portion of Wise's Brigade, including the 46th Regiment, was temporarily attached to General Holmes' Division on June 30. Moving to New Market, Wise was ordered to advance down the River Road. On July 1, at Malvern Hill, Wise's Brigade was engaged on the Confederate right during the battle. Late in the evening of July 2, Wise was ordered to return to Chaffin's Bluff.

When the army was reorganized after the Seven Days', Wise's Brigade was attached to General D. H. Hill's Division, Longstreet's command. On July 23, Wise's Brigade was detached from Hill's Division and assigned to the Department of Richmond. While the Army of Northern Virginia moved to oppose Pope in northern Virginia, Wise's Brigade remained at Chaffin's Bluff. On August 16 the paroled members of the Blues, who had been captured at Roanoke Island, were exchanged. They rejoined the company on the 22nd, and 1st Lieutenant Fred Carter was promoted to captain.

With the exception of a few minor skirmishes, the company saw little active field duty for the balance of 1862. Winter quarters were established at Chaffin's Farm on the 23rd of November, where the company remained until January 7, 1863. On that day, it marched to Richmond. Here the company remained on provost duty until May 11, when it rejoined the regiment at Chaffin's Farm. The company record book indicates that the company did not remain in the city all that time. The following entries indicate it was called out to engage the enemy:

> April 16th. Made several excursions through Charles City County after the Yankees. Camped several times in New Kent County at a place called Barhamsville. The inhabitants were very kind although nearly everything had been destroyed by the Yankees.
>
> We started on a march for Williamsburg to drive out the Yankees. They hearing we were coming were largely re-inforced. Our general in command concluded not to attack them then, and we were ordered to return to our old camp....
>
> May 2nd. It having been reported that a fight had commenced at Fredericksburg, we were ordered to prepare to leave by the Richmond, Fredericksburg & Potomac Railroad.
>
> May 3rd. Leave Richmond, stopped at South Anna Bridge in afternoon. The Yankees on a raid, enter Ashland and tried to draw us away from the bridge. At night several fires caused by the Yankee incendiaries were plainly seen from our position. The object in the first instance

was to draw us away from the bridge, but their main object was deviltry, stimulated by Yankee greed. The bridge was saved by the exertion of the R. L. I. Blues, bivouacked in the open field without tents or blankets.

May 10th, 1863. Seventieth Anniversary of the Blues. Not celebrated as usual on account of the War for National Independence. Also announcement of the death of General Jackson (Stonewall) cast a gloom over the spirits of the company....

May 11th. Marched back to old camp at Chaffin's Farm.

Three days after its arrival at Chaffin's Farm, the company moved toward New Kent Court House. Moving to Barhamsville, the company encamped until May 23, when it moved to Saltville. Detachments were sent out as scouts, and on June 4 the company took part in the general movement on Williamsburg. After advancing as far as Barhamsville, orders were received countermanding the move on Williamsburg and ordering the company to Glennis, on the Pamunkey River. On June 17 the Blues returned to Chaffin's Farm. When reports were received of a Federal advance up the Peninsula, the 46th Regiment moved to Long Bridge on June 28. On July 1 it returned to Chaffin's Farm. Here it remained until September 11, when Wise's Brigade was ordered to South Carolina for duty in the defense of Charleston.

Moving to Richmond, the Blues entrained on September 14th and arrived at Charleston late on the 19th. Wise's Brigade was assembled at the depot and moved to Camp Duke, on the Wappoo River, about three miles southwest of Charleston. On October 22, General Wise was assigned to command the district south of the Ashley River and west of Wappoo Cut. On November 4 the 46th Regiment was ordered to James Island; and, on the 7th, it was moved to Fort Johnson, James Island. For the next few weeks the men were under heavy shell fire. They remained on James Island until relieved on the 14th of November, when they returned to Camp Duke.

The company remained at Camp Duke until December 10, when it marched to Adams Run. The next day it moved to Jacksonboro, near the Edisto River. Here it remained until February 21, 1864, when it marched to Jacksonboro, where "it took cars for Rantowles Station, our regiment having been removed to Church Flats near that place." At Adams Run, on February 23, the following entry was made in the company record book:

> General Wise said that the Blues were the damnest hardest set of men to manage he ever had anything to do with, but they were perfect devils in a fight, and if he had a hazardous job on hand, he knew he could depend upon them in any emergency for prompt execution if they did not perish in the attempt. The whole camp would follow him to the very Devil if he requested it, provided he knew the road.

On May 3, 1864 General Wise's Brigade was ordered to proceed by rail to Richmond. Leaving on the 5th, the troops moved by way of Charleston and Wilmington, and arrived at Weldon, N. C., on the 8th. Leaving Weldon at midnight on the 8th, the troops proceeded to Petersburg, where they arrived about 8 p.m. on the 9th.

General Wise was assigned to command the Petersburg District under General Beauregard on May 10. On the 15th, Wise's Brigade was assigned to General W. H. C. Whiting's Division and took part in Beauregard's campaign to bottle up Butler at Bermuda Hundred. Moving to Swift Creek, the Blues formed a part of the line of skirmishers as Whiting's Division crossed the creek on the morning of the 16th. Contacting the enemy skirmishers on Timberry Creek, the Confederates drove them back to Walthall Junction, where they encountered a larger Federal force. Advancing his division, Whiting drove the Federals from the Junction. During this engagement, the Blues suffered one killed and four wounded. On the next day, the command moved forward and effected a junction with the balance of Beauregard's command. The 46th Regiment entrenched their position at Bake House Creek. On the 22nd of May, Wise's Brigade was moved to the left of Beauregard's line to the James River, near Dr. Howlett's house. Here, on June 2, the company took part in a general operation to drive in the enemy pickets and gain more suitable ground to establish new entrenchments.

On June 3 the 46th Regiment was withdrawn from the entrenchments and ordered to Petersburg, where it encamped at Dunn's Farm, about two and a half miles from the city. While the regiment received a brief rest, a portion of the Blues was deployed on picket duty. On June 9, Wise's Brigade, supported by Dearing's cavalry, and the local Militia and Home Guard, successfully repulsed a Federal attempt to capture Petersburg. On June 12, Grant began moving his army toward Petersburg, and on June 15 General W. F. Smith's Corps moved upon the Confederate works at Petersburg. Wise's Brigade stubbornly held the first line of works until about 7:30 p.m., when they were forced to retire to a second line. During the night, reinforcements arrived from the Army of Northern Virginia. The next day, three Federal corps renewed the attack and succeeded in making a lodgment, but could not drive the Confederates from the works. On the 17th, the Federals, now reinforced by an additional corps, renewed the attack. About dusk, a portion of the Confederate line was broken, but reinforcements arrived on the field from the Army of Northern Virginia and closed the breach. Selecting a shorter line in rear of his front line, Beauregard withdrew the entire Confederate line to the new line during the night of June 17-18, 1864. Reinforced by Longstreet's Corps, the defenders of Petersburg successfully halted the Federal advance on the 18th. From June 15 to 18 the Blues lost three killed, eleven wounded, and one missing. Among those killed was Captain Carter, who died on the 17th from wounds received on the 15th. Following the death of Captain Carter, 1st Lieutenant Charles Purcell Bigger was promoted to captain.

Following the establishment of the line with the arrival of Longstreet's men, General Beauregard's men were incorporated into the Army of Northern Virginia. Wise's Brigade was assigned to General B. R. Johnson's Division. This division occupied the lines on either side of Pegram's salient. On July 30 the Federals exploded a mine under the salient in an effort to breach the line. The Blues were "some two or three hundred yards" from the crater, and delivered a flanking fire on the advancing Federals. About 11 a.m., the company moved about the length of the company to the left. Here it remained, firing into the Federal flank as reinforcements closed the breach and a new line was formed in rear of the crater. During this action, the Blues lost one killed and seven wounded.

The Blues remained in the Petersburg line until it was evacuated on April 2, 1865. From June 18, 1864 to April 2, 1865 the company saw active duty in the trenches and on picket, frequently engaging in skirmishes with the enemy pickets. In October, the Colonel, Lieutenant Colonel, and several members of the 46th Regiment were captured when the regiment relieved another regiment late in the evening. Believing the advancing Federals to be the retiring pickets of the relieved unit, the Confederates allowed the Federals to advance to the trenches before discovering the error. A brief skirmish ensued, during which the officers and men were captured before the Federals were driven out. On November 17, 1864 Captain Bigger retired, and 1st Lieutenant Ezekiel J. Levy was promoted to command the company. Captain Levy resigned on February 2, 1865, and 1st Lieutenant George W. Jarvis was promoted to captain.

Early in March 1865, Wise's Brigade, still serving in General B. R. Johnson's Division, was ordered to the extreme right of the line at Hatcher's Run. Evidence proved the Federals were moving to turn Lee's right. To contain them, Lee ordered Pickett's Division, reinforced by two brigades from Johnson's Division, and three divisions of cavalry to Five Forks. The two remaining brigades of Johnson's Division, Wise and Wallace, were ordered to actively demonstrate against the enemy in their front. On March 29 they advanced against the Federals near Burgess' Mill. After a stubborn fight, the Confederates were forced to retire to their entrenchments. Again on the 31st they advanced against the Federals in their front. Again they were forced to retire. On the night of the 31st, Wise's and Wallace's brigades moved to Sutherland Station on the South Side Railroad to reinforce Pickett at Five Forks.

The next day, news reached them of Pickett's defeat at Five Forks, and under orders, they withdrew to Namozine Creek. Here they were engaged on the 3rd of April when Sheridan's cavalry assaulted their position. Retiring that night, the brigades were engaged the next day at Deep Creek, near Mannsboro. Following this engagement, the two brigades rejoined the army retreating westward. General Wise later reported that his brigade "passed on by Amelia Court House, Jetersville, and Deatonsville, zig-zagging from right to left, and from left to right, and skirmishing the whole way until we came to the forks of Sayler's Creek, near Jamestown, and the High Bridge, on the 6th of April." Here, on that same day, the brigade was actively engaged during the battle at Sayler's Creek and managed to escape capture by cutting its way out before being surrounded. Moving to Farmville, Wise's brigade rejoined the army. The final events were recorded in the company record book:

> We crossed the river, near Farmville, arrived there about nine o'clock in the morning of the 7th of April. Some of the Yankee cavalry had been in there ahead of us. We marched through, when the enemy commenced shelling us again. We then took up our line of march for Lynchburg, but did not get any further than Appomattox Court House. We arrived there about 4 o'clock Saturday evening and went in camp. In a short time the enemy charged on our artillery camp and spiked several guns, so we had orders to advance on the enemy; remained under arms all night. The next morning we renewed the fighting; drove them some distance back. We then received orders to cease firing as General Lee would be forced to surrender to overwhelming numbers. The orders were brought by a Yankee general with pomp and stuffed full of self-conceit, accompanied by one of our men as his pilot. He said he had orders for our surrender from General Gordon who commanded the corps that we were in. The men could not or would not believe him, and insisted that it was a Yankee trick. Some said shoot him. Others said take him prisoner. Some of our officers sent him back with a squad of men to see if it were true. They came back with elongated faces and said it was a lamentable fact. We were then marched back to camp.

Sixteen men remained with the army when it was surrendered on April 9, 1865.

## RICHMOND LIGHT INFANTRY BLUES

### CAPTAINS

Bigger, Charles P.
Carter, Fred
Levy, E. J.

Wise, O. Jennings
Wise, William B., Sgt. Major.

### LIEUTENANTS

Bagwell, Edmund R., 2nd Lieut.
Gregory, E. J., 1st Lieut.
Hopkins, George H., 2nd Lieut.
Jarvis, George W., 1st Lieut
Maule, W. L., 2nd Lieut.

McDowell, Robert J., 2nd Lieut.
Sanxay, Richard S., 2nd Lieut.
Scott, James A., 1st Lieut.
Warden, William R., Lieut.

### NON-COMMISSIONED OFFICERS AND PRIVATES

Adler, Henry, Pvt.
Aige, (unknown)
Bailey, William C., Pvt.
Bayton, L. B.
Bell, William T. R., Pvt.
Bernard, Byron W., Pvt.
Berry, Andrew J., Pvt.
Beveridge, Wm. H., Pvt.
Blackburn, Edward W., Pvt.
Blake, James A., Pvt.
Blankenship, Thomas H., Pvt.
Bringle, (unknown)
Briqut, Francis D., Pvt.
Briscoe, Richard, Pvt.
Brunson, John, Pvt.
Burr, Henry D., Pvt.
Butler, James H., Pvt.
Carter, R. Curtis, Pvt.
Carter, Robert M., Pvt.
Chamberlayne, R. C. M., Pvt.
Chapman, C. W., Pvt.
Chesterman, William D., Pvt.
Cleveland, George D. B., Pvt.
Cochran, John H., Pvt.
Copeland, Richard
Cox, A. Judson, Pvt.
Cox, James T., Pvt.
Crafton, John A., Pvt.
Crawford, William T., Pvt.
Crouch, Andrew, Musician
Dann, Patrick H., Pvt.
Dodson, Joseph H., Pvt.
Duesberry, A. B., Pvt.

Duesberry, Richard H., Pvt.
Dugan, Joseph, Pvt.
Duke, A. K., Pvt.
Duke, W. H., Pvt.
Duke, William B., Pvt.
Epps, Charles H., Pvt.
Epps, George W., Pvt.
Ewell, William H., Corpl.
Ezekiel, Ezekiel M., Pvt.
Fosque, George B., Pvt.
Fosquey, W.
Frayser, Samuel, Pvt.
Gamble, Francis D., Pvt.
Gibson, Charles A., Musician
Gilham, Richard B., Pvt.
Glinn, Peter D., Jr., Corpl.
Goolsby, John C., Pvt.
Gregg, James H., Pvt.
Griffin, Fendall W., Pvt.
Grill, George W., Pvt.
Hall, John T., Pvt.
Harter, S., Pvt.
Hauser, (unknown)
Hawkins, J. F., Pvt.
Hermans, Edgar, Pvt.
Hewitt, Thomas B., Sgt.
Hexter, Simon, Musician
Hix, Richard J., Pvt.
Hobson, C. C., Pvt.
Howlett, James, Pvt.
Howlett, James B., Pvt.
Iaege, Finton, Pvt.
Isaacs, Abraham, Pvt.

Johnson, Robert M., Pvt.
Johnson, W. F., Pvt.
Johnston, Francis, Pvt.
Kayton, Lewis, Pvt.
Kellan, James, Pvt.
Kelly, Henry T., Pvt.
Kuper, George A., Pvt.
Landrum, Wm. R., Pvt.
Langley, Christopher T., Pvt.
Lawrence, James R., Pvt.
Lee, W. C., Pvt.
Levy, Alex H., Pvt.
Levy, E. G., Pvt.
Levy, Isaac J., Pvt.
Levy, Joseph, Pvt.
Lipscomb, William T., Pvt.
Littrell, George, Pvt.
Locknane, James M., Pvt.
Lovenstein, William, Pvt.
Lumpkin, George T., Pvt.
Lyon, Thomas W., Pvt.
Makourz, Wladislaus, Pvt.
Martin, William H., Pvt.
Maze, George, 3 Cook
McFarland, James, Pvt.
McGill, Thomas W., Pvt.
McRoberts
Medlicott, James R., Corpl.
Miller, Henry M., Pvt.
Mountjoy, James M., Pvt.
Mugler, Philip, Pvt.
Mulligan, Thomas
Napier, Edward S., Pvt.
New, F. Aubry, Pvt.
Nolan, E. F., Pvt.
Nott, Robert, Pvt.
Nute, William W., Pvt.
Omenhauser, John J., Pvt.
Pardigon, C. F., Pvt.
Partello, Dwight, Pvt.
Payne, Thomas, Pvt.
Perkins, F. J., Pvt.
Pierce, Andrew J., Pvt.
Place, Henry, Pvt.
Poulson, James, Pvt.
Poulson, Thomas H. G., Ord, Sgt.
Powell, Francis L., Pvt.
Rade, William, Pvt.
Rady, J. M.,
Ralston, Robert, Pvt.
Reid, Robert, Pvt.
Robertson, James E., Pvt.
Robinson, John S., Pvt.

Roy, Churchill B., Pvt.
Rush, William W., Pvt.
Ruskell, William, Pvt.
Sarvay, Rufus H., Sgt.
Saunders, James H., Pvt.
Sherrer, Samuel
Ship, James A., Pvt.
Slater, John C., Pvt.
Smith, Henry I., Pvt.
Smith, J. Wesley, Pvt.
Snead, William D., Corpl.
Southall, Henry C., Pvt.
Southall, William A., Pvt.
Spradling, Alexander V., Pvt.
Steele, William, Pvt.
Swank, William L., Musician
Taylor, Samuel H., Pvt.
Taylor, Robert, Teamster
Thompson, Charles H., Corpl.
Thurston, W. S., Pvt.
Timberlake, L. W., Pvt.
Timberlake, Wilson H., Corpl.
Todd, G. W., Pvt.
Tompkins, H. B., Pvt.
Tower, Charles H., Pvt.
Trueheart, Lewis T., Pvt.
Trundle, B. H.
Tyler, Alonzo, Pvt.
Tyler, George C., Pvt.
Tyree, William H., Sgt.
Valentine, Robert S., Pvt.
Walker, William M., Pvt.
Wasserman, Levi, Pvt.
Watkins, J. Polk, Pvt.
Weisiger, R. Wilmer, Pvt.
Wellington, J. Howard, Pvt.
White, Alexander A., Pvt.
White, Silas A., Pvt.
Wickers,
Wiesiger, George, 1 Cook
Wilkerson, Joshua J., Corpl
Wilkinson, Charles, Pvt.
Williams, James L., Sgt.
Williams, John, Pvt.
Willis, Edward B., Pvt.
Willis, James Henry, Pvt.
Wilson, Charles H., Pvt.
Wilson, Lewis, Pvt.
Wilson, William B., Pvt.
Woolcott, Augustus
Yancey, Francis M., Pvt.
Yarrington, Charles W.,
Yeatman, William W., Pvt.

## RICHMOND SHARPSHOOTERS

Organized early in May 1861, the Richmond Sharpshooters enlisted on May 14 for one year with Robert A. Tompkins as captain. Soon after being mustered in, the company was assigned to the 23rd Regiment Virginia Infantry as Company H. On June 6, the regiment, under Colonel William B. Taliaferro, was ordered to Staunton. From Staunton the regiment proceeded to Laurel Hill, where it became a part of General Robert S. Garnett's command.

When the regiment joined Garnett's command, the Confederates were regrouping in an effort to establish a defensive line against an advancing Federal force. The Richmond Sharpshooters were actively engaged in the skirmishes around Laurel Hill from July 7 to July 10, losing two men killed. Following a Confederate defeat at Rich Mountain on July 11, General Garnett withdrew his force from Laurel Hill. The 23rd Regiment brought up the rear of Garnett's column, and was engaged at Carrick's Ford on July 13, where the Richmond Sharpshooters lost nine men—one killed, one mortally wounded, and seven captured. Following this engagement, in which General Garnett was killed, the Confederate force retreated northward through Hardy County, Md., and thence moved southward, finally reaching Monterey after seven days of marching. At Monterey the remnants of Garnett's command joined a Confederate force under General Henry R. Jackson of Georgia.

On July 20 General W. W. Loring was assigned to command the force at Monterey, designated as the Army of the Northwest. On July 23 the regiment was reported at McDowell, and on August 16 it was ordered to move to the Greenbrier River on the Monterey Line. Upon its arrival the regiment was stationed at Camp Bartow, near where the Parkersburg pike crosses the Greenbrier River. The forces on this end of the Monterey Line were under General Henry R. Jackson, while General Loring commanded the forces opposing the Federals in the vicinity of Cheat Mountain. On September 8 the 23rd Regiment was assigned to the 5th Brigade, Colonel William B. Taliaferro commanding, Army of the Northwest. Remaining at Camp Bartow, the regiment took part in the movements of General Jackson's command during the Cheat Mountain campaign, September 11-17, 1861. According to the plan of attack, General Jackson was to advance his entire force after a force under Colonel Rust stormed the Federal position. Colonel Rust failed to deliver the assault which was to initiate the general advance and the complex plan failed to produce any lasting results. General Jackson advanced and gained the first summit, but withdrew after Colonel Rust's attack failed to develop. Jackson's force returned to Camp Bartow, where it remained when General Loring moved with a portion of his army to support General Floyd in the Kanawha Valley area.

While General Loring was absent with a portion of his command, General Joseph J. Reynolds, commanding the Federal force at Cheat

Mountain, decided to advance against General Jackson's positions at Camp Bartow. On October 3 the Federals succeeded in driving in the Confederate pickets, but were unsuccessful in their efforts to cross the Greenbrier River and storm Camp Bartow. The Richmond Sharpshooters were engaged during the battle and lost one man wounded. The Federal attack hastened General Loring's return from the Kanawha Valley area. Taliaferro's Brigade, consisting of the 1st Georgia, 3rd Arkansas, 37th Virginia, and 23rd Virginia, was ordered to garrison Monterey on November 22. From Monterey the brigade moved to join General T. J. Jackson's command at Winchester early in December, along with the balance of Loring's army.

With his force, General Jackson moved to reoccupy Romney. On January 2, 1862 he advanced on Bath and occupied the town on the 3rd and 4th. After bombarding Hancock on the 5th, Jackson moved on Romney and occupied the town on January 10. Leaving Loring's army at Romney, Jackson returned with his original force to Winchester. However, early in February, Jackson was directed by the Secretary of War to order Loring's command back to Winchester. With the commands united, Jackson withdrew from Winchester on March 11 and retired to Woodstock. He then moved on a Federal force at Kernstown where he was engaged on March 23. Now brigaded with the 37th Virginia, under Colonel S. V. Fulkerson, who was commanding the brigade, the 23rd Virginia was actively engaged at Kernstown, losing three killed, fourteen wounded, and thirty-two missing. After an unsuccessful attempt to drive the Federals, Jackson retired to Newtown. On April 2, 1862 Captain Robert A. Tompkins was dropped from the rolls, and when the Richmond Sharpshooters were reorganized for the war on the 21st of April. 1st Lieutenant Emmett C. DePriest was promoted to captain.

After the action at Kernstown, Jackson, now reinforced by Ewell's command, moved down the Shenandoah Valley. At this time the 23rd Regiment was reported in Taliaferro's Brigade, Army of the Valley, and participated in Jackson's famous Valley Campaign. After defeating the Federals at McDowell on May 8, where the 23rd Regiment lost six killed and thirty-five wounded, Jackson moved against a Federal force at Front Royal and defeated it on May 23. On May 25, at Winchester, Jackson routed the Federals under General Banks. Jackson then withdrew up the Valley to avoid being cut off and to meet a Federal thrust from western Virginia. The regiment was engaged at Port Republic on June 8-9 when Jackson defeated General Shields.

With the defeat of the Federals in the Shenandoah Valley and the presence of McClellan's army in front of Richmond, General Lee ordered Jackson to move to Richmond for an attack on McClellan's right. The series of battles which followed succeeded in driving McClellan from in front of the capital, are known as the Seven Days'. Throughout this campaign, June 26-July 1, the 23rd Regiment served in Taliaferro's Brigade, Jackson's Division, Jackson's command, and lost six men wounded.

After the engagements around Richmond, Lee dispatched Jackson's command to confront a Federal force under General John Pope moving in the direction of Gordonsville. On July 23 the 23rd Regiment, under Colonel Alex G. Taliaferro, was reported in Brigadier General William B. Taliaferro's Brigade, Jackson's Division, Jackson's command. Moving with Jackson's command, the regiment was actively engaged at Cedar Mountain on August 9, when Jackson defeated Pope's advance. During the battle the regiment lost three killed and fifteen wounded. Lee, finding McClellan evacuating the Peninsula and moving to reinforce Pope, determined to join Jackson in an effort to defeat Pope before he could be reinforced. A move was made on August 21, but Pope retired behind the Rappahannock. Sending Jackson around Pope's right to attack his base of supply at Manassas Junction, Lee reasoned that Pope would retire to protect his line of supply. Jackson executed the move and retired to Groveton. Pope retired to confront Jackson, and Lee moved with Longstreet to join Jackson. These moves resulted in a Confederate victory in the Battle of Second Manassas, August 29-30, during which the 23rd Regiment lost one killed and thirteen wounded.

Lee now determined to move his army into Maryland, and the 23rd Regiment, still serving in Jackson's Division (now commanded by General J. R. Jones), encamped near Frederick, Md., on August 7. Three days later the regiment moved with Jackson to capture Harpers Ferry, which surrendered on the 15th. Jackson left one division to carry out the necessary administrative work while he marched with the rest of his command to join the army at Sharpsburg. Arriving on the field at Sharpsburg on the 16th, Jackson's command was ordered to the left of the Confederate line. On the morning of the 17th Jackson's troops bore the brunt of the initial Federal assault. Heavily engaged, the 23rd Regiment later reported a loss of eight killed and thirty-five wounded.

Lee retired from Sharpsburg during the night of September 18-19 and moved his army to the vicinity of Winchester where it was allowed to receive a much needed rest. In late October, McClellan moved his army across the Potomac River east of the Blue Ridge. Lee divided his army and moved Longstreet east of the mountains, leaving Jackson in the Shenandoah Valley to guard the mountain passes and threaten McClellan's communications. On November 9 General Ambrose E. Burnside assumed command of the Federal army and began shifting the army toward Fredericksburg. Lee moved Longstreet to that town and succeeded in occupying the heights just west of it before Burnside's army was up, thus preventing him from taking the town. Jackson was ordered from the Valley when it was determined that Burnside intended a move on Richmond from Fredericksburg. Jackson's force was placed south of the town to guard avenues of advance should Burnside determine to move south, avoiding a crossing at Fredericksburg. When Burnside began crossing the Rappahannock at Fredericksburg on December 11, Lee moved Jackson up on Longstreet's right to extend his line southward along the heights just west of the town. Taliaferro's Brigade, now commanded by Colonel E. T. H. Warren, 10th Virginia, was moved to Hamilton's Crossing and placed "in rear of the Hamilton House, in support of the batteries on the hill." Burnside launched his attack on December 13 and failed to break through the Confederate line. Taliaferro's Brigade remained in rear of the Hamilton House, and "saw nothing of the enemy." Defeated, Burnside withdrew to the north bank of the Rappahannock. After the battle, Taliaferro's Brigade was moved to Skinker's Neck, where it went into winter quarters.

In April 1863 General Raleigh E. Colston was assigned to command Taliaferro's old brigade, and on April 29 the brigade moved from Skinker's Neck to Hamilton Crossing as Lee regrouped his army to meet General Hooker's move up the north bank of the Rappahannock. After crossing the river, Hooker moved his army to Chancellorsville where he halted to prepare his advance on the rear of Lee's lines at Fredericksburg. Lee had made his dispositions to meet Hooker, and on May 1 Jackson's command moved to reinforce the forces opposing Hooker. After a spirited engagelorsville. During the night of May 1-2 Jackson moved his command across Hooker's front and came up on his right flank. Jackson deployed his troops into three lines, Colston's Brigade going into position in the second line to the right of the turnpike. Late in the afternoon of May 2, Jackson's forces drove in Hooker's right and advanced until strong Federal resistance, darkness, and confusion resulting from the intermingling of units when Jackson's first two lines became one, forced the Confederates to discontinue the advance and dig in. On the 3rd, Lee's two wings united and succeeded in driving the Federals from Chancellorsville. Hooker withdrew his troops to a defensive position north of Chancellorsville, and Lee was forced to withdraw troops to confront a Federal force under General John Sedgwick moving toward Chancellorsville from Fredericksburg. Surrounded on three sides with the river to his right, General Sedgwick withdrew across the river. Lee returned with his troops to Chancellorsville, only to find that Hooker had withdrawn across the Rapidan and was in the process of moving back to his old positions across the river at Fredericksburg. Lee then withdrew his command and reoccupied his old positions at Fredericksburg. The 23rd Regiment was actively engaged throughout the Chancellorsville campaign, and reported a loss of ten killed, seventy wounded, and two missing.

Following Jackson's death, the Army of Northern Virginia was reorganized into three corps. On May 28 General Colston was relieved and Brigadier General George H. Steuart was assigned to command the brigade, which was now in Major General Edward Johnson's Division, Ewell's Corps. On the move into Pennsylvania the 23rd Regiment was assigned to guard the division trains as the division broke camp near Hamilton's Crossing on June 3. The regiment, therefore, did not participate in the fight at Winchester on June 14-15. Moving with Ewell's Corps, the division crossed the Potomac at Boteler's Ford on June 18. At Greencastle, Pa., Steuart's Brigade was ordered to McConnellsburg to collect horses, cattle, and other supplies, and rejoined the division at Carlisle. General Johnson reported that on June 29 the division "countermarched to Greenville, thence eastwardly, via Scotland, to Gettysburg, not arriving in time, however, to participate in the action of the 1st instant." As Ewell's Corps arrived on the field at Gettysburg, it formed the left of Lee's army.

Late on the 2nd, Ewell ordered General Johnson to move against the Federals on Culp's Hill; and Steuart's Brigade, on the left of Johnson's line of advance, was the only brigade to make a lodgment during the bitter night fighting. Early the next morning a Confederate attack was repulsed and Ewell's men broke off the fighting as Pickett's men prepared to assault the Federal center. Following the repulse of this attack, Lee determined to retire. On the night of July 4-5 the Army of Northern Virginia began the long march back to Virginia. By August 31, 1863 the Richmond Sharpshooters were encamped near Orange Court House, Va., where the company clerk reported that the company had lost two men wounded in the fighting on Culp's Hill.

The activities of the Richmond Sharpshooters for the balance of 1863, which included the Bristoe and Mine Run campaigns, were reported by the company clerk on the muster rolls as follows:

September-October 1863, dated October 31, 1863
Station: near Brandy Station

> This company marched from camp near Orange Court House to camp near Raccoon Ford about the 18 or 19 September 1863—distance twenty-five miles. On the 8th day of October the company marched from there to Bristoe Station, Orange and Alexandria Railroad, and then marched back to the present camp, arriving about the 22nd October 1863. This company was not engaged in battle, a portion only being engaged in a skirmish without losing any men. Distance in last named march, eighty miles.

November-December 1863, dated January 1, 1864
Station: Camp in the field

> This company was engaged at the battle of Panes [Payne's] Farm—no one hurt—November 27. Laid in line of battle five days on Mine Run. Nothing else worthy of note transpired in the past two months.

Early in January 1864 the company went into winter quarters near Pisgah Church. On February 6 it was engaged with the enemy at Morton's Ford, and returned to camp after the enemy retired. On February 29 the company clerk reported that "every man of this company reenlisted for the war that was present at the time the proposition was made to the regiment."

On May 1, 1864 the company left its winter quarters to go on picket at Morton's Ford. While there, orders were received to "march in the direction of Fredericksburg." Actually, the company rejoined the 23rd Regiment, Steuart's Brigade, Johnson's Division, Ewell's Corps, as the corps moved to oppose Grant in the Wilderness. Blocked in his efforts to turn Lee's flank in the Wilderness, Grant moved toward Spotsylvania Court House. As the advance of Grant's army arrived at Spotsylvania Court House it found the way blocked by elements of Lee's army. Both commanders concentrated their armies at Spotsylvania. In establishing his defensive line, Lee adhered to the terrain. At one point his line resembled a horse shoe. General Edward Johnson's Division occupied the trenches in that portion of the line. In a pre-dawn attack on May 12 Grant's forces succeeded in penetrating Johnson's line and overran the Confederate position, capturing many prisoners, including Generals Johnson and Steuart. The Confederates succeeded in closing the breech, but not before the Federals had moved their prisoners to the rear. During this engagement the regimental flag of the 23rd Regiment was captured, and the Richmond Sharpshooters lost two killed, two wounded, and eleven captured, including Captain De Priest and 1st Lieutenant James W. L. Jones. The command of the company now devolved on 2nd Lieutenant Clinton De Priest. On May 14 the remnants of the Virginia regiments of Johnson's Division were consolidated into a brigade and attached to General Early's Division. On May 19 Brigadier General William Terry was assigned to command the brigade, still in Early's Division, which was now commanded by Major General John B. Gordon. By the end of May, General Early was assigned to command Ewell's Corps because of the latter's absence due to illness. Thus, by the end of May, the remnants of the 23rd Regiment were in Terry's Brigade, Gordon's Division, Early's (Ewell's old) Corps. Remaining with the Army of Northern Virginia, the regiment now moved with Gordon's Division as Lee moved to block Grant at North Anna, Hanover Junction, and Cold Harbor.

On June 12 General Early was ordered to proceed with his corps to reinforce General John C. Breckinridge in the Shenandoah Valley, who was retiring before a superior Federal force under General David Hunter. Arriving at Lynchburg, Early's troops joined those under Breckinridge in defense of that place on June 18. Hunter then retired westward and Early began moving down the Valley after an unsuccessful attempt to overtake Hunter. At Staunton, on June 26, Gordon's Division was temporarily attached to Breckinridge's command, and moved under that officer on the campaign to Washington. On July 9 Gordon's Division was actively engaged at the Battle of Monocacy. Following this victory, Early moved on Washington, arriving before the defenses of the city in the evening of the 10th. Finding the defenses strengthened by reinforcements, Early withdrew back into the Shenandoah Valley. At Winchester, on September 19, Early's forces were driven from their positions around the town, and on the 22nd were again driven from a defensive position at Fisher's Hill. Retiring up the Valley, Early reorganized his small army. Breckinridge left the army under orders to return to the Department of Southwestern Virginia, leaving his divisions under Early. In October, Early advanced against the Federals under Sheridan, and on October 19 assaulted the Federal positions at Cedar Creek. Although initially successful, the Confederate attack was halted by a Federal stand. Counterattacking, Sheridan's forces routed Early's command. Defeated, Early retired to New Market. On October 27, 2nd Lieutenant De Priest was captured and the Richmond Sharpshooters were left without any officers. The April 30-October 31, 1864 company muster roll was made out on October 29 by 2nd Lieutenant Joseph W. Waddy, Company A, 23rd Virginia, and reported only six men present. The movements of the company for the period covered on the muster roll were reported as follows:

> From Richmond it marched to Salem via Charlottesville and Lynchburg, and then down the Valley via Lexington and Winchester within a few miles of Washington City, engaging in various fights and skirmishes, namely Kernstown [July 23-24], Monocacy [July 9], etc., etc., losing one killed. Was engaged at Winchester [September 19], Fisher's Hill [September 22], and Cedar Creek [October 19], and then marched to New Market where it is now in camp.

From April 30 to October 31 the company had "marched in all about 1,200 miles."

Gordon's Division broke camp at New Market on December 6 under orders to rejoin the main army in the Richmond-Petersburg defenses. Marching via Harrisonburg, the division took the train from Waynesboro on the 9th. From Richmond the troops moved to Petersburg where they went into the lines. The Richmond Sharpshooters went into winter quarters near Burgess' Mill, Dinwiddie County. On January 10, 1865, when the November-December 1864 muster roll was made out, the company was still in winter quarters near Burgess' Mill, and only six privates were reported present.*

When the Petersburg lines were evacuated on April 2, the remnants of the Richmond Sharpshooters joined the retreat westward. Only three members of the company remained to be paroled at Appomattox Court House on April 9, 1865.

---

* This muster roll was made out by Captain Richard P. Jennings, Company E, 23rd Virginia. All six men present had enlisted in the Richmond Sharpshooters on May 1, 1861.

# RICHMOND SHARPSHOOTERS

## CAPTAIN

Tompkins, Robert A.
DePriest, Emmett E.

## LIEUTENANTS

Baber, Edward S., 2nd Lieut.
Crump, Edward C., 2nd Lieut.
DePriest, Clinton, 2nd Lieut.
Jarvis, R. H., 2nd Lieut.

Jones, James W. L., 1st Lieut.
Ludman, Christian, 1st Lieut.
Wilson, John J., 2nd Lieut.

## NON-COMMISSIONED OFFICERS AND PRIVATES

Allen, William L., Pvt.
Alley, John B., Pvt.
Allumes, James, Pvt.
Beazley, Cornelius C., Pvt.
Beazley, Joseph W., Pvt.
Blake, John H., Pvt.
Bland, Ira R., Pvt.
Brandt, William, Pvt.
Briquet, Samuel, Pvt.
Brooke, Charles B., Pvt.
Brown, N. C., Pvt.
Burch, James, Pvt.
Burch, William R., Pvt.
Burke, Francis, Pvt.
Burns, John W., Pvt.
Carline, Philip, Pvt.
Chappell, John T., Corp.
Childress, Charles P., Pvt.
Clarke, William T., Pvt.
Cousins, Thomas E., Pvt.
Crowley, James, Pvt.
Davis, William J., Pvt.
Dittell, Ferdinand, Pvt.
Eggleston, William H., Pvt.
Faudree, Joseph J., Sgt.
Folkes, Thomas H., Pvt.
Ford, Fleming H., Pvt.
Fordham, Edward, Pvt.
Freitag, A. Theodore, Sgt.
Fulton, Robert A., Pvt.
Fuqua, Richard H., Pvt.
Gentry, Watkins L., Pvt.
Goff, Charles H., Pvt
Griffin, John H., Pvt.
Groeber, Adolph, Pvt.

Hardiman, Richard H., Pvt.
Harris, William H., Pvt.
Haupt, Simon, Pvt.
Hetzler, Frederick, Pvt.
Hickey, William E., Pvt.
Higgason, Morgan, Pvt.
Hoffnagle, Edward H., Pvt.
Hoffnagle, John, Pvt.
Horwell, Charles N., Pvt.
Johnson, Alfred, Pvt.
Johnson, J. J., Pvt.
Jordan, William B., Pvt.
Kell, Jacob, Pvt.
Langford, Charles H., Pvt.
Larkin, John, Pvt.
L'Ecuyer, Anthony P., Sgt.
Lindsay, George W., Sgt.
Lynch, John, Pvt.
Mahoney, William E., Pvt.
Martin, Charles, Pvt.
Mattern, George T., Pvt.
McDowell, Alonzo, Pvt.
McGann, Thomas M., Pvt.
McKinney, Icelius, Pvt.
McRae, Arthur N., Pvt.
Miller, Charles, Pvt.
Miller, George, Pvt.
Minter, James H., Pvt.
Mitchell, James H., Pvt.
Mull, Watson D., Pvt.
Mundie, James M., Pvt.
Murphy, Patrick, Pvt.
Nichols, John J., Pvt.
Normant, Samuel W., Pvt.
Parcley, Philip, Pvt.

Parcley, Solomon, Pvt.
Pearman, Robert H., Pvt.
Perrin, Henry A., Pvt.
Phillips, Sampson, Pvt.
Puryear, Henry H., Pvt.
Rhinehardt, Gustavus, Pvt.
Richardson, William J., Pvt.
Roach, James, Pvt.
Roberts, John, Pvt.
Ryan, Robert E. J., Pvt.
Schofield, John, Pvt.
Schwartz, George, Pvt.
Sheppard, John, Pvt.
Snead, John, Pvt.

Snyder, John, Pvt.
Tills, Joseph S., Pvt.
Tompkins, Herbert B., Pvt.
Turner, James H., Pvt.
Tyler, John H., Pvt.
Wall, Frank, Pvt.
Watkins, William H., Pvt.
Waul, William C., Pvt.
Williamson, Charles L., Pvt.
Wingfield, William J., Sgt.
Wright, John A., Pvt.
Wynant, Richard, Pvt.
Wynant, William, Pvt.

## RICHMOND ZOUAVES

The organization of the Richmond Zouaves, which had begun about May 16, was completed on June 1, 1861. By the 7th of June the company was reported as having seventy partly uniformed members. Edward Mc Connell, Jr., a Civil Engineer graduate from the Virginia Military Institute with the Class of 1857, was elected captain. On June 10 the company was mustered into service; and on the next day marched from their headquarters at Corinthian Hall on Main Street, between Ninth and Tenth, to Camp Lee, the camp of instruction at the Hermitage Fair Grounds on the western edge of Richmond. When the 44th Regiment Virginia Infantry was organized under Colonel William Scott about June 14, the Richmond Zouaves was included, and designated as Company E.

The uniforms for the Richmond Zouaves were made by the ladies of the Monumental Episcopal Church, and the following extract from an article, which appeared in the Richmond Whig on June 10, suggests that the company was outfitted in a typical colorful Zouave pattern uniform, consisting of a blue jacket and orange baggy trousers:

> At drill hours our Armory [Corinthian Hall] presents quite an animated scene, and uniforms other than the blue and orange, mingle cum toga civile. To-night, two of the Zouaves Francais were present and expressed themselves well pleased at our appearance and movements. All thanks to the courteous Frenchmen, whether we deserve the compliments or not.

The two Frenchmen were apparently from Lieutenant Colonel George Auguste Gaston Coppens' Battalion of Louisiana Zouaves, which had arrived in Richmond on June 7. The battalion, comprised of many nationalities, was uniformed in a red fez, blue jacket with gold braid trim, and red baggy trousers with white gaiters. It seems unlikely that members of this already notorious command would have praised the Richmond Zouaves had the Virginians been wearing anything other than Zouave pattern uniforms. We do know that during June white canvas leggings were made for Captain McConnell's company by contract with a Mr. F. Thomas of Richmond. The Zouaves were equipped with a unique knapsack, which could be unfolded to serve as a raincoat or small tent. It was patented in the Confederate States by a Mr. Reith, a salesman for Messrs. Kent, Paine & Co., a dry goods firm in Richmond. Reith had previously served with the British Army in Africa and in the Crimea. The Zouaves were issued flintlock muskets in June; however, by July 20 the company was rearmed with percussion Springfield rifled muskets.

The 44th Regiment left Richmond by railroad late on July 1, 1861 to join the command of Brigadier General Robert S. Garnett at Laurel Hill, headquarters of the Department of Northwestern Virginia. On July 10, the regiment arrived at Beverly in Randolph County, sixteen miles from Laurel

Hill; and on the 11th it started for Garnett's headquarters but was called back to aid Lieutenant Colonel John Pegram at Rich Mountain, eight miles east of Beverly. Colonel Scott, as requested, placed the regiment, which then numbered about 570 men, on the Buckhannon Turnpike, between Rich Mountain and Beverly. It was expected that a portion of the Federal force would move by a county road, around Pegram's right, to the Buckhannon Turnpike, and then attack Pegram's command from the rear, cutting them off from Beverly and Garnett's forces at Laurel Hill. After waiting for some time for the appearance of the enemy on the county road, Colonel Scott learned that the Federals had struck Pegram's left flank instead. The 44th moved at double-quick time up the road toward Rich Mountain, but did not arrive in time to assist Pegram, whose command was cut off and captured. Colonel Scott, perceiving that he was far outnumbered, decided against attacking the enemy and marched the regiment back to Beverly. From Beverly, Colonel Scott proceeded on to Huttonsville, and during the night of July 12, while crossing Cheat Mountain, 2nd Lieutenant Robert McConnell, brother of Captain McConnell, and two enlisted men of the Zouaves, were killed by an overturning wagon. On the 13th, at the Greenbrier River, Colonel Scott's command was joined by Colonel Edward Johnson's Georgia regiment. The retreat continued to the Alleghany Mountains, where they met Brigadier General Henry R. Jackson, who conducted the troops to Monterey.

On July 24, 1861 General Jackson, commanding the Army of Northwestern Virginia, reported that Colonel Scott's regiment was among the units left at Monterey, and that "without tents or camp equipage, and with but the clothing upon their backs...this force is far from efficient." In August the 44th Regiment, attached to Colonel William B. Taliaferro's Fifth Brigade, Army of Northwestern Virginia, left Monterey for Camp Bartow in Pocahontas County. The camp was located where the Parkersburg-Staunton Turnpike crossed the Greenbrier River.

General Jackson's command at Camp Bartow was attacked on October 3 by a Federal force estimated at 5,000. Although heavily outnumbered, Jackson was successful in repulsing the enemy after a struggle of about four and a half hours. Taliaferro's Brigade, which held the center of the defenses, was exposed to a considerable amount of artillery fire, but sustained a remarkably small number of casualties, having two killed and six wounded.

By November 3 the Richmond Zouaves, still at Camp Bartow, had dwindled from three officers and fifty enlisted men present for duty in late August, to two officers and thirty-four enlisted men present for duty. The company at this time had received some clothing, and it is doubtful that much of their Zouave clothing was still in evidence.

On April 22, 1862, the Army of the Northwest, under Brigadier General Edward Johnson, was divided into two brigades. As senior officer Colonel Scott was placed in command of the brigade to which the 44th Regiment was assigned. On May 1, 1st Lieutenant Edward M. Alfriend was appointed captain of Company E, replacing Captain McConnell, who, because of a long continued absence due to ill health, was dropped from the rolls effective January 1, 1862. Charges of breech of arrest had also been preferred against him by Lieutenant Colonel Hubbard of the 44th Regiment. McConnell was later commissioned as captain of cavalry in the Virginia State Line, but resigned in January 1863 in order to have the War Department investigate the charges that had been preferred against him by Hubbard. He was found not guilty, and, by order of the Secretary of War on March 20, 1863, Captain McConnell was reinstated in the Provisional Army of the Confederate States and given permission to resign.

General Johnson's two brigades formed the advance of the combined forces under Major General Thomas J. "Stonewall" Jackson on the 8th of May in the engagement with Milroy near McDowell, about twelve miles east of Monterey. The 44th Regiment, holding the center of Johnson's line, was at first bitterly engaged in the fighting, but was withdrawn by Colonel Scott and placed as reserves, in a depression where the men were ordered to lie down. However, as the fighting grew more intense, and when Colonel Scott's attention was directed elsewhere, a large number of the regiment left the safety of the depression and joined in the fighting with the 58th Virginia; the balance of the regiment joined another brigade. Casualties in Scott's Brigade were light in comparison with those suffered by the others. The 44th Regiment had two killed and seventeen wounded.

After the battle near McDowell, Scott's Brigade, attached to Ewell's Division, continued on the march with Jackson, and on June 8 participated in the battle at Cross Keys. The 44th Regiment numbered about 130 in this engagement, and had one killed and three wounded. On the 9th of June the regiment, with Ewell's Division, marched seven miles to Port Republic, where Scott's Brigade was severely engaged, losing 30 killed and 169 wounded. The 44th's loss was fourteen killed and thirty-four wounded. In their reports of the action at Port Republic, General Ewell and Colonel Scott singled out the gallantry displayed by 2nd Lieutenant N. Dixon Walker of the Zouaves.

The 44th Regiment served throughout the Seven Days' Battles, June 26-July 1, 1862, with the Fourth Brigade, Ewell's Division, Jackson's Army of the Valley District. General Elzey, commanding the brigade, was wounded at Gaines' Mill; and on July 1 the command of the brigade was given to Brigadier General Jubal A. Early. During the Seven Days', the 44th Regiment had two killed and sixteen wounded.

In July, General Jackson proceeded with Ewell's Division to Gordonsville to oppose General Pope, who was reported to be moving from Orange Court House. On August 9, Ewell's Division engaged Bank's Corps at Cedar Mountain. The 44th Regiment, with part of the 52nd Regiment, was detached from Early's Brigade and employed on the flanks of the army to prevent surprise attacks by the enemy's cavalry. Moving northward with Jackson on August 16, the 44th Regiment was engaged in the battles near Manassas, August 26-September 1. The army crossed the Potomac River into Maryland on September 5-6, and on the 14th, moved against Harpers Ferry. After the capture of Harpers Ferry, Jackson proceeded toward Sharpsburg, where, on the 17th, the 44th Regiment suffered two killed and thirty-two wounded.

In early October 1862 the Richmond Zouaves were assigned to the 19th Battalion Virginia Heavy Artillery. The transfer was apparently later declared as illegal, and in December Captain Alfriend's company was back with the 44th Regiment near Fredericksburg, where, during the battle of December 13, the regiment had two killed and thirteen wounded.

Colonel Scott resigned on January 14, 1863, and Major Norvell Cobb was placed in command of the regiment. He did not, however, receive his promotion as colonel until late in the summer of that year. At the end of February 1863, Company E, stationed at Corbin's Neck, near Fredericksburg, had two officers and eighteen enlisted men present for duty out of an aggregate strength of thirty-four.

In early 1863 the 44th Regiment was assigned to Brigadier General J. R. Jones' Brigade, Trimble's Division, Jackson's Corps. The regiment, under Major Cobb, saw much fighting at Chancellorsville in May. On the 2nd of May it participated in Jackson's flank march. Upon reaching the Plank Road the regiment was divided with Major Cobb commanding a portion on the right of the road and Captain Thomas R. Buckner commanding on the left. On May 3 the regiment advanced with the brigade to the enemy's works, and was exposed to a terrific fire from artillery and infantry. In the course of the day's fighting, Lieutenant Walker of the Zouaves, who had been cited for gallantry at Port Republic, was killed while carrying the colors in advance of the regiment.

After Chancellorsville, the army was reorganized, and Jones' Brigade was placed in Major General Edward Johnson's Division of Ewell's Corps. In June the army moved northward into Maryland and Pennsylvania, and although the brigade reached Gettysburg late in the afternoon of July 1, they were not committed to action until late on the following day. Major Cobb was wounded and Captain Buckner assumed command of the regiment. In the two days of fighting at Gettysburg the 44th Regiment suffered about fifty-six casualties. On the night of July 13 Johnson's Division recrossed the Potomac near Williamsport and reached Drakesville on the 15th. The division went into camp near Orange Court House about August 1. The Richmond Zouaves at this time had one officer, Captain Alfriend, four noncommissioned officers, one musician (drummer) and only eleven privates present for duty.

The 44th Regiment, with Jones' Brigade, was engaged in the Battle of the Wilderness, May 5-7, 1864, and on May 12 they were in the thick of the fighting at the salient on Ewell's line at Spotsylvania. Only a small number of the regiment escaped capture with Johnson's Division when the Federals broke through the Confederate line at the salient on the 12th of May 1864. Nothing specific is known about the history of Company E after May 12, but there may well have been a few survivors who continued with the remnants of the regiment until the end of the war. The fragments of General Johnson's infantry regiments, remaining after Spotsylvania, were formed into a brigade under Brigadier General William Terry, and served with Gordon's Division, General Early's Army of the

Valley District, during the summer of 1864. The 44th Regiment's battle-flag was reportedly captured at the Cedar Creek disaster of October 19, 1864. The remnants of the brigade were sent east during the winter and served with the main army at Petersburg.

# RICHMOND ZOUAVES

## CAPTAINS

McConnell, Edward, Jr.
Alfriend, Edward M.

## LIEUTENANTS

McConnell, Robert H., 2nd Lieut.
Omohundro, John W., 2nd Lieut.
Regan, John, 2nd Lieut.

Waldman, George R., 1st Lieut.
Walker, Noah Dixon, 1st Lieut.

## NON-COMMISSIONED OFFICERS AND PRIVATES

Alexander, George W., Pvt.
Anderson, Joseph, Pvt.
Andrews, A. G., Pvt.
Andrews, Vincent T., Pvt.
Baldwin, William, Pvt.
Ball, W. H., Pvt.
Banks, J. W. T., Pvt.
Baxter, Henry, Pvt.
Behan, Joseph, Pvt.
Bird, William P., Sgt.
Bond, Benjamin F., Pvt.
Brickelman, Henry, Pvt.
Brock, Henry, Pvt.
Brockwell, J., Pvt.
Brown, Alvin, Pvt.
Buchanan, William, Pvt.
Burke, Patrick, Pvt.
Burton, George, Corp.
Byrnes, Thomas, Pvt.
Cadigan, John, Pvt.
Caine, Michael, Pvt.
Carter, Henry M., Sgt.
Clark, John J., Pvt.
Cottrell, Edward D., Pvt.
Courtney, Edward, Pvt.
Cox, Alexander C., Pvt.
Crivellari, Mathew J., Pvt.
Crivellari, Thomas, Pvt.
Cullen, Peter, Corp.
Curley, Michael, Pvt.
Davis, John B., Sgt.
Deaning, Cornelius, Pvt.
Digney, Henry, Pvt.
Edwards, William J., Pvt.
Elwood, James, Pvt.
English, Charles L., Corp.

Feeney, Barney, Pvt.
Fenderick, Rudolph, Pvt.
Finley, Edgar S., Pvt.
Finley, James, Pvt.
Forbes, Edward J., Corp.
Furguson, James, Pvt.
Gelowsky, Lewis, Pvt.
Gerard, Augustus P., Pvt.
Goodwynn, James A., Pvt.
Gotsmyer, George A., Pvt.
Grant, Clinton D., Corp.
Graves, James S., Pvt.
Griffith, John, Pvt.
Grubbs, Euell B., Pvt.
Grubbs, R. D., Pvt.
Harper, James, Drummer
Haywood, James L., Pvt.
Healy, Alfred A., Pvt.
Hodgson, Talfair, Pvt.
Hughes, Tel., Pvt.
Hynes, James, Pvt.
Jones, John E., Pvt.
Keaton, Edward, Pvt.
Kelly, John, Pvt.
Kennedy, Edward, Pvt.
Kent, John W., Pvt.
King, Edwin F., Pvt.
King, John N., Pvt.
Lando, Charles C., Pvt.
Langaioni, Mariano, Pvt.
Lloyd, Thomas, Pvt.
Loomis, John, Pvt.
Lowenthal, Reinhart, Sgt.
Mathews, Herbert, Pvt.
McConnell, S. E., Corp.
McElroy, Patrick, Pvt.

McIntyre, John, Pvt.
Meer, Reuben, Pvt.
Mulhuen, James S., Pvt.
Parke, John F., Pvt.
Payne, John H., Pvt.
Phillips, Henry J., Pvt.
Pierce, Richard, Pvt.
Pleasants, Westmore H., Pvt.
Poole, William H., Pvt.
Pyle, Augustus J., Sgt.

Redmond, Morgan, Pvt.
Regan, John, 1st Sgt.
Sharpe, David E., 1st Sgt.
Shepherd, Alick, Pvt.
Simmott, Henry, Drummer
Trayler, Z. T., Pvt.
Walters, John, Pvt.
Ware, John R., Pvt.
Wiley, George W., Sgt.
Williams, William, Pvt.

## VARINA ARTILLERY

About June 1, 1861 the Varina Troop (Henrico Mounted Rangers) was reorganized as an artillery company under Captain John P. Harrison. The company was assigned to a battalion of volunteers under Major John P. Wilson, stationed at Fort Powhatan, on the south side of the James River, about twenty miles east of Petersburg. In late July 1861 the battalion moved further down the river to Hardy's Bluff, on Burwell's Bay.

By the end of October 1861, Lieutenant Colonel Fletcher H. Archer had been detached from the 3rd Regiment Virginia Volunteers and placed in command of Wilson's Battalion. Archer's Battalion Virginia Volunteers, known also as the 5th Battalion Virginia Infantry, was comprised of six companies, of which the Varina Artillery was designated as Company D.

Captain Harrison died of typhoid fever on October 17, 1861 and on October 24, 1st Lieutenant James H. Akin was elected captain to succeed him. At the end of October the company had—besides Captain Akin—one second lieutenant, four sergeants, four corporals, two musicians (drummer and fifer), and twenty-nine privates, present for duty. The company was armed with flintlock muskets and their uniforms consisted of gray caps, jackets and pants.

On November 26, 1861 the battalion moved into winter quarters. The Varina Artillery was one of the two companies assigned to the battery, called Fort Huger, which was erected during July near Stonehouse Wharf Landing at Hardy's Bluff. The battery was reported in March 1862 as consisting of thirteen guns—one 10-inch rifled Columbiad, four 9-inch Dahlgrens, two 8-inch Columbiads, and six "hot-shot" 32-pounders mounted on naval carriages.

Captain Akin's company manned the guns at Fort Huger on May 8, 1862 in an engagement with Federal gunboats, and on May 13 evacuated the fort. The company marched, with the battalion, thirty miles to Zuni on the Norfolk & Petersburg Railroad, and on the 14th marched seven miles to Broad Water Bridge on the Blackwater River, where they encamped for several days. From there the battalion marched to Ivor, on the Petersburg railroad, and remained there until May 24 when they proceeded by rail to Petersburg. On May 28 the battalion moved by rail to Richmond and on June 1, with Huger's Division, was engaged at Seven Pines, where the Varina Artillery had one killed and one wounded. After Seven Pines the company occupied a position on the lines near the York River Railroad. At this time the company was commanded by Lieutenant C. W. Everett. Captain Akin, because of ill health, tendered his resignation which was accepted on July 26, 1862. Between April and June 1862, the flintlocks of the company had been replaced by percussion muskets.

The 5th Battalion, attached to Armistead's Brigade, occupied rifle pits in the woods between the railroad and the Williamsburg Road; and on June 25 the battalion was engaged in repelling the enemy's attack on the brigade front. On June 29 Armistead moved down the Charles City Road and at about 10:00 a.m. July 1, the battalion, under Captain William E. Alley, was assigned a position in line with the brigade at Malvern Hill, remaining there throughout the battle. Although the battalion was not actively engaged, they were exposed to considerable artillery fire. Casualties, however, were light, amounting to only one killed and five wounded.

Presumably, the 5th Battalion was with Armistead's Brigade, Anderson's Division, Longstreet's Corps, throughout August 1862 and participated in the campaign against General Pope. On September 6, 1862 the battalion was ordered to be disbanded and all men between the ages of eighteen and thirty-five were enrolled and transferred to the 53rd Regiment Virginia Infantry, Armistead's Brigade.

# VARINA ARTILLERY

## CAPTAIN

Akin, James H.
Harrison, John P.

## LIEUTENANTS

Braxton, Augustine M., 1st Lieut.
Braxton, Robert C., 2nd Lieut.
Cox, James T., 1st Lieut

Everett, Charles W., 2nd Lieut.
Yarbrough, James E., 2nd Lieut.

## NON-COMMISSIONED OFFICERS AND PRIVATES

Adams, Robert E., Corpl
Bartley, George J., Pvt.
Britton, John, Corpl.
Britton, Robert, Pvt.
Carter, Clauborne, Pvt.
Carter, Elias, Pvt.
Carter, Joseph W., Pvt.
Carthright, Geo. A., Pvt.
Clark, Daniel, Pvt.
Clarke, Robert, Pvt.
Claytor, Thomas, Pvt.
Davis, William A. J., Pvt.
Dodson, Thomas R., Pvt.
Doggett, Henry H., Pvt.
Duffy, Thomas, Pvt.
Duke, John H., Pvt.
Dunavant, John, Pvt.
Ellis, Robert, Pvt.
Enroughty, Jervas, Pvt.
Foster, John, Pvt.
Foster, Josiah, Pvt.
Foster, Larkin, Corpl.
Garrity, James, Pvt.
Garthright, George A., Pvt.
Gentry, Mathew G., Pvt.
Glenn, James F., Pvt.
Goode, Howard, Pvt.
Goodman, James, Pvt.
Green, Robert, Pvt.
Griffin, Robert W., Sergt.
Grove, N. L., Corpl.
Hanvey, Charles, Sergt.
Hobbs, James C., Pvt.
Jacob, Lewis A., Sergt.
Jones, John, Pvt.
Jordan, George, Pvt.
Jordan, Thomas, Pvt.
Jordon, Archer, Pvt.
King, R. L., Pvt.
Knight, Joseph, Pvt.
Lawford, James, Sergt.

Mahoney, Patrick, Pvt.
Martin, Albert, Pvt.
Martin, Moses, Pvt.
Mayo, James E., Pvt.
McRea, William, Pvt.
Melton, Thomas J., Pvt.
Oakley, Robert, Pvt.
Parker, Henderson, Pvt.
Penney, Thomas L., Pvt.
Pierce, Adolphus, Pvt.
Pitts, William E., Pvt.
Pollard, Fielding, Pvt.
Pollard, Philip, Pvt.
Pollard, Richard Corpl.
Riley, William, Pvt.
Ritter, Richard C., Sergt.
Robinson, Peter, Pvt.
Robinson, Willis W., 1st Sergt.
Roke, Peter, Pvt.
Roper, Jas R., Pvt.
Schinault, Temple, Pvt.
Schools, George, Sergt.
Sharp, James W., Pvt.
Sharp, William H., Pvt.
Skelton, Alexander, Pvt.
Smoot, Richard, Pvt.
Smoot, Robert, Pvt.
Southall, Henry, Pvt.
Taylor, Joseph F., Pvt.
Throgmorton, John M., Pvt.
Throgmorton, Joseph, Pvt.
Timberlake, Robert, Corpl.
Trueman, Claiborne T., Pvt.
Trueman, Richard, Pvt.
Tucker, Archer B., Pvt.
Tucker, Richard, Pvt.
Turner, Albert C., Pvt.
Wade, Robert, Pvt.
Warner, Gidwell, Pvt.
White, John, Pvt.

## VIRGINIA GUARD

The Virginia Guard was organized in May 1861, and was mustered into State service on May 25, 1861 for twelve months service, with Samuel T. Bayly as captain. Soon after being mustered in, the company was assigned to the 20th Regiment Virginia Infantry — commanded by Colonel John Pegram — as Company A. This regiment was accepted into Confederate States service about July 1, 1861. However, before being accepted into Confederate service, eight companies of the regiment had been ordered to proceed to Staunton on June 6. The remaining two companies left Richmond on June 26 to join the regiment, which had moved to join Brigadier General R. S. Garnett's command at Laurel Hill.

Arriving at Laurel Hill on June 21, the eight companies went into camp. On July 1 at 2 a.m., seven companies under Major Nat Tyler moved to Rich Mountain. Arriving at 12 noon on July 2, the companies went into defensive positions in preparation for the expected Federal advance. Colonel Pegram arrived at Rich Mountain on the 7th with the remaining three companies of the regiment. The day before, Federal forces under General George B. McClellan had driven the Confederate picket from Middle Fork bridge, between Buckhannon and Rich Mountain. Underestimating the Federal strength, Pegram contemplated a night attack. However, perceiving signs of a flank attack, he posted pickets on top of the mountain. Early on the morning of July 11 he learned that six regiments of Federal infantry were already on their way to seize a position on the summit of the mountain commanding his fortifications. Sending a small force to reinforce the picket on the mountain at Hart's House, Colonel Pegram requested General Garnett to order Colonel William C. Scott's 44th Regiment Virginia Infantry to hold the road to Beverly in his rear. The Federals assaulted the position at Hart's House about 11 a.m. on the 11th. Colonel Pegram moved the remainder of his regiment to support the force at Hart's. Considering the situation too desperate to warrant an attack, he ordered Major Tyler to assume command of the balance of the regiment and to join General Garnett at Laurel Hill or Colonel Scott on the road to Beverly. Colonel Pegram moved to join the balance of his command under Colonel J. M. Heck, while Major Tyler moved to join General Garnett or Colonel Scott. Defeated, the Confederates withdrew from Rich Mountain and a general retreat began. Colonel Pegram tried to join General Garnett at Laurel Hill, but the latter began withdrawing at midnight on the 11th upon receiving news of the defeat at Rich Mountain. Colonel Pegram was cut off from the forces under Garnett, and on the 13th he surrendered his command, which contained two companies of the 20th Regiment. These troops were paroled and allowed to return to their lines. Major Tyler's command retired to Monterey, where the remnants of Garnett's command assembled. Only two companies of the regiment remained at Monterey, while Major Tyler proceeded to Staunton with six "remnants of companies" and the two paroled companies. On July 22, Major Tyler reported his presence at Staunton with remnants of companies A (Virginia Guard), B, C, D, E, and F, and companies G and H on parole. Under orders to "proceed to general headquarters," Major Tyler proceeded with his command to Richmond, where it encamped at Hermitage Camp of Instruction.

On August 31, 1861 Captain Bayly reported on the company muster roll:

> "I certify that many of the articles which were drawn for this company were lost at the battle of Rich Mountain, July 11, 1861; that all the books, rolls, and accounts of some of the arms and accoutrements, also the tents of the company and camp equipage, were unavoidably lost at the same time."

Companies A to E, 20th Regiment Virginia Infantry, were disbanded on September 10, 1861 by Special Orders No. 270, paragraph 5, Adjutant and Inspector General's Office, dated September 5, 1861. Thus the Virginia Guard was dissolved.

# VIRGINIA GUARD

## CAPTAIN

Bayly, Samuel T.

## LIEUTENANTS

Brander, Thomas A., 2nd Lieut.
Burwell, William P., 1st Lieut.
Hollidy, Alexander Q., 2nd Lieut.

## NON-COMMISSIONED OFFICERS AND PRIVATES

Adkins, Andrew J., Corpl.
Allen, Robert, Corpl.
Amey, William, Pvt.
Bayly, John, Pvt.
Bender, William, Pvt.
Brown, Alfred, Pvt.
Brown, John Thompson, 1st Sgt.
Burch, William, Pvt.
Burrows, John, Pvt.
Butler, John, Pvt.
Cannon, Patrick, Pvt.
Caughlin, Patrick, Pvt.
Conner, Alexander, Pvt.
Conner, Jeremiah, Pvt.
Connolly, Patrick, Pvt.
Constantinie, Charles, Pvt.
Constelo, Timothy, Pvt.
Crawford, Jacob, Pvt.
Cronin, Stephen, Pvt.
Dauser, John, Pvt.
Davidson, Reuben P., Pvt.
DeBlassiere, Charles, Corpl.
Dennis, John, Pvt.
Diacored, John, Pvt.
Dillman, Jacob, Pvt.
Donoghue, Joseph P., Pvt.
Driscal, James, Pvt.
Eaves, William, Pvt.
Ford, James W., Pvt.
Furgurson, Robert, Pvt.
Gaines, Thomas, Pvt.
Gordon, Daniel M., Pvt.
Gray, Howard, Sgt.
Hogan, James, Pvt.
Huefner, Fred W., Pvt.
Jelks, Green M., Pvt.
Johnson, George W., Pvt.
Jones, Jamos H., Pvt.
Kirby, Robert, Pvt.
Langley, Edward, Pvt.
Lord, George H., Pvt.
Lyle, Mathias, Corpl.
Mack, Thomas, Pvt.
Martin, Thomas, Pvt.
McCullock, William, Pvt.
McLellan, Daniel, Pvt.
McMahan, Timothy, Pvt.
Miller, Jacob, Pvt.
Mitchell, John, Pvt.
Nailor, James, Pvt.
Newby, Young, Pvt.
Parie, Otto, Pvt.
Perdie, William, Pvt.
Rowly, Sewell, Pvt.
Russell, Christopher, Pvt.
Smith, Jacob, Pvt.
Smith, William A. J., Sgt.
Smith, William H., Pvt.
Talley, Robert H., Sgt.
Thiebes, William, Pvt.
Thompson, Frederick, Pvt.
Tool, Michael O., Pvt.
Welsh, Daniel, Pvt.
Wynne, Julius, Pvt.